NONINDIFFERENT NATURE

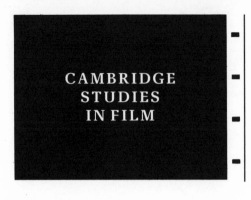

CAMBRIDGE
STUDIES
IN FILM

NONINDIFFERENT NATURE

SERGEI EISENSTEIN

Translated by

HERBERT MARSHALL

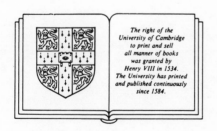

The right of the
University of Cambridge
to print and sell
all manner of books
was granted by
Henry VIII in 1534.
The University has printed
and published continuously
since 1584.

CAMBRIDGE UNIVERSITY PRESS

CAMBRIDGE

NEW YORK   NEW ROCHELLE   MELBOURNE   SYDNEY

Published by the Press Syndicate of the University of Cambridge
The Pitt Building, Trumpington Street, Cambridge CB2 IRP
32 East 57th Street, New York, NY 10022, USA
10 Stamford Road, Oakleigh, Melbourne 3166, Australia

First published 1987

Printed in the United States of America

Library of Congress Cataloging-in-Publication Data
Eisenstein, Sergei, 1898–1948.
Nonindifferent nature.
(Cambridge studies in film)
Translation of: Neravnodushnaia priroda.
1. Moving-pictures – Aesthetics.   2. Moving-pictures –
Psychological aspects.   3. Aesthetics.   4. Arts –
Psychological aspects.   I. Marshall, Herbert,
1906–   .   II. Title.   III. Series.
PN1995.E5313   1987   791.43   86–33457

British Library Cataloguing-in-Publication Data
Eĭzenshteĭn, Sergeĭ
Nonindifferent nature. – (Cambridge
studies in film).
1. Moving-pictures
I. Title
791.43′01   PN1995

ISBN 0 521 32415 7

Contents

Portrait sculpture of Sergei Eisenstein by Fredda Brilliant, 1937 (acquired by the Ministry of Culture of the USSR for the Eisenstein Museum).

Introduction
by Herbert Eagle

Sergei Eisenstein dedicated *Nonindifferent Nature* to "poor Salieri," who, in Alexander Pushkin's dramatic poem, laments: "...True tone I smothered, dissecting music like a corpse; I test with algebra pure harmony...." It was Eisenstein's intent, though, to vindicate Salieri by arguing that the spontaneous and intoxicating act of artistic creation *must* be followed by "ever-increasing, precise knowledge about what we do." Thus, *Nonindifferent Nature* not only represents the most advanced stage of Eisenstein's thinking on the structure of film, but it is the creator's attempt to demonstrate, once again, the validity of his own personal lifelong synthesis of creative art *and* theoretical analysis, a synthesis not always viewed positively by official Soviet criticism.

Eisenstein's films of the 1920s, *Strike, Battleship Potemkin, October* (*Ten Days That Shook the World*), *The Old and the New* (*The General Line*), captured the attention of the world with their daring approach to film montage. Eisenstein clearly was not satisfied to represent the world from without, as if through an illusionist window on "reality"; he wanted to assault the viewer with his own particular perceptions, under-standings, and emotions. The mental state to be produced *in the viewer*, and not the object to be represented, was at the center of Eisenstein's film practice and of his later theories. He broke down "reality" into signs and symbols and reassembled it into films that, to this day, represent a unique approach to the art.

By the late 1920s, however, Eisenstein's experimental work was no longer a preferred form for the conservative bureaucracy that ultimately prevailed in Soviet cultural policy and ushered in the officially sanc-tioned style of "socialist realism." Eisenstein remained a hero of Soviet culture on the international scene, but at home his planned films were delayed or shelved. Scholarship, theorizing, and teaching occupied his attention increasingly, as film scripts and projects awaited authoriza-tion. Beginning in late 1928, and for two decades afterwards, Eisenstein articulated and broadened the theories of montage for which he is now so famous. Because Eisenstein considered the cinema to be the highest
vii

stage of the arts, a complex synthesis of literature, drama, the visual arts, and music, his theoretical speculations, backed by prodigious reading, ultimately became a theory of culture and art as a whole. In his expositions and discussions, examples came from the works of writers, painters, sculptors, and musicians as often as they did from filmmakers, and his sources ranged from psychologists, natural scientists, and philosophers to theoreticians and historians of art, music, and theater. This breadth of interest, and Eisenstein's constant emphasis on art as communication through signs, led the Soviet linguist V. V. Ivanov to devote a major portion of his *Notes on the History of Semiotics in the USSR* (1976) to Eisenstein's thought.

Eisenstein's work on montage as a collision of signs began appearing in 1928 with an article on Kabuki theater and an afterword to a book on Japanese cinema. In these articles, Eisenstein drew close parallels between the principles of montage and the ideograms of Japanese writing, where separate signs, originally representational, are super-imposed to create new signs whose meaning is the result of a metaphorical operation (for example, the ideographs for "knife" and "heart" are combined to form the ideogram "sorrow"). In Kabuki Eisenstein was fascinated by the "decomposition" of reality into independent visual and aural signs and their free recombination: A verbal text is read offstage; onstage an actor mimes, while elements of makeup represent character traits and emotional moods. In essence, Eisenstein was in agreement with the Russian formalist theoretician Yuri Tynyanov, who wrote: "The visible person, the visible thing, is only an element of cinema language when it is given in the quality of a semantic sign."

In his articles of the late 1920s (including the famous programmatic statement, signed by his colleagues the directors Pudovkin and Alexandrov, about the function of sound in cinema *not* being reduced to the mere recording of dialogue), Eisenstein emphasized the *collision* of disparate and conflicting elements in montage in order to produce, in the synthesis, new concepts and emotions. Eisenstein coined such phrases as "overtonal montage" to refer to modulations on such levels as lighting and color, and "intellectual montage" to describe collisions produced by the juxtaposition of objects with rich cultural implications (thus, Eisenstein, in *October*, seeks to discredit Orthodoxy by juxtaposing its religious icons and idols with Asian and African statues, which for his European audience would connote the primitive and the superstitious).

In the mid-1930s, Eisenstein turned increasingly to the problem of modeling "inner speech," of creating in cinema an analogue for both the "thematic-logical" and the "image-sensual" aspects of thought. According to Eisenstein, cinema could recover the organic and syncretic qualities of primitive culture, simultaneously integrating impulses along a number of different tracks. These concerns led Eisenstein to the problems of "*pathos* constructions" and of "vertical montage," which are the principal themes of *Nonindifferent Nature*.

Although the first outline for the entire monograph *Nonindifferent Nature* dates from 1945, the articles that clearly anticipate it appeared during 1939–41, the period of Eisenstein's collaboration with the composer Prokofiev on the film *Alexander Nevsky*. Three articles from that time were, in fact, revised and included in *Nonindifferent Nature*: "On the Structure of Things" [published first in the journal *Iskusstvo kino* (*The Art of Cinema*) in 1939], "Once More on the Structure of Things" (which appeared in the same journal in 1940), and "Poor Salieri" (written as an introduction to a planned edition of Eisenstein's articles but unpublished until its appearance in the posthumous *Collected Works* of Eisenstein in 1964). In 1940, Eisenstein also wrote three articles for *The Art of Cinema* entitled "Vertical Montage," which form an important introduction to some of the considerations in *Nonindifferent Nature*. (These articles constitute most of the volume entitled *The Film Sense*, published in English in J. Leyda's translation in 1942.) The remaining portions of *Nonindifferent Nature*, which constitute the majority of the monograph, were written by Eisenstein in the years 1945–7, after his work with Prokofiev on *Ivan the Terrible*. The volume is thus highly representative of Eisenstein's most pressing artistic concerns during the very active and energetic final decade of his life. It also brings to the fore quite eloquently those central concerns that unify Eisenstein's work from the 1920s to the 1940s.

From the earliest period of his work in theater and film, Eisenstein wrote of techniques for causing the viewer to experience the emotions linked to a particular content; even then these techniques involved the use of separate elements of mise-en-scène, gesture, and sound to carry the chain of emotions to the audience. In his famous article "Montage of Attractions," published in the journal *LEF* in 1923, he stated: "The attraction (in our diagnosis of the theater) is every aggressive moment in it, i.e., every element of it that brings to light in the spectator those senses or that psychology that influence his experience." In Eisenstein's directorial practice, as in that of his teacher Vsevolod Meyerhold, "leaps from one type of expression to another" were common – from elements of the set to features of costume to the acrobatic movements of the actors. The "vertical montage" that Eisenstein devised fifteen years later was an application of this same principle to the cinema. He wrote in 1939: "The juxtaposition of these partial details in a given montage construction calls to life and forces into the light that *general* quality in which each detail has participated and that binds together all the details into a *whole*, namely, into that generalized *image*, wherein the creator, followed by the spectator, experiences the theme."

In "On the Structure of Things," Eisenstein designated by the term "*pathos*" the heightened emotional state produced by works of art. Such works must possess qualities that arouse passion in their receivers. Eisenstein asserted that this could occur only by means of "a compositional structure identical with human behavior in the grip of *pathos*" (taking the term in its original Greek meaning). Such behavior entailed a leap out of oneself, *ex stasis*, ecstacy: "To be beside oneself is unavoidably also a transition to something else, to something different in quality, to something opposite to what preceded it." The problem then was to fuse the structure of human emotional behavior with the receiver's experience of the content.

Eisenstein looked to both physiological and psychological manifestations of emotions, from irregular breathing, quickened heartbeat, and emphatic gesture to metaphorical and poetic speech. The structural elements of such phenomena would have to be recreated in the composition of the work of art. Seeking them, Eisenstein analyzed his own films *Battleship Potemkin* (1925) and *Alexander Nevsky* (1939), as well as Emile Zola's prose, Alexander Pushkin's poetry, and the painting *The Boyarina Morozova* by V. I. Surikov. From these comparative studies, Eisenstein derived two key principles: organic unity and the leap to a new quality.

Although the notion of organicity might seem to be somewhat of a cliché, Eisenstein took the concept quite literally and specifically: "The organic unity of a work, as well as the sense of organic unity received from the work, arises when the law of the construction of this work corresponds to the laws of *the structure of organic phenomena of nature*." In *Battleship Potemkin*, Eisenstein found that all five parts of the film, as well as the film as a whole, are governed by the same structural law (evidence of a general organic order). In each part, revolutionary brotherhood grows from a small incipient "cell" into a manifestation of greater intensity or larger scale, and there is a turning point (Eisenstein terms it a "caesura"), when the action "leaps over" from a quieter protest to a more angry and violent clash: The approaching execution under a tarpaulin of resisting sailors "leaps over" into the shipboard mutiny; the mourning for the martyred sailor Vakulinchuk "leaps over" into an angry demonstration; the peaceful fraternization between ship and shore turns suddenly into a massacre with the scream of a woman and the appearance of a rank of firing tsarist troops at the top of the Odessa steps. From the points of transition at these caesuras Eisenstein derived an important principle:

And it is also remarkable that the jump at each point – is not simply a sudden jump to *another* mood, to *another* rhythm, to *another* event, but each time it is a transition to a *distinct opposite*. Not contrastive, but *opposite*, for each time it *gives the image of that same theme from the opposite point of view and at the same time unavoidably grows out of it.*

The caesuras in each of the film's parts echo a central caesura in the film as a whole: the sequence of mourning for the dead Vakulinchuk. At this point, the stormy actions of rebellion are replaced by near stillness, and the theme of universal revolutionary embrace must begin to build again to its climaxes in the second part of the film: the spread of the rebellion to the city, and then to the entire tsarist fleet.

It was "the leap to a new quality," however, that became for Eisenstein the most important characteristic of the *pathos* construction. It was to this subject that he devoted the series of chapters written in 1946–7, entitled "Pathos," which comprise most of the first half of *Nonindifferent Nature.* These studies constitute a detailed elaboration of the leap into a new and opposed quality (in particular, the leap from the literal into the metaphorical) and of the merging of opposites into the organic unity of the whole. Eisenstein points to instances of these structures in his films *The Old and the New* (1929) and *Ivan the Terrible* (1944), as well as in the work of various writers (Zola, Whitman, Zweig, Pushkin), performers (the actor Frédérick Lemaître, the poet Mayakovsky reciting his own verse), and artists (Claude Monet, Vincent van Gogh, El Greco, Leonardo da Vinci).

Eisenstein argues that in *The Old and the New*, his filmic paean to collectivization and the mechanization of agriculture, *pathos* constructions per se are more distinguishable than they are in *Potemkin* where the theme of revolution itself already carries much of the *pathos*. The task in *The Old and the New* was to create the *pathos* of the machine through expressiveness and composition alone; Eisenstein's techniques led French critics of the day to refer to the film's "epic lyricism" over "those terrestrial gifts that derive their inspiration from the machine" and its rendering of "everyday phenomena...in themselves insignificant" with "Dionysian lyricism." Eisenstein focuses his attention on the sequence "Testing of the Milk Separator" in which he embodied, structurally, the property of continually leaping from one state to another of different quality. What played a crucial compositional role was the ability of the wide-angle lens to distort perspective, enabling objects "to go beyond themselves, beyond their natural bounds of volume and form." As the collective farmers wait to see if the separator will work, Eisenstein moves from group shots to two-shots to close-ups of faces. "Their movement is caught up by shots of spinning disks and the feed pipes of the separator, appearing all the more frequently at various angles." "Shots of intensifying hope" use gradually brighter lighting, whereas "shots of aggravated suspicion" gradually become darker. As the change from bright to dark frames occurs more often, the disks spin faster and faster. A drop at the end of the separator pipe begins to swell.

Finally the drop falls, hitting the bottom of the pail in a starlike spray. Eisenstein describes the ensuing montage as follows:

And now unchecked, at furious pressure bursting from the body separator, a jet stream of thickened white cream thuds into the pail.

By now, through editing, the spurts and spray pierce through the stream of enthusiastic close-ups with a cascade of snow-white streams of milk, a silvery fountain of unchecked spurts, a fireworks display of unceasing splashes.

And then, as if in answer to the involuntary comparisons emerging on the screen, after the explosion resulting from the first spurts of milk, the sequence of these milk streams is interjected by what appears to be foreign matter flooded with light... Aquatic pillars of shooting fountains.

The fountains of milk then leap over into a new dimension, into images of an actual fountain, and then leap again into an image of fireworks, produced by coloring separate shots of the shooting water streams and intercutting them rapidly. The sequence finally reaches a purely formal climax: a totally black field with intermittent "lightening" flashes of white. As Eisenstein puts it: "...the structural system itself skipped over from the sphere of the *representational* to its opposite sphere of the *nonrepresentational*." Nonrepresentational leaps on the level of color also occur in *Ivan the Terrible* (Part II), where the sequence of the boyar conspiracy (in gray tones) leaps over into the banquet sequence wherein the tsar sets in motion his passionate and bloody response (in a color sequence dominated by reds and golds), and then leaps again into the murder in the cathedral (almost entirely in stark contrasts of black and white).

In Zola, Eisenstein finds that the emotionally moving descriptions are produced by a hyperbolic multiplication of everyday objects possessing a particular quality – the descriptions seem to "eject out of one another" in a rising level of frenzy. The repetitions represent a diversity of manifestations of a single thesis. Then, suddenly, the metonymic accumulation of detail leaps into metaphor. Zola ends by describing not the literal event but his own emotional passion over it.

Eisenstein argues that the unity of opposites is strikingly portrayed in the style of the great nineteenth century French actor Frédérick Lemaître, the literal meaning of whose words was often completely contradicted by the emotional qualities of his delivery. Thus, the qualities that Lemaître could convey were often described by his contemporaries as, in fact, oppositional pairs: "energy and sensitivity," "cunning and good nature." Eisenstein terms this "the dynamic unity of mutually exclusive antithetical principles within a character." The same can be said of Dostoyevsky's heroes, for "one is often struck not only by the duality, but especially by the at times unmotivated collapse of a character into another extreme...." This, says Eisenstein, is what inspired him in his creation of Ivan the Terrible: "...the construction of *pathos* effects by the direct charging of elements ecstatically exploding into each other with constantly increasing intensity...."

Two of the most intriguing analyses in the *pathos* section of *Nonindifferent Nature* concern the art of El Greco and of Piranesi. In both cases, Eisenstein describes meticulously the structural "explosion" of an early variant to yield a more ecstatic (and justifiably more famous) later variant. He explores the harmonic transition of certain forms into other forms; a sequence of forms "overflowing" into new forms. Entire movements in art show a similar mechanism: The Gothic "explodes" the preceding features of Romanesque architecture; impressionism and cubism explode the contours and the spatial bounds of realism's objects.

Artists make such leaps, notes Eisenstein, when they themselves are overcome by ecstacy, obsessed by certain ideas. This ecstacy, which approaches madness (in El Greco and in Piranesi), is akin to the state induced by opiates, for "the dynamics of these construction elements overflowing into each other promote the feeling of emotional seizure."

Eisenstein, with his training in civil engineering and his early experience as a set designer, is himself obsessed by the symbolic meaning of architectural forms, a potential he utilizes so brilliantly in *Battleship Potemkin* and in *Ivan the Terrible*. He compares architectural composition to cinematic montage, sees in Gothic churches ecstacy embodied in stone, and in the buildings of the reign of Tsar Nicholas — "the image of absolutism." Architecture speaks in "the strongest figurative rhetoric of its epoch...of its system or of its inner aspirations."

Eisenstein's own personal ecstacy over Piranesi's work is reflected in this discussion, where insights are expressed not only in structural diagrams of the spatial and graphic "explosions," but also in the poetic and metaphorical quality of Eisenstein's prose. The inspiration of Piranesi is evident as well in Eisenstein's set designs for *Ivan the Terrible*, where a system of receding "wings" forces our eyes deeper and deeper into the distance, while at the same time the foreground of shots is occupied by close-ups of parts of heads. All of this, Eisenstein asserts, is based on the effect of the telescope, of one thing thrusting out another. He draws analogies also to recent "accelerations upon accelerations" in science: nuclear chain-reaction explosions and multistage rockets, in which a new leap in magnitude accompanies each successive stage.

From architecture and science, Eisenstein returns again to literature (via Gogol's little known article in the miscellany *Arabesques* on "The Architecture of Our Time.") Gogol's preference for the ecstatic Gothic is no accident, states Eisenstein, for the very same process of forms metamorphosing into other forms, of contrastive metaphors leaping from one dimension to another, is as characteristic of Gogol's prose as it is of Gothic architecture.

Eisenstein finds the tendency of things to grow out of one another in a diversity of other cultural phenomena as well: in the structure of toys (like the chain of sticks that, in changing their angles, produce a jack-in-the-box thrust, or like the Russian *matrushka* dolls that emerge out of one another), in the practice of Yucatan cultures that built pyramids directly over previous pyramids, in the spiral repetition of features in design motifs in many cultures. Moreover, notes Eisenstein, there are important similarities between the structure of *pathos* and the structure of comedy. When there is a sign of growth, but, instead of a leap into a new quality, we get merely the repetition of the same thing, the effect is comic. Thus, concludes Eisenstein, the formula for construction of extreme versions of phenomena is the same, whether in science or in art: ". . . this formula is nothing but the moment (instant) of the culmination of the dialectic law of the transition of quantity into quality."

"Why are *pathos* constructions in all of these varied art forms essentially the same?" asks Eisenstein. Because they must correspond to a basic "formula for *pathos*" in the emotive (nonlogical) centers of the brain. They depend not on psychological factors, but on a psychic state. The basic laws governing change in natural phenomena are imprinted in this psychic state, which in turn determines the structuring of the material in an ecstatic work of art. The art work's ecstatic structures in turn produce a vivid experience in the receiver.

When the artist is first inspired by some object that produces in him an intensity of experience, his ecstacy, in itself, is objectless and formless; it cannot be described verbally. However, the artist reconstructs the process of ecstatic movement through his structuring of the material of his theme, thus communicating the very same *pathos* to his audience. Thus, the process, for Eisenstein, is rooted in the more primitive functions of the brain. Ecstacy is a state prior to thinking, and there is no means of expressing that state other than by simple signs, that is, either by an analogue of the state (in semiotics, an "icon") or by a recreation of a part of the state itself (the semiotic "index").

As a postscript to the "Pathos" study, Eisenstein concluded the first half of *Nonindifferent Nature* with a revised version of his article "Once Again on the Structure of Things," first written in 1940. The subject of the article is "the way the general dialectic position on the *unity* of opposites is applicable to the area of composition." As a twenty-six-year-old filmmaker, Eisenstein reminds us, he was faced with the challenge of surpassing the highly popular American films of the day, with their clever intrigues and their glittering "stars." Instead of using a direct assault, he went in the opposite direction: the rejection of traditional plot and the denial of the isolated individual as hero (the masses themselves become the basic dramatis personae). Of course, on a deeper level, these "formally" opposite solutions reflect basic ideological oppositions.

A decade later, in the film *Chapayev* (1934), which dates from the period of Soviet film's return to classical narrative, the *pathos* embodied throughout *Potemkin* by a leap away from plot and the hero is now accomplished by means of a reversal of the leap. The hero Chapayev, although the main protagonist, does not push forward ahead of the others; he remains a man of the people. What is conventionally spoken in elevated emotional speech, he, instead, talks in simple conversational words. If Eisenstein's style was a leap into the poetic, the Vasiliev brothers (directors of *Chapayev*), accomplish a leap from poetic expectations into conventional speech.

The second half of *Nonindifferent Nature*, actually written in 1945, consists of the extended study "The Music of Landscape and the Fate of Montage Counterpoint at a New Stage." It is the culmination of Eisenstein's work on the subject of "vertical montage" and polyphonic structure, a study begun in a series of essays in *Iskusstvo Kino* during 1939–40 and published in English in 1942 as *The Film Sense*.* Eisenstein used the term "vertical montage" to indicate the process of superposition and integration of the various structural levels of cinema: landscape and scenery, mise-en-scène, gesture, music, lighting, and color. In the articles on verticle montage, Eisenstein claimed that all of these levels should reflect the dominance of a unified theme, one which governs all the choices in all the participating "lines":

The juxtaposition of these partial details in a given montage construction calls to life and forces into the light that *general* quality in which each detail has participated and which binds together all the details into a *whole*, namely, into that generalized artistic *image*, wherein the creator, followed by the spectator, experiences the theme. (*The Film Sense*, p. 11)

Eisenstein's work with Prokofiev, with the cinematographers Tisse and Moskvin, and with the actors in *Ivan the Terrible* was to embody this process, for the architectonics of the set, the framing, the lighting, the camera angles, the costuming, the intonation and gestures of the actors, and the musical score all figured in a montage construction wherein integration had to take place not only horizontally (in collisions from shot to shot) but also vertically:

Through the progression of the *vertical* line, pervading the entire orchestra, and interwoven horizontally, the intricate harmonic musical movement of the whole orchestra moves forward.

When we turn from this image of the orchestral score to that of the audio-visual score, we find it necessary to add a new part to the instrumental parts: this new part is a 'staff' of visuals . . . where shot is linked to shot not merely through

---

* S. Eisenstein, *The Film Sense*; J. Leyda, ed. and trans., Faber & Faber, London, 1953.

one indication – movement, or light values,...or the like – but through the *simultaneous advance* of a multiple series of lines, each maintaining an independent compositional course and each contributing to the total compositional course of the sequence. (*The Film Sense*, pp. 74–5)

In the last period of his life, with his work on *Ivan the Terrible*, on *Nonindifferent Nature*, and on a series of essays on the use of color in cinema, Eisenstein turned increasingly to the specific problems of vertical montage – the problems of identifying and elaborating the features according to which such a synaesthetic montage could proceed. In the second part of *Nonindifferent Nature*, Eisenstein is inspired by the use of nature in Soviet silent cinema, where it was hardly "indifferent," but served to create emotional mood through an "inner plastic music." This task fell to landscape because it was "the least burdened with servile, narrative tasks." Like music, it could express emotionally what was inexpressible by other means and, like later musical sound tracks, it could interweave with the narrative portions of the film.

Indeed, the silent films of Eisenstein, Pudovkin, Dovzhenko, and Kozintsev and Trauberg often began with a landscape "prelude," setting up certain motifs that would then resonate with landscape inserts later in the film. Eisenstein himself, in his writing on "overtonal" montage in 1929, had provided a detailed analysis of the "harbor mist sequence" in *Battleship Potemkin*. After the body of the martyred sailor Vakulinchuk (leader of the successful rebellion) is taken to shore and placed in a tent, there is a seascape suite consisting of shots of the fog-enshrouded harbor, with outlines of ships, buoys, and seagulls barely visible through the mist. Eisenstein analyzed the modulations of gray lighting, the vibrations of the light within the fog (echoed by the rippling motion of the waves), as homologous to the mood of sorrow.

In "The Music of Landscape," Eisenstein parallels such cinematic techniques to those of Chinese and Japanese poetry, based on the calligraphy of symbols that are, in themselves, ideograms. It is not so much a poetry of sound as a poetry of graphics, "music for the eye." Just as words with different meanings and different sounds can rhyme *graphically* in this poetry, so elements of landscape or background can rhyme visually with one another, a process Eisenstein terms "plastic rhyme." Such "plastic" correspondences produce semantic effects; the images in which they occur stand in the same figurative relationship induced for rhymed words in poetry.

In Chinese landscape painting (scroll painting), one finds such "musical" composition, based on the interplay of a limited set of symbolic elements of nature (which correspond to the musical notes in Eisenstein's analogy) appearing in various combinations along the scroll (just as they would in the measures of a musical score). The art historians whom Eisenstein quotes consistently discuss these scroll paintings in musical terms, for the identical landscape motifs and elements are combined as they would be in a polyphonic composition: The theme goes through numerous variations, built upon resonances and "echoings."

The complementary principles of segmentation and continuity figure in Chinese landscapes as they do in a number of disparate cultural forms (Eisenstein cites, for example, Indian spiral painting and Greek "ox-furrow" writing). Elements that are distinct in their oppositions to one another are integrated into a continuous whole along a linear chain; they form a polyphonic stream. Film art, for Eisenstein, not only embodies these properties but raises them to the greatest complexity in terms of the number of different kinds of "lines" or different signifying systems that are integrated.

In all of these art forms, Eisenstein contends, it is the human personality and its attributes that are conveyed in metaphorical terms, whether through the details of landscape (as in Chinese painting), through the fantastic anthromorphism of nature (as in mythology), or through the disparate voices of narrators and characters (as in the "polyphonic" novel as analyzed by Bakhtin). Thus, the compositional devices themselves must also be rooted in the nature of the human mind and human behavior.

Eisenstein's excursions into anthropological theory are quite fascinating, for he contends that artistic syntax is dependent on two instinctive principles that provide the foundation for human culture: plot as pursuit (manifested early in culture as hunting) and interweaving (appearing in the construction of baskets). The hunt can easily be seen as the basis for adventure and mystery plots, but many other narratives retain the quest or riddle structure as well (somewhat later, the French structuralist theoretician Roland Barthes would also name the drive to answer questions, what he called the *hermeneutic code*, as one of the fundamental structures of literature). The inclination to interweave, that is to say polyphonic structure, Eisenstein locates in diverse human activities, from the tying and untying of knots, to the magician Harry Houdini's escapes, to the word weaving of poetry, to the plot complications of novels and plays:

Something of this longing of each knot to be unraveled corresponding to the yearning to tie knots, as we have seen, sits deeply in the psyche of man....

It is all the same, whether it occurs in the graphic knots of Leonardo and Durer,

in the frequencies of vibrations of vowels that wind into the phonetic knots of Dante,

or in the peripeteias of the arrangement of the sequence of scenes that attract equally Pushkin, Joseph Conrad, and Orson Welles!

These are the methods that Eisenstein himself employed in *Ivan the Terrible*, developing the image of the tsar as a unity in variety, expressed through the integrated flow of his graphic contour and makeup, and the lighting and camera angles for the shots. The visual properties of the image (the "landscape" in the broadest sense of the term) echoes the emotional state of the tsar. Eisenstein indeed sees his work on *Ivan the Terrible* as the third (and culminating) stage of film montage. During the first historical stage, there was the shooting of long-shots, from one setup and with no editing; the second stage (exemplified by his own work in the 1920s) exhibited a separation of distinct signifying elements, but with a use of sharp divergence and opposition in their combination (Eisenstein's famous "collision montage"); only in the third stage (*Ivan the Terrible*) is there harmonious counterpoint that eschews "paradoxes and excesses." Eisenstein's disavowal of his work of the 1920s as excessive should be taken here with a grain of salt; because the "collision" theory of montage was related to the Russian formalist valorization of "making strange" as the basis of art, and because that formalism had been condemned with the onset of the Stalinist period, Eisenstein might be seen as politically circumspect in distancing himself somewhat from this "formalist" period. Thus, Eisenstein tells us in 1945 that many of the devices in *Battleship Potemkin* could be described as the "exposed nerve" of montage, whereas the "harbor mist sequence" represents "a fused structure of contrapuntal currents" that anticipates the polyphonic montage of *Ivan the Terrible*.

But Eisenstein does not want to completely disavow the shock tactics of his early "montage of attractions"; rather, he now sees those diverse sensual attractions as more primitive realizations of what can be achieved, in the third stage, through more subtle audiovisual means: "This is one more reason why we are not only interested in analyzing what has been done in *Ivan the Terrible*, but also in tracing retrospectively how what was done in this direction in *Ivan, is derived in method from what had been done in Potemkin*." Thus, what Eisenstein in the 1920s termed collisions of opposed elements to form attractions, he now calls a "systematic unity of diverse components." The basic principle of an integrative montage structure, a synthesis of diverse "contrapuntal" stimuli, remains the same. Eisenstein simply expands and reformulates his ideas so as to put some distance between his theories of 1945 and his politically disreputable "formalist" past.

The centerpiece of Eisenstein's discussion of polyphonic montage is his analysis of the mourning scenes in *Potemkin* and *Ivan the Terrible*. In the latter film, Ivan is mourning the death of his beloved Anastasia. She has been poisoned by his aunt Ephrosinia Staritskaya, but Ivan does not know this. He sees the death as possibly a condemnation from God. He is subdued, repentant, depressed, and, at this scene's nadir, virtually crushed (he seems to cower below the funeral bier). Suddenly, from somewhere deep within himself, a resistance, a rebellion, a self-affirmation arises – at the scene's climax. This complex interplay of moods and drives is rendered by diverse levels of the audiovisual montage. The sharp camera angles (the sequence opens with a panning shot from above that reveals Ivan kneeling at the foot of Anastasia's catafalque), the graphic lines of the mise-en-scène, Ivan's gestures, and a multivoiced sound track all contribute to the vertical montage. Eisenstein breaks down the movements of Ivan into a "distinctive orchestra of parts," a decomposition of the human figure into signs. The elements of mise-en-scène are a poetry of significant shapes, of light and shadow, which match the timbres, melodies, and rhythm of the sound track.

That track itself is very complex, interweaving several voices: a choir singing a funereal dirge, Metropolitan Pimen (Ivan's enemy) reading about man's hubris and insignificance (passages from the Book of Lamentations), Malyuta (Ivan's loyal servitor) reporting the defection of Ivan's "friend" Prince Kurbsky to the enemy, the encouraging words of Ivan's *oprichniki* (personal guard) the Basmanovs, and Ivan's own voice – which varies greatly in its modulations. The respective voices of Pimen and Malyuta ultimately constitute an antithesis that develops along two lines:

The line of *death and constraint of will* enters with the immobile face of the dead Anastasia, passes into the constrained, immobile shots of Ivan, develops in the theme of Pimen's reading ("*exhausted* from wailing," "my throat *dried out*," "my eyes grew weary"), and is crowned by shots of the vehicle of the theme of death and its actual culprit – the poisoner Staritskaya.

The line of affirmation – Malyuta's line – is taken up by the Basmanovs (father and son), the inflammatory nature of the old man's speech passes into the fiery "Two Romes fell, and a Third stands" of the tsar, and ends with the flight of servants in the real fires of the torches.

Quite clearly, Eisenstein feels that every level of a physical manifestation can be broken down into distinctive features, systems of opposites. To grasp something, we might analyze and describe these oppositions (as the theoretician does) or we might extract a synthetic image, a gestalt that captures the basic tonality of the whole complex (as the artist does). The latter method underlines Eisenstein's theory of typecasting ("the process of selecting types"). He searched for faces where the expressive "resonance" is "absolutely *precise*, like a chord or note," and "this precision...expressed with maximum clarity and directness, so that a certain image of a completely defined human characterization could be formed from a short, momentary appearance to the viewer's perception." Thus, for example, in the "suite" of shots of grieving faces over Vakulinchuk's body, each face bears not only a note of grief but also a sign of social class and of other everyday life experiences. The effect of this suite is a portrait of the universality of the grief over Vakulinchuk's death.

Eisenstein stresses that vertical montage also affects linear montage to a significant degree, since each "line" must realize its own rhythmic pattern, must carry its own melody, while at the same time integrating itself with the other accompanying lines.

In discussing the vertical montage in *Ivan the Terrible*, Eisenstein also has frequent recourse to analogies with the structure of verse, strongly echoing the views of the Russian formalist theoretician Yuri Tynyanov, who in the 1920s compared the "turn" from one shot to the next with the turn from one compact verse to the next. Accents within each shot come from the various visual and audial lines (changes in light tonality, actor's abrupt gestures, sudden shifts in vocal intonation or music); these accents, in Eisenstein's view, are most effective when the visual accent counterpoints the musical accent, so that the pattern produced is analogous to that of bricklaying (where the junctures of the bricks at one level should not coincide with the junctures on the next). The effect is akin to enjambement in poetry, where the metrical and syntactic orders of organization do not coincide, thus producing the special semantic tensions of the verse form. In film editing where the accents on the various levels regularly coincide, states Eisenstein, the correspondence becomes mechanical and a comic effect is likely to be produced.

At the conclusion of *Nonindifferent Nature*, Eisenstein brings the two halves of his study together by identifying "emotional landscape" as another bearer of *pathos*, since it provides an image of "the mutual immersion of man and nature into the other. . . . in the miracle of a genuinely emotional landscape we have a total unity in the mutual interpenetration of nature and man with all the overflowing variety of his temperament." Such a total unity of a landscape with the soul of its creator is achieved in works such as El Greco's *Storm over Toledo*.

In the "Epilogue" to *Nonindifferent Nature*, Eisenstein sought to justify his own role in the development of Soviet cinema in the light of the theories he presented in the volume:

Ancient writings contained a whole series of books under the general title "didactic."

I also look on my films as being "didactic" to a certain extent; that is, those which, besides their immediate aims, always contain researches and experiments in form.

These researches and experiments are made so that – in another interpretation and from another individual point of view – they could be used later collectively by all of us working on the creation of films in general.

Characteristically, Eisenstein admits, on the one hand, the validity of the criticism that he sometimes carried his structural passions too far; on the other, he asserts a much more important fact: Those very experiments and his postanalysis of them had an immense and indelible impact on the development of the cinema as an art form.

University of Michigan, Ann Arbor   H. E.

Acknowledgments

I wish to first express gratitude to my fellow translator Roberta Reader of Harvard University for her conscientious and painstaking work on Eisenstein's text and notes.

I wish to express also my thanks to Southern Illinois University at Carbondale, its President Albert Somit, its Dean of Communications and Fine Arts Keith Sanders, and the Head of Research Projects Michael Dingerson, for giving me the facilities of secretarial and mechanical aid, including word processing, to produce such a book. Additional thanks go to Alan Cohn and Carol Palmer of the Humanities Division, SIU Library, and to Michaelann Goodman and Karen Engelhardt, my indefatigable typists, and Brenda Yuccas who brilliantly coped with the word processing. My colleague Mr. Samuel Sorgenstein deserves also many thanks for his conscientious work on the indexing of *Nonindifferent Nature* and his expert assistance in editorial work for the Center.

I want to acknowledge also assistance that is often forgotten, that of the publisher's editors Ms. Elizabeth Maguire, Mr. Michael Gnat, and Ms. Ernestine Franco, whose conscientious and diligent supervision of my manuscript through the press was essential for its emerging as a beautiful book.

Finally, my eternal thanks to Fredda Brilliant, my wife, fellow-artist, and fellow-writer, whose help in all my work is indispensable.

Herbert Marshall

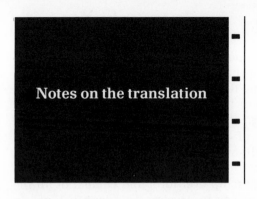

Notes on the translation

Eisenstein's language and style

Everyone who has attempted it knows that translating Eisenstein is a most difficult task. His subject matter is unusual, complex, and erudite in the extreme. He was an original thinker, creating new concepts that are couched in new terminology, with words often stretched to new usages, as, for instance, the words "montage" and "pathos," or with neologisms invented by Eisenstein himself. A further complication is caused by Eisenstein's fluency in four languages. He was able effortlessly to switch from one to another, writing them in the original, or absorbing them into the Russian language. Then, too, his reading was so universal and voracious that he frequently quoted from unexpected and often unknown sources, and the Russian transliteration of a foreign word sometimes makes it very difficult for the translator to find out how the original word was spelled. This applies especially to languages that depend on pronunciation, like French; and when Chinese or Japanese is quoted, the original and the English forms may be poles apart.

I have tried my best to make sure that the English forms are correct, but despite the most painstaking checking and research, there may be errors.

On top of all this, his style was at times far from lucid, its significance difficult to decipher, and, when translated, after much discussion and analysis and research, it remained overly complicated and convoluted. He jumped from association to association in a myriad of directions; he partly explained this himself, saying at one point, "Here I slip into a fatal unrestricted verbiage in all directions, away from the immediate actual basis of the article," and elsewhere, "Some chapters begin with one thing. Then follows an accidentally emerging reminiscence and, finally, a whole chain of free association. Beginning a chapter, I never know where it will take off to."

Now, if this weren't enough, there is another formidable obstacle to understanding: the assumption that the reader will have a general knowledge of the complex and often confused background of Russian

xxiii

history in general and of certain periods in particular, for example, the reigns of Ivan the Terrible, Peter the Great, Nicholas I, and Nicholas II; World War I; the two revolutions; the civil war; foreign intervention; the NEP (the New Economic Policy of Lenin); the nature of the Communist Party and its internal struggles, its treatment of art and culture; the internecine battles over styles of art, labeled formalist and socialist realist; the aims of the Proletcult and such slogans as "the living man"; the growth of Stalinism and its totalitarian structure and terror; the growing control and total dictatorship over form and content of all the arts; the necessity for Soviet citizens to develop the "double-think" in order to survive, and the way an artist has to utilize the double entendre, metaphor, and allegory to express what he really feels, as compared with how the Communist Party orders him to feel or think or act. Eisenstein was a master at this kind of writing: There is hardly an overt word of criticism of the Communist Party in any of his writings, but deep down it is there – as his autobiography *Immoral Memories* will reveal to those who can read between the lines.

Then there is a special development of Eisenstein's style into what I call "cinematic montage" – his deliberate habit of breaking down his sentences into montage pieces of very short length. So the reader must not be surprised to find a sentence broken into several lines set, paragraph fashion, sometimes after a comma, sometimes not, and starting with a lower-case letter, then breaking off at another comma, again to a new line, with still no period or capital letter.

That is the essence of Eisenstein's literary style – the continuity and clash of lines, as if they were film shots, to form a cinematic sequence of words. This explains why he used a great deal more inversion than is usual in prose; it is a fundamental ingredient of the structure of poetry and often the basis for bringing to the end of the line a rhyme word. Like other writing techniques, its quality depends on the skill of the writer: It can be consummately skillful, the art that conceals art; or it can be painfully awkward and obvious. I hope that my translation has done its best in conveying Eisenstein's cinematic style.

Footnotes and endnotes

The translator has kept the original endnotes, by and large, which are usually by the Russian editors of the Soviet edition. As they were intended for a Russian readership they were not always necessary or applicable or were political polemics. So though, by and large, the translator has kept the original endnotes, in certain places they have been edited with the aim of objectivity. The same numeration of the endnotes has been kept so that any interested party can check with the original.

When possible the translator has tried to find standard English translations of quotations that are given, of course, in a Russian translation in Eisenstein's text, though sometimes he quotes the original text, particularly in German, English, or French.

All parenthetical text reference citations have been treated as footnotes. These footnotes are either S. Eisenstein's, the Russian editor's, or the translator's (whose additions are given in brackets). Modern transliterative spellings were used for names except for those in common use and previously established.

Regarding Eisenstein's own footnotes, these have been kept untouched and, like the whole text, translated as faithfully as possible.

H. M.

Photo portrait of Sergei Eisenstein, 1931.

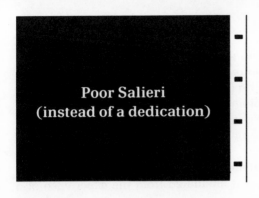

Poor Salieri
(instead of a dedication)

> ...True tone I smothered, dissecting
> music like a corpse. I test with
> algebra pure harmony...
>   — Pushkin, "Mozart and Salieri"

For some time I have pondered to whom I should dedicate my first book. For favored girls, it is too businesslike. My students, regardless, will use it as a textbook. My friends, even so, will support me. Enemies will attack it anyway.

As it is, I always dedicate all of my endeavors to the working class. Past generations don't need it. Future generations will go further...

So, I am left with one person, in whose memory I would like to dedicate this work, Salieri.

Pushkin's poor Salieri.

He dissected music like a corpse...

And in this lay something really terrible.

Like a corpse.

To come to a stop, to be terminated, without movement and without life.

All because there was, as yet, no cinematography, because the one art had not come into existence that would have made it possible, without taking its life, or killing its sound, or dooming it to be a lifeless corpse, to tune into and study, under dynamic conditions and Mozartian joie de vivre, not only its algebra and geometry, but also its calculus and differentials; without which, on the level of cinematography, art cannot go very far.

Such is the first reason why I am not afraid of dedicating my book to Salieri.

The second lies in the fact that, no matter how caustic is the venom of my opponents, when I create, I fling the "crutches" of conformity to the devil, a term used by Lessing;[1] and I call to mind the words of Goethe: "Grau ist die theorie..."[2]

1

["Theory, my friend, is gray, but the tree of life grows green"] and then plunge headlong into spontaneous creativity.

However, never for a moment do I lose sight of the great importance of the necessity, outside of those moments of creative intoxication, of ever-increasing, precise knowledge about what we do, and especially me. Without this, neither the development of our art, nor the education of youth is possible.

And, I repeat, never and nowhere has preconceived algebra stood in my way. Everywhere and always, it emanated from the experience of a finished work of art.

Therefore, as well as a dedication to the tragic memory of the searcher, Salieri, this volume is simultaneously dedicated also to the memory of Mozart's spontaneous joie de vivre.

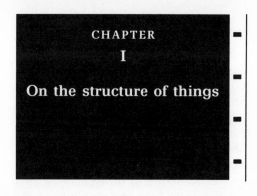

CHAPTER

I

On the structure of things

Let us assume we are to present grief on the screen. There is no such thing as grief "in general." Grief is concrete, thematic; it has a vehicle when a character is grieving; it has a consumer when sorrow is presented, so that the viewer also grieves.

The latter doesn't have to be always present in the depiction of grief: The enemy's grief after suffering defeat evokes joy in the viewer, who identifies himself with the victor.

These ideas are childishly obvious, but in them are contained the most complex problems of the structure of a work of art, for they touch on the most vital aspect of our work: *the problem of representation and the relationship to what is being represented.*

Composition is one of the most effective means of expressing this relationship, although this relationship is not only achieved through composition and it is not the only task of composition.

In this article I will be concerned with the special question of how the embodiment of this relationship is achieved specifically by narrow compositional means. The relationship to what is represented is achieved by the manner in which this representation is presented. And immediately the question arises concerning the methods and means with which one must treat the representation so that there is a relationship between *what* it shows, *how* the author relates to it, and how the author wishes the viewers to perceive, feel, and sense what he is representing.

Let us trace this phenomenon from the point of view of composition; that is, let us look at a case when the task of embodying the author's attitude is served first by composition, understood as the law of structuring what is being represented. This is extremely important for us, for very little has been written on the role of composition in film, and those features of composition that I have in mind here have almost never been mentioned in literature at all.

The object of representation and the law of structuring by which it is presented may coincide. This is the simplest case, and one can more or less cope with a compositional problem of this type. This is a structuring of the simplest type: "grievous grief," "joyful joy," "a marching march," etc. In other words: The hero grieves and nature, lighting, sometimes the composition of the frame, less often the rhythm of montage, and most of all the music pasted onto it, grieve with him in unison. The same thing occurs when we are dealing with "joyful joy," etc.

Even in these simplest cases it is extremely clear what the source of composition is and where it gets its experience and material from: *The composition takes structural elements of the represented phenomenon and from them it creates the law of the structure of things.*

In addition, it mainly takes these elements from the structure of the *emotional behavior of the human being in relation to the experience of the content* of one or the other phenomenon represented.

It is just for this reason that genuine composition is immutably, deeply human: whether this be the "bouncing" rhythm of the structure of cheerful episodes, the "monotonously drawn-out quality" of the editing of a sad scene, or the "glittering with joy" lighting resolution of a shot.

Diderot deduces the compositional *principles* of vocal music, and later instrumental music, from the bases of intonation of living emotional human speech (at the same time also from audial phenomena perceived by him in surrounding nature).[1]

And Bach – master of the most complex compositional passages in music – affirms a very similar *human approach* to the bases of composition, as a direct pedagogic prerequisite:

...On testimony coming to us from Bach's pupils, he taught them to look at the instrumental voice as they would a personality, and at the polyphonic instrumental composition as a conversation between these personalities, while setting up a rule that each of them "speak well and in time, and if they have nothing to say, it would be better to remain silent or wait their turn..."[*]

On exactly the same basis of the mutual play of human emotions, on the basis of human experience, cinematography builds its structural passages and most complex compositional structures.

Let us take as an example one of the most successful scenes in *Alexander Nevsky* – the episode of the attack of the German "wedge" on the Russian militia at the beginning of the "Battle on the Ice."

All the nuances of an experience of growing terror are heard in this episode, when in the face of imminent danger one's heart contracts and one holds one's breath.

The structure of the "galloping wedge" in *Alexander Nevsky* is precisely "copied" from a variation within the process of this experience.

This is what dictated the rhythms of growth, caesura, the increase in tempo, and the retardation of the passage.

---

* E. K. Rozenov, *J. S. Bach i ego rod* (*J. S. Bach and His Kind*), Moscow, 1911, p. 72.

The intense throbbing of an excited heart dictated the rhythm of the galloping hooves:

visually depictive – this is the *jump* of the jumping knights.

compositional – this is the intense *beating* of the excited heart.

In the successful production, both of them – the representational and the compositional system – merged *here* in an unbroken unity of a threatening image – the beginning of a battle not for life, but for death.

And the event unfolded on the screen "according to the graph" of the flow of this or that passion and, by this "graph," coming back from the screen, involved the emotions of the viewer, raising them to that same tangle of passions that determined the compositional scheme of the work.

This is where the secret of the genuinely emotional effect of true composition lies. Using as its source *the structure of human emotions, it unmistakably also appeals to the emotions*, unmistakably evokes the complex of those emotions that engendered it.

In all aspects of art – and in film art more than anywhere else – it is exactly in this manner and mainly in this way that what Lev Tolstoy wrote about music is achieved: "It, music, immediately, directly transports me into that spiritual state in which the one who wrote the music found himself."*

This – from the simplest instances to the most complex – is one of the possible *types* of the structure of things.

But there is also another case when an author, instead of a resolution of the type "joyful joy," must solve, for example, the theme of "life-affirming death."

How can that be done here?

It is quite obvious that in such cases the law of the structure of things is no longer provided *exclusively* by elements *directly* flowing out of natural and common emotions, states and feelings of a person that accompany the given phenomenon.

However, the law of composition still remains the same in the given case.

But the search for the *primary scheme* of the system of composition will lie not so much in the emotions accompanying *the object represented* as initially in the emotional *relationship to the object represented*.

But this case is quite rare and not obligatory in general. Usually in such cases a very curious and often unexpected picture arises of the transmission of the phenomenon by a structure not at all common under

* L. N. Tolstoy, "The Kreutzer Sonata," XXIII [in *Six Short Stories*, M. Wettlin, trans., Dell, New York, 1963 – HM].

"normal" circumstances. Literature is overflowing with examples of this in all its nuances.

Here this method appears also in such primary elements of compositional treatment as the structure of artistic images, resolutions possible through a system of analogies.

And from the pages of literature we have images of quite unexpected compositional structures in which phenomena are presented that "in themselves" are completely normal. In addition, these structures are not defined, nourished, or called to life by formalistic exaggerations or extravagant researches.

The examples I have in mind relate to the realistic classics; they are classics because it is by exactly these means that the clearest judgment concerning the phenomenon, the clearest *relationship* to the phenomenon, was embodied in them with extreme clarity.

How many times in literature do we come across a description of the "adultress"! By what variety of situation, position, and figurative comparisons are they adorned – there are hardly more impressive pictures than those where the "criminal embraces of the lovers" are figuratively equated with...murder.

...She felt so guilty, so much to blame, that it only remained for her to humble herself and ask to be forgiven; but she had no one in the world now except him, so that even her prayer for forgiveness was addressed to him. Looking at him, she felt her humiliation physically, and could say nothing more. He felt what a murderer must feel when looking at the body he has deprived of life. The body he had deprived of life was their love, the first period of their love. There was something frightful and revolting in the recollection of what had been paid for with the terrible price of shame. The shame she felt at her spiritual nakedness communicated itself to him. But in spite of the murderer's horror of the body of his victim, that body must be cut in pieces and hidden away, and he must make use of what he has obtained by the murder.

Then, as the murderer desperately throws himself on the body, as though with passion, and drags it and hacks it, so Vronsky covered her face and shoulders with kisses.

She held his hand and did not move. Yes! These kisses were what had been bought by that shame! Yes, and this hand, which will always be mine, is the hand of my accomplice.*

In this excerpt from *Anna Karenina* (part 2, Chap. XI), in the figurative system of its comparisons, the whole scene is totally resolved with magnificent cruelty from the very depths of the author's relationship to the phenomenon, rather than from the feelings and emotions of its participants [as, for example, this very same theme in numerous

* [*Anna Karenina*, L. Maude and A. Maude trans., Norton, New York, 1970, p. 135 – HM.]

variations had been resolved by Zola in the course of his *Rougon-Macquart* (1871–93)].

Tolstoy attached an epitaph to his novel: "Vengeance is mine; I will repay, saith the Lord."

M. Sukhotin, in a letter to Veresayev[2] of March 23, 1907, cites Tolstoy's words on the significance of this epigraph, which had excited Veresayev:

> ...I must repeat that I chose this epigraph...in order to express the idea that the evil that man commits has as its consequences all bitter things that come not from people, but from God, and which Anna Karenina also experienced within her.[3]

In the second part of the novel, from where this excerpt has been taken, Tolstoy had the task of showing "the evil that man commits."

The writer's temperament forces one to feel it in forms of the highest stage of evil – as crime.

The moralist's temperament forces one to assess the evil act of the highest degree of crime against a person as – murder.

Finally, the artist's temperament forces an evaluation of the characters' behavior to come through, helped by all the means of expression available to him.

The crime – murder, having become *the basic expressive relationship of the author* to the phenomenon – becomes at the same time *the determinant of all basic elements of the compositional treatment of the scene.*

It dictates the images and analogies: "...what a murderer must feel when looking at the body he has deprived of life. The body he had deprived of life was their love..." etc., etc.

It dictates as well the images of the characters' actions, prescribing the embodiment of the actions, characteristic of love, in forms characteristic of murder.

"...Then, as the murderer desperately throws himself on the body, as though with passion, and drags it and hacks it, so Vronsky covered her face and shoulders with kisses," etc.

These extremely precise "stage directions," defining the nuance of behavior, are chosen from thousands of possible ones, just because they are the only ones that correspond, in this particular case, most fully to the author's relationship to the phenomenon itself.

The idea of evil being expressed compositionally through the image of crime – of murder, by which the given scene has been resolved – is encountered in other works of Tolstoy as well. This image is a favorite one of his, and close to him.

Not only the "adulterer" but also "animal relation" under conditions of inter-marriage relationships is built on the same figurative system of composition.

In the "Kreutzer Sonata" we meet the same thing. Two excerpts from Pozdnyshev's story will give a clear idea of this. The second one (about children) broadens the framework of the example, creating even greater surprises by its outer compositional structuring, which, however, result entirely from the inner relationship to the theme.

I was amazed by our hatred for each other. But nothing else could have been expected. It was the mutual hatred of two parties to a crime – to the instigation and perpetration of a crime. For was it not a crime indeed when she, poor thing, became pregnant the very first month and still our animal relations went on? Do you think this is all irrelevant to the story? You are wrong. It is all part of the story of how I killed my wife. At the trial they asked me how I killed her and what I killed her with. Fools! They thought I killed her on the 5th of October with a knife. It was not then that I killed her, it was much earlier....*

...And so the coming of children poisoned our life instead of improving it. Furthermore, the children were a new cause of dissension. This became evident as soon as they appeared, and the older they grew, the oftener they were a means and an object of dissension. They were not only an object of dissension, they were a weapon of struggle as well. We fought each other with our children. Each of us had his favourite child and used it as his weapon. My thrusts were usually directed against our eldest boy, Vasya; hers, against Liza....

They, poor things, suffered dreadfully from this, but we were too much engrossed in our constant state of war to think of them.[†]

As we have seen, no matter what example we might take, the method of composition remains always the same. In all cases its basic determinant remains primarily *the author's relationship*. In all cases the prototype for composition remains *the action* of man and *the structure* of human actions.

The decisive elements of the compositional structure are taken by the author from the bases of his relation to the phenomenon. It dictates the *structure* and character by which the actual representation is unfolded. The representation, losing nothing in its reality, emerges from here with immeasurable enriched significance and emotion.

It is possible to bring in one more example. It is curious because in it, in the delineation of the two characters represented, not only are the structure and features in contrast to the ones usually and tritely characteristic of them, but by means of construction...an exchange of structures is consciously produced!

These characters are a German officer and a French prostitute.

The structure of the image of the "noble officer" is assigned to the prostitute.

The structure of the image of the prostitute in its most unattractive

---

* L. N. Tolstoy, "The Kreutzer Sonata," XIII, op. cit. p. 316.
[†] Ibid., XVI, p. 328.

resolution is the skeleton of the treatment of the German officer.

This original *chasse-croise** was done by Maupassant in the well-known story "Mademoiselle Fifi."

The structure of the image of the Frenchwoman is woven out of all the characteristics of nobility connected with the bourgeois presentation of an officer.

And it is quite natural that by the very same method the German officer is revealed in his *essence – in his prostitutelike nature.*

From this "nature" Maupassant took only one feature – her destructiveness for the "moral foundations" of bourgeois society. This is interesting since from this aspect Maupassant took a similar scheme as something ready-made, well known, and fresh in our minds. His German officer is cut according to the image created by Zola.

The officer with the nickname "Mademoiselle Fifi" is, of course, Nana.

Nana not as a whole, but Nana in that part of the novel where Zola raises this image to great destructive power for respectable families and at the same time describes Nana's destructive caprices, when she breaks the family porcelain presented to her by her admirers. The generalized presentation of the destructive quality of the courtesan for families and for society in this scene is also "made concrete" in the particular episode with the *bonbonniere* of Saxon china and the pile of other valuable gifts, which seem to serve as a symbol of "high society," mockingly smashed by Nana's whims.

The structure of the officer's behavior is completely identical to the structure of Nana's behavior in this scene. The name "Nana" and the nickname "Fifi" emphasize this unmistakable connection. This is not contradicted by the fact that French diminutives of names are generally formed by doubling the characteristic syllable: Ernest – "Neness," Josephine – "Fifina," Robert – "Beber." Instead this only emphasizes our supposition.[†]

But in the novella as a whole we have a good model of how a common, everyday depiction is compositionally reworked in a necessary direction that definitely corresponds to the structural skelton.

Here we are concerned with cases that are quite obvious, apparent, and easy to interpret. However, those very same principles lie in the deepest elements of compositional structure, in those depths reached only by the scalpel of very pedantic and profound analysis.

And it turns out that everywhere the basis is that very same

---

* A dancing figure with cavalier and lady exchanging places.
† It is interesting to note that Maupassant, as if blind, destroying a similar association, "motivates" the nickname of "Fifi" by the fact that its bearer – the Marquis Wilhelm von Erich (the officer) – had the habit of expressing his disdain for everything around him with the exclamation: "Fi, donc!" ("Fi, how disgusting!"). However, this does not change the matter, and probably only emphasizes that same association.

humaneness, human psychology, nourishing the most complex composi-
tional elements of form, in exactly the same way it nourishes and defines
the content of the work for itself.

I would like to illustrate these positions in two quite complicated and, it would seem, formally quite abstract examples that apply to the composition of *Battleship Potemkin.*

For the theme of the structure of things and composition in the widest sense of the word, they will serve as examples and confirmation of what was stated above. From the point of view of *Potemkin* they will serve as *research material for the film itself.*

When Potemkin is discussed, usually two of its features are observed: the organic unity of its composition as a whole, and the *pathos** of the film.

Organic unity and *pathos*

Let us take two of the most outstanding features of *Potemkin* and try to discover by what means they were achieved, especially in terms of composition. The first feature will be examined in the composition of the film as a whole. The second will be examined in the "Odessa Steps" episode, where *pathos* achieves the greatest dramatic tension. Later, we will generalize this for the entire film as well.

Our analysis will be concerned with how the organic unity and *pathos* of the theme were resolved by means of the composition itself. In the same way one could analyze how these same elements were resolved by other elements, as, for example, by the actors' performance, by the treatment of theme, by the color range of the film, by use of landscape, by treatment of mass scenes, etc.

However, we will confine ourselves here to one particular problem, the problem of *the structure of things*, making no pretense to a thorough analysis of all aspects of the film.

However, it is in an organic work of art that the elements contributing to the work as a whole permeate every feature composing this work. A single norm pervades not only the whole and each of its parts but also each element that is called to participate in the creation of the whole. One and the same principle will nourish every part, appearing in each of them with their own special qualitative distinctions. And only in this case can one speak of the organic unity of a work, for here we understand an

---

* [Greek πάθος (*pathos*) – "a passion, emotion, such as love, hate." (H. G. Liddell and R. Scott, *Greek–English Lexicon*, 7th ed., Oxford University Press, Oxford, 1961, p. 584); but because Eisenstein is specifically signifying *Ex stasis*, ecstasy, inspiration, we shall continue to use the particular term throughout the rest of the book, set in italics to emphasize Eisenstein's specific meaning – HM.]

organism as Engels defines it in *The Dialectics of Nature*: "...an organism is, of course, a higher unity..."*

These considerations immediately lead us to the first theme of our analysis – to the question of the "organic unity" of the structure of *Potemkin*.

Let us approach this question by proceeding from the premise set forth at the beginning. The organic unity of a work, as well as the sense of organic unity received from the work, arises when the law of the construction of this work corresponds to the laws of *the structure of organic phenomena of nature*.

It is quite obvious that here we are concerned with a sense of the compositional organic unity of the whole. This feeling cannot be withstood even by those viewers who, because of their class allegiances, have sharply negative attitudes toward the topic and theme of the work; that is, those viewers for whom neither the topic nor the theme is at all "organic." This is exactly what happened with *Potemkin* in bourgeois auditoriums. However, let us make more precise the concept of organic unity of the structure of a work in the sense used here.

I would say there are two types of organic unity.

The first is characteristic of any work in general that possesses wholeness and an inner law.

In this case organic unity is defined by the fact that the work is governed by a definite law of structuring, and all its separate parts are subordinated to this law.

Based on definitions of German aestheticians, I would call this type of organic unity *the organic unity of a general order*. In the given case it is quite obvious that we have in this principle a copy of the one by which natural phenomena are constructed and about which V. I. Lenin said: "...The particular does not exist outside of those relations which lead to the general. The general exists only in the particular, through the particular..."†

But the actual law by which these natural phenomena are structured in this given case doesn't necessarily coincide with the law by which this or that work of art is structured.

The organic unity of works of the second type occurs when not only the actual *principle of organic unity* is present but also the actual canon of law by which natural phenomena are structured. This could be called the organic unity of a *particular* of exceptional order. It is this that we find particularly interesting.

Here we have a case where the work of art – *an artificial work* – is

---

* F. Engels, *The Dialectics of Nature*, 5th ed., Sotsekgiz, Moscow–Leningrad, 1931, p. 151.
† V.I. Lenin, *Works*, XIII, Gos. Izd. Polit. Lit., Moscow–Leningrad, 1958–65, pp. 302–3 [Russian].

structured according to the same laws by which *nonartificial* phenomena – "organic," natural phenomena – are structured.

And in this case not only is a realistic theme proper but the forms of its compositional embodiment also fully reflect the laws peculiar to reality.

It is obvious that a work of this type has a very particular effect on the perceiver, not only because it is raised to the same level as natural phenomena but also because the law of its structuring is also the law governing those who perceive the work, for they too are a part of organic nature. The perceiver feels organically tied, merged, and united with a work of this type, just as he feels himself one with and merged with the organic environment and nature surrounding him.

To a greater or lesser degree this feeling is inevitable in each of us, and the secret consists of the fact that in each case both *us and the work* are governed by *one and the same canon of law*. The nature of this law will also be examined in both our examples, which analyze, it would seem, two different and independent questions but which, however, in the end, come together.

The first example will be based on an analysis of this law under static conditions; the second will be examined under dynamic conditions.

Thus in the first example we will discuss the divisions and *proportions* of the structure of the work. In the second, we will discuss the *process* of the structure of things.

Thus the resolution of the first question concerning the organic unity of *Potemkin's* structure must begin with an interpretation of whether this structure is subordinate to the first condition – *the organic unity of a general order.*

Potemkin looks like a chronicle of events but acts as a drama.

The secret of this effect is that in it the chronicle stages of events have been timed to the strict composition of tragedy. In addition, it is the composition of tragedy in its most canonical form – the five-act tragedy.

The events, taken almost as bare facts, are divided into the five acts of tragedy, in which the facts have been chosen and selected in a sequence where they answer those demands that classical tragedy imposed on the third act as opposed to the second, on the fifth act as opposed to the first, etc., etc.

The advantage and law of selection of the five-act construction of tragedy, of course, is also not accidental, but the result of prolonged natural selection; however, we will not dwell on this here. It is sufficient that as the basis of the initial division of our drama, it was this very structure, validated by the centuries, that was selected. This is even emphasized by the fact that every "act" has its own independent title.

Let us briefly mention these five acts.

Part I – "Men and Maggots": Exposition of the action. The situation on the battleship. Maggoty meat. Discontent among the sailors.

Part II – "Drama on the Quarterdeck"[4] "Hands on deck!" Refusal to eat the maggoty soup. Scene with the tarpaulin. "Brothers!" Refusal to shoot. Mutiny. Revenge on the officers.

Part III – "The Dead Man Appeals": Mists. Vakulinchuk's corpse in the Odessa port. Lament over the body. Meeting of insurrection. Raising the red flag.

Part IV – "The Odessa Steps": Fraternization of the shore with the battleship. The yawls with provisions. The shooting on the Odessa steps. The battleship firing on the "Germans' H. Q."

Part V – "Meeting the Squadron": Night of expectation. Meeting the squadron. Engines. "Brothers!" Refusal of squadron to shoot. Battleship passes victoriously through the squadron.

Based on their action, the episodes of each part of the drama are quite different, but a double repetition pervades them and seems to cement them together.

In the "Drama on the Quarterdeck," a small group of mutinous sailors – a small fraction of the battleship – shout "Brothers!" on encountering the muzzles of the rifles of the firing squad directed at them. And the muzzles are lowered: The whole organism of the battleship is with them.

In "Meeting the Squadron," the mutinous battleship as a whole – a small fraction of the fleet – hurls the same cry "Brothers!" on encountering the muzzles of the admiralty squadron guns directed at them. And the muzzles are lowered: The whole organism of the fleet is with them.

From a cell of the battleship organism to the organism of the battleship as a whole; from a cell of the organism of the fleet – of the battleship – to the organism of the fleet as a whole – this is the way the revolutionary feeling of fraternity develops thematically. And it is repeated by the structure of the work, which has as its theme fraternity and revolution.

Over the heads of the battleship's commanders, over the heads of the tsar's admirals of the fleet, finally over the heads of the censors of bourgeois countries surges the fraternal "hurrah" of the film as a whole, just as within the picture the feeling of fraternity flies from the mutinying battleship over the sea to the shore.

The organic unity of the film, conceived in a cell within the film, not only goes on, spreading through the film as a whole, but it goes far beyond the limits of the film itself.

Thematically and emotionally perhaps, it might be sufficient to discuss its organic unity, but we wish to be stricter concerning the form.

Let us look closely at the structure of the work.

Its five acts, connected to the main direction of the theme by the theme of revolutionary fraternity, otherwise bear little resemblance to each other. But in one respect they are absolutely *identical*: Each part distinctly divides into two almost equal halves. This is particularly clear in the second act.

The scene with the tarpaulin – the mutiny.

Mourning for Vakulinchuk – the angry meeting.

Lyrical fraternization – the shooting.

Nervous awaiting the squadron – triumph.

Moreover, at points of a "break" in each part, there always seems to be a pause – a type of "caesura."

In one case – it is several shots of clenched fists in which the theme of mourning over the murdered man jumps to the theme of rage (Part III).

There is the subtitle "SUDDENLY," cutting short the scene of fraternization in order to transfer it to the scene of the shooting (Part IV).

The motionless rifle muzzles are there (Part II). The gaping muzzles of the guns are here (Part V). And the shout "Brothers!" breaking the deathly pause of expectation in an outburst of fraternal feelings is in both parts.

And it is also remarkable that the jump at each point – is not simply a sudden jump to *another* mood, to *another* rhythm, to *another* event, but each time it is a transition to a *distinct opposite*. Not contrastive, but *opposite*, for each time it gives *the image of that same theme from the opposite point of view and at the same time unavoidably grows out of it*.

The outburst of the mutiny after the maximum point of tension under the muzzles of the guns (Part II).

Or the outburst of anger organically bursting out of the theme of the masses' mourning for the murdered man (Part III).

The shots on the stairs as an organic "conclusion" of the reaction to the fraternal embraces of the insurgents from the *Potemkin* and the population of Odessa (Part IV), etc.

The unity of a similar law, recurring in *every act* of the drama, is significant in itself.

But if we look at the work as a whole, then we will see that the same thing occurs in the whole structure of *Potemkin*.

Actually, near the middle, *the film as a whole is divided by the dead pause of a caesura*; the stormy movement of the beginning pauses totally so that it can gather momentum a second time for its second half.

The role of a similar caesura in terms of the film as a whole is played by the episode of the dead Vakulinchuk and the Odessa mists.

For the film as a whole, this episode plays the same role of the pause before a transition that is played by separate shots within the separate parts. Actually, from this moment on, the theme, having broken the circle bound by the sides of one mutinous battleship, also explodes, enveloping the whole city, which is *opposing* the ship topographically but merging with it emotionally, only, however, to be cut off from it by soldier's boots on the steps at the very moment when the theme returns again to the drama at sea.

We see how organic the development of the theme is, and at the same time we see that the structure of *Potemkin*, which has evolved out of the theme, is *united in the work as a whole* in exactly the same way it is *united in its basic parts*.

The law of organic unity of a general order, as we can see, has been completely observed.

Let's examine further and check: Is the law of organic unity not carried deeper? Do we not observe in the structure of *Potemkin* not only the principle but the very formula of that basic law that exists as a phenomenon of organic nature.

For this we must penetrate into the very nature of this basic law, define it and then check: Does the compositional structure of *Potemkin* correspond not only in *principle* but even to the very "formula" itself by which the processes of the phenomena of nature take place?

Obviously if the question is put like that then it would first of all concern *proportions* by which *Potemkin* is structured and to what degree the structural *rhythm of these proportions* will correspond with the rhythm of the *basic laws of natural phenomena.*

For this we must recall and determine what are those "formulas" and geometrical forms, in which is expressed the characteristics of organic natural phenomena, their organic wholeness, and the indications of organic unity of the whole and its parts.

The easiest of all is to reveal and determine the basic phenomena that differentiates living organic nature from other phenomena. This phenomenon is *growth*, and around the formula of growth, as a basic sign of organic phenomena, we shall concentrate our search. We deliberately speak now of *growth*, and not of development, which is about the primitive evolutionary aspect of phenomena, as distinct from the laws of development having another, more complex behavioral graphic. We will speak below about this second phase of development in contrast to growth, which takes place organically not only in natural phenomena but also in society.

However, what is the "formula" of growth as the primary typical sign of organic nature?

In the area of determined proportions, in the dynamics of this phenomenon expressing itself in statics, the formula emerges, which in aesthetic studies is usually termed "the golden section."

In school we called a similar proportion the division of a segment in the relationship of the middle to the extremes.

Let us pause here for a moment, and in a brief digression let us try to show how in the formula of the golden section the *actual curved* growth of natural phenomena crossbreeds with the mathematical image for expressing the idea of *growth*.

In investigating the "formulas" and the generalizing image of the curve that would express the idea of organic growth, researchers into this question have gone in two directions.

On the one hand, they went along the simplest path – comparative measurements of *actual growing objects of organic nature*.

On the other hand – they used "pure" mathematics in search of a formula that would express in a mathematical image the idea of a second necessary sign of organic unity, that is, the principle of *the unity and inseparability of the whole and of all its merging parts*.

Wreaths of leaves and flower stems, pine cones and sunflower seeds served as objects of measurement for the first. The latter proved to be one of the most graphic images for observation: The trajectory of curving growth is apparent in the sunflower seed, as in the prepared sketch.

The measurements and conclusion of the curve, generalizing all particular cases led to the following position: The process of growth flows along a turning spiral, and this spiral is logarithmic.

Logarithmic spirals are varied, but they all have the same feature, that the consecutive vectors arranged as *OA, OB, OC, OD*, etc. in the sketch form a *geometric progression*, that is, for the logarithmic spiral the following series will always occur:

$$\frac{OA}{OB} = \frac{OB}{OC} = \frac{OC}{OD} \cdots = m$$

for any meaning *m* (see Figure 1).

It is obvious that every logarithmic spiral carries within itself the image of the idea of uniform evolution.*

However, it is also very obvious that the actual curve of growth out of *all possible ones* turns out to be the *only* definite one, and in addition, one that will be able to link the vectors between themselves and (according to the second condition of organic unity) establish yet one more connection, that is, between consecutive vectors – a connection that is also characteristic of the unity of the whole and its parts.

And both series of quests meet at this point: the path of the actual

---

* Except in cases when this spiral turns into a circle, straight line, or point, in the presence of the corresponding $OB = OA$, $OB = O$, $OB = \infty$.

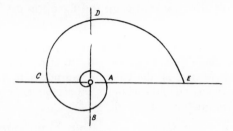

Figure 1.

measurements and the path of the quest for the mathematical image for the idea of the unity of the whole and its parts.

The mathematical expression of this idea excited the ancients also.

The first approximation to the expression of this is given by Plato[5] in answer to the question: How can two parts form a whole (*Timaeus*, VII)?*

But it is not possible for two things to be fairly united without a third; for they need a bond between them which shall join them both. The best of bonds is that which makes itself and those which it binds as complete a unity as possible; and the nature of proportion is to accomplish this most perfectly. For when of any three numbers, whether expressing three or two dimensions, one is a mean term, so that as the first is to the middle, as is the middle to the last; and conversely as the last is to the middle, so is the middle to the first; then since the middle becomes first and last, and the last and the first both become middle, of necessity all will come to be the same, and being the same *with one another all will be a unity*. (I quote according to G. Timerding).[6]

If we add to this the condition that the larger is at the same time a whole, that is, the sum of the smaller and the middle, then this will also be a formula, embodying most fully the idea of the connection of the whole and its parts, which are presented as two segments, in its sum composing this whole.

We have known of this concept since our school days – "the division of a segment in the relationship of the middle to the extremes," or the so-called golden section.

"*Sectio aurea*" – this is what Leonardo da Vinci called this section. In the endless series of scholars and admirers studying this fascinating problem of the golden section, from antiquity up to our own day, da Vinci has an honorable place in the definition of its characteristics.

Its characteristics are really those characteristics we have been looking for.

* [*The Timaeus of Plato*, R. D. Archer-Hind, ed., Ayer, New York, 1973, p. 97 – HM.]

Professor Grimm writes in "Summing up the Exceptional Features of the Golden Section":*

...2. Only the golden section, of all divisions of the whole, gives a constant relationship between the whole and its parts; only in it do both preceeding members[†] exist in full dependence on the basic magnitude and on the whole, while the relation between them and to the whole is not accidental, but a constant relation equal to 0.618...in any meaning of the whole.

Obviously, this is the maximally accessible approximation of a mathematical scheme to that condition of organic unity of the whole and its parts in nature as Hegel defined it in those pages of the "Encyclopedia" with which Engels operates in *The Dialectic of Nature.*[‡]

...They say, it is true, that an animal consists of bones, muscles, nerves, etc. However, it is immediately clear that this does not have the same sense as the statement has that a piece of granite consists of the above-named substances. These substances are quite indifferently related to their combination and can exist very well even without this combination; various parts and members of an organic body are maintained only in their combination and, separate from each other, they cease existing as such.[¶]

...Members and organs of a living body must not only be examined as its parts, since they present themselves in such a way that they are presented only in a unity, and by no means relate indifferently to the latter. These limbs and organs become simple parts only under the hand of anatomy, but it then no longer is a matter of living bodies, but of corpses.[#]

It is natural to ask where the connection actually is between the golden section as *the most perfect mathematical image of the unity of the whole and its parts* and the logarithmic spiral as *the most perfect linear image of the expression of the principle of proportional evolution in general.*

This connection is vital, and consists in this, that of all possible ones the only logarithmic spiral that outlines not only the image of the *principle of evolution* in general but is in accord with the actual growth of natural phenomena, is the one in which the relationship

$$\frac{OA}{OB} = \frac{OB}{OC} = \frac{OC}{OD} \quad \text{etc. are equal to 0.618,}$$

that is, that for every AC, BD, etc. the corresponding OB, OC, etc. serve as the greater of the two segments into which they are divided by the golden section.

Thus we see that this curve, which is actually present in all cases of

---

* *Proportion in Architecture*, Moscow, 1935, p. 33.
† That is, both segments composing the whole.
‡ International Publishers, New York, 1940, pp. 340–1.
¶ Hegel, *Works*, Vol. II, Sotsekgiz, Moscow–Leningrad, 1930, p. 215.
# Ibid., p. 227.

growth – and is equally true for a section of a tree trunk as well as for the curve of a conch shell, for the structure of an animal's horn and for the section of human bones – is inseparable from this remarkable plastic image of the idea of growth, and each of its three vectors of the type *OA, OB, OC* is found in a proportion that most closely embodies the mathematical image of the unity of the whole and its parts.

Thus in symbols and proportions in the sphere of mathematics, the idea of organic unity is also embodied, which by all signs coincides with process and facts of organic nature.

Thus, in the area relating to proportion, "organic" proportions are the *proportions of the golden section.*

Such an excursion in and of itself, of course, is fascinating. However, it is undoubtedly too specialized to dwell much longer on questions touched by it, or to treat them in greater detail. Moreover, for our theme the most important is the conclusion: What is important is that the sought-for condition of organic unity of the proportions of the two segments of one line – both in relationship to each other as well as in their relationship to this line as a whole – demands that the division of this line into two should pass through the point of the so-called golden section. The golden section consists of a division of the whole line *into two such constituents, where the smaller relates to the larger as the larger does to the whole.*

Expressed by whole numbers, the proportion of the distance of *the point of the golden section from the ends of the segment* is expressed in sequential approximations by the following series:

$\frac{2}{3}, \frac{3}{4}, \frac{8}{13}, \frac{13}{21}$, etc.,

or the infinite fraction 0.618…for *the greater segment, considering the whole as a unit.*

The structure of a work whose proportions are combined according to the golden section has extremely exceptional effective influence in art for it creates a sense of maximum organic unity.

The finest monuments of Greece and the Renaissance were built in accordance with this principle. The composition of the most interesting paintings are impregnated by it. In the area of the plastic arts in general, the golden section and the compositional use of it is extremely popular.

It is quite obvious that there is nothing "mystical" at the basis of its particular and exceptional effect. We tried very hard to show why this effect is so characteristically organic, and why it is just this law that produces the greatest response within us: With all the fibers of our organism, if not our soul, we, part of a single law of the simplest movement – growth – correspond to what has been presented to us in a work of art.

Once upon a time the "blood" tie of man with a future building was established physically – by the bloody remains of a human sacrifice that were buried on the spot of future temples and walls. However, beginning with the Greeks, the blood relationship of this tie passed from the physical body and bones of a man into the unity and community laws that pervade equally both the living human body and those unsurpassed masterpieces of Greek architecture, whose proportions have been resolved by the golden section.

As we have said, questions of the golden section have been worked out very thoroughly in the area of the plastic arts.

They are less popular in application to the other arts, although here they probably have an even greater area of application.

However, something similar also exists in the sphere of poetry. An analysis of the structure of musical works I learned mostly from E. K. Rozenov's unfinished or unpublished works, giving a very high percentage of "hits" of the golden section in music.

Examples from poetry are numerous. Pushkin is particularly full of them. I will choose at random two of my favorite brilliant examples: In them the hits of the golden section in the lines themselves are parried by the sign of the full pause – the period. The period occurs *within the line* only in the area of the golden section.

The first example has been taken from the second canto of *Ruslan and Lyudmila*:

```
...From the doorstep of my hut
So I saw, amidst summer days,
When behind the timid hen,
The arrogant sultan of the hen-coop,
My rooster, ran around the yard
And with lustful wings
His sweetheart he embraced;                    A
Over them in sly circles
The old thief of the chicken village,
Having taken destructive measures,
Rushed, floated, the gray kite,
And fell like lightning on the yard.
He screamed, he flew.‖ In...terrible claws
Into the darkness of safe crevices
He carries away the poor rogue.
In vain, struck with grief
And cold fear                                  B
The rooster calls out to his beloved...
He sees only flying feathers,
Brought by the flying wind.*
```

* [My translation – HM.]

The golden section passes along the thirteenth line (out of twenty), cutting it into two segments of literary material, of which the larger is exactly 0.62 of the whole volume (the golden section: 0.618). From the content itself, it is obvious that it is just at this spot that the *thematic* division of the mass into two parts occurs, from which it clearly follows that the golden section is by no means an abstract "mind play," but that it is closely connected with the content.

The extent to which it is sharply distinguished can be seen by the fact that in the whole example – this is the only line interrupted within by the mark of "full punctuation" – the period.

A second example:

On horseback, in the wilds of the naked steppes,
The king and the hetman both dash. A_1
They flee.‖ Fate bound them.
Danger is near and fury
Gives strength to the king. A_2 A
His heavy wound
He forgot.‖His head dropping,
He gallops, pursued by the Russians, B_1
And the crowd of faithful servants B
Can barely follow after him.* B_2

The basic golden section falls after the word "forgot." $A:B=6:4$; more precisely, $6.25:3.75$.

The masses A and B also break up according to the golden section, within the same exemplary degree of approximation.

The division of *the whole mass*, and also the division *within* the mass. And again cut off by full stops – periods, again single instances when the period is *inside the line.*

One the word "servants," where the mass B is divided according to the golden section, instead of a period we are dealing with a purely intonational accent, which arises obligatorily in the reading and produces a *corresponding pause* before the word "faithful" (like an "imaginary period").

The data of both examples (1817–20 and 1829) have also been examined in order to show that these elements of "organic unity" are equally characteristic of Pushkin in completely different stages of his work.

It seems to me that a "check" of works of film art for the golden section has never been made.

And it is even more curious to note that it is *Potemkin*, empirically well

* *Poltava*, 1829, 3rd canto [my translation – HM.].

known for the "organic unity" of its structure, that is completely constructed according to the law of the golden section.

It was not accidental that we said above that the division of each separate part into two, as well as of the entire film as whole, lies *approximately* in the middle. It lies much closer to the proportion 2 : 3, which is the closest approximation to the golden section.

Actually, it is just at the ratio 2 : 3, between the end of the second and beginning of the third part of the five-act film, that the basic caesura of the film lies: the *zero* point of a pause in the action.

To be more precise, the theme of the dead Vakulinchuk and the tent enter the action not at the beginning of the third part, but at the end of *the second*, adding the missing 0.18 to the six points of the remaining part of the film, which gives the result 6.18, that is, the precise proportion corresponding to the golden section. The very same displacement into an analogical porportion of the point of caesura is the break *OB* in separate parts of the film.

But, probably, the most curious thing of all is that the law of the golden section is observed in *Potemkin* not only for the *zero point* of movement – it is also true for the culmination point. The culmination point is the red flag on the mast of the battleship. And the red flag is raised also. . . at the point of the golden section! But the golden section, considered this time from the *other end* of the film – is at the point 3 : 2 (that is, at the point dividing the three first parts from the two last parts – at the end of the *third part*. In addition with a sweep into the fourth part, where the flag also figures at the beginning of the fourth part).

Thus, in *Potemkin* not only each separate part, but the film as a whole, and in both of its culminations as well – at the point of complete stasis and at the point of maximum movement – strictly follows the law of the golden section – the structural law of the organic phenomena of nature.*

This is the secret of the organic unity of its composition, and here is the affirmation in practice of those hypotheses about composition in general expressed at the beginning.

In order that these hypotheses about composition once and for all be made "propositions about compositions," let us analyze the question of the second distinctive feature of *Battleship Potemkin* – the question of its *pathos* and those compositional means by which the *pathos* of the theme is embodied in the *pathos* of the picture.

However, before turning to the question of *pathos*, let us note that *Potemkin* is not alone in the fact that both the moment of culmination as

---

* I think the nature of tragedy, striving, as we have shown above, toward the five-act structure, is related to this fact: The naturalness of the division of the material of the five acts into the most organic proportions 2:3 and 3:2 is expressed in the given case by whole acts.

well as of counterculmination occur at the interval from the beginning and end of the film at the point of the golden section – once counted from the beginning, and the second time – from the end.

In this respect *Potemkin* is by no means alone. In any contiguous art it is possible to find examples of how *two* striking points of the compositional structure *both* prove to be at points of the golden section. In this case these points prove to be counted off in the exact same way from different ends of the basic mass, which they divide.

Let us examine an example of such a "double golden section" from painting.

This example is particularly interesting because it is taken from a work disputed by no one as the greatest representative of the realistic direction in painting.

And the fact that we see it in this very painting will serve as a reproach to those prejudices that hold one everyday truth for realism, that the strictness of composition in painting is definitely not important and perhaps even harmful!

An analysis of works of the truly great masters of realism reveal something quite different. The problems of composition tormented them in their creativity as incessantly as problems of embodiment of the truth of life, for with sincerity full felt and with total emotional expressiveness truth was embodied by all the means available to the artist. But this has already been thoroughly discussed. Let us proceed to an example.

This picture is *The Boyarina Morozova.**

The artist is V. I. Surikov.

That picture and that artist, about whose truthfulness Stasov wrote (in 1887):

...Surikov has now created a picture which, in my opinion, is the best of all our pictures based on a theme from Russian history... The strength of truth, the strength of historic authenticity with which Surikov's new picture breathes is astonishing...[7]

And linked to this fact, the very same Surikov wrote the following about his stay at the Academy of Art:

...I am more occupied with composition than anything else. There they called me the "composer": I studied all the naturalness and beauty of composition. At home I presented myself with problems and solved them...[8]

Surikov remained a "composer" his whole life. Any of his paintings is a living confirmation of this.

And the most outstanding is *The Boyarina Morozova.*

---

* [The wife of a boyar, who was a nobleman of the first rank in the court of the tsar, with the exclusive privilege of possessing land and serfs – HM.]

Here the combination of "naturalness" and beauty in composition has been presented perhaps most richly.

But what is this combination of "naturalness and beauty," if not the "organic unity" in the sense we spoke of above?

But wherever it is a question of organic unity, there...look for the golden section in the proportions!

The same Stasov wrote on *The Boyarina Morozova* as a "soloist" surrounded by a "choir." The central "part" belongs to the boyarina herself. The center portion of the picture is assigned to her role. It is bound by the point of highest flight and the point of lowest descent of the picture's theme. This is the upward ascent of Morozova's arm with the two-fingered sign of the cross as the highest point. And this is the hand helplessly stretched toward that same boyarina, but this time – the hand of an old woman – of a wandering beggar, a hand from under which the end of the sleigh slips out along with the last hope of salvation.

These are the two central dramatic points of the Boyarina Morozova's role: the "zero" point and the point of maximum upward ascent.

The unity of the drama seems to be designed by the circumstance that both these points are confined to the decisive central diagonal, determining the whole basic structure of the picture.

They do not *coincide* literally with this diagonal, and it is precisely this that distinguishes a living picture from a dead geometrical scheme.

But the *striving* toward this diagonal and the connection with it is evident.

Let us try to determine spatially which other decisive dividing lines pass close to these two points of the drama.

A small sketch – a geometrical diagram (see Figure 2) will show us that both these points of the drama include between them two vertical dividing lines that pass at 0.618 ... from each edge of the rectangle of the picture!

The "lower point" completely coincides with the dividing line AB, going to 0.618 ... from the left edge.

And how does one treat the "highest point"? At first glance we have an apparent contradiction: Actually section A_1B_1 as it goes to 0.618 ... from the right edge of the picture, passes not through the hand, not even through the head or eyes of the boyarina, but appears somewhere in front of the boyarina's mouth! That is, in other words – it is a decisive dividing line, a means of attracting maximum attention, as if passing through the air, for no purpose, in front of the mouth.

Agreed, it is in front of the mouth.

Agreed, it is through the air.

But we cannot agree it is "for no purpose."

On the contrary!

The golden section cuts here at the main point. And the unexpected-

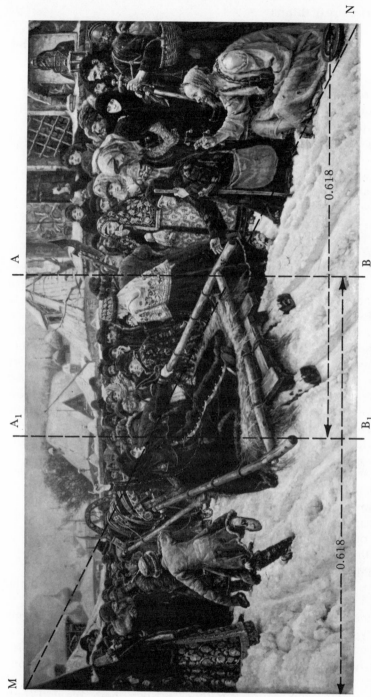

Figure 2. *The Exile of Boyarina Morozovs* by V.I. Surikov, 1887 (State Tretiakov Gallery, Moscow). Eisenstein's breakdown of its composition reveals the artist's use of the Golden Section.

ness is only that *the very thing that is most important* – is unportrayable plastically.

The golden section A_1B_1 passes through the word that flies from Boyarina Morozova's mouth.

For it is not the arm, not the burning eyes, not the mouth – which are the main thing – but *the flaming word of fanatic conviction*.

It is in this, and precisely in this, that Morozova's greatest strength lies.

That same Stasov writes about it, saying it is "that same woman of whom Avvakum,[9] the head of the fanatics of that time, said in those days, that she was 'a lion among sheep'."

However, the hand – is depicted. The eye – is depicted. The face – is depicted.

The voice – is not.

What is Surikov really doing? At the place where the "plastically not depictable" voice would burst out, he does not put any detail capable of attracting the viewer's attention. But he forces the viewer's attention to remain excitedly on this spot, for this spot is not a plastically depicted point of transversal of two decisive compositional divisions, leading the eye along the surface of the picture, but namely – a basic compositional line of a diagonal and a line that passes through the golden section. Here by means of compositional division Surikov goes beyond the frame of a narrowly depictive plastic exposition, and he does this in order to allow one to feel what it would be impossible to show by means of any plastic depiction! He attracts attention not only to the Boyarina Morozova, not only to her face, but also seems to attract attention to the words of the flaming invocation bursting from her lips.

As we can see, the true highest point as well as the lowest, as in the case of *Potemkin*, both appear on the axes of the golden section.

It is curious to note that the resemblance goes even deeper.

We just revealed the transition in Surikov from dimension to dimension on "the point of highest ascent." The undepicted sound is applied at this point.

Something quite analogous occurs at "the point of highest ascent" in *Potemkin* as well: At this point the *red* flag appears; at this point the black–gray–white light range of photographs is suddenly hurled to another dimension – to paint, to *color*. Depiction by light becomes depiction by color.

Let us keep this in mind and now turn to an analysis of the principles of *pathos*, where similar phenomena will be given the required attention.

We will not discuss the nature of *pathos* "as such" here. We will limit ourselves to examining a work of *pathos* from the aspect of the viewer's perception of it, or more exactly, from the aspect of its effect on the viewer. And, proceeding from the nature of the effect, we will try to define those special features of construction that a composition of *pathos* must have. After that we will verify these features in an interesting example and will not deny ourselves the satisfaction of finishing with a few general conclusions.

In order to do this, we must first outline the effect of *pathos* in a few words. We will intentionally do this as glibly and tritely as possible. Then the most obvious and characteristic features will come out immediately.

The most primitive way appears to be a simple description of the most superficial signs of the external behavior of a viewer overcome by *pathos*.

However, these signs also appear to be so symptomatic that they immediately lead us to the basis of the problem. According to this sign, *pathos* is what forces the viewer to jump out of his seat. It is what forces him to flee from his place. It is what forces him to clap, to cry out. It is what forces his eyes to gleam with ecstasy before tears of ecstasy appear in them. In word, it is everything that forces the viewer to "be beside himself."

Putting it more elegantly, we might say that the effect of the *pathos* of a work consists in bringing the viewer to the point of ecstasy. Such a formula adds nothing new, for three lines above we said exactly the same thing, since *ex stasis* (out of a state) means literally the same thing as "being beside oneself" or "going out of a normal state" does.

All the signs mentioned strictly follow this formula. Sitting – he stood up. Standing – he jumped. Motionless – he moved. Silent – he shouted. Lusterless – began to gleam (eyes). Dry – became moist (tears). In every case there occurred a "going out of a state," "being beside oneself."

But this is not sufficient: "To be beside oneself" is not "to go into nothing." To be beside oneself is unavoidably also a transition to something else, to something different in quality, to something opposite to what preceded it (no motion – to motion, no sound – to sound, etc.).

Thus, just from the most superficial description of the ecstatic effect, which produces a construction of *pathos*, we can see what basic feature the construction must have in a composition of *pathos*.

In this structure the condition of "being beside oneself" must be observed in all of its features, as well as the constant transition to a different quality.

To be beside oneself, to be out of the usual balance and state, to move to a new state – all this, of course, contributes to the conditions necessary for the effect of any art capable of captivating us.

And the aspects of artistic works, apparently, are grouped *according to the degree* and to what measure this is available to them.

In this series the condition of having this general quality in the highest degree belongs to productions of *pathos*. Apparently the construction of *pathos* is the culminating point on this common path.

And apparently it is possible to examine all other varieties of the composition of artistic works as certain *diminishing* derivatives of *a maximum case*, maximally "being beside oneself" – a case of the *pathos type of construction*.

Let no one be afraid that, in speaking of *pathos*, I have not once touched on the question of theme and content. The discussion is not of *pathos* content in general but in what way *pathos* is realized in composition. The same fact may enter into a work of art in any aspect of its production: from a cold exposition of content to a genuine hymn of *pathos*. And the nature of the artistic means that raises the "resonance" of an event to *pathos* is also important here.

Undoubtedly this is primarily conditioned by the author's relationship to the content. But composition as we understand it here *is also a construction that primarily serves as an embodiment of the author's relation to the content* and at the same time forces the viewer also to relate to this content.

Therefore, in this article we are less interested in the question of the "nature" of *pathos* in one phenomenon or other, for that is always socially relative. We also will not dwell on the nature of the *pathos* relationship of the author to any particular phenomenon, since that also is obviously socially conditioned. We are interested (in the a priori presence of both) in the limited problem of how this "relationship" to the "nature of phenomena" is realized by composition in the construction of a work of *pathos*.

Thus, following the same position, which has already justified itself in the question of organic unity, we will agree that to achieve maximum "being beside oneself" in the viewer, we must propose to him a corresponding "prescription," following which he will arrive at the desired state.

The simplest "prototype" of similar imitative behavior will be, of course, a figure behaving ecstatically on the screen, that is, a character seized by *pathos*, a character who in one sense or other is "beside himself."

Here the structure will coincide with the depiction. And the object of depiction – the *behavior* of the figure *himself* will agree with the conditions of the "ecstatic" structure. Let us examine this in the form of speech. *Nonorderly* in its usual flow, the structure, imbued with *pathos*, quickly takes on the imprint of a growing rhythmic quality; not only prosaic but also *prosaic* in its forms, it soon begins to sparkle with forms and turns of speech that are characteristic of *poetry* (startling comparisons, vivid figurative expressions), etc., etc. No matter what form of speech or other expression of the person be taken at that moment, in everything we will find that progression *from quality to a new quality*.

This is the first step on this path of compositional possibilities. The situation will be more complicated and more effective when this basic condition isn't limited just to the human being but, going "beyond the limits" of the human being, will spread both to the milieu and surroundings of the character, that is, when the surroundings themselves are presented under those same conditions of "frenzy." One can find this in Shakespeare. In this respect the example of Lear's "frenzy" is classic, frenzy going beyond the limits of the characters into "frenzy" of nature itself – into the storm...

"Being beside oneself" – a transition to the following dimension with the aim of evoking a *pathos* effect – is generally characteristic of Shakespeare.

Let us recall such a characteristic example of "pathosization"* of the fact that "the king will drink to Hamlet's better breath," in the words of King Claudius, raising his goblet to Hamlet in the scene of the duel with Laertes.

The king shall drink to Hamlet's better breath
...Give me the cups;
And let the kettle to the trumpet speak,
The trumpet to the cannoneer without,
The cannons to the heavens, the heaven to earth,
Now the king drinks to Hamlet. Come, begin...

(V.ii)

Here the "method" of *pathos* is almost reduced to a "device." And this is very valid: The king raises the goblet to the man who, according to his information, must perish in the duel from a tiny scratch of the poisoned rapier!

Thus the king's tirade of *pathos* is not a sincere burst of feeling but an exclamation that has been constructed technically and with great care according to the "prescription" for speeches of *pathos*!

This is also the reason for revealing the device, and the choice of the actual means, because of the fact that Englishmen, instead of *pathos*, here use "bathos" – excessive pomposity.

What is more important for us is that here, in an extremely "accentuated" manner, is the method of how *pathos* is constructed by Shakespeare.[†]

Let us not forget that he is true to his method at moments of the highest tension in his tragedies.

---

* An equivalent of the neologism created by Eisenstein – HM.
[†] We will find an analogous example later, in the last section of this work, in the descriptions of the somewhat exaggerated manner of acting *pathos* by the great Frédérick Lemaître.[10]

Thus, from *English* the exclamation jumps into *Latin*: "And you, too, Brutus!" – ("Et tu, Brute!") on the lips of Julius Caesar, dying from the assassins' daggers at the foot of Pompey's statue.

Equally clear examples, which are also resolutions based on any environment *common* to us, can be found in abundance among the naturalists of Zola's school and especially in Zola himself.

In Zola the environment being described, the merging of its details, the phases of the events in each separate scene are always chosen and presented in such a way that from an *everyday and physical aspect* they prove to be in the necessary state in terms of the *structure*. This is true for any compositional structure of his, but it is particularly apparent in those cases when Zola falls into *pathos* and raises those events to the level of *pathos*, which in themselves are often not necessarily filled with *pathos* at all.

In Zola it is not in the rhythm of prose, not in the system of images and analogies, not in the structure of a scene, that is, *not in the purely* compositional elements of episodes where the structural norm necessary for a scene operates, but in agreement with its formula, the phenomena and people depicted behave according to the dictates of the author.

This is so typical of Zola's manner that one might consider this as a specific mode, a characteristic method of this school of naturalists.

Thus, in this case what is most important is *the selection of* phenomena, *which by themselves flow ecstatically*, which of themselves are "beside themselves," that is, are taken for the moment of description just at such moments of their existence.

This device coincides with yet a second, although rudimentary compositional device: the phenomena represented in this way are so *intermixed that one of them in relation to the other begins to sound like a transition from one intensity to another, from one "dimension" to another.*

And only in the third and last place does this school sometimes also apply those same conditions to elements that are purely compositional: to such a movement within an exchange of prose rhythms, within the nature of language or the general structure of the movement of an episode or chain of episodes.

This part of the work historically falls instead to the lot of the schools that displaced the school of "naturalism," schools that in their enthusiasm for this aspect of a work, in many cases accomplished this and are accomplishing this, even to the detriment of a high-quality "Rubenesque" concreteness of depictions, which is so characteristic of Zola.

But after all has been said, let us now turn to the basic object of our investigation – to the "Odessa Steps."

Let us examine the system of how the events are presented and grouped together in it.

First of all, *having noted the frenzied state of the people and masses being depicted*, let us trace what structural and compositional features are necessary.

Let us do this in terms of *movement*.

First, there are the *close-ups* of the figures rushing chaotically, then the *long-shots* of the figures rushing chaotically.

Then the chaotic movement passes over into the stamping of soldiers' feet rhythmically descending the steps.

The tempo quickens. The rhythm grows.

And now the increasing rush of movement *downward* is suddenly reversed upward, the *dizzy* movement of the masses downward passes into the *slow, solemn* movement upward of the solitary figure of the mother with her dead child.

The masses. Dizziness. Downward.

And suddenly:

A solitary figure. In triumphant slowness. Upward.

But only for a moment. And again a reverse leap to the movement downward.

The rhythm grows. The tempo quickens.

And suddenly the tempo of the *flight of the crowd* jumps into the next stage of fast movement – to the *rolling* baby carriage. It rushes with the idea of rolling down into the next dimension – *from rolling understood "figuratively" to actually physically rolling*. This is not only a different state of *tempo*. This is also a *leap in the method of illustration* from the figurative to the physical, which occurs within a presentation of rolling movement.

Close-ups leap to *long-shots*.

Chaotic movement (of the masses) to *rhythmic movement* (of the soldiers).

One aspect of the speed of movement (people rushing) – to the next stage of that same theme of fast movement (the rolling baby carriage).

Movement *downward* – to movement *upward*.

Many volleys of *many* guns – to *one* shot from *one* muzzle of the battleship.

Step by step – a leap from dimension to dimension. A leap from quality to quality. So that in the last analysis it is no longer a single episode (the carriage) but *the entire method of the exposition* of a whole event also completes its leap: The narrative of exposition as well as the *roaring (jumping) lions* is hurled into a figurative method of construction. Visual rhythmic prose seems to jump over into visual poetic speech.

As we have seen, the steps of the staircase, along which the jump action is carried downward, strictly repeats the jump in steps from quality to quality, in terms of the intensity and dimensions leading upward.*

And, as we can see, the theme of *pathos*, here rushing down the staircase in the *pathos* of the shooting, also permeates completely the basic structure by which the events have been plastically and rhythmically composed.[†]

Is the episode on the steps unique in this respect? Does this feature remove it from the general method of construction? Not at all. In it are those features characteristic of the method, only sharpened as it were into a culmination, as the episode itself has been sharpened, culminating in its tragedy for the film as a whole.

Moreover, this compositional feature has something else that is quite a surprising supplement for a silent film.

I was somehow forced to write that, in terms of practicing sound film, I am like the last guest arriving at a wedding: I am the youngest director of sound film and entered this area later than anyone else.

On closer examination this is not really true.

My first work on sound film was in 1926.

And it concerned that same *Potemkin*.

The fact is that *Potemkin* – in its fate abroad – was one of the few films provided with music written especially for it, that is, in silent cinematography it comes extremely close to the way any sound film is arranged.

It is not a question here, however, of the fact that Edmund Meisel[12] wrote special music for *Potemkin*. There were even cases when silent films had been shot with certain music in mind (this is particularly the case of operettas, when, for example, *Ein Walzertraum* by Ludwig Berger[13] was apparently shot to the music of Strauss.)

But in our case what is important is *how* the music for *Potemkin* was written.

It was written as one works with sound track now.

More truly, *as one should work* with the sound track, always and everywhere, with the creative cooperation and friendly cocreation of the composer and the director.

Actually, despite everything even now sound film music is almost always "close by the film" and doesn't basically differ from former "musical illustrations."

---

* Incidentally we draw attention to the fact that the compositional structure of the "Odessa Steps" is identical to the behavior of *man* overcome by *pathos*, as we have described him above.

Chaos is changed to rhythm, prose by poetic turns of speech etc.

† For lack of space, we are only analyzing compositional "highways" here. However, the fabric of *Potemkin* will sustain any "microscopic" analysis as well (see, for example, the analysis of fourteen montage pieces of the encounter between the skiffs and the battleship, published in the article "On the Purity of Film Language.")[11]

However, it was different with *Potemkin*. Admittedly not in everything and it was far from being complete: I was not in Berlin long enough while the music was being composed (1926). But, nevertheless, it was long enough to make arrangement with the composer Meisel about the decisive "effect" of the music for *Potemkin*.

And especially about the "music of the machines" in the encounter with the squadron.

For this episode I demanded categorically that the composer reject *the usual melodic quality* and the emphasis on *the bare rhythmic percussion beat*, but, by these demands, I essentially *forced the music as well in this decisive spot to "jump over" into a "new quality": into a noise structure.*

At this point *Potemkin* stylistically explodes beyond the limits of the system of "silent picture with musical illustration" into a new area – into *sound film*, where true models of this aspect of art live in a unity of fused musical and visual images,* *which thereby created a single audiovisual image of the production.*

It is mainly due to these elements, *anticipating the possibility of the inner nature of the composition of sound film*, that the scene "Encounter with the Squadron" owes its shattering effect, and being cited in all anthologies of cinematography abroad equal to that of the "Odessa Steps."

I am particularly interested here in the fact that within this area, which in the general structure of *Potemkin* is also a jump into a new quality – in the *very treatment of the music itself* the same permeating condition of *pathos* construction is observed – the condition of a qualitative leap that, as we have shown in *Potemkin*, is inseparable from the organic theme itself.

Here the silent *Potemkin* gives a lesson to sound film, affirming again and again the position that for something organic, a single law of structure permeates it decisively in all its "manifestations" and in order that it not be "on the run" but becomes an *organic part of the film*; the music also must be governed not only *according to those same images and themes* but also by the same basic laws and principles of structure that govern the thing as a whole.†

It is amusing to recall that even its first actual showing was to end with its own particular "being beside oneself" *of the film as a whole*. This was in the Bolshoi Theater of the USSR in December 1925 – on the

---

* As we have seen, our "Claim" coming out two years later[14] (in 1928), establishing the question of an audiovisual image, also had certain pragmatically verified experience behind it.

† In many of its parts we were also able to achieve this in sound film – in the first of our sound films, *Alexander Nevsky*. We accomplished this here thanks to the cooperation of such a remarkable and brilliant master as S. S. Prokofiev.

twentieth anniversary of the Revolution of 1905, in whose memory the film had been made.

According to the director's idea, the last shot of the film – the oncoming nose of the battleship – had to cut. . .the surface of the screen: The screen had to be cut in two and reveal behind it an actual memorable solemn meeting of real people – the participants of the events of 1905.

By this device *Potemkin* would complete a series of analogical cases of the past.

Once, as Kasimir Malevich[15] later told me, in the same way a curtain was torn open revealing the first performance of the Russian futurists in a theater on Officer Street.[16] But this was not crowned by a whole performance and by its logical completion; here there was also no expression of inner *pathos*, but instead the constant clatter of plates and nothing more than another "slap in the face of public taste."[17]

On a very different date – on the memorable July 14, 1789, a completely different great surge of social *pathos* ripped open a gauze curtain that separated the audience from the actors in the Parisian theater *Des Délassements Comiques*.

In its insatiable battle against popular (folk) theaters, the *Comédie Française*,[18] whose director was Plancher-Valcour, obtained from the government the restoration of all types of oppressive rules that, according to its privileges, the *Comédie* had the right to impose on small theaters: a prohibition against actors speaking, a prohibition to have more than three actors on stage at the same time. Added to this was the primitive and absurd condition that the actors be separated from the audience by a permanent gauze curtain of tulle.

On July 14 the news of the taking of the Bastille reached Plancher-Valcour, and in a burst of true *pathos* he punched his fist through the tulle curtain and tore it in two with the exclamation: "Long live freedom!" On January 13, 1791, the revolutionary government decreed the freedom of the theaters.

(See: L. M. Bernardin, La Comédie Italienne en France et le Théâtre de la Foire et du Boulevard 1570–1791, Paris, 1902, p. 233)*

And, finally, one may also add the most famous case in literature of an explosion of *pathos* accompanied by the ripping of a curtain – ". . .the veil of the temple was rent in twain from the top to the bottom" at the moment of the completion of the tragedy of Golgotha.[19]

Potemkin does have ill-matched ancestors!

And it is difficult to say which of these associations and memories contributed to the formation of my conception, which, however, in itself

---

* It is curious that in spite of this decree, the absurd order about the gauze curtain again was revived at the beginning of the nineteenth century. Because of the demands of the large theaters, this measure was adopted by the Francon Theater, the theater in the Montabor Hall, and a series of other auditoriums.

was a pure expression of that same *pathos* by which this film was inspired, realized, and completed through montage.

And now it is appropriate to recall what we spoke of above, concerning the *actual character* of those two parts, into which each of the five acts of *Potemkin's* drama is divided according to the proportions of "the golden section."

We spoke of the fact that the action inevitably "leaps" and "hurls itself" through the caesura, and we did not use this term accidentally, but because each time the diapason of the new quality, into which the first half passed, was the *maximum* possible: Each time it was a leap *into the opposite* (see above).

Thus, it appears that in all decisive compositional elements we encounter a basic formula of the ecstatic everywhere: a leap "beside oneself," which unavoidably becomes a leap into a new quality and most often encompasses a diapason leap into the opposite.

And just as in the golden section and its proportions we spoke of above, so here in the actual *course* of the production we have the same secret of the organic: For a transition by leaps from quality to quality is *not only a formula of growth* but *also a formula of development* – development involving us by its regularity no longer only as *single "vegetative" units, subordinate to the evolutionary laws* of nature, but as *units that are both collective and social, consciously participating in its development,* for we know that this leap, which we are now discussing, also exists in certain aspects of social phenomena, in those revolutions by whose path social development and social movements proceed.

And now one could say that for the third time we have before us the organic unity of *Potemkin, for the leap that characterizes the structure of each compositional link in the whole is the introduction into the structure of composition of the most decisive element of the content of the theme – a revolutionary explosion as one of the leaps, by which the uninterrupted chain of progressive conscious social development is realized.*

But:

a leap. A transition from quantity to quality. A transition into the opposite.

All these are elements of the dialectic course development, into which they enter according to the laws of dialectical materialism.

And this is the source of both the structure of a complex production as well as of any structure of *pathos* – one might say that a structure of *pathos* is that which compels us, in repeating its course, *to experience the moments of culmination and becoming* of the norms of dialectic processes.

The *moment* of culmination is understood here in the sense of those points in a process through which water passes at the *moment* of becoming steam, ice – water, castiron – steel. This is that same being beside oneself, going out of a state, a move from quality to quality, ecstasy. And if water, steam, ice, and steel could psychologically register their own feelings at these critical *moments* – moments of achieving the leap, they would say they are speaking with *pathos*, that they are in ecstasy.

Much higher forms of the experience of *pathos*, much higher forms of ecstasy are available to us. We and only we of all the inhabitants of the earthly sphere have been given the greatest thing of all – actually to experience step by step each moment of the steady process in which the greatest achievements in social development are taking place.

We have been given even more – the collective participation in the greatest turning points in the history of Man and the opportunity to experience them.

This experience of a moment of history is imbued with the greatest *pathos* and sense of unity with this process. A sense of being in step with it. The sense of collective participation in it.

Such is *pathos* in life.

Such is its reflection in the methods of *pathos* in art. Here, born out of the *pathos* of the theme, the compositional structure repeats that single basic principle by which organic, social, and all other processes of the formation of the universe are achieved, and cooperation with this principle (whose reflection is our consciousness, and the area of application – our whole being) cannot but fill us with the highest feeling experienced by man – *pathos*.

The question remains by what means can the artist pragmatically achieve all these compositional formulas?

Is there a recipe for its exposition? A standard? A prescription? A master key?

In every true production of *pathos* these compositional formulas are definitely in operation. But they are not achieved by a priori compositional calculations alone.

Skill alone, craftsmanship alone, the total mastery of one of their techniques is insufficient.

For genuine organic unity and for genuine *pathos* as its highest form these are all necessary, but alone are not enough.

A production will become organic and achieve the highest organic unity – in the sphere of *pathos* as we understand it – only when the theme of the work, its content, and its ideas become an organically inseparable whole with the thoughts, feelings, the very being and existence of the author.

Only then will organic unity appear in the strictest forms of the structure of a work, only then does it remain for a master, proficient in his skill, to bring it to the final brilliance of formal perfection.

And then, and only then, will a genuine organic unity of the work occur, entering the circle of natural and social phenomena as an equal member, as an independent phenomenon.

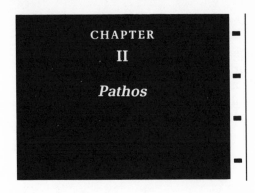

The milk separator and the Holy Grail

In analyzing the composition of *Potemkin* we established a definite principle according to which the structure of *pathos* is formed.

We discovered that the primary indication of *pathos* in composition is a state of continuous "ecstasy," a continuous state of "being beside oneself," a continuing leap of each separate element or sign of the work of art from quality to quality, in proportion to the quantitative growth of the ever-heightening intensity of the emotional content of a shot, sequence, or scene in the work of art as a whole.

We were successful in showing that the composition of *Potemkin* unfolds in precisely this way, both in its whole and in its separate parts.

The resolution of the composition, according to this formula, came about quite intuitively and naturally, as the most organic form into which the ecstatic experience of the theme could be molded.

However, having completed the film, there and then to scrutinize, reveal, and formulate this compositional method, even in the sphere of signs, was, of course, impossible for me to have done and was not done.

It became necessary to make yet another solution in the composition of *pathos*, of a similar nature, and, only after – having juxtaposed the results of both these solutions – would it have been possible to find some common denominator and to dare to view it as a basis on which a definite method could be formulated, according to which *pathos* in composition is structured in general.

Besides which, to determine the *pathos* structure of *Potemkin* in *Potemkin* itself, strangely enough, was hindered to a certain extent by the *pathos* of its very material, its very subject, its very themes, and its very situations.

The discovery of the method for infusing *pathos* into the material by *means of composition* was drowned here in the *pathos of the very theme*.

It was absolutely necessary to compare the structure of this composition with some other examples and cases from the sphere of *pathos formation*.

Furthermore, the most desirable example here would have to be such where *pathos was involuntarily infused* into certain material that, in itself (per se), contained no *pathos* at all.

We were fortunate to come across just such an example immediately upon the completion of *Potemkin*.

This did much to further our understanding of methods for structuring works of *pathos* in general.

These very years saw the birth of the collective farm system and mighty state farms, which in the future were to play such a gigantic role in the economy of our country and the building of socialism. Such grandiose social perspectives could not but be a source of inspiration.

At the same time, the theme of industrialization of agriculture could not but be appealing in itself. One must keep in mind that in those years the image of industry was one of the most popular with the artists of our generation.

With regards to this film,* it cannot be said that the first part of our task was solved profoundly or effectively enough.

And this, no doubt, is because priority was given to the "*pathos* of the machine," rather than to the social analysis of those profound processes, which our villages experienced in their transition to forms of collective farm economy.

However, if this film as a whole did not live up to the vastness of its theme, then in the sphere of methodological research into the problem of *pathos*, that so interested me, it turned out to be precisely what I needed.

It was our film *The Old and the New* (with a variant title, *The General Line*, 1926–9), which acquired its fame by heralding the "*pathos* of the milk separator."

Much had been, and still is being written on this film, particularly about our enterprising treatment of an object of agricultural equipment in an ecstatic light and how in reponse to the allusion of the separator being lit by an "inner light," as if an image of the Holy Grail,[1] I retorted at the time: "What the hell do we need that Spanish vessel for...".[2]

But in this direction the film did achieve a certain degree of *pathos*.

Some additional confirmation of this aspect from general "eyewitness" reports, made soon after viewing the film, would be beneficial. Let us quote a few excerpts from among the sea of printed matter that gushed out in reply to the cascade of milk, which streamed forth from the screen in this film [Fig. 3].

First here are a few lines taken from *Histoire du Cinéma* by Bardeche,[3] Paris, 19(35).

...It is not to be wondered at that, from considering men as the members of a

---

* [That is, *The Old and the New* – HM.]

group almost as if they were animals,* the Soviet film at one stage in its evolution should have come to take nature as its principal character...It is certainly true that nature, that agricultural labor, are noble themes which literature has forgotten for two thousand years. It is not the novels of peasant life which carry on the tradition of Hesiod[4] and of Virgil[5]: They lack that mixture of precision and of poetry which constitute the true "Georgic." Eisenstein and Dovzhenko are the true Virgils....†

Here pretty photographs alone would have been insufficient, it was necessary for the cinéaste to resurrect in himself the ancient poets so that he himself became a singer of man's struggle with the soil, a comtemporary Hesiod.

I intentionally draw my next citation from a Belgian...Catholic magazine, which doubtlessly can be considered more competent in matters of exultation, ecstasy, and *pathos*.‡

Here are its comments on the effect of *pathos* achieved in the film:

...Epic lyricism propels *The General Line*, singing and glorifying fields, milk, bread, the fruits of the earth ("Exaltation des eléments terrestres"), those terrestrial gifts that derive their inspiration from the machine (just as our eye finds its inspiration in a similar "machine," the camera). The powerful rhythm of the changing seasons, the fertile harvest, the vital force of the atmosphere itself, invoke their exultation and all is depicted with hitherto unprecedented wealth. A drop of cream, a bundle of rye, or a spark of molten metal – all these revelations of inner dynamism, hidden in the nature of these phenomena, in appearance seemingly everyday phenomena and in themselves insignificant, all these swell into Dionysian lyricism[6] with Eisenstein.¶ Even these most modest features of everyday life become imbued with *pathos*, are transformed and exalted into the category of majestic phenomena of the elements, caught by the screen and spread before us...

A French magazine, *Le Mois* (Paris 1931), goes even further in its evaluations. Here, the "modest" separator scene is thought of in terms of an ecstatic orgy. We read:

...Suddenly, right before our eyes, milk condenses and turns to cream!: Eyes sparkle, teeth shine through breaking smiles. A joyfully smiling, peasant girl, Martha, stretches out her hands to capture the flow of cream, vertically streaming toward her; cream splatters all over her face; she bursts into a fit of laughter, her joy being sensual, almost animal in nature. One almost expects her to cast off all her clothes in a frenzy of passion to wallow naked in the flood of well-being produced by the spouting torrents of cream...

---

* Here is meant the films of the "masses" – *Potemkin* and *Ten Days*, characteristic of the previous stage or the evolution of Soviet cinema. The "Cinema of the Militant Revolution," as distinguished from the ensuing stage or the "Cinema of Peaceful Construction" as designated by Bardeche.

† Here is meant *Earth* by A. P. Dovzhenko, made immediately after *The Old and the New*. It is particularly pleasant for me to quote here this note on his work.

‡ *La Nouvelle Equipe*, No. 1, 1930.

¶ "Lyrisme dyonisiaque d'Eisenstein"(!)

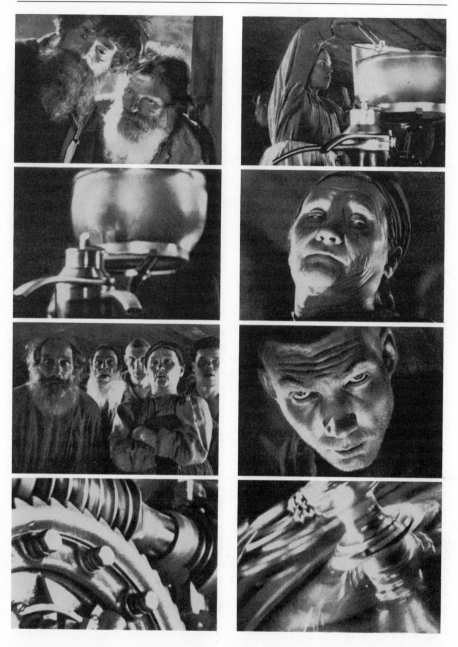

Figure 3. The "Separator (Milk Churn)" sequence from Eisenstein's film *The Old and the New* (also known as *The General Line*). The immobile numerals ("4–38–50–CHLENOV ARTEL") become dynamic with increasing size and speed of cutting, graphically demonstrating the increasing numbers of collective farm members.

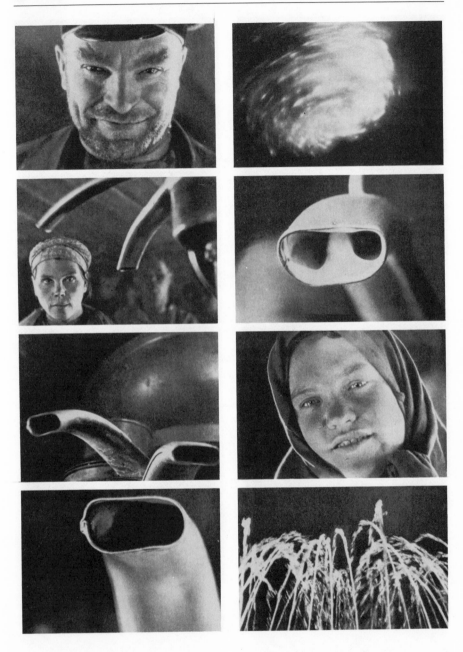

Caption to Figure 3 (*cont.*)

Caption to Figure 3 (*cont.*)

At this point, one is inadvertently reminded of an episode in Dovzhenko's film *Earth*, which is mentioned, immediately following *The Old and the New*, by Bardeche in *The History of Motion Pictures.*

If, in the present resolution of the separator scene by compositional means it was possible to attain such a degree of ecstatic frenzy, that at any moment one expected the heroine of the film to throw herself into an orgiastic dance, then in Dovzhenko's film, in its first edited form, we do, in fact, find an analogous scene where a woman, casting off her clothes, whirls about the cottage in a frenzy. This "naked wench," as she was named by critics, was naturally met "with bayonettes". This, of course, was to be quite expected, because such an image in general, and such a concept of her actions in particular, appeared completely out of place, a "foreign body" in the everyday setting of a Ukrainian village undergoing collectivization. It would have been quite different had the film had for its subject matter the joyous, religious celebrations of Dionysus or the zealous festivities of the religious, Russian, self-flagellating sect, the "Khlysty." As it was, the "naked wench" was censored from the film.*

We will have further cause to allude to the above episode when we begin analyzing the reasons for *expression of pathos through composition* rather than *through the exultation of the participants through "acting."*

It is obvious from the "evidence" brought forth that the end result of using purely compositional means does not yield to "histrionic" means and it even invokes that very image of ecstacy in the "feelings" of the spectator, seemingly natural in the given situation but which is in no way relevant in similar circumstances!

On the whole, it appears to me that this "evidence" is more than sufficient to enable us to confirm the degree of "ecstatic" effect attained in certain scenes throughout the film and in the separator scene in particular!

Unless, perhaps, it is worth mentioning in addition something from a review by Krasna Kraus in the magazine *FilmTechnik* (1930). The latter noticed the pictorial peculiarity of the film, in presenting everything in three-dimensional plasticity "either very close, or else very distant (long-shots)," i.e., the same basic characteristic sign of ecstasy, in this case along the line of scale, everywhere *seeming to extend itself beyond the well-balanced norms*, so that if there is a long-shot, it becomes a "super-long-shot", if it is a close-up, it becomes a "super-close-up."

However, as this was all so long ago, it might be beneficial to briefly

---

* About this ill-fated "naked wench" I have had occasion to write elsewhere at some length in my essay on D. W. Griffith.

help the reader recollect what and how this took place in the film as a whole...*

The central, more successful, and, as always, more illustrative for the method itself was indeed the separator scene. From the film's very birth, the separator justifiably became its "catchword"[†] under which were "programmed" its specific cinematographic qualities.

I have already written much on the subject matter of the film,[7] but here I must write, for the first time, of the pure research significance of this central episode, which depicts around the separator a tense play of hope and doubt – "will the milk thicken or not thicken" culminating, finally, in a burst of joy, coupled with that first spurt of cream and a whirlwind buildup of mass registration for membership into the milk cooperative.

Here we find a perfect example of thematic *pathos*, lacking any external elements of *pathos* in the setting of the scene itself, structured instead around the manipulation of a certain apparatus, capable of separating milk from cream and cream from milk, according to laws of centrifugal and centripetal force.

Here is where instilling *pathos*[‡] in the subject matter demanded strictly that, by expressiveness and composition alone, the appearance of the first drop of thickened milk be made just as thrilling and exciting a scene as the episode of the meeting of the *Potemkin* with the admiral's squadron. To build the anticipation of this first drop of thickened milk to an intensity similar to the suspense of waiting – will there or will there not be a shot from the muzzles of the squadron – and in the end to find the plastically compositional means for expressing the idea of joy, when that trying moment of "testing the separator" is crowned with triumphant technological success.

For here there was no scene of masses scurrying down the Odessa steps during the shooting,

no squadrons, with gaping muzzles, deployed in an advancing front on the solitary battleship,

no beat of the engines during the moments of highest intensity,

no flight of hundreds of sailors' caps, tossed into the air when the admiral's squadron sailed by without a single shot.

We find here instead, an almost empty log cabin, used by the Milk Cooperative.

A handful of doubting peasant men and women.

A trio of enthusiasts: an "activist" Martha Lapkina, a fair-haired

---

* [SME proposed to add here a short summary of the content of *The Old and the New*, but did not – HM.]
† [English word appears in Russian original – HM.]
‡ [In Russian, *patetizatsi* (pathetication), a word invented by SME – HM.]

member of the Young Communist League, a regional agriculturalist.

Finally, a faintly glimmering "milk machine."

And yet at the same time the theme has somehow a mighty sense of "community" with all parts of the film about the rebellious battleship.

The community of spirit in the emerging consciousness of class solidarity and collectivism, which in the historical moment of *Potemkin's* fate unites into one the battleship and the squadron and just as significantly, in the everyday setting of one village, amidst millions like it in our motherland, is created a similar miracle in the merging of separate proprietors into a single, collectivized economy.*

Both scenes are not only saturated with equal *pathos*.

But in spite of the difference in eras, circumstances, and the obvious scale of events, they are united by a common theme – the theme of collective unity.

Such a kindred community of theme could not help but demand common methods for its fulfillment.

Therefore – the wake of *Potemkin* – the theme could not but determine for itself the basic compositional structure and scenes with the separator, which, according to the same formula of explosion, following an uncurbed buildup of intensity, bursts into a system of successive explosions, emerging one from the other, just as in a rocket missile or in the uranium chain reaction of an atom bomb.

This fact consequently determined the choice of circumstances (anticipation of that first drop of thickened milk) resembling the climactic scene (anticipation of that first salvo) in *Potemkin*.

And all this because the scheme "of a chain reaction" – buildup of intensity – explosion – leaps from explosion to explosion – gives a clearer structural picture of the leaps from one state to another, characteristic for the ecstasy of particulars accumulating into the *pathos* of the whole.

And yet, at the same time, here we had material quite different in subject, in situation, in setting, in details, and elements of the scenes.

A solution just as direct, as "spontaneous" and as extemporaneous... this scene, subsequently juxtaposed with the scenes from *Potemkin*, could not help but reveal the essence of this very formula as the basis of the method upon which the *pathos* of both these scenes was structured.

Precision in formulation, as previously stated, came later from a comparison of the completed films.

However, it is of interest to note to what degree this feeling of continuity of both sequences was clear to the directors themselves even at the scenario stage of *The Old and the New*.

If, by itself, the editing resolution of *pathos* in the separator sequence

* The true tragedy of forced collectivization was inevitably ignored by SME as by most Soviet intellectuals during Stalin's reign of terror – HM.]

was basically determined on the editing table, followed, as a result, by subsequent necessary additional shots (fountains, subtitles of the numbers increasing in size), then the link between the inner dynamics of the structure of this sequence with corresponding structures in *Potemkin* can be detected, if only through the fact that in the script itself of *The Old and the New*, precisely at this point, a direct reference was made to...*Potemkin*!

In this scene of anticipation for that drop of thickened milk from the separator, a word-for-word insertion reads: "...Thus waited the *Battleship Potemkin*, its encounter with the squadron..."

Such, for example, in this particular sequence, unlike the cut-in and cut-out fragments of the "Battleship," are the delivery pipes of the separator in shots photographed in such a way that they plastically echo the empty, menacing gun muzzles so terrifyingly protruding from the screen into the audience in *Potemkin*.*

(Such a method of filming was completely in keeping with the overall style of this film. Let us not forget it was precisely here that this particular method was used intentionally, openly, and ironically. Such was also the case in the satiric exposure of another "machine" – a "Bureaucratic Machine" – the carriage of a typewriter, filmed in gigantic proportion, filling the entire screen, which came hurling toward the camera and, before it was "exposed," appeared to be a crane, or some sort of grandiose, industrial structure.)

This trick of artistic "plasticity" in its turn lies wholly within the system of plastic means of expression, so abundantly used in the film as a whole.

It was in the particular film that, for the first time, the expressive possibilities of plastic distortion of the 28" lens were systematically used and thoroughly researched.

The peculiarity of this lens – its ability to show with equal depth of focus the most prominent object in the foreground, as well as the whole depth of background – is well known and is often used for simple demonstration.

However, this characteristic of the lens is accompanied by still another, which previously had carefully been skirted, or at least carefully avoided during the late 1920s.

It is – the ability of this lens to produce perspective distortion.

---

* It is interesting to note that the effect of such a gun muzzle directed at the audience, after the showing of the film, was used in two theater productions of the recent season – one in Moscow, the other in Berlin (during the production of a play by Bernard Shaw). In the first case the whole prow of the ship with jutting-out gun muzzles turned to face the audience; in the second the long barrel of a single gun emerged and progressed to full length. [The Moscow production was of the play *Roar China* by Sergei Tretiakov in the Meyerhold Theatre – HM.]

It consists of the fact that by the use of this lens the perspective reduction of objects in depth sharply speeds up, contrary to the natural norms our eye is accustomed to.

This phenomenon is especially striking to the eye when objects in the foreground are pushed forward exceptionally close to the lens; or better still, in those cases when one and the same object is positioned so that one of its ends is in close proximity to the camera, whereas the other stands far away from it. Examples are soles of feet absurdly out of proportion, jutting out into the audience; or a figure, placed directly facing the camera so that from it protrudes a bow-shaped stomach, while the head and legs remain lost in the "background," etc.

It is quite natural that with greater or lesser degree of marked "outspokenness" such possibilities of the lens can't help but be interwoven into our method of filming, in which "being beside oneself" – from one state into another – stood at the basis of the theme about peasants becoming collective farmers, and this determined also the whole mechanics of expressive means, following the ecstatic formula of being beside oneself.

Here the application of the distortive quality of the 28" lens was used in all possible variations.

In some instances, it was an almost imperceptible change in actual forms of nature by the enlargement of their mass. Such, for example, were the cruppers of kulak horses, which Martha attempted in vain to acquire from a kulak for ploughing, before she is forced to harness her own cow to her antiquated plough. Beside these horses the poor frail Martha appears particularly small and helpless.

In other instances the distortive qualities of the lens were used more openly: either in the manner of "Gogolesque" hyperbolization (as in the "style of Mantegna,"[8] the sleeping carcass of a kulak was filmed from foot to head) or by a sort of monumentalization – as in filming separate parts of a bull or, in depth, the bull itself from his hind legs to his horns, in the scene of the "Bull's Wedding," creating the impression that the bull was some sort of semimythological, massive creature, reminiscent of Jupiter, once kidnapping Europa in that guise.[9]

And finally, in a pointedly ironic exposure of the method, after the successful, initial "mystification" by the previously mentioned typewriter.

One way or another, in all these cases – in various doses and various degrees of manifestation – the 28" lens invariably was helpful in propelling objects..."to go beyond themselves," beyond their natural bounds of volume and form.

In this the theme of man resounded anew, with its own "plasticity," where aided by industry – under a new socialist regime – by means of his own creative effort, the age-old established norms and forms "of the idiotism of village life" (Marx) were forced to go "beyond themselves," into new aspects, forms and qualities of socialist agriculture.

Analyzing the film as a whole in the light of these facts, we see that "intrinsically" the separator scene carried a completely distinct ideological *pathos*-imbued theme.

Furthermore, I think the choice of the milk – cream conversion scene as a central episode was not entirely by chance. Be that as it may, that drop of milk, undergoing a qualitative transformation into a drop of cream, as in a drop of...water, as it were, concretely mirrors the fate of a cluster of disunited individual peasant-owners. These peasants, impressed by the performance of the separator (which represents opportunities and resources of mechanized agriculture) just as suddenly undertake a gigantic qualitative leap in the area of social progress, from individual landownership to collective agriculture, evolving from "muzhiks" into collective farmers.

And, at the same time, the very problem posed as to the "*pathos* of a separator," following the problem of *pathos* of the mutinous battleship, could not help but reveal a certain paradox in its purely exterior features and characteristics.

Such a paradox in the posing of the problem itself could not help but demand a certain paradoxicality also in the sphere of the expressive means of similar intentions.

As already stated, the paradoxicality here was more in appearance than in the essence, and it was therefore, natural that in the sphere of embodiment a similar paradoxicality had to, of itself, color the more external elements of composition.

This rendered the entire structure of composition particularly obvious, since the paradoxicality of applied means inadvertently "exposed" here the very nature of the method and means by which *pathos* could be "created."

It gave *The Old and the New* a big research advantage over *Potemkin*, where these means of influencing were embedded so organically in the very mesh of the work that, at first glance, without being compared with other instances and examples, they appeared completely imperceptible.

If now, in retrospect, we were to take a look at these two films side by side, it might appear that all this commotion over "the *pathos* of the separator" was raised with the sole purpose of conducting a scientific experiment whose objective, it would seem, was to discover the nature of *pathos* in composition!

In fact, such was not the case.

During the period of my work with the film, I was least of all preoccupied with formal problems or methods, instead the entire... *pathos* of creation was directed toward one end – by all possible and impossible means to raise to the level of *pathos* what appeared to be a gray and banal theme about agriculture, but which in its very essence, bore an idea of highest *pathos* – the creation of the collective farm structure.

Kindled by an internal flame, the separator could be said to have been a central artistic image, condensing in itself both the theme as a whole, and its treatment.

As practical experience revealed, in the realization of our goal by all "possible or impossible means," a lion's share expressive means fell precisely on means...."impossible" and paradoxical.

Just by these means alone, taken from the very environment itself and from the materials of the separator setting, "to raise" this scene to the degree of ardent ecstasy was, of course, impossible and turned out to be a failure.

Rather it demanded...a leap beyond the sphere of expressive means and the possibilities of this particular environment.

We have seen that precisely the same thing occurs in the "Odessa Steps" finale, where, after using all the expressive means connected with the firing sequence, the very principle of these means "leaps" into another dimension – from the category of a situation drama to the category of metaphor (see above).

At this point one may naturally ask: Why not resolve this scene of ecstatic rapture over the separator by means of pure "behavioral" acting?

First of all, here the theme centers on the triumph of the underlying idea and not on a Dionysian Bacchanalia, which seizes a certain group of people witnessing a miracle.

This consideration, more than any other, determined the basic necessity of resolving this scene not through ordinary external means of behavior, but by means of a plan other than that of common, everyday action.

To this may be added still another factor, the everyday acceptable range of "ecstatic" joy, manifested in behavior itself, would have been here too modest and have an insufficiently dynamic diapason.

A wild dance around the separator in the manner of *The Night on Bald Mountain** would be as equally incongruous and inappropriate in a setting of a dairy co-op as it would if applied to the rational, restrained character of our peasant, if he were not inflamed by elemental forces and passions of quite another militant character than the range of his feelings at a first encounter with the separator.

If, for example, we had before us a scene depicting Moses, who with one blow of his staff brought forth spurts of water from a lonely cliff in the desert, and thousands of people dying of thirst threw themselves at these spurting streams,[10]

or a frenzied dance of apostates around a biblical "golden calf,"[11] or

* From Moussourgsky's opera: "Sarochinsky Fair."

Shakhsi-Vakhsi, a procession of hundreds of religious fanatics in delirium beating themselves with sabres,[12]

or even the self-inflicting torture of the "Flagellants,"[13] – then we would have something from which to develop a picture of masses, seized by *pathos* through the ecstasy of their own behavior!

But that's not all!

At the moment when the separator scene is reached, the possibilities of means for achievement of ecstatic behavior are already exhausted within the film itself.

The separator scene is preceded by one depicting an Easter religious procession and a prayer for rain in a sun-scorched field.

Here, free reign is given to the frenzied, fanatical, religious ecstasy of those genuflecting believers, who crawling on their knees, with fruitless chants incite heaven for the miracle of rain, while they sink beneath the weight of the icons into the dust of the parched earth.

We had to clash and juxtapose these two different worlds of *pathos* and ecstasy – the world "of the old" and the world "of the new," succeeding it – the world of helpless servile submission to the mysterious forces of nature, compared with the world of organized technology, equiped to withstand blind forces.*

And this internal juxtapositioning of two contrasting elements of ecstasy and *pathos* also demanded varied methods for their embodiment. And the expressive means for the embodiment of these adjoining scenes naturally "stratified" into various areas, according to different dimensions of functional means.

The Easter religious crusade and the "prayer for rain" absorbed primarily the playacting – or, better said, "theatrical" – means of influence through human behavior (not ignoring, of course, all the other possibilities within the arsenal of cinema methods and techniques).

The separator scene, after all, basically relied on pure cinematographic means, impossible on such scale and form in the other arts (not ignoring, of course, the other necessary elements for this scene, as behavior, and acting, presented in a particularly parsimonious and restrained manner).

Such "delimitation" of means of expression had meaningful importance from the point of view of *pathos* in composition (as we know it now), because in this sequential system of expressive means there was a similar displacement ("a leap") from one dimension to another – from the dimension of cinema – acting ("theatrical" cinematography) to the dimension of "pure" cinematography, of independent, unique, and unmatched means and possibilities.

---

* The large-scale size of dairy and cattle farming, apart from other values, is yet another form of guaranteeing economic self-defense of peasant economy against nature's misfortunes.

The entire system of expressive means "somewhere near the middle of the reel" (just as in *Potemkin*) would "leap" completely into another, new counterdimension.

What, in fact, was the course of the structuring, to which we have added here such a thorough and detailed analysis?

Up to the moment when the first drop of "thickened" milk* appears, hitting the empty pail, the play of tension is built upon the means provided by the entire, available arsenal of montage methods.

This is a play of doubts and aspirations, suspicion and confidence, plain curiosity and unconcealed anxiety, passing through a whole series of ever-enlarging close-ups – from group shots, "three-shots," or "two-shots," to the single person.

This series of faces is intercut with shots of the heroine – Martha Lapkina, the agronomist and the young Communist Leaguer, Vasia, who turn the handle of the separator at an ever-increasing tempo.

Their movement is caught up by shots of spinning disks and the feed pipes of the separator, appearing all the more frequently at various angles.

Hardly perceptible and as if by accident "the play of doubts" is echoed by the tonality of the shot.[14]

As if by accident and hardly perceptible, shots of intensifying hope gradually brighten, whereas shots of aggravated suspicion – darken.

With the increase in tempo pieces are cut shorter – fragmentation of the change from bright to dark frames occurs more often. The disks spin faster and faster, and as if caught up by them, light fragmentation of edited cuts slide into actually revolving "sunbeams", in close-up (done with the help of a technical device – splinters of a mirror pasted on a spinning sphere).

At the appropriate moment, this entire edited sequence is intercut by the muzzle of a separator pipe. For just the right instant it remains empty. For just the necessary length of time at its lower edge, a drop begins to swell.

(Changing faces flash in close-up.)

For the necessary length of time the swollen drop trembles.

(The disks of the separator mechanism revolve at a frantic speed.)

At any moment the drop will fall.

(The close-ups flash, intercut with the revolving disks.)

The drop breaks off.

It falls!

---

* Incidentally, we mustn't forget to point out here that the purely objective aspect of the scene also bears within itself a subject of *pathos* in the fact that "ordinary" milk leaps into a higher qualitative milkiness, into...cream!

And the tiniest spray, starlike scatters, hitting the bottom of the empty pail.

And now unchecked, at furious pressure bursting from the body separator, a jet stream of thickened white cream thuds into the pail.

By now, through editing, the spurts and spray pierce through the stream of enthusiastic close-ups with a cascade of snow-white streams of milk, a silvery fountain of unchecked spurts, a fireworks display of unceasing splashes.

And then, as if in answer to the involuntary comparisons emerging on the screen, after the explosion resulting from the first spurts of milk, the sequence of these milk streams is interjected by what appears to be foreign matter flooded with light. . .aquatic pillars of shooting fountains.

Once again, as in *Potemkin* a metaphor bursts into the action, "fountains" of milk spurt from the separator – fountains of milk, echoing the folklore images of "rivers of milk" and "a land flowing with milk and honey" – symbols of material well-being.

And once again, as in *Potemkin*, simultaneously with the increase in intensity of movement, leaping over into the next dimension (fountains shooting more energetically, glittering more brightly than streams of milk!). Within the very method of show and tell, there is a similar leap from dimension to dimension: from an exposition by subject to an exposition by metaphor ("fountains of milk").

But montage does not stop there, it makes a new leap, into a new image – the image of "blazing fireworks."

Seizing upon the shimmer of the water fountain, the splendid shimmer of the milk streams, montage elevates the level of this shimmer to a new heightened class of intensity – to a shimmer of soaring fire sparks, sparks not only kindled by light, but flickering with multicoloredness with a new quality – color.

The technical method of realizing this idea turned out to be the grandnephew of the method of hand coloring the red flag in the same *Potemkin*.

From the image of fireworks we took only the element of changing multicoloredness and echoing it; the technical method itself came about through a flooding of pure color – by variously coloring separate cuts of shooting water streams. The monochromatic splendor of the intercuts of shooting fountains lept into another dimension – to a color coruscation exactly as it occurs at dusk when fountain squares blaze into many colors from the beams of multicolored projectors.*

---

* Within the compass of this film similar short cuts of color expositions were edited into the ecstatic moment of the paroxysm of the "Bull's Wedding," where the usual "everyday" scene at the coupling stable took place.

But even this did not exhaust the montage "fury" of the scene.

Flashing dizzyingly on the screen for a time, these color cuts would again swing over into cuts that are...colorless.

Because for *chromatic* cuts, the leap into *achromatic* ones is a new leap, again, into a new quality!

For this time, it was not at all a return to the gray cuts of monotone photography.

Chromatic cuts shifted into a system of new achromatic cuts, but such cuts, it seemed, split the color of gray monotype photography in two: a totally black field and a totally white stroke of lightening on this black background.

Compared with *Potemkin* this seems to be carrying to a nonrepresentational degree of "suprematism"[15] a similar fragmentation of the gray tone – there, where *Potemkin* remains within the bounds of concrete white highlights of night lights on the black surface of night waters, in the night scene on the eve of the encounter between the battleship and the squadron.

Furthermore, in *The Old and the New*, in similar abstract shots, from piece to piece, the white zigzag on the black canvas grows in leaps, becoming augmented and more complicated.

Plastically this was a new turn in color resolution: to go from a multiversity of color bursting forth from single-tone photography, not *back* to gray monotoneness, but *forward* – to the pure graphics of black and white.

Simultaneously, the structural system itself skipped over from the sphere of the *representational* to its opposite sphere of the *nonrepresentational*: white zigzags over a black background.

But that's not all, the nonrepresentational white zigzags, plastically ever increasing in size, carried instead, a new trait – the idea of growth, expressed not by means of the number of pictorialized objects, but through the meaning of the sign.

Because they increased not only in external size but first of all in internal meaning of that augmenting quantity, which they were to express.

These white zigzags were augmented not only in size but also by the quantitative inner meaning of *arabic numerals*: 5–10–17–20–35, numerals that increasing in their quantitative meaning, simultaneously with the enlargement of the plastic size of the ciphers, tap out a triumphant rataplan of the growing quantity of people enlisting in the dairy cooperative.

A "rataplan" resulted from the fact that a flowing sequence of *dynamic* shots was followed by a movement of a "pit-a-pat of peas" sequence of *static* shots of *immobile* numerals, succeeding one another in edited cuts.

And here again was a displacement and a leap into its opposite!

At the same time this was especially interesting because here the maximum *dynamics* was determined by means of an edited sequence of short cuts, clipped into small pieces and in themselves immobile – i.e. *static*!

The very finale of this scene, where the direct dynamics of the edited changing white zigzags of ever-increasing size, bore simultaneously, in the very content of these ciphers, the idea of quantitative growth expressed in signs, and thereby appeared as fundamental in the very nature of *pathos* – a similar fusion into a whole – in one sweep – the sphere of feeling and consciousness of man, overcome by ecstasy.

The abstracted final concept of numbers – the enumeration of the members of the dairy cooperative – was reversed into the revelry of sensual presentation, from which, in the course of the unfolding of that very scene, it passed through stages of becoming, from fact to image, from image to concept, leading the spectator through the sphere of feeling to the sphere of conception and fusing both spheres into a unified all-embracing *pathos*.

And recreating thus, on the shortest bit of film, the process in which there actually occurs the transformation of feeling into concept, this final scene could not help but captivate in its own manner, profoundly and invincibly, the consciousness and feelings of the audience.

Precisely here, and after what has been said above, it is quite natural – as a digression – to express the supposition of what would occur if we were faced with a reverse situation.

If, instead of a complete, harmonious synthesis between the outlined aspect and the inner meaning, there occurred just the opposite – a complete "bifurcation," a complete "dissection" between the essence and the sign, with a subsequent arbitrary collision of them "head-on" in a forced and unnatural conjunction.

As if there was every right to assume that the construction of the reverse principle of *pathos* must also give the reverse effect of *pathos*: that is, a comic humorous effect. We know in which possible states of human behavior such a dissociation between the sign and its meaning could take place in our comprehension.

This occurs in moments of intense "shock."

I had reason to quote a perfect example of this, in another place and for another reason.[16]

Such a similar psychological observation, of course, could belong only to the pen of such a brilliant analyst as Lev Nikolaevitch Tolstoy.

And indeed, in the pages of *Anna Karenina*, we find the description we need.

This is the famous passage where Vronsky, after learning of Anna's pregnancy, stares senselessly at the dial of his watch, incapable of connecting the outlined position of the hands with any idea of what time it is.

In moments of such a condition, a person, as they say, "is not quite himself".

And this state "of being not quite oneself," has a more sharply ironic form in Russian, "*ne v svoiye tarelke*,"* which is, as it were, the passive and detrimental – reverse – aspect of "exalting us," the active *pathos* of "being beside oneself."

The shock itself – is the same crooked mirror of qualitative jump which, at some instant "becomes unhinged" and overturns a certain established "order of things" and circumstances, previously appearing stable and indestructible.

It is quite natural to suppose that the reflection of such a situation, in the principles of composition, would give the effect of what we may label "*antipathos*," implying by this term not just a "mild humor" or "a good-natured grin," but rather a phenomenon that is comic in appearance and profoundly significant (perhaps even tragic) in essence.

We find ourselves here in an extremely advantageous position because, in this case, we can supply a very concrete example, a genuinely comic situation (i.e., comic in the above sense), built on just this kind of split between a sign and its meaning.

This situation belongs to one of the more famous comic creations of recent years.

It is one of the more pointed satirical scenes, in depth of meaning, in Chaplin's *Dictator*.

This is the scene in which we find Chaplin playing a small-town barber who upon his return home is found painstakingly erasing some kind of absurd white zigzags, smeared by some unknown hand on the windows of his small barbershop.

Meanwhile, these absurd zigzags are really not so absurd as ominous, because the essence of the letters "J," "E," "W," – when put together spell "Jew" and that very word written on the shop window is the image and symbol of fascist racial oppression.

And, at the same time, in essence, in depth of inner meaning, this is precisely that raving absurdity and filth – later to become bloody filth – that the little barber took these inscriptions to be.

Therefore, "the external split" between the inscriptions and their meaning is again joined in their deeper meaning and forces the apparently external comedy of the situation to reverberate with *pathos* of the true essence of this scene's social background.

However, getting back to the separator, we must add that the culminating scene of the "calvacade" of ever-increasing numbers in

* [Literally, "not in one's own plate" – HM.]

essence overcomes still another "hurdle"; it achieves still one more leap in the sphere of method and the means of expounding the subject matter.

First was the leap from *object exposure* to *image exposition*.

But the "cavalcade of ciphers" goes further, achieving incidentally a second leap, from the sphere of *representation* to the *sphere of nonrepresentation*, and it makes a decisive third leap from the sphere of *image exposition* to the sphere of *concept exposition*.

Because *the idea of quantity* is expressed here not through the *object exposure* of a "mass scene," not through the metaphorical *imagery* of a "stream" of people flooding the collective farm* but through a pure concept, expressed by *numbers*.

Second, the very chain of representational shots leaps over into a chain of black and white numerical subtitles.

True, one should keep in mind that the play on the dimensional enlargement of projected numerals, echoing the growth of their quantitative meaning, conveys by means of this abstract idea of quantity, an exclusively sensual dynamism, and by this means establishes, as it were, a transitional chain of relationships between the preceding sensuous images and the succeeding abstract concepts.

The most curious thing in all this, however, is that film directors went about making this intricate sequential scheme quite intuitively, not having the slightest theoretical knowledge of the principles of how to construct a work of *pathos*, how to "instill" *pathos* into the work, when the author himself is overcome by the *pathos* of the theme.

And at the same time we see that step by step the system of leaps and displacements from one sphere to another, from one dimension to another, is maintained in a strict qualitative succession of mounting intensity with an almost mathematical precision.

However, what was most important was that here, and simultaneously in *Potemkin*, were already two examples of the structure of *pathos*.

And from a comparison of these two differing examples, resolved under different circumstances, with different material and different subjects,[†] the principles of structure, into which organically flows the author's feeling of *pathos*, began to emerge with great ease from the particular applied examples of the "inspired" solution of these problems, transposing themselves into concrete forms of structural *pathos*.

These are the same principles to which the entire previous chapter has been devoted.

---

* An example of such a treatment would be something like the parallel editing of moving "streams" of people and say, a surging ice-flow, as Pudovkin did in the last part of his film *Mother*.

[†] Furthermore the material of one, as was stated above, was not only "as such" imbued with *pathos*, but graphically so, whereas the other no less clearly demanded a conscious imbuing of *pathos* by compositional means.

As a supplement to the chapter on *pathos* composition in *The Old and the New*, I would like to briefly focus the reader's attention on the moment of the leap, analyzed above, from pieces of ordinary "gray" photography to colored pieces and from colored further – once more – to uncolored, but now not "gray" pieces, but to pieces decisively demarcated into black and white (in numerical subtitles).

[...]* The color scheme "gray–color–black and white," developing in the separator scene, over a length of several feet, is "reborn," amplified,[17] and extended, by one and the same author, to the length of whole sequences in the color conception of the film *Ivan the Terrible*.

Thus, two reels of the scene of conspiracy against Ivan's life in Staritsky's mansion were maintained in a markedly gray gamma, followed by – color "fireworks" – again two reels depicting the feast in Alexandrov Sloboda and finally again in two reels – the scene depicting the murder of Vladimir Andreyevitch in the cathedral, totally executed in black (pierced by a scintillating streak of the brocade robes of the doomed prince and by moving dots of candle lights in the hands of the *Opritchniks'* choir).

This "intrusion" of color, as if a watershed between the gray and black and white, was not of itself to link the colored section in part one of the history of Ivan the Terrible with its entirely colored third part (although in two parts, this film was conceived, according to its inner units, as a trilogy – a triptych).

Highlights of all this taken together, however, is incorporated in its entirety in one and the same *Potemkin*, where gray similarly predominates, differentiated into black and white (of this more in detail later), and where in a moment of color fanfare, at the culminating point, bursts forth...the red flag!

It is interesting to note that *Potemkin* in this case does not stand alone as an example of *pathos*.

Those same years offered another example of *pathos* in the play of black and white exploding into red.

This same color formula was also used by Mayakovsky in another aspect, but for exactly the same aim.

One of his most pointed impressions on America (which he visited in 1925) he embodied in the poem "Black and White," about an old Negro who works as a shoeshine boy in Havana. It depicts the racial prejudice in the United States that had so infuriated Mayakovsky.

From the Negro's, Willie, point of view the entire world is differentiated into two colors: black and white:

* [As per Russian original – HM.]

The white
eats
          the pineapple ripe,
the black —
          rotten and specked.
Clean white work
          is done by the whites
dirty black work —
          by the blacks.

However, only one factor, incomprehensible to the Negro, Willie, throws this sharp demarcation off balance:

Why must sugar also,
          whiter than white,
be made by
          a blacker than black?*

In answer to his question, he is given a slap across the face by the pure white sugar king, who is "whiter than a herd of clouds."

Scarlet blood floods the black face and oozes onto the white clothes.

Thus, the confrontation between black and white in a social conflict explodes into a red color — the color of blood, inflamed by the color of social protest — the color of revolution.

Twenty-two supporting columns

Thus the norms by which I constructed my films of *pathos* were self-determined.

However, before believing that these principles were as binding as a general law, I first tried to verify their validity in other areas.

After having "caught" and understood the principles of the structuring of *pathos* in film, as described above, I immediately tried to test these principles in contiguous, related fields of art.

And first I examined them in literature.

And in literature I first observed them in the novels of Zola.

I knew very well and loved very much the *Rougon-Macquart* cycle.

I remembered very well that the great novelist set each of the twenty novels in the well-defined and self-enclosed material of a precisely delineated and limited environment.

(The Parisian market; the railroad; coal mines; the undergrowth of an abandoned park; the stock exchange; the city of Paris as a whole; a large store; a house with bourgeois apartments, with an imposing red carpet

* [My translation — HM.]

running up the broad main staircase; or a house with wretched inhabitants, with streaks of paint streaming from the miserable dye works over its besmeared threshold, which in the colors of these streams repeated the peripeteias of the dramas within the house, etc., etc.)

And I remembered very distinctly that in each of these novels (each time in material typical only of the environment chosen for it) invariably the exact same basic situations of man's animal existence are resolved: love and death.

For each time Zola compels the corresponding environment, which is always new, to repeat "in unison" the culmination of these "decisive" moments of human existence, an endless number instructive for any director who does not limit himself only to the expressiveness of his characters, but extends it to the atmosphere and surroundings as well. It is instructive for every artist who concerns himself with the emotional expressiveness of his production's "material formulation," and most of all – for the film director who has this problem facing him in every shot of his film.

In addition, we must not forget that, within each separate novel, the material and the basic environment chosen for each novel proceed each time in their own particular way through the entire spectrum and range of human dramas, with which the narration is saturated.

Here on a high level occurs what was accomplished by the most typical impressionists, the contemporaries of our novelist who were so close to him in spirit.

And the stock exchange, the palace of deputies, the interior of a cathedral, or a signalman's cabin were also altered symphonically in tone with the social drama that was unfolding within them. This is exactly similar to the manner in which the same *Cathedral* by Claude Monet[18] burns with dozens of colored variations. On numerous canvases it catches the peripeteias of the same age-old drama of the battle of light and dark, this daily combat of the ancient Ormazd and Ahriman,[19] whose alternate success lies on its Gothic facade with constantly changing contours of bright spots amidst clefts of darkness, from the crimson dawn of the rising sun to the violet twilight of the conquest of night.*

But there is more.

I still remembered very clearly that besides these obligatory themes of love and death in each novel (and again mainly through the environment and the material on which the novel is built), Zola at some point falls into an ecstatic litany,[20] a hymn of *pathos*, forcing the concrete tale

---

* It is interesting to recall that lawn tennis, which is now so popular, was once a purely mystery-cult game: A ball, having flown past in the sunlight (always half in light and half inevitably in darkness), signifies both kingdoms, which change place eternally – the kingdom of Light and the kingdom of Darkness: the triumph of Ormazd and the triumph of Ahriman.

through titanic generalizations into sublimating forms of the ecstatic dithyramb.

Interrupting the story of Nana's adventures in the chapter of the "golden fly" or in the dizzy scene of the steeplechase, he raises the material of the novel to an unrestrained typhoon of gilded prostitution, into which it is transformed before our very eyes and in which the gilded Second Empire of Ratapoile[21] and Rigalbouch[22] chokes and flounders, so that it may then burn down in the expiating fire of the auto-da-fé of the blazing, fiery ball of the conflagration of the Tuileries Palace and the city of Paris perishing in the flames on the pages of *The Rout*.

In *Earth* like a stream – no, a deluge! waves of city filth soar upward, readily swelling and hurling over into generalized images and symbols of vice, greed, and depravity, rushing down endlessly like cascades onto the virgin soil of village communities not yet totally corrupted.

And in the increasingly inundating streams of these waves rushing down looms the image of the ultimate demoralization of French society in the era of Napoleon III.

These are the whirlwinds of financial catastrophes and stock market crashes raised to the level of hurricanes in *Money*; the dizzy dreams of Father Mauraut, intoxicated by the sensual atmosphere of the overgrown park of Amada and the wild, sunburnt girl jumping through his bushes and grass; the symphony of cheese and mountain avalanches of nightly gorging tumbling into the eternally hungry belly of Paris.

Are these not the gigantic canvases of *pathos* to which the material environment and objects of the Second Empire were elevated so that through them the image of the beginning of the destruction and collapse of the bourgeoisie would thunder, in the same merciless way as the other giant novelist Balzac, through a gallery of titanic living human images, engraved the image of the bourgeoisie as the rising class?!

Is it not also characteristic that in the center of Balzac's attention are the individual and the people, producing and captivating objects, but in Zola it is the environment and objects that have captivated, swallowed, and enslaved the living person-creator?

In those marvelous 1920s when I focused on a detailed analysis of Zola, it was easy to collect twenty enthusiasts.*

It was easy within the walls of the "free workshop" in the Film Institute to distribute all twenty novels of Emile Zola among them.

And it was even easier, while forcing quotations from twenty separate novels to "beat their heads against each other," novels containing

---

* Among these young enthusiasts at that time were those who are new bending under the burden of honors and laurels, young people like the brothers Vasil'ev (long before *Chapayev*),[23] Alexey Popov (long before the Red Army Theater),[24] G. V. Alexandrov (long before *Circus, Volga-Volga,* and *Spring*),[25] Maxim Shtraukh,[26] who had not yet played the role of Lenin, and many others.

different material that solved *identical* situations, to understand what methods and what techniques were used by the father of naturalism to accomplish this.

Besides the unusual scholarly "comfort" that came from the fact that we were dealing with the work of a novelist whose method could be compared in twenty parallel aspects, we also appreciated the "naturalism" by which the method itself was realized. This, however, is not the place to analyze or evaluate the "naturalistic method."

This is especially true since the connotation of this term today hardly applies to the method to the amazingly figurative and, I would say, poetic and musical construction of Zola's works. The term is inextricably linked with concepts of "frailty of form," bordering on compositional "amorphousness," and not only with an unintelligent documentation of surrounding reality's external phenomena, with no attempt to discover and represent its social significance.

This is also not the place to discuss in any great detail how the author of this polemical slogan understood everything that he included within it.

We were more interested in another topic at this point.

What was relevant was the limited means of expression with which Zola basically operated in his works.

It would be useful here to conceive of the term "naturalism" mainly as related to that characteristic of his novels by means of which he achieves his expressive effects, whether it be simply emotional effects or those "going beyond themselves," those of *pathos*.

What is more important is that, in order to achieve these emotional effects, Zola does not really *transform* natural phenomena, the environment, the situation, or objects, so that through his literary style or literary techniques he would compel them to resound emotionally in the thematic key which he requires.

He does not so much arbitrarily "alter" them, through description and exposition, as "select" them, in the aspect in which they can actually be found in the given circumstances.

Of all the possible elements of the environment or phenomena, he chooses just that situation and just those objects in just that state that at the given moment are most "in unison" with that emotional (and often even physiological) sensation that he wants to evoke in the reader.

The state in which the objects and elements of the environment are represented (as well as their participation in the scene), in selected conditions and circumstances quite normal for them, is substantiated in everyday reality and is appropriately "natural." The novelist can place any scene into any surroundings.

He can order any weather outside the window for it.

He can furnish it with any kind of furniture.

He can illuminate it by any source of light.

An author of another school, for this purpose, limits himself to an environment most appropriate to the everyday living conditions, or by an environment most easily associated with a particular situation.

For Zola this is not sufficient.

Of all possible elements of the environment, surroundings, and objects of the situation, he selects those and only those that, by their nature, appearance, or state, are found in the same nuance of mood or atmosphere of the scene.

In Balzac the character itself permeates the situation. The nature of the character. The house of the old man Grandet is Grandet himself, expressed through the beams, boards, barrels, and locks.

All this is even clearer and more obvious in Gogol's hyperboles; for example, in *Dead Souls*. Nozdrev's yard, which resounds with numerous dogs barking, the pile of junk in Pliushkin's "den," also stand for Pliushkin and Nozdrov, inasmuch as Sobakevich's household resembles Sobakevich.

...When Chichikov looked sideways at Sobakevich, he struck him this time as being very much like a medium-sized bear. To complete the resemblance, the frockcoat he was wearing was exactly the color of a bear's coat, his sleeves were long, his trousers were long, he walked flat-footedly, lurching from side to side, and he was continually treading on other people's toes.... Chichikov stole another glance at him as they passed through the dining-room: "A bear, a regular bear!" What a strange resemblance – he was even called Mikhail Semyonovich, the name Russian peasants give to a bear...In a corner of the drawingroom stood a paunchy walnut bureau on four ridiculous legs – a regular bear! The table, the armchairs, the chairs, all of them were of the heaviest and most uncomfortable shape; in short, every object, every chair, seemed to be saying: "I'm a Sobakevich, too!" or "I, too, am very like Sobakevich!"*

In Zola the situation reflects the nature of the character in the same way (let us recall Nana's boudoir), and in addition (and this seems to be essential) the situation and setting, environment, and landscape all compose an eternally changing symphony that, like music, is especially designed to convey the atmosphere, the changing mood, and the psychological state of the protagonists acting within it.

The well-known "incompleteness" of the depiction of characters in Zola here seems to be fully written, drawn, and played by this orchestra of the material environment surrounding them.

Balzac's characters always appear (just as Balzac himself) like the portrait of the fat grandee attributed to Velasquez. They, too, are imposingly round, and similarly stand out from the background of the

---

* [Nikolai Gogol, *Dead Souls*, David Magarshack, trans., Penguin, Baltimore, 1961, pp. 103, 105 – HM.]

wall; the nature of their faces and bearing is also fully depicted down to the smallest detail; they, too, stand firmly on their feet and clasp in their hands what has been put there by him.

Zola's approach is quite different.

These are really "torsos," but only torsos in those cases when they are separated from the surroundings into which they have grown, or, more precisely, from the surroundings out of which they seemed to have grown.

Indeed, no one would ever think of calling Manet's[27] *Girl behind the Bar* a "torso," although in the painting she has no legs. This is because it would not occur to anyone to separate her from the reflection in the mirror that completes the depiction of the expression of her face or from the counter that has replaced the lower part of her body: Similarly, no one would call the waitress in another of his canvases . . . "one-breasted" just because, in place of her left breast, the round head of someone at the table protrudes in the foreground!

In any case, in order to achieve these changing emotional effects in a situation taking place in the same environment – Zola painstakingly selects from "all possible ones" those particular details and those hours or moments and those very conditions of temperature and light that repeat emotionally the same psychological nuance with which Zola is trying to overwhelm the reader at a given moment.

He extends the hot atmosphere of a lover's quarrel to a warm or burning-hot environment and situation.

But he does not depend mainly on literary style to "heat up" the environment and situation – through a complicated system of metaphoric constructions, rhythmic refinements, or the timbre or the sound of cleverly arranged words.* Instead, Zola puts his heroes into a real situation with objects from the surroundings that are in the physical state he requires.

This is the little iron stove burning so hot it induces stupor in the small room in *The Human-Beast*. This is also true of the red (warm!) tone required in the general course of events. As it increases, this tone inundates the wall and radiates naturally from the burning, red-hot walls of this stove.

This is the stupefying, once again animal, hot atmosphere of the feathers and down of a slaughtered bird in the cellar of the Parisian market.

Or the monstrous sultriness at the moment of the interruption of the harvest amidst the immeasurable spread-out fields in *Earth*.

No one prevented the author from selecting, as a sign of everyday

---

* It was just with an emphasis on this aspect of expressive techniques that the subsequent leading literary trend – the symbolists – "swept away" the school of naturalism later on.

reality, a "cool little forest" instead of a sultry field, and a pantry with sausages instead of a cellar with a slaughtered bird for the scene he required.

To what extent the emotional intoxication of the atmosphere would be diminished after having lost the elements of animal warmth and heat – is for the reader himself to judge!

In exactly the same way Zola builds up the desired crescendo of any nuance of expression, of any range of phenomena, increasing according to their effect. He will achieve this, not by increasing the employment of stylistic devices, but mainly by stringing out such realistic, everyday (and mostly naturalistic) details that, by their nature, as signs of everyday reality, increase proportionally to the impression they produce.

And from what has been discussed here it already seems obvious what "didactic" significance this method of literary style has for filmmakers in particular. However, this is true, of course, only for those who achieve a consistent symphonic unity of the whole through all the elements of their pictures.

Here we have a profoundly conceived method and a whole school of experimentation with the organization of the environment and behavior in the emotional passages required by the theme.

With this as a starting point, the filmmaker extends this method to those devices specific to film that will produce the desired effects.

He extends "coldness" and "warmth" to the range of light with which he correspondingly floods the material chosen by him, in a shot that echoes (or is in contrast) to the person experiencing it.

He extends the convulsive zigzag of the shots of the hostile city landscape to the montage "ragtime"[28] of the corresponding sequence[29] of this film.

To a point where he also learns to compel the material, which is in itself neutral, "natural," and "raw" before the camera, to "sing" in the tone he requires through camera angle, shooting, and editing.

But by this time he has already come down from the school bench of Emile Zola's "naturalistic method" and has passed to the next class of cinematic techniques of expression.

To clarify how this is done, one may use examples from *Potemkin* where crescendo is often constructed according to this principle (besides the rhythmic and editing devices that play an extremely important role in the film). For example, the increasing menace of the battleship preparing for combat has been created in this way.

The stages are arranged consecutively one after the other in proportion to the increasing intensity of danger.

The gangways are raised.

The shells are transported.

The cannons are aimed.

The muzzles are raised.

The machines begin to pound.

All these elements are not presented arbitrarily but in strict succession, and at the same time, as we have seen, being very careful that their effective force continually increases: Each element in turn plays its "role" and, having played it to the end, yields its place to the next one, which produces a more intense effect.

The same thing occurs on the Odessa steps.

First the crowd, stumbling, runs down.

Then they roll down the stairs, to be precise there are 194 of them.

And finally, rolling, downward, rushes – the baby carriage.

This does not mean, however, that for the sake of an "'objectivistic" stylistic method, Zola in any way ignores other types of literary effect.

Not at all!

And actually on the contrary.

Therefore, having described above the method of exploiting the "natural" state of objects as well as the emotional effect accompanying it, we then cautiously discussed this method as a sacramental formula "in its fundamentals."

As is commonly known, this formula usually "frees your hands" for any assertions that do not coincide "substantially" with the substantial!

If we take rhythm, for example, whole passages in Zola's novels are written in almost rhythmic prose: Somewhere in a booklet I happened to see a page describing a procession of coal miners that was written in the genre of narrative verse – as a sequence of consecutive stanzas in one of the heroic verse meters.

However, what is particularly interesting here is not the actual fact of "rhythmic" prose, but those moments in which Zola's prose has taken on a rhythmic imprint.

Those moments, where "simple exposition" is transformed into exposition with a rhythmic imprint, turn out to be moments inevitably linked with the exposition of events...of *pathos* (for example, the scene mentioned above in *Germinal*).

Zola uses metaphor, simile, and tropes just as often and just as brilliantly.

This occurs again in moments when [the aid] of the technique of simple and direct descriptive narration is insufficient for the attainment of – an effect of *pathos*.

And the method based on a documentary style makes a qualitative leap into another "dimension" of narration – into narration based on similes, metaphors, and metonymies.

But the "leap" here is not limited only to the fact that one method gets to a state of "being beside itself" and hurls itself into another.

Faithful to his basic technique, Zola chooses as the objects of comparison only those in such a state that will make the material capable of evoking *pathos* at the moment chosen by him.

And the actual "state" of the described objects is a state...of being beside itself.

The material of the figurative level of comparison is also a "being beside oneself."*

Here, for example, is a passage from *Ladies' Delight* [*Au bonheur des dames*]:

It was a gigantic sale like a fair. It seemed like the store trembled and *hurled out* its surplus onto the street.

...Gold, silver and bronze, *flowing out* of bags, *tearing* purses, formed an enormous pile of net receipts, still warm and full of the life with which it emerged out of the buyers' hands...

The goods *are hurled out*.
The money *flows out*.
The bags *are torn*.
Cold metal takes on *animal warmth*.

...On that day a special display of corsets was arranged. It consisted of an entire army of headless and legless mannequins, which under silk displayed only torsos and flat doll chests full of unhealthy lewdness...

In the lifeless torsos of the mannequins, unhealthy lewdness is aroused.

But now the fabric enveloping them and the mannequins themselves begin to become alive and move:

People examined them, women who were stopping shoved each other in front of the windows, the crowd was acting rude because of its eager desire. And the material became alive under this passion of the street: The lace slightly trembled, fell down and mysteriously hid the womb of the store; even pieces of cloth, thick and square, breathed with temptation; coats drooped more and more on the mannequins, which had come alive, and a large velvet mantle, supple and warm, swelled as if it were on human shoulders, on a heaving chest, on trembling thighs...

And now endlessly repeating themselves in mirrors, the mannequins not only come alive but are incarnated into women:

...The rounded breasts of the mannequins expanded the material, the broad hips emphasized the slender waists...Mirrors on both sides of the store window, according to a prearranged plan, endlessly reflected and multiplied the mannequins, populating the street with these pretty women on sale, whose price was marked on their heads...

* [Eisenstein bases this concept on the Greek *ex stasis* meaning ecstasy, a "going out" of a particular state, going beyond its limits, "being beside oneself" – HM.]

And a woman-mannequin now rushes from the show window display into the evening streets of the city:

...A large velvet mantle, made of silver fox, displayed its curved profile of a headless woman who rushed in the pouring rain to some festival, in the dark Parisian twilight.

And the enlivened fabric – is no longer fabric, but a living woman's body:

...All this muslin and cambric, dead, scattered over the counters, flung and piled up, began to live with the life of a body, became fragrant and warm from the aroma of love. The white cloud became sacred, having undergone its night baptism and, soon as it whirled away, the rosy gleam of a knee, glittering on the background of whiteness, drove people out of their minds...

...The silk department represented a large room prepared just for love... Here were all the milk-white nuances of the body of an adored woman, beginning with the velvet hips and ending with the fine silk of the thighs with the gleaming satin of the breast...*

And likewise women turn into fruit in *The Belly of Paris* [*Le Ventre de Paris*]

...Apricots lying on moss were taking on the color of amber, with the burning tones of the setting sun that gilds the nape of a brunette where her small locks curl. Cherries, set out berry by berry, were like the too-narrow lips of smiling Chinese women; those from Montmorency were like the fat lips of a plump woman; English cherries – more oblong and serious; heart cherries – with ordinary skin, black, ruined by kisses.[†]

And the "womb" of woman, her maternal belly, lends its figurative name to the gigantic belly of Paris in the title of the novel, devoted to the hub of its central market. When it becomes necessary to take the belly beyond the limits of the commonplace, to raise it to the level of *pathos*, then another sacred edifice – a cathedral, temple, tabernacle[30] – is at the author's disposal.

In them blossoms, in them overflows, by them flickers and burns the gigantic figure of the "supernatural" woman on Claude's canvas. The real Christina "arose" and was incarnated into this figure. She was "almost dead" and "lifeless," prostrate at the feet of the conqueress in the fatal battle of the two women – the wife and the creation – for the soul of the artist (*The Masterpiece*) [*Le Oeuvre*].

...Then Christina pushed the door open and rushed forward. The invincible fury, the anger of a wife insulted in her own home, deceived here while she was sleeping in the next room, drove her.

* [Translated from Eisenstein's Russian – HM.]
[†] [Translated from the French – HM.]

Yes, he was with the other woman; he was painting her stomach, her thighs, as if seized by the madness of love, a visionary whose tormenting need for the real was hurling him into the exaltation of the supernatural.

These thighs took on a golden hue like the columns of a temple, her stomach turned into a heavenly luminary that sparkled with bright, yellow and red tones, blinding and symbolic.

...Who had painted this idol of an unknown religion? Who had created it out of metal, marble, and semi precious stones? Who placed the symbolic unfolding rose of her feminine nature between the precious columns of her thighs, under the holy vault of her stomach?

And later (after Claude's suicide):

Oh, Claude...Oh, Claude, She took you away, she killed you, murdered you, the cursed, despised creature.

In the abundance of suffering all the blood rushed back from her heart, and breathless, she lay on the earth as if dead, like a white remnant, pathetic and destroyed...

Above her shone the woman in the symbolic radiancy of the idol.... (*The Masterpiece*)*

The well-known formula at every step!

And not only as a whole, but in every part.

Claude's palette of pure colors becomes a conglomeration of semi-precious stones:

This is such an unusual picture in which it seemed that semiprecious stones were sparkling for some kind of religious worship.

And the valuable semiprecious stone has been chosen here for comparison because it is a stone originating rays of colorful glitter.

Even in these examples it is already apparent that the method of achieving the style of *pathos* in literature is not different from the ecstatic formula we discovered in film.

However, this statement achieves its full impact, as I noted above, where Zola is suddenly hurled into a debauch of generalized *pathos*.

Here also, due to his characteristic method of exposition, which we tried so carefully to discuss above, it becomes especially clear that all the material of the scene he describes or all the material for the corresponding comparisons (invariable in scenes of *pathos*) occurs in states of "being beside one-self," in states of "frenzy," in states of "ecstasy."

In addition, this material is arranged sequentially, according to the degree of increasing intensity of frenzy, in such a way that, placed in a row side by side along the rising line of this intensity, the materials seem to eject out of each other.

* [Translated from Russian – HM.]

It also does not matter what is the nature of the material from the environment.

And it does not matter whether these are details of an actual situation, or a chain of phenomena and objects chosen for comparison, or the same elements used for depiction taken totally out of the everyday setting, or out of the atmosphere of delirium, dream, or hallucination.

Let us begin with the debauch of the miners woven entirely out of definite, everyday details, on their payday in the tavern of the widow Désire from *Germinal*.

This scene "in itself" does not have anything heroic about it, nothing that "by tradition" would require the emotional frenzy of *pathos*. But by Zola's will and the skill of his literary mastery, this scene, filled and oversatiated with everyday details, with the density of the "Flemish" style, is "sublimated" to a scale worthy of Rabelais[31] and of the frenzied *pathos* of the ancient bacchantes.

Again, as in the case of *The Old and the New*, it is in just such material (in itself not necessarily emotionally heightened by *pathos*) that the method of his development of *pathos* can be seen very clearly.

The air thickens, through the haze of the fumes, into clouds of tobacco smoke and seems to congeal in an endless number of paper garlands.

Breasts burst out of corsages.

Sweat pours out like steam.

Milk flows from mothers' breasts into the hungry lips of the infants pressing to them.

Children urinate under the tables.

In the yard, adults vomit streams of beer that have been poured uncontrollably into their throats.

The cornet blasts the air with its roar.

And the rosy color of skin pours over into the gold shimmering of the gradually unclad bodies, and from here it glides over to the glittering gilding of the golden shields hung on the walls with the names of saints: St. Eloi, patron of ironworks; St. Crispin, patron of shoemakers; and St. Barbara, patroness of coalminers.

Let us not forget that, like a diamond (a stone that has emerged into a shimmering effect), gold is also a color that has spilt over with bright rays of light.

But here is the description itself, permeated by the leitmotif of overabundance, brimming to the top:

...On Fair nights the day's celebrations ended up at the Bon Joyeux dance. This was run by widow Désire, a stout matron of fifty, round as a barrel but still so fresh that she had six lovers, one for each weekday, as she put it, and all six together on Sundays. She called all the miners her boys, and grew quite sentimental at the thought of all the rivers of beer she had poured out for them these thirty years. It was also her boast that not a single haulage girl became pregnant without first having lost her virtue at her establishment. There were two rooms at the Bon Joyeux: the bar, containing the counter and tables, and, leading out of it on the same level through a wide archway, the dance-hall, a huge room with a wooden floor in the center only and a brick surround. It was adorned with two chains of paper flowers, crossing the ceiling from corner to corner, and caught up at the intersection by a wreath of the same flowers.

...On this particular Sunday dancing was in full swing by five o'clock, with broad daylight coming through the windows. But it was about seven before the place filled up. A stormy wind had sprung up outside, raising clouds of black dust which blinded people and sizzled in the pans of frying-fat....

...As darkness fell, the musicians played like mad, and nothing could be seen but jigging haunches and bosoms in a confusion of waving arms. A great shout greeted the appearance of the four lamps, and everything was suddenly lit up – red faces, hair coming down and sticking to the skin, skirts flying and wafting a strong smell of sweating couples. Maheu called Etienne's attention to Mouquette: Round and fat like a bladder of lard, she was gyrating dizzily in the arms of a tall, thin trammer. Evidently she had consoled herself by picking up a man...

They could have supper later on; nobody was hungry, for their stomachs were all swimming with coffee and blown out with beer...

...A quadrille was ending in a cloud of reddish dust, the walls were splitting, a cornet was giving vent to high-pitched whistlings like a railway engine in distress, and when the dancers stopped they were steaming like horses...

...They stayed until ten. Women kept coming in to find their men folk and take them home; droves of children tagged on behind, and mothers, giving up any pretence of delicacy, took out breast that hung down like long, yellow sacks of oats, and smeared their chubby offspring with milk; whilst the children who could already walk, blown out with beer, crawled about on all fours under the tables and shamelessly relieved themselves. All round there was a rising tide of beer, widow Désire's barrels had all been broached, beer had rounded all paunches and was overflowing in all directions, from noses, eyes – and else-where. People were so blown out and higgledy-piggledy, that everybody's elbows or knees were sticking into his neighbour and everybody thought it great fun to feel his neighbour's elbows. All mouths were grinning from ear to ear in continuous laughter. The heat was like an oven and everybody was roasting, so they made themselves comfortable by laying bare their flesh, which appeared golden in the thick clouds of pipe smoke. The only nuisance was when you had to go outside; now and again a girl would get up, go to the other end, lift her skirt by the pump and come back. Underneath the paper chains the dancers could no longer see each other for sweat, and this encouraged pit-boys to catch hold of backsides at random and throw haulage girls on their backs. But when a girl fell down with a man on top of her, the cornet drowned their fall with its frenzied tootlings and feet trampled all over them as though the dance itself had buried them alive.

...So they all went back together, passing for the last time the fair, the pans of congealing fish and chips, the pubs from which the last glasses of beer were flowing out into the middle of the road in streams. The storm was still threatening...the laughter became louder and louder. From the ripe corn there was arising a breath of passion; a good many children must have been made that night...*

We can see that all the material has been taken in a state of overabundance, flowing out of its state, flowing out of one environment into another — "beside itself."

The beer runs out of their noses and eyes. Children urinate under the tables. There are wenches at the pumps. Milk pours from mothers' breasts. The remnants of beer run in streams onto the passing road. Everybody's elbows or knees were sticking into his neighbor. Walls tremble, fall down, bodies swell, and, having become naked, burst from their coats. Bellies expand forming the contour of a circle...

There are objects that in themselves are incapable of outpouring, but even those are chosen by physical signs of descriptive details, arranged in a sequence, as if passing over consecutively from stage to stage.

The air. At first it becomes filled with sweat. With reddish dust. With the tobacco smoke of the pipes and the dancers smoking like horses. Finally it is so full of perspiration that the dancers can no longer see each other. The air seems to turn into a solid mass. Paper flowers, garlands, hang in this haze as if the limit of the potential solidification of the air.

The treatment of sound is also intentional here: the cornet roaring like a locomotive.

Its roar is presented at that level of sound at which it is no longer perceived as producing sound, and begins to act like motion, like a pure motor. Like movement that no longer produces sound, but shifts, overturns.

We know this kind of rumbling of Turkish drums "that do not resound" but only shake the environment, the air, windows, and walls; pipe tubas rending the air and tearing the drum membranes; the whistle of sirens, of locomotive pipes cutting the ear and the material environment. In the same way the roaring "piston" cuts the atmosphere of the Bon Joyeux. And that is why it makes sense that no violin or flute is employed in this passage.

And over all this solemnly reigns the hostess of the Bon Joyeux, this tavern Circe, who bursts out of the embraces of her six lovers into generalization. Her name embodies the satisfaction toward which the frantic revelry of the participants in her tavern are rushing:

Desire — *Désire* — longing.

Here the "eruption" is presented in its simplest "natural" form and inseparable from those phenomena for which it is typical to "erupt" in such a way when in a certain state.

The actual selection of these phenomena may, of course, seem

* *Germinal*, Pt. III, chap. 2 [Emile Zola, *Germinal*, Leonard Tancock, trans., Penguin, New York, 1954, pp. 161–2 – HM.]

peculiar, but it would be difficult to separate it from the truly captivating effect of this scene as a whole, whose ecstatic carnivorousness would be worthy of Breughel,[32] Rubens,[33] or Rabelais. However, we must depart from this kind of "naturalistic fresco" and move into the realm of the poetically inspired narration of "elevated" material. Yet even here we will immediately encounter – the exact same selection of phenomena. The difference will lie only in the fact that in this case these phenomena will be separated from their naturalistic, everyday concreteness and will be employed metaphorically and abstractly; that is, in terms of their purely dynamic application to such areas that are not "realistically" connected with such phenomena in ordinary circumstances.

As an example of this, we may introduce the ecstatic "outpouring" of Shelley[34] on the subject of Francis Bacon[35] in his *Defence of Poetry.**

Lord Bacon was a poet. His language has a sweet and majestic rhythm, which satisfies the sense, no less than the almost superhuman wisdom of his philosophy satisfies the intellect; it is a strain which *distends*, and then *bursts* the circumference of the reader's mind, and *pours itself* forth together with it into the universal element with which it has perpetual sympathy.

As we can see, even here, although on a different level, there is the very same "selection" of phenomena and states:

"superhuman" wisdom,

"bursts" the circumference of the human mind,

"pours itself forth"...into the universal element...

But of course *pathos* is even more inflammatory in those cases where the scenes are thematically suffused with the *pathos* of social protest, even if it be in those limited representations by means of which Zola was able to draw the images of revolution and its victory.

The heightened intensity of these descriptions is characteristic in that Zola "hurls himself" there beyond the limits of merely "naturalistic" description; that here in the description, figurative comparisons occur in their full magnitude.

In this way, for example, in *The Career of Rougon* there is the description of a scene of *pathos*, the night attack of the "small army" of insurgents against the provincial town of Plassans. On the following pages of the novel, merciless punishment awaits them for participation in the uprising, but at this moment they are at the peak of the upward flight of the revolutionary explosion.

Suddenly Silvère raised his head. He threw back the folds of his cloak and listened carefully...

...Already several moments from behind the hills, in the midst of which the

* [*The Prose Work of Percy Bysshe Shelley*, Harry Buxfon Forman, ed., vol. 3, Reeves and Turner, London, 1880, p. 107 – HM.]

road to Nice disappeared, a vague rumble approached. It was like the distant jolting of a convoy of carts. The Viorne covered these vague sounds with her grumbling. But little by little they grew stronger, began to resemble the tramping of an army on the march. Soon in the increasing peal one could distinguish the noise of the crowd, the strange blowing of a tornado, measured and rhythmical. It seemed that these were the strokes of lightning of an advancing storm, shaking the drowsy air with its approach...Suddenly from behind the bend appeared the black mass. The threatening *Marseillaise*, sung with a passionate thirst for vengeance, burst out...

"It's them" – screamed Silvère in a burst of joy and enthusiasm.

...The crowd surged in a grand, irresistible explosion. Nothing could have been more threatening, more sublime than the sudden appearance of several thousands of people on the dead, icy tranquility of the horizon. The road, which had turned into a torrent, rolled in living waves which seemed to be inexhaustible. Constantly from behind the bend appeared new black masses whose singing continued to swell the enormous voice of this human storm. When the last batallions appeared, a deafening explosion resounded. The *Marseillaise* filled the sky as if blown by the mouths of giants playing on monstrous trumpets which hurled it, vibrating with the coldness of brass, to all ends of the valley. The sleeping village awoke immediately. It shuddered like a drum beaten by drumsticks; it resounded in its very bowels, repeating with its echoes the ardent notes of the national anthem. Now not only was the crowd singing: from all parts of the horizon – from the distant hills, from strips of cultivated land, from the meadows, from clusters of trees and the smallest bushes came the human voices. A wide amphitheater arising from the river to Plassans, a gigantic waterfall along which streamed the blue radiancy of the moon, was covered by an invisible, immeasurable crowd welcoming the insurgents. Along the shores of the Viorne, by the waters speckled with mysterious reflections of melted tin, there was not a dark pit where the people hidden did not catch up the refrain with extreme anger. The fields in the shaking air and ground screamed vengeance and freedom. And all the while, as the army descended along the slope, the roar of the crowd rolled in a resounding wave, cut by sudden peals which shook even the stones of the road.*

Here the springboard of action is somewhat broader than the sturdy halls of the widow Désire.

The river, hills, sky, and icy tranquility of the horizon.

But this in no way changes the stylistic method.

We need only take the expressive means from a more intense register and from a broader range.

The basic object of plenitude expands here to the fullness of the space of the heavens.

And for its plenitude, dust, sweat, and the warmth of the dancers, and the cornets, do not suffice.

* [*La Fortune de Rougon (The Career of Rougon)* from the French edition, *Oeuvres complètes*, Cercle du Livre Précieux, Paris, 1967, pp. 38–40; available in English, trans. E. A. Vizetelly, Chatto & Windus, London, 1898 – HM.]

There is the rumble like "the distant jolting of carts," the Viorne covering the heavenly sounds "with her grumbling," the threatening *Marseillaise* – "the deafening explosion of the *Marseillaise* filled the sky as if blown by the mouths of giants playing on monstrous trumpets that hurled it, vibrating with the coldness of brass, to all ends of the valley. ...It resounded in its very bowels, repeating with its echoes the ardent notes of the national anthem..."

If in the *Bon Joyeux* the basic leitmotif was the increasing effusion of liquid and the material filling up of the atmosphere, then here the basic means of achieving frenzy is by filling the air with sounds from the environment, by a flow of sound going beyond the limits inscribed by the horizon.

But the horizon – is the limit.

And no one and nothing may be hurled beyond its contours.

But here Zola's splendid resourcefulness finds a brilliant way out.

Having struck the limits of the environment and incapable of penetrating it, the sound elements of Zola are not hurled through these limits, but are bounced back from them!

Zola introduces...an echo!

...The village...trembled like a drum beaten by drumsticks; it resounded in its very bowels, repeating with its echoes the ardent notes of the national anthem...from all parts of the horizon – from the distant hills, from strips of cultivated land, from meadows, from clusters of trees and the smallest bushes...The fields in the shaking air and ground screamed vengeance and freedom...

By its pressure the sound wishes to explode the horizon encapsulating it.

But it is not allowed to do this.

And its ecstatic pressure is hurled back by the hills and the wall of trees not *beyond* the limits of the horizon, but back – inside, in the form of an inhuman, that is, superhuman echo.

In the above passage, what is especially notable is the disproportion that occurs between the actual significance of the moving detachment (two to three thousand people subsequently ingloriously and senselessly perishing) and the "superhuman," almost cosmic significance Zola lends this fact through his emotionally heightened treatment of *pathos*.

And among these devices, the most important appears to be the small detachment of two to three thousand people that he transforms, through the element of sound, into a crowd of millions by numerous interweaving, colliding echoes striking against each other!

Thousands grow into millions.

And this reveals what is basic to Zola's conception. He presents this event, not on the scale of excitement proportional to the quantity of the actual number of participants, but in correspondence to the social significance he himself sees in this event, in the social conception of the action of the army (even though a small one) to which he wishes to submit his reader.

This reminds me of my own quarrel (also in the realm of sound and music) with the composers who selected the music for *The Old and the New*.

They would not agree to add music of the magnitude of *Die Gotterdammerung*[36] to an ecstatic religious procession.

"But this is only a village religious procession. Why such pretentions for its music?"

I required music that was not based on the number of chimes in the village bell tower or the actual number of singers, but based on the degree of religious frenzy of this group of people, however small, lost among the immeasurable fields that were languishing from the drought.

There is, of course, no end to the number of strange anecdotes on the theme of musical compilations during the silent film epoch.

I recall how the late L. Sabaneyev[37] shouted because of the music that had to be written for *Potemkin*:* "This is impossible! How can you write music to worms on a carcass of meat!"

He could not be convinced that the musical image here had to symbolize the tide of the growing indignation of the mass of sailors, boiling with the revolutionary rise of the whole nation's indignation at the heroic time of 1905.

There are also examples of the opposite extreme.

In the film *October* when, during the July days, the Palace Bridge was lifted to cut off the workers' districts from the center, on the order of Kerensky's Provisional Government, the corpse of a white horse harnessed to a cab was helplessly hanging from the bridge where it had been wounded.

The music was to be selected by Fayer.[38]

"A horse in the sky?...Ah! It's the 'Ride of the Valkyries'!..."

However, – back to Emile Zola.

The following example is from *The Rout*.

Here it is no longer a question of the beginning of an uprising of a small army accompanied by the sound of the *Marseillaise* marching to a battle with tyranny.

---

* How remarkable! Among my old papers from the period of the production of *Potemkin* I found a document, yellowed with age, from the Committee for the Commemoration of 1905 at the Central Institute of Culture, USSR (headed by M. I. Kalinin), where the decision was taken to commission S. S. Prokofiev to write the music for the anniversary film. Going abroad at that time, one of our comrades was asked to contact Prokofiev and invite him to join the project. Because of the extremely short notice, Sergey Sergeevich was not able to undertake this work. Nevertheless, in my mind I date the beginning of our collaboration from the memorable year 1925.

Here we can see the culminating moment of the battle of the people rising against their enslavers.

We see the unfurled canvas of the Apocalypse[39] of the destruction of the Second Empire, perishing symbolically like Sodom and Gomorrah[40] in tongues of flame devouring the Tuileries Palace.

And again on the "natural" level there are the twisted iron, the bursting fireplace, exploding barrels of powder.

And on this level the dance of flaming tongues is hurled into the metaphor of a fiery ball:

And once again a leap into the rank of imagery.

...On the left burned the Tuileries Palace. With the advent of night the Communards ignited the palace on both sides, by the pavilion of Flora and Marsan. The fire quickly reached the Pavilion of the clock toward the center of the palace where they had prepared a whole mine made of barrels of powder piled up in the Hall of the Marshals. At that moment out of the smashed windows of the intervening buildings burst puffs of reddish smoke, in which there sometimes appeared long blue streams of flames. The roofs began to burn from the fiery tongues and gaped, like volcanic earth, under the pressure of the inner conflagration.

But the Pavilion of Flore, which had ignited first, burned especially brightly: It burned with a terrible crackling from the lowest story to the vast garret. The kerosene that they poured on the parquet, the curtains, and the upholstery made the flame so strong that the iron railings of the balconies twisted, and the tall fireplaces burst, with their enormous stucco suns, now red hot.

...Maurice laughed madly in delirium.

A lovely holiday in the State Council and the Tuileries...the facade is illuminated, the chandeliers burning, the women dancing...Yes, dance in your smoking skirts, with your flaming chignons.

...Suddenly a horrible crackling was heard. The fire, coming in the Tuileries from both ends, reached the Hall of the Marshals. Barrels of powder were ignited: The Pavilion of the clocks flew into the air like a powder house. A huge sheaf rose, a plume, occupying the entire black sky, a burning bouquet of terrible fireworks.

Bravo!*

The limits of metaphor, image, and simile are broader. Retaining the characteristic feature of real objects going beyond themselves, they are at the same time not constrained by the conditions of the possibilities of everyday reality, notwithstanding their total nonverisimilitude to everyday reality.

The broad implications of the direction we are pursuing are achieved by Zola when the material at his disposal is totally free of the bonds of everyday verisimilitude.

---

* *The Rout*, part III [*La Debacle*, Garnier-Flammarion, Paris, 1892, pp. 524–6 – HM].

At this point the objects of the narration finally behave in a state of frenzy.

They finally go beyond themselves.

But under the conditions of the naturalistic limitations that the father of naturalism set for himself, this is of course possible where their nonverisimilitude is strictly motivated by everyday life.

Here, of course, it cannot be merely a question of just any real event, even if it be splashed by a cascade of frenzying metaphors.

Here only the realm of delirium and hallucination remains, similarly documented in a naturalistically figurative way and also created figuratively in strict correspondence with what these images may be and are.

An example is the shattering and voluptuous picture of Father Mouret's hallucinations, in which the conflict between the ascetic ecstasy of the young priest and the strong, sensual *pathos* of the call of the flesh breaking into his soul culminates in the grandiose collapse of the church, plunged into the dust under the unrestrained pressure of victorious nature:

. . . The priest was standing, beset by hallucinations. He believed that at this new blasphemy the church had collapsed. The ray of the sun, which inundated the high altar, slowly spread, illuminating the walls with its red fire. Red flames rose higher, licked the ceiling and were extinguished in the bloodred glow. The church suddenly became dark. It seemed as if the fire of the sunset burst through the roof, shattered the walls, opened gaping holes on all sides for the attack from outside. The dark skeleton of the church rocked, waiting for some terrible assault. Night quickly approached.

Then from far away the priest heard a murmer rising from the valley of Artaud. Earlier he had not understood the ardent language of this burning soil, where knotted grapevines twisted, stunted almond trees, old olive trees stretched their mutilated limbs. He passed amidst this passion with the serenity of his ignorance. But today, instructed in the flesh, he caught every breath of the leaves gasping under the sun.

And now at first on the distant horizon the hills, still warm from the setting sun, trembled with the deafening tramping of an army on the march. Then the scattered rocks, the stones of the road, all the pebbles of the valley also rose up, rolling, growling, as if some fateful force pushed them forward. Behind them the expanse of red earth, the rare fields conquered by blows of the spade, flowed and began to rage like escaping rivers carrying in their waves seeds, sprouts of roots, the copulations of plants. And soon everything began to stir: Grapevines crawled like huge insects: The sparse wheat, dry grass, lined up like batallions armed with tall lances: Trees began to run, straightening their limbs, like warriors preparing for combat: Falling leaves marched, the dust of the road marched. The hordes recruited new forces at every step, people in heat whose breathing was approaching like a tempest of life, with a fiery flame, carrying everything before it in the whirlwind of an enormous childbirth. Suddenly the attack occurred. At the edge of the horizon the countryside hurled itself onto the church, the hills, the stones, the earth, the trees. The church crashed at this first shock. The walls split, the tiles flew apart. But the grand Christ, swinging, did not fall.

There was a short respite. Outside voices arose more furious than before. Now the priest distinguished human voices. It was the village, Artaud, this handful of bastards, on a rock with the obstinacy of weeds, which send a wind swarming with living creatures.

Artaud fornicated with the earth, planted by degrees a forest of people whose trunks devoured every space around them. They came right up to the church, they burst through the door with one thrust, threatened to occupy the nave with the spreading branches of their race. Behind them in the thicket of bushes rushed animals, bulls trying to smash through the walls with their horns, a herd of donkeys, goats, sheep, beating down the church into ruins like living waves; clouds of woodlice and crickets attacked the foundations, gnawed them with their teeth like saws. And from the other side crowded Desirée's barnyard whose dung gave off suffocating fumes: The large rooster Alexander sounded the assault on his bugle, the chickens dug up stones with blows of their beaks, rabbits dug burrows right under the altars; a hog, having been fattened up to the point it could not move, snarled, waiting for the holy ornaments to turn to warm ashes so it could wallow in them. A terrible murmur approached, a second assault was made. The village, the animals, all this flood of life in an instant swallowed the church, under a fury of bodies, making the beams give way. The females in the scuffle released from their entrails a continuous childbirth of new fighters. This time a corner of the wall was brought down; the ceiling gave way, the window frames were smashed, the smoke of twilight, growing increasingly darker, entered through the gaps that yawned frighteningly. On the cross the great Christ barely held on by the nail of his left hand.

The collapsing wall was greeted with general rejoicing. But the church still remained firm in spite of its wounds. It stubbornly persisted, mute, somber, clinging to the smallest stones of its foundation. It appeared that this ruin in order to remain upright only needed the most slender pillar to hold up the smashed roof by a miracle of balance. Then Father Mouret saw that the coarse plants, which grew on the slopes, set to work, these terrible calloused plants in the dryness of the rocks, knotted like serpents of hard wood. Lichen the color of rust, resembling inflamed leprosy, first ate the lime. Then thyme forced its roots among the bricks like iron wedges. Lavender forced through their long hooked fingers under the masonry, and with an uninterrupted movement made it even looser. The juniper, rosemary, prickly holly all rose higher, thrusting invincibly. And the herbs themselves, these herbs whose dry blades passed under the portal, straightened up like steel pikes, burst through the portal, advanced along the nave where they raised the flagstones with their mighty pincers – This was a victorious riot, revolutionary nature built barricades with the toppled altars, demolished the church that for centuries had thrown too great a shadow...

Then suddenly it was over. The rowan, whose tall branches had already reached the vault, burst in through the broken glass with the flood of its formidable verdure. It placed itself in the middle of the nave. There it spread immeasurable; its trunk became colossal so that the church burst like a belt that was too tight. The branches spread to all sides with their enormous knots, each carried a piece of the wall, a fragment of the roof; and they continued to multiply...Now the giant tree touched the stars. Its forest of branches was a forest of human limbs, legs, arms, torsos, stomachs; hanging women's hair, men's heads burst the core with the laughter of new buds. High above pairs of lovers swooning at the edge of their nests filled the air with the music of their pleasure and the odor of their fecundity. A last burst of the hurricane, which had flown to the church, washed the pulpit, the confessional, which had scattered into powder...The tree of life burst through the sky. And it projected beyond the stars.

Father Mouret, like the damned, applauded furiously at this spectacle. The church was conquered. God no longer had a home. Now God would no longer bother him. He could rejoin Albine, for she had triumphed. And how he laughed at himself, he who only an hour ago confirmed that the church would devour the earth with its shadow!...*

It is interesting that in his fruitless search for expressions with which to characterize the creative figure of another master of *pathos*, Walt Whitman,[41] the English historian John Addington Symonds, unable to find adequate words, turns to the last possible device, to metaphor.

And among them he turns to the same tree *growing into the earth and the sky*:

...He is an immense tree, a kind of Yggdrasil,[42] stretching its roots deep down into the bowels of the world, and unfolding its magic boughs through all the space of the heavens...†

But this same image is probably also characteristic of the creative figure of Zola as well. And this is because, like his own unembraceable tree penetrating the "limits of the firmament" and "projecting beyond the stars," Zola is hurled in exactly the same way beyond the limits of his own method during the last stage of his literary activity.

This explosion into a new quality, into a new method, is exactly what Zola's work is like after the *Rougon-Macquart* cycle.

If within every novel from the *Rougon* cycle we discover at a certain moment a leap into ecstatic frenzy, then Zola's works following the *Rougons* show the same ecstatically frenzied leap in respect to the whole set of preceding novels, and this is equally true of the theme and material as well as of the style.

I have in mind two cycles: *Three Cities* (*Lourdes*, 1894; *Rome*, 1896; *Paris*, 1897) and *The Four Evangelists* (of which three were written: *Fruitfulness*, 1899; *Work*, 1900; and *Truth*, 1903; Zola died without having written the fourth novel – *Justice*).‡

---

* *The Sin of Father Mouret*, pt. III, chap. 9 [from the French, *La Faute De L'Abbé Mouret*, Cercle du Livre Précieux, Paris, 1966, pp. 238–41 – HM.].
† [John Addington Symonds, *Walt Whitman: A Study*, George Routledge & Sons, London, 1906, p. 156 – HM.]
‡ I do not feel at this point like evaluating the objective merit of these novels, which, both intellectually as well as artistically, cannot be compared in many ways with the *Rougon-*

At the same time the very nature of this new quality into which Zola's creative method is transported in these last novels seems to have exactly those same features that occurred in the novels of the preceding period, where objective naturalistic narration of events would suddenly leap into the style of an ecstatic hymn.

In this new series of novels the naturalistic objective story gives way to a generalized inspired prophecy, so that the last novel becomes transformed into a social-utopian hymn.

Extremely precise naturalistic pictures and images of the most recent *past* "history of a *single family* during the time of the Second Empire" become the imagined pictures of a utopian *future*, and at the same time, of *all of France.*

But it is not a question of *France* alone.

It is a question of *humanity* as a whole, for whom France must be only the prototype – the "messiah, atoner, savior."

It is interesting to note that for the realization of this great mission Zola thought France had to become truly democratic. And it seems that the spirit of prophecy of the "age of democracy" – Whitman – soars above Zola when he writes: "In order that France becomes the future, it is necessary that she now represent democracy, truth, justice against the old world of Catholicism and monarchy..."

In his notes to the unwritten *Fourth Evangelist – Justice –* Zola writes: ..."I will introduce *Humanity,* the nations being united, returning to one family; the question of race, having been studied and solved, a universal world at the end..."

It is sufficient to open any serious work on Zola's creation of this period to read that in this last phase of his work Zola decisively rejects his "original poetics of artistic objectivity."

The time had passed when Zola "demanded from the artist impartial, scientific-objective depiction of the contemporary period," toward which he had aimed in his own work of the earlier period.

And Zola now considers himself a prophet, a social reformer. After the positive "experimental-naturalistic" novel, the *Rougon-Macquarts,* Zola will write the antireligious novel *Three Cities* and the social-utopian novel *The Four Evangelists.*

And even both cycles of his last novels are connected by a "leap" not

---

Macquarts. I am now mainly interested in the peripeteia of the actual method of Zola, the novelist, the reason being that beginning with the classics of Marxism, enough has been written in great detail on questions of the social value, the significance and insignificance of his creative contribution to world literature.

In Zola's work I am most interested in the methodological precepts of separate parts of his work. And in a general evaluation of his work, this does not prevent my reader from agreeing with Henri Barbusse's other evaluation of Zola, to whom he devoted an entire book.[43]

But in Zola's work and technique I am particularly concerned with pursuing the affirmation of those principles of the style of *pathos* that were discussed above!

only with the *Rougon-Macquarts* but also with each other. *Three Cities* is a transitional stage from the "historical" to the "utopian" novel, and within each of these novels in turn that same leap inevitably occurs: ..."All these novels begin in the difficult and tormenting present period and arrive at bourgeois-utopian happiness..." that is, they are hurled from a situation in which the true horrors of reality exist into an imagined realm where they are overcome."*

All the internal features of Emile Zola's literary style also undergo a pronounced transformation.

The hidden solemnity of the rhythm of separate passages in Zola's earlier works (we noted above the page from *Germinal* which can easily be rearranged into the stanzas of a poem) here begins to envelop the novel as a whole and is overtly apparent.

The structure of *Fruitfulness* may serve as an example.

The theme of the novel is, in Zola's words, "Fruitfulness in the course of an entire century, the multiplication of a family around one man, a great oak..." The growth of the noted "tree of the Rougon-Macquarts" seems to have been compressed into one novel. The visible manifestation of the dynamic quality of this growth derived from this ("This extremely broadens my limits, provides movement, the intensive development of a family").

The cinematographer proceeds in the same manner, when through time-lapse photography he condenses into several seconds the process of the growth of plants that takes several days and – wonder of wonders! – as living movement and life before our eyes a rose blossoms, seeds sprout, young shoots actually stretch toward the sun and, like snakes, wind their roots in search of nourishing soil.

Thus on the pages of one novel Mathieu and Marianne "are fruitful and multiply" with such success that on the day of their diamond wedding anniversary, the seventieth year of their marriage, they are surrounded by 158 heads of children, grandchildren, and great-grand-children, and the family as a whole, counting the wives of children and grandchildren, compose a total of 300!

And reiterating this emergence out of each other of one generation from another that is constantly being repeated...

---

* This quotation is taken from the work of B. Reizov, "The Utopian Novels of Zola" (the Russian journal *Literaturnaya Ucheba* [*Literary Studies*], Moscow, 1934).

Wherever I can, I purposely cite passages from other studies that do not have any direct relation to our theme. And this is for the sake of objectivity, so that I might totally avoid not only deliberate but also subconsciously slanted "preferential treatment" of the analyzed material for the sake of those viewpoints with which I am concerned. The quotations, characteristics, and descriptions introduced below are taken from the same work of B. Reizov.

...periodically, like a refrain, through the entire novel several almost unchanging phrases are repeated, returning the reader to one fundamental idea, persistently driving the basic thesis of the novel into his head. These refrains follow each chapter, each scene of the novel. The main refrains are three – the first beginning with the words:

...During those four years at Chanteble the Froments had been ever founding, creating, increasing, and multiplying, again and again proving victorious in the eternal battle which life wages against death...* etc.;

the second refrain:

And 'twas ever the great work, the good work, the work of fruitfulness spreading...

and finally the third:

...Then two more years rolled on. And during those two years Mathieu and Marianne had yet another child..."

These refrains are repeated dozens of times, and sometimes come one after another in succession. But besides these basic refrains, separate images and similes, which also carry the author's basic idea through the book, are repeated constantly...

...Carried to their utmost limits in *Fruitfulness*, these repetitions produced a numbing, and sometimes simply comic impression. Probably as a result of this Zola significantly limited their application in the following novels..."[†]

But another interesting point is that in these last novels Zola carries the technique of producing effects beyond the boundaries of those limits noted above – "in essence" – through the selection of factual material presented in the state required by the author.

Zola also undergoes a "shift" in the devices described: He begins to more vehemently disturb the structure of the fabric of literary style.

The "timidity" of the initial attempts of such "musical-poetic" passages passes over here into "excess."

Zola himself writes about the "musicality" of this device and the leap from "timidity" to "excess" in his use of it:

...What you call repetitions is encountered in all of my books. This is really a literary device I first used timidly and I then perhaps developed excessively. I think this makes a work more solid, it lends it more unity. It is somewhat reminiscent of Wagner's leitmotif and, after asking for an explanation of its role from your musician friends, you will then be aware of it in my literary device as well... (Letter of 24 October 1894)

---

* [Emile Zola, *Fruitfulness*, trans., Ernest Vizetelly, Doubleday, Pate & Co., New York, 1900, p. 20 – HM.]
[†] [V. Reizov, op. cit. – HM.]

An allusion to the superheightened *pathos* of Wagner and to one of his most distinctive devices in his technique of ecstatic writing would be particularly relevant at this point.

It would probably be even more valid for Zola to refer to the Bach fugue. In any event, this brings us again directly to the problem of *pathos* in *Potemkin*.

As far as the problem of *pathos* is concerned, then Wagner, and even more so Bach, reveal to us another new aspect of the "formula of *pathos*" that also develops into a new quality, growing out of the first formula. Similarly the prototype corresponding to it, from features characterizing processes of the dialectic, is contained as a whole and grows out of the principle of the unity of opposites.

This principle of unity in variety – is that form of the embodiment of the principles of the dialectic on which the principle of the Bach fugue is basically constructed and, as we see below, the principle of so-called montage cinematography, which was above all the cinematography of *pathos*.

I will write later about the principle of the fugue in my own work, when I compare the structure of *Potemkin*, *Alexander Nevsky*, and the first part of *Ivan the Terrible*.

I will also discuss the "organic nature" of the form of the fugue.

At this point it is sufficient to mention that because of its similarity to the principle of unity in variety, this principle is especially close in its application to works of *pathos*.

Let us not digress from Zola, about whom we still have a few words to say. They refer to the nature of Zola's utopia, which, of course, suffers from the narrowmindedness of the inevitable fetters of petty bourgeois, albeit rebellious, images, which imposed the same imprint on the one-sidedness of what appeared to him as total "objectivity" in the composition of a picture of real life in his "naturalistic" description.

Nowhere in his work does Zola rise above Fourier's teachings, which were not perceived very profoundly, and for whom Zola's last novels could serve as very extensive illustrated commentary.

But we are interested here not so much in the actual elements of his preaching as in the picture of how the "narrator" is projected into the preacher.

Gogol accomplishes that same leap in tragic form.

Especially since we know from Zola's biography that in *The Dreyfus Trial* this "armchair" novelist accomplishes this same "jump" into the realm of public political battle, from "words" to immediate "activity," to intervention in life.

This same path of going beyond the limits of literary activity into the sphere of one's own biography was accomplished more profoundly and more significantly by our own Lev Tolstoy. In him also the third link (after the activity of the writer and the activity of the prophet, the next step is no longer a creative act but an active deed) is a *"departure"* that, having exploded his "teachings," necessarily resulted in projecting him into biographic activity.

However, let us not digress into new generalizations and new material, especially since we will have to concern ourselves later with a particular example of this phenomenon.

Let us limit ourselves only to the fact that, through detailed analysis, the well-constructed colonnade of Zola's ten pairs of novels became the solid support in film of a method also found in literature, albeit within the limits of one literary school.

Page after page it was justified in all the convolutions of the literary Himalayas of Zola.

Some day I will probably get everything in order and will publish a detailed analysis of Zola's novels from the point of view in which we are really interested. At this time it was important to me that, in my first inroad into how the various materials are constructed in the contiguous arts, I came across confirmation of the correctness of the *pathos* style principle found in the practice of independent creative work in film.

...We shall briefly focus on two literary examples from two authors deliberately practicing *pathos*. In one case the device is so apparent (as the passion of *pathos* is so apparent in Zola's utopian novels) that on the one hand it "numbs the mind" and on the other hand it sometimes arouses derision.

It concerns the American singer of the "the coming democracy" – Walt Whitman.

And especially his hymns of *pathos* that are so clearly and obviously constructed on a literal embodiment of the principle of unity in variety, for which the venomous Pitkin[44] included the author in his *A Short History of Human Stupidity*, and Lee Masters in his excellent book[45] on Whitman quite scornfully designates the compositional device of these poems as..."catalogs."

This device is important for us because it clearly demonstrates the principle in which we are interested. After this it will be much easier to observe it in those constructions where it is more deeply embedded in the very fabric of the works.

I am speaking here about the "Song of the Broad Axe."

The principle is applied here in an almost naively apparent manner.

And moreover, to me the sound of the work is shattering and stupefying.

This is a hymn to the American – to the pioneer, conveyed through a hymn to the tool basic to him – the axe, with which he subdued the continent of the New World in the name of culture.

And the principle of heightening the *pathos* effect of this primeval tool is unusually simple.

For page after page Whitman enumerates everything made and constructed by the axe.

The gallery of the vast ocean of the activity of man, the builder of life, passes before us.

And this variety fuses that basic tool with which everything is created into a grand image of unity...

the primitive axe of the pioneer – the broad axe.

This axe seems to have been smashed into a thousand fragments of the particular cases of its application.

And step by step the song itself composes it again into a new unity.

The static unity of the axe as an instrument, which has been smashed into myriads of fragments, is reassembled, but not into a dead instrument but into a living, dynamic image of human activity.*

The image of the axe developed into the image of the creating hand. The hand grew into the Man-Giant, the builder of the New World, the primogenitor of the new ideal of true democracy (as it appeared to Whitman).

Similarly in mythology the earthly Bacchus used to be torn apart so that the parts might be reunited into the divine Bacchus.[46]

Other mythological figures such as Osiris,[47] the Phoenix,[48] etc., etc., went through the same process of *pathos* intensification by a transition from one level to another, from one dimension to another.

At the beginning of this work we briefly noted that the ecstatic structure is like a copy of the behavior of someone seized by ecstasy.

This statement is much more concrete and precise than simply a "*façon de parler,*" than a "*bon mot*" or "turn of phrase."

Actually, the constructions of *pathos* similar to Whitman's "Song of the Broad Axe" reproduce one of the strongest phases of ecstatic experience in their structure.

This is the moment in which one experiences the feeling of unity in variety: the feeling of a single generalizing law that extends through all the variety of single (apparently) accidental phenomena of nature, of reality, of history, of science.

A work of *pathos* with an analogous structure tries in every way possible to recreate a similar "state of things"; [it] behaves as though it were a copy, and as in a piece of writing, for example, as the reader follows it he passes through the same stages of gradual accumulation of

---

* We should compare what we wrote above with the one large sail in *Potemkin* disintegrating into fragments of separate sails of separate skiffs, and again reassembling not into a sail, but into...the bright red flag over the battleship.

data, suddenly at a certain moment of narration he is inflamed with the feeling of its unity.

This is experienced as well by the scholar, who has come across a single law penetrating and seizing all the plenitude of individual and varied data of experience.

This is also felt by the artist, especially in those cases when not only his individual work suddenly arises out of all the parts that flowed together in it, uniting and sublimating these separate parts into an organically whole work of art, but even more so, in those cases when the creator (of very high caliber) experiences the whole of his opus as a great unity.

A similar moment is commonly known from Balzac's biography. It is the moment when the concept of *The Human Comedy* is suddenly born from the accumulation of plans already made for the future. This concept unifies them as a whole, and all the novels (written and conceived, realized or "planned") are composed into a single whole – into his "Madelaine," the figurative name he intentionally gave this unified whole after the largest cathedral in Paris.

Let us recall this moment, even if it be in the form of Emil Ludwig's description:*

...He was already well into his thirties and had just come to realize the full measure of his strength when, on looking back over a number of single, unrelated novels, he got the idea of bringing into one system all his past and future work, of writing the moral history of his period. Balzac fully realized the importance of this moment, wherein he ceased to be a writer of stories and became a writer of history. He immediately ran with this idea to his sister, swinging his Spanish cane, playing a drum-call, and crying: "I am breaking through all obstacles! Salute! I am now on the road to genius!"

In this way Balzac entered on the path of the creation of what turned out to be *The Thousand and One Nights of the West.*

And I must repeat that the mutual experience of this moment of the formation of unity in variety, through creating a work of art, is achieved by establishing an exact copy as the basis for it, an exact reflection of the structure of the process of "descending" to a man of "genius," the ability to see the law of unity in this chaos of chance, and to reveal and bring out by oneself this law of unity from all the variety of what is actually real and exists.

The most literal embodiment of this scheme is the construction we see in Whitman's "Hymns."

Another ecstatic uses this device, the author of the numerous pages of

---

* *Genius and Character*, Kenneth Burke, trans., [Harcourt, Brace & Co., New York 1927 – HM].

pathos in *Amos* and *Jeremiah*, less originally with less surprise, but moving in the same direction – Stefan Zweig.[49]

Here we will only allude to an example taken from his early works and that directly echoes the example from Whitman described above.

It has been taken at random from his "cycle of lyric statues" of 1913, which under the general title *Ruler of Life* (*Die Herren des Lebens*) combines eleven poetically outlined images.

Some of them are connected with the images of definite individuals: There is "The Sculptor" (related to Rodin), "The Martyr" (an image of Dostoyevsky, to whom Zweig frequently turned), "The Conductor" (in memory of Gustav Mahler[50] – "The Emperor" (Franz Josef I).[51]

One can only rarely guess the allusion in the others.

These are "The Singer," "The Pilot," "The Fakir," "The Confessor," "The Seducer," and "The Dreamer."

For Zweig this is a gallery of a single image seemingly shattered into fragments, the image of an active ruler who once more grows into a truly gigantic figure when separate "statues" are composed into a common whole!*

If the device unifying the entire cycle is of this type, then Zweig confines this device within the separate lyric poems out of which it is created.

For example, the image of his "Emperor," of a ruler of the fates of millions of lives and territories subject to him, is "raised" by Zweig out of an endless repetition of a flourish of the pen with which the aged Franz-Josef prescribed his will, signing his hand to the royal decree in the approaching hours of dawn in the castle of Schönbrun...

"And every flourish – creates destinies."

This one will become a Captain.

That one a Judge.

Another a count with a seven-pointed crown.

Out of the earth a cathedral will arise, and into it will rush streams of the devout.

The door of a prison opens, and into bits bursts the scaffold that had been prepared for executing those who had been pardoned.

War is declared. And like lightning the news is carried throughout the land. Rifles gleam. Cannons roar. Trains dash.

A new flourish – and the earth rearing up becomes calm.

---

* My task here does not include a critical evaluation of this synthetic image and its objective value. It is quite clear that it, as well as the individual images composing it, are certainly prewar images and concepts. And moreover, "prewar" relating World War I, which so profoundly transformed Zweig's Weltanschauung. I am limiting myself here to only an analysis of the devices and methods with which Zweig composed what he saw in the symbolic image of an earthly ruler under the conditions that existed in prewar Europe in exactly the same way Whitman saw the epoch of the Civil War in America.

Again the prosperity of the world. Etc., etc.

"The Seducer" is constructed in the same way (probably it is one of the first sketches for the future "Casanova").

Here through thousands of sacrifices he is constantly searching for the eyes of that first unique and inimitable woman whom he first loved.

For him the sky is now sown with stars, but the horizon is embraced by the luminaries of feminine images. And in one loving embrace he would like to smother the earth, fusing with it, etc.

The image of the inexorable rise of the pilot is constructed by the same technique. The pilot comes into contact with the bosom of the music of the spheres as newer and newer images of ascent and height accumulate in relation to his rise into the heavens.

It is interesting to note that this scheme was already the basis for the construction of an image of *pathos* in the eighteenth century by such a remarkable ecstatic as the Ukrainian philosopher Gregory Skovoroda:

Arise, if you will, on level ground and set up a hundred mirrors around you. At that moment you will perceive that your one corporeal form possesses hundreds of shapes, and as soon as you remove the mirrors, all copies are concealed. However, our corporeal form is also only the shadow of the true man. Like a monkey, through humanlike activity this creature images the corporeal activity of an unseen and eternal power and divinity of that man where all our forms are like mirrorlike shadows.

The archaic phraseology of this very exalted utterance adds, of course, to its inevitable comic flight. "Corporeal form" in the sense of a membrane, an "envelope," a "cover", in Skovoroda necessarily evokes associations connected with the word "bolvan"* from an entirely different semantic field – "fool," "ignoramus," "know-nothing," "stupid," etc.

The strong "ambiguity" of the feeling of this text arising from such an "unforeseen" course of associations could not escape the attention of that great lover of wit, our Leskov.[52]

We all know the given passage from Skovoroda not in its original, of course, but in the epigraph to *The Rabbit's Forfeit*, whose satirical essence is expressed magificently in the ambiguous sound this old quotation has for the contemporary ear.

In general the ironic reinterpretation of canonized forms of *pathos* is a device frequently found in Leskov.

In a similar way his amazing skill raises the naively trivial and the apparently anecdotal to levels of true *pathos*.

Both this as well as Leskov's other skill testifies to his very precise

---

* [*Bolvan* means "idol, graven image" in old Russian, but "fool" in contemporary Russian – HM.].

mastery of the method of *pathos*. He does not blindly submit to this method, but has it under very conscious control.

Thus on the one hand there is the *Sacred Tales* of Leskov and on the other – *The Sealed Angel*, saints' lives, legends, and fairy tales (for example, "Malan'ya – the Head of a Ram").

However, . . . we must discuss one more author.

When we read Zweig we automatically recall the author who sometimes wrote "in this manner," but somewhat earlier.

This is Pushkin.

And especially Pushkin of *The Covetous Knight*.

While reading about the emperor's "flourish of the pen" in Zweig, I recalled the sequence expounding the omnipotence of the owner of gold.

I have only to wish it – and a palace will arise . . .
I have only to whistle, and to me obediently, slavishly
Bloody villainy will crawl . . . *

In reading the "Song of the Broad Axe," you will recall how in Pushkin the pile of gold "accumulates" from numerous acts of numerous people, and

. . . of how many human cares
Deceptions, tears, prayers, and curses
It is the ponderous representative!

All the gold composing this mountain is a concrete fragment of the dramatic episode through which the riches and power of the greedy miser is constructed.

Here is an ancient doubloon . . . here it is. Just now
A widow gave it back to me; but first
With three children a halfday before my window
She stood on her knees, wailing.
It rained, and stopped, and rained again –
The hypocrite was not moved . . .

Or

And this one? This is the one Thibault brought to me –
Where did he get it, the idler, the rogue?
He stole it, of course, or, perhaps,
There, on the highway, at night, in a grove . . .
etc.

These separate images were retained in my memory since childhood. You reach out your hand for the little volume of Pushkin so you can copy out after him another stream of images in which the Pushkin "catalog" of enumerations dazzles in the tone of Whitman.

---

* [This and subsequent passages from Pushkin are my own translation – HM.]

And now you come up against an unexpected and curious phenomenon.

It turns out not to be "another stream" or "catalog of enumerations."

And after each pair of the above excerpts it is not applicable to put as
we have above..."etc."

There is no "etc." there at all.

And now we can discover the great mastery of Pushkin, who so
brilliantly was able to clothe a small fraction of an enumeration into an
extremely refined formal variety.

Whereas Whitman would have spent innumerable pages providing
countless "biographies" of the "widow" or "Thibault" type relating to the
source of each "gold piece," Pushkin proceeds in a different way.

He does not force the poem to be composed of separate sketches, in the
way a pile of gold is formed out of separate pieces of money or a
mountain is composed of separate handfuls of earth.

This process, which had been developed by Whitman within the
actual structure of the poem, is "tightened" in Pushkin into a poetic
image of the description of such a process, which he expresses as a
simile within the poem itself:

...I read somewhere,
That a tsar once ordered his warriors
To take handfuls of earth and throw them into a pile
And a proud hill arose – and the tsar
Was able to gaze with joy from the heights
At the valley covered with white tents
And at the sea where ships sped.
So I, bringing handful after handful
Of my habitual tribute here to the cellar,
I erected my hill,* and from its heights
I can gaze at everything that is subject to me.
And what is not subject to me?

After such an introduction, only two to three, more precisely – four
actual enumerations are sufficient, so that they may merge in the reader's
mind with the enormous quantity of handfuls of earth the warriors bring:
The fantasy of the reader will finish drawing for him everything that
Whitman would have "written out" in an analogous situation.

But Pushkin is capable of much more.

A uniform enumeration of even four episodes of exactly the same type
frightened him by their possible monotony.

---

* It is interesting that among the variety of the devices of *pathos* Pushkin uses the same
"unity of opposites" – the cellar and the hill – just as it is used in a tirade of *pathos* by
Derzhavin: "I am – a slave, I am – a king, I am – a worm, I am – a god" or by Tynyanov[53] in
The Waxen Personage where the *pathos* of the scene of the departing Peter reaches
"equalization" in the generalized unification of deeds mighty and deeds insignificant, as if
they were of equal and identical significance.

He makes the "allotment" of the enumeration according to two different "measurements," inextricably connected with each other.

Some episodes (more precisely, two) will compose the image of the bearer of power.

Others (two) compose the image of his pedestal – the gold mountain.

The bearer and the pedestal in a certain sense oppose each other, and at the same time are still identical. Both pairs of "episodes" are constructed inwardly according to this type of opposition. They belong in pairs to the contrasting parts of the image of the owner and his pedestal.

A festival of virtue and sleepless labor and
"bloody villainy."
The helplessness of the weak widow
and the criminal activity of the rogue Thibault.

At this point the "enumeration" stops. And once more, as in the beginning, it "is gathered" again into a simile where it is as if some gigantic whole is being described, forming out of minute, varied "partial" units:

. . . Yes! if all the blood, sweat, and tears
Poured out for everything kept here
Suddenly issued forth from the earth's bowels,
That would be the Flood once again – and I would drown In my faithful cellars.

In the repetition of the image of the whole forming out of the parts, Pushkin presents it in new material. And in material not only new but antithetical. The gathering "solidity" of the hill and the streams flowing together into one "deluge."

The movement within the action of the flood is similar: It rises out of the bowels (upward) and floods. . .the cellar.

And what is particularly interesting at this point is that Pushkin selects extreme opposites.

The "mountain" and "water" – this is a classical pair of contrasting opposites.

In Chinese painting, for example, the term "landscape" literally means "a picture of mountains and water."

Moreover, in the Chinese concept this rarely means the description of the most frequent landscape "subjects."

According to Chinese teaching, "water" and "mountain" express two constant opposing elements: the static unchanging and the eternally moving.

The mutual penetration of these contrasting "principles" create all aspects of phenomena and engender the process of their formation.

The interaction of different bearers of these principles in harmonious interaction also defines the basis of composition in the aesthetic of Chinese painting, and of landscape paintings in particular.

We discussed this question in great detail in another part of this work.

Now it is merely interesting to note how the principle of the unity of opposites has been resolved by Pushkin by separating them into the most strongly expressed extremes, approaching the concepts of "cosmic opposites" in the ancient teaching of China.

Their unity (as shown above) is achieved by the uniformity of the image in which first the formation of a hill from handfuls of earth is presented and the second time a flood arising out of the merging streams.

It is interesting that this principle of contrast has also been observed in the "behavior" of a flood.

A flood arises out of a movement opposite to what we usually associate with its representation: It is born not out of streams coming down from the sky, but it rises out of waters coming out of the "bowels of the earth"!

Images connected with concepts of movement, and among them – with the direction of movement, are very frequent in Pushkin and help considerably to further the dynamic feeling of his images, similes, and descriptions.

Pushkin's discretion in this question proves his great resourcefulness, if we compare the construction of the poems of our great poet with the style of the American Longfellow.[54]

The lack of diversity and variety in the poetic meter make his work almost unreadable today.

The monotony of the poetic composition of *Hiawatha* is almost hypnotizing.

Of course, one of the most recent publishers of his poetic legacy, Louis Untermeyer, correctly writes:

Longfellow is not for those who demand ecstasy; yet what he lacks in force is made up in finesse. The verse is delicate, at times even thin; but it has an unusually even tone, an extraordinarily fine-grained texture. Such poetry is not heaven-shaking; it rarely strives for passionate heights. Nor does it probe psychological depths. But it maintains itself on its own unperilous level; it persists quietly in the mind as well as in the heart. It expresses a kindliness which is spontaneous, and a homeliness which is winning because it is so straightforward. It retains its popularity because it is unaffectedly clear, unashamedly tender, and unshakably serene.*

[...]† There is good reason that in the general chorus of ecstasy, when the first collection of his poems were published (*Voices of the Night,*

---

* See "The Poems of Henry W. Longfellow," in *The American Poets*, L. Untermeyer, ed., Heritage Press, New York, 1943.
† [As per Russian original – HM.]

1839), one strongly negative exclamation was heard, and this exclamation belonged to the young and still unknown journalist by the name of – Edgar Allan Poe![55] This lack of passion, lack of poetic ecstasy in the themes and aims of the author make his application of an emphatic repetitious structure even more destined to failure for the contemporary (not to him, but to us) reader.

The repetition of accumulation through the diversity and variety of a single thesis, single image, single poetic meter – is an integral sign of the style of *pathos.*

But its application to [material] of a non*pathos* orientation, let alone having no diversity and variety, produces an extremely monotonous effect – an impression that is difficult to destroy when reading the cited *Song of Hiawatha* in our time.

What has been said here about Longfellow makes even more apparent what is unique about Pushkin's skill, which so clearly shows us how through the great variety of the ways in which it develops, the naked structure still retains its total original dynamic effect. Moreover, the structure also avoids monotony and is prevented from being totally obvious, which would give the possibility of "examining the device" and in this way would undermine its immediate effect.*

However... is this "all"?

And this doubt leads us to the observation for which we disturbed the covetous knight in his underground cellar.

If we compare all three examples – the baron's monologue, Zweig's "emperor," and "*Song of the Broad Axe,*" then in the end result they turn out to be completely different in their general structural basis.

On the one hand we see the most realistic classical proportions of the *pathos* style delineation of the baron in Pushkin;

On the other – the almost hysterically broken, convulsive ecstasy of Zweig.

And finally, third, we see the cosmic, all-embracing *pathos* of Whitman, who is not without a certain flight of "barbarity" in his primitive power.

It would not be complicated to briefly characterize the premises on which the very different forms are based.

In the first place there is Pushkin, who in true classical perfection

---

* The same thing was accomplished on the Odessa steps in relation to the soldiers' feet. By editing they cut through the masses being shot at, repeating this many times. This repetition provides the "rhythmic drum" necessary for the feeling of crushing movement that is always at the rhythmic basis of such scenes (for example, the gallop, jump, leap of the knight "snouts" in *Alexander Nevsky*) at the same time each of these pieces is distinguished from the other – by size, shooting angle, or shot – each time introducing a new feeling and new accent into the theme of the marching feet of the soldiers, and at the same time it thematically retains the unity of their merciless movement down the steps.

culminated a whole stage of Russian culture and revealed the paths for a new movement and for the rise of the next stage of literature.

Next is Zweig, who more or less repeated the feeling of sunset of the broken prewar culture of Western Europe on the very eve of the war, which brought with it the collapse of its system of governments and concepts.

And finally Walt Whitman – the representative of the young American nation just at the time of the Civil War between the North and the South, after it had finally got on its own feet, with an unrestrained appetite on the one hand, and with utopian democratic ideals on the other.

It is natural that every historical stage dictates to the master of its epoch a given treatment with a given norm.

The most elaborate variety of style in one.

The baring of the device as if hacked out by the pioneer's axe in the other.*

A convulsive, spasmatic construction in the third.

Each sings with the voice of his stage of cultural development.

But something else is more interesting for us at this point.

A different stage of development dictates a different voice.

A different voice here affects the different use of one and the same norm.

And this historically different treatment of it determines a different objective stage of the intensity of the effect.

The emotional "degree" of resonance of all three – is very different.

The lion in old age

Thus, the method we have analyzed in a contiguous area – in the area of literature – was entirely justified. But we must do more.

And we could not but set out into new explorations in new areas – all with the same aim of verifying and being convinced of the correctness of what we discovered.

What scope for "regaining the city,"[56] how tempting for the eye, ear, taste, smell, and touch that is too curious!

We were bold enough to suggest that the method we discovered was true everywhere.

So it follows – with qualitative corrections due to the peculiarities of one area or another, we shall discover it in all areas of art.

Let the area of the actor's performance be material for our next excursion.

---

* [The "baring of the device" is a concept from the Russian formalists of the 1920s where a work of art was not supposed to "substitute reality." Instead the perceiver was supposed to be consciously aware that what he was perceiving was a work of art, and one means of producing this effect was to expose the devices typical of a particular art form – HM.]

I intentionally do not want to linger on examples of tragedy and drama.

Here the field is too broad and clear.

It is confirmed by the fragments of Claudius's speech given above,[57] the last utterance of Caesar, who, in the paroxysm of his last moments, switches from English to Latin: "Et tu, Brute!"; by scenes from *King Lear* (where, one should note, Gloucester "recovers his sight" only after he goes blind, as Hegel has already pointed out)*; by prose transported in moments of *pathos* into poetic meter – and not only in Shakespeare; by the official "you" transported within same monologue into the inflamed "thou," in the pathetic tirades of Victorien Sardou[59] in *The Count de Rizor*, and, finally, in Shakespeare himself by the wonderful leap at the climax of *Macbeth*, when the concrete course of the exposition of the tragic events are transported onto the unexpected level of metaphor: "till Birnam forest come to Dunsinane" or into the trick of a biological interpretation of another "sign" – "not of woman born," because of the fact that Macduff came into God's world by means of a Caesarean operation.

The excerpt from Claudius's speech was particularly striking because of its extreme pomposity.

And how well this speech can be compared here with lines "descending" from king to worm, repeated later by Ambrose Bierce[60] in *The Devil's Dictionary*, in the idle fashion of aimless "nihilism in general," and therefore doomed, only chasing its own tail, locked unavoidably into a terminal circle – so much so that on the path around its circumference it should not be swallowed bit by bit, in the form of a "reverse" formula, according to which progressive links of a single chain of development hurled out of each other:

> . . . EDIBLE, *adj*, Good to eat, and wholesome to digest, as a worm to a toad, a toad to a snake, a snake to a pig, a pig to a man, and a man to a worm.†

For the sake of clarity let us look into the area of the actor's performance for an example of a somewhat "elevated" manner, not yet poisoned

---

* Oedipus acts just the opposite – having gained insight into the truth, he blinds himself.

The heroine of one of the most unrestrained melodramas of David Belasco[58] acts in quite a different way – the blind Andrea. In the course of the action she gains sight. But this apparently occurs only so that in the pathetic finale (when she gives away the royal crown to the son of her beloved Caezo, whom she punished with her own hand) in a burst of despair she returns to the sun the light given to her as a gift. In this finale she again blinds herself. And she does this by looking at the flaming solar disk with eyes wide open. (*Andrea* – a Romantic tragedy set in the fifth century A. D. – written by David Belasco and John Luther Long and first produced in New York on January 11, 1905.)

† [*The Collected Works of Ambrose Bierce*, Vol. VII, *The Devil's Dictionary*, Neale, New York, 1909–12, 12 volumes. N.Y. and Washington, 1911, p. 79 – HM.]

by the poison of "simplicity," so characteristic of the stage technique of our century.

Where would we look for such example?

Of course, in the romantic theater!

And among the leading figures of this theater, of course, in the grandest figure of this theater – the great Frédérick, who, like kings, was called by his first name in the enthusiastic reviews of his contemporaries – Frédérick Lemaître.

What could be more magnificent for its time than the *pathos* of this king of melodrama, this flamboyant lion and total master of the Parisian stage, whose lavalike temperament at its crest bore the romantic madness of the violent plays of Victor Hugo, Alexandre Dumas,[61] Félix Pyat,[62] and Guilbert de Pixerécourt?[63]

Kean, Don Caesar de Bazan, Father Jean, Buridan, Toussaint-L'Ouverture, Robert Macaire[64] – what a gallery, what triumphs!

The period of blossoming of his fame was so amazing, so thrilling, so blinding, that neither Theophiles Gautier[65] nor Jules Janin[66] in the roar of their own applause, took on, for posterity, the task of analyzing with a cold scalpel the mysteries and secrets of the totally shattering effect of the mastery of this "Roscius of the Boulevards,"[67] as the great Frédérick was called, or should have been called, by the great Balzac.

Therefore it is not in the period of his glory, but it is in the declining years of his career, not in the blinding reflection of the stage, but in the domestic salon, not in the dithyrambs of an enthusiastic critic, but in the descriptions of the timid first encounter of a novice with a titan of the past – that it is better to seek significant signs of the actor's technique of this master of stage *pathos*.

There is a little book of memoirs of the actor and very productive dramatist Pierre Berton,* whose name is much less popular than the names of his plays – especially of one.

Berton (as well as Charles Simon) is the author of the very touching *Zaza*[68] (1898), so charmingly played quite recently in the movies by Claudette Colbert and Herbert Marshall.

Forty years before the writing of this play, in 1858, Pierre Berton – a sixteen-year-old youth who had just begun to dream about a theatrical career, the grandson of the famous actor and teacher of generations of actors – Samson,[69] the godson of the disciple of his grandfather – Rachel,[70] and subsequently a friend of Sardou, Dumas-fils,[71] and Bizet – met the great Frédérick for the first time in his life.

The great "lion" of the stage was already in his declining years.

And here are the cursory notes of the young novice Berton on the aging Lamaître and on several features of his stage manner, so unexpectedly

---

* *Souvenirs de la vie de Théatre*, Paris, Lafitte et Cie.

revealed before him in the setting of the "terrible" bourgeois salon, glittering with the cheap luxury of the gold and purple upholstery, where the great "comédien" received him in a regal crimson and gold dressing gown:*

This parlor, grotesquely bourgeois and flashy, was all in red and gold.

The gilt of the furniture, which was a repulsive style from a repulsive epoch, framed the crimson upholstery trimmed with yellow fringe; the doors were hung with the same type of portieres. In all its aspects this was the typical mise-en-scène of the fourth act of a melodrama, when this fourth act takes place at a banker's – the parlor of Robert Macaire in the period of his brilliance and glory. I waited for ten minutes, vainly trying to find on the walls, on the tables, on the fireplace the smallest sign of any kind of work of art, when suddenly, having turned around at the sound of opening doors, I saw the great artist in person coming forward to greet me. A remarkable phenomenon, unforgettable and typical, which even now, half a century later, stands before me idelibly in all its minutest details...

Frédérick was quite tall, well-built, with hair freely flowing on his wide shoulders, with small hands and feet. The elegance and confidence of gait spoke of the harmonious development of this man. He was dressed in a silk dressing-gown of such a bright scarlet color for a moment all the crimson upholstery of the salon faded...

...He moved toward me with a noble and measured gait and alone seemed like a whole cortege, lacking only its solemn music. His feet moved into first position, toes to the side, hiding the refinement of his feet in luxurious, gold-embroidered slippers...

...The dressing gown, streaming in its splendor from his shoulders, trailed after him like the train of a courtly cape, and the bottom of the figure was confined by a thick plaited belt, which could have so nicely enveloped the whole, but, instead, hung on one end and, winding like a snake, trailed along the carpet like the tail end of a procession, still lost in the other room at the moment when the artist was already standing in the center of the parlor.

The great Frédérick came up to me with that same gait with which Don Sallust in *Ruy Blas*[72] approached the Spanish queen in order to touch her regal hand with his lips...

...His hand, plastic and elegant, played not with a dagger, but only with my grandfather's letter. We exchanged only a few insignificant words. His speech addressed to me was very simple. Having spoken to me of how greatly he was flattered by the epistle of his old friend, he offered me two tickets for the next performance, which I accepted with delight.

But these few words on his lips took on a most unusual significance, totally incommeasurable with the subject they were touching. It seemed as if he commanded not just two balconies, but the fate of the entire empire.

---

* This weakness for gilt and crimson as well as Oriental luxury and "Damask silk" was also shared by another "lion" Balzac, who his whole life tried to furnish his changing "abodes" with a similar luxury.

Every syllable bursting from his lips spread into the richness of the whole independent word; intervals, filled by mysterious profundity, separated words from each other and gave them such significance that they began to appear to be whole phrases, and the simplest phrases – long monologues. This strange manner of pronouncing words appeared in the realm of declamation to be like the optical phenomenon of a lens through which a tiny insect seems to us to be the size of an elephant. Just as form generally attracts content to itself, so here the richness of the pronunciation of the words elevated the thoughts. A simple "Good day, sir," seemed to contain a whole world within it, and banal phrases which I had listened to with confusion took on the rich value and sonority of the verses of Victor Hugo. I left him bewitched and full of thankfulness for having, already in my first impression, learned a great deal about the temperament, nature and manner of the great actor's performance. (pp. 47–58)

Commentary is really not necessary at this point.
It could not be said better:
a syllable grows into a word,
a word – into a phrase,
a phrase – into a monologue.

The aging Frédérick here, in the setting of the dimming luxury of the crimson salon, gives to the young proselyte one of the secrets of the great tradition of *pathos* in performance by actors of the romantic school.

In another place in his little book, Berton tries to establish the reasons for which this unusual manner of declamation arose in Lamaître. He attributes it to a totally unexpected phenomenon within the exceptional artistic talent of the great actor.

Nature had given him everything and had left out only one thing. As it turns out, Frédérick had a weak voice and had extreme difficulty in pronouncing words.

"...This organic shortcoming" writes Berton, "this defect of vocal apparatus, forcing him to a slow and emphasized pronunciation of the text, to the exaggeration of gesture and glance, made of him that ideal performer of the great works of romantic theater that authors could only dream about..."

These observations do not essentially change anything.

And the physical defect, which partially determined the manner of Lemaître's declamation, according to the testimony of Berton himself, made him the most ideal instrument for pronouncing tirades of *pathos* by Hugo and others.

Similarly both of Mayakovsky's dentures (a secret once jealously guarded by us in the bowels of *LEF*, but now after a quarter of a century, hardly necessary to hide any longer), of course, did not in any way determine either the basic rhythmic (even more so...thematic) aspirations of our greatest poet, but also this situation couldn't help but leave its imprint on his basic declamatory manner, which in turn to a certain extent could not but affect "in reverse" a modification of the rhythmic treatment of this verse.

This situation undoubtedly intensified even more the placard garishness and lapidary-pounding quality of the stamp of his verse style, consciously chosen by the poet for other motives.

Likewise the individual acting defects and difficulties of Stanislavsky-the-actor – in the process of his overcoming them – produced many valuable things in the development of the "system" of Stanislavsky-the-teacher.

It is sufficient to compare his classic work on the actor's technique with the memoir data from his book *My Life in Art* to become convinced that whole sections of "the system" developed, formed, and achieved a theoretical basis for their necessity as a result of similar particular individual features of its creator. In those cases when these difficulties coincided with those of "acting in general," the methodological "solutions" found in them were brilliant. In those cases when they seem to be narrowly individual, they engender within the "system" paragraphs that are not very convincing, but because of reverence for the whole work, the "systems" are just as diligently taught by popularizers in spite of their very relative need for those in whom the specific natural deficiencies of Constantine Sergeyevich are lacking.

In this little book from which we took the scene just described – several pages later – that same Pierre Berton introduces a well-known anecdote about Lamaître.

At a certain point Frédérick became too inclined to the use of strong drink. It happened quite frequently that he performed in an unsober condition. Usually the great actor, whom the adoring public invariably saw as their idol, got away with this.

But sometimes the idol went too far, and then he was attacked by the uncontrollable anger – not common in our generally restrained viewers – of the effusive French theater auditorium.

So it was on that evening.

...The public demanded an apology from him. Frédérick refused. The storm of dissatisfaction grows. The director, under the threat of having to return money to the public, rushes to the stage from where he unsuccessfully tries to calm down his spectators and then behind the wings, from where Frédérick, shaking with rage, hurls his curses at the auditorium. The case was serious. The artist dared to hurl to his viewers' faces the extremely frank exclamation: "A herd of fools!" Obviously this was too much. And this obvious situation finally convinces the guilty person himself.

"Alright, o.k. – I'll apologize to them! You'll see!"

The director runs onto the stage and proclaims that the great actor admits his guilt and apologizes the auditorium.

The door at the back of the stage opens wide, and Frédérick Lemaître, always grand even in an unsober state, moves to the footlights.

Having seen him, the whole hall lets out a general "Ah!" of satisfied self-esteem and calms down into complete silence.

First of all, with his usual grace, Frédérick does the traditional bow to all three sides. Then he utters the following meek phrases: "Gentlemen, I have just told you that you are all – idiots; this is true. I bring you my sincere apologies; I – am not right!" And the thunder of the applause covers his words...

But it is not for the fine use of words that I have brought in this anecdote here, this magnificent model of the composition of ironic *double entendre*, where the true sense of the words is directly opposite to the external sense, which the phrase apparently seems to have.

I bring in this example here because, on the plane of irony, that very same method by which the great actor secretly and effectively formed not only his stage behavior but also the actual concept of the dynamics of the characters and images of his heroes, is connected to this example mechanically and nakedly (and therefore also ironically).*

And this method – even in this area, is that same unity of mutually exclusive opposites that we constantly note in *pure form* as the basis of the marks and principles of a composition of *pathos*.

The testimony I set forth is not secondhand and is not from other descriptions.

It has pleased fate to give me into my own hands a small quarter of a sheet of paper dotted with the original tiny pearls of the handwriting of Félix Pyat – the original letter sent to the actor by the dramatist after apparently quite stormy and heated squabbling and wrangling on the eve (as is apparent from the text)...

This letter, which I came across at the sale of the library of the late Jamais,[74] dated February 10, 1842 – three months before the premiére of *The Parisian Ragpicker* – is also charming because the atmosphere is still trembling with the recent, apparently heated, quarrel between the dramatist and the actor.

In the course of the letter, Félix Pyat is restrained, respectful, and even flattering, and only in the signature "amitiés quand même" (my best feelings, in spite of everything) does not feel that Frédérick flatly has his own way, and Félix Pyat must submit to his will.

What was it Frédérick insisted on?

This is emphasized by a nervous line in Félix Pyat's letter, who usually signs his other letters with the words: "my best feelings" (amitiés), "a thousand and one expressions of my best feelings" (mille et une amitiés – a letter of 1849), or "heartfelt embraces" (je vous embrasse cordiale-ment).

---

* We only briefly noted the connection between pathetic and ironic composition here. Perhaps we should also touch on the similar proximity later on, below. But the conflict of the secret of this outer "similarity" and also basic "antithesis" of both – we will save for another time, when the task of comic construction enters into the problem of our compositional analysis.[73]

But here is the actual text of the letter:

Dear Friend,

Here finally is the text of *Father Jean* you have been waiting for. I have felt so bad recently that I was in no condition to send it to you any sooner. Please be kind enough to confirm its receipt and read it when you have time.

If, as you said to me several times after lunch, you want to put into this role *energy and sensitivity* (énergie et sensibilité), *cunning and good nature* (causticité et bonhomie) – all the treasures of your great talent – I will not doubt for a moment in my personal success and will be completely indebted to you for it.

My best feelings, in spite of everything (amitiés quand même). Félix Pyat... *

In the underlined words we can clearly see the theme of the argument.

And by reading it attentively, we will immediately catch the basic mainspring by which Frédérick revealed "the treasures of his great talent."

We have before us three antitheses.

And the fusion of similar antitheses opposing each other into an organic whole, through the ardor of his actor's gift, also apparently lies at the basis of the effect of *pathos* with which the great Frédérick's performance sparkles.

The instantaneous transition of contrasting features of character into each other and the merging of these opposites into the organic unity of the role is probably the basic thing the great actor was able to achieve inimitably, and why the disclosure of similar elements within a role was also apparently at the basis of what attracted him to certain roles and that he so persistently demanded from his playwrights.

The merging of opposites into a unity, and the transition of them into each other, as one of the main signs of the *pathos* method is also one of the essential features of creating *pathos* in general, as we have followed it step by step.

...And one must only emphasize that it is a question here not of the effect of contrasts, as might appear at first glance, but about the dynamic unity of mutually exclusive antithetical principles within a character, forcing him as well to burn and be consumed by great *pathos*.

And didn't one of the greatest masters of *pathos* in the field of poetry, Walt Whitman, speak of this magnificence when he wrote:

Perhaps I am contradicting myself?
Well – I am so great that I can contain contradictions within myself.

Let these strokes as well as the mountains and mountains of what Whitman has written besides them enter the circle of "testimonial

---

* The letter, as far as I know, has apparently been published here for the first time.

evidence," to be used as a justification of the basic norms of the creative forms of *pathos* examined by us.

It is interesting how much this conception has in common with the activity of the other masters of *pathos* – the Greeks.

Thus, according to Pliny's testimony,[75] the gigantic wall fresco of Zeuxis[76] was created on the basis of this principle. He had come from Heraclea to Athens in 424 and depicted the Athenian nation in all its "ruthlessness as well as its mercy, its haughtiness as well as – its humility, its aggressiveness and shyness, its pettiness and magnanimity," and through this he revealed for the first time to the Athenians the complexity and contradictory nature of their own character.

But, recalling the giants of Greek tragedy, who embodied this contradictory nature of the Greek national character, it is impossible not to recall another gallery of superhuman passions that surpasses them in scope, "tearing them apart," the internally contradictory images and characters of world literature of the pre-October epoch.*

Such are the tragic images of Dostoyevsky.

Beginning with Raskolnikov, going from the greatest ruin and grief down to the crudest dirty work,

through his haughty women with their bustles and parasols with frills, these Petersburg kindred sisters to the ancient Medea,[77] Phaedra,[78] or the mother of the Horatii,[79] able at a single moment to inhumanly humiliate the strongest of this world of – "millionaires," and in another to grovel in the dust of self-humiliation at the feet of a nonentity, who is not worthy of their spittle,

through the ascetic and saint who is capable of "stinking,"[80]

to Ivan Karamazov, whose "second" nature is so intense, that is materializes before his very eyes and enters with him into the most clever casuistry of metaphysical discussion...and to the hero, bearing the stigmata of the duality of the radiant knight's martial invincibility, with the gentle meekness of the idiot doomed to impotence – in the conflict between his own last name Myshkin (little mouse) with his first name...Lev (lion), which Dostoyevsky gives his hero.

Not only thanks to the scope of passion, not only in the vigor of a certain theatricality of these characters of Dostoyevsky, elevated on buskins,† as if illuminated by the unnatural light of electricity (as Maikov[81] said of them), the ancient theater reminds one of Dostoyevsky, and Dostoyevsky – of the ancient theater.

In one as well as the other, one is often struck, not only by the duality

---

* [That is, before 1917 Russian Revolution. – HM.]
† [High, thick-soled, laced boots worn by actors in ancient Greek and Roman tragedy, also known as cothurni – HM.]

but especially by the – at times – unmotivated collapse of a character into another extreme, incompatible and unreconcilable with it, into another antithesis.

Among the Greeks this is sudden, lapidary,

the first wooden step from the initial dramaturgical taboo, as if it were being dictated to the persona – the actor – by the unchanging constraint of the form of the persona-mask in which, without changing form and character, he originally performed the tragedy from beginning to end...

Then arose the possibility of change. They surmised that it was possible to change the mask. But the jolt from this change of mask to mask remained as a rigid jump that, without nuance, without transition, was forced to create a character that was suddenly transformed into another antithetical depiction of his passions.

Through Seneca[82] the imprint of this "handicap"* was transformed into pre-Shakespearean Elizabethan drama, where the lack of flexibility and multifacetedness of transition within a character was no longer determined by the persona-mask disappearing from the stage but continued the tradition inside the dramatic texture itself, which was doomed to "blanc et noir" [black and white] characters, lacking nuances, as vestiges of the limitations of the stage technique of the Greek theater's two-mask characters.

And only by the arrival of Shakespeare in the sixteenth century and, even more, of Dostoyevsky – in the nineteenth – was tragedy able to be raised from the stage of opposite halves to complete unity in the antitheses composing the natures of their characters, by which the unsurpassed dynamics of their inner tension is achieved, and the psychological outbursts of transport from adoration to denigration of the adored, from hate to love, from meekness to beastliness and that "divine frenzy" in which all the depths of their *pathos* is revealed.

One could multiply page after page on this theme.

But what is more important, perhaps, is to note its invariable, inherent attractiveness.

The combination of a similar duality in the unity of one and the same nature of an extraordinary person fascinated me personally. This was in the character of the man I chose after my first experience making a mass film without hero or plot, when for the first time I tried to make a film about a man I imagined to be superhuman.

I have in mind the image of Tsar Ivan the Terrible, contact with whom brought me so much joy and so much sorrow, as if the work on him was fated to carry the imprint of his unique disposition.

I was fascinated by the image in which Belinsky so "furiously"

---

* [As per Russian original ("handicap'a") – HM.]

sketched him in his critical response to the third part of Nicholas Polevoy's *Russian History for First Reading*:*

...Several different opinions of Ivan the Terrible reign among us: Karamzin represents him as a type of double, in one half of which we see a certain angel, holy and without sin, and in the other – a monster, vomited by nature at a moment of discord with itself for the ruin and torment of poor humanity, and these two halves are sewn in him, as they say, with white thread. The Terrible was a riddle for Karamzin; others present him not only as evil, but also as a limited man; several see a genius in him. Polevoy can be found somewhere in the middle: In him Ivan is not a genius, but simply a remarkable man. We cannot agree with him at all...We understand this madness, this bestial bloodthirstiness, these unheard-of crimes, this pride, and along with all this, these scalding tears, this tormenting despair, and this humiliation in which all of Ivan's life manifested itself; we also understand that only angels can turn from spirits of light into the spirit of darkness...Ivan is didactic in his madness; this was a fallen angel who, in his falling, reveals...the strength of an iron character, and the strength of a high mind...

Belinsky here correctly stands up against the adopted tradition of the division of Ivan into two: into the "blessed" Ivan of the period preceding the creation of the *oprichnina* (in 1564) and Ivan "the tyrant" after this event – both sewn "with white thread."

Belinsky sees an organic unity in the transition of the image from the "meek" to the "terrible," although he also interprets this transition too subjectively and does not emphasize the inevitability of this transition aimed at realizing a single, unchanging, persistant historical task facing Ivan – the unification of Russia – whose unity the self-interested feudal nobility so violently resisted [...]

Probably the very attractiveness of the dynamics that such a character reading furnishes the figure of Ivan, not only attracted me, but to a certain extent, because of the magnificence of the inner conflicts, prevented an adequate exposition in my film of those objective political results in which was expressed the overcoming of these inner contradictions within Ivan himself.

In the actual modeling of this "character," new to my experience, was expressed my sympathy not so much for Shakespeare as for Elizabethans of a more archaic type: Marlowe,[83] Ben Jonson,[84] and especially Webster[85][...]

Not only a certain graphic dual color of a basic nature "single into two," but equally the nature of Ivan's environment is really contained more in the "canon" of Ben Jonson's teaching about humors,[86] which, on the other hand, is also characteristic for the construction of *pathos*

* Moscow, 1835.

effects by the direct charging of elements ecstatically exploding into each other with constantly increasing intensity [. . .]

However, leaving Greek and Elizabethan materials, let us return again to the Russian, and let us do so in relation to a very important point, which is touched on here very appropriately, in connection with the construction of a character of *pathos* the type of Pyat – Lemaître, as a unity-in-contradiction image.

. . .Somewhere above, in the preceding chapter, we showed briefly that the form of *pathos* is essentially no more than a stage in the state of expressive means in relation to the degree of the author's perception of his theme's *pathos*, the stage in which this form, of course, acquires marks of a new quality, but at the same time, clearly retains features of continuity from the previous (lower) stages of intensity, which can be felt and revealed through the features of this new quality.

In the example just analyzed of Félix Pyat's letter, this is easy to reveal, if the antithesis synthesized in it is compared with the too-well-known formula, "seek in the villain where he is good," so inseparably linked to the teachings of another great master of theater – C. S. Stanislavsky.

The theater of Stanislavsky, the theater of semitones, of Chekhovian nuances and lace patterns of refined emotion – of course is in no way the theater of great naked passions, which was the French theater of the nineteenth century.

Moreover, it was conceived and was essentially an active protest against that very theatrical style in which glittered Frédérick Lemaître and the leading pleiade of romantic actors of the French theater.

And I think that here, in the fusion of Stanislavsky's realistic theater and Pyat–Lemaître's theatre of *pathos*, one senses with utmost precision the progression of their methods, dividing them by the degree of intensity with which the principle of the inner contradictoriness of images occurs in them.

At one extreme here the character is cut into opposites, in a flight of *pathos* uniting its opposites in the unity of an ardent, vivid image.

At the other extreme – a no less vivid, and perhaps even more real and undoubtedly more common, image that sets off the leading [sign] of the permeating feature – by division into "good" or "evil" – by dabs of complementary tones from opposite palettes, and thereby it attains the living reality of the results.

The multifaceted play of vivid colors here, and the merging of all contrasts of the palette into a single golden-white ray of the inspired image of *pathos*, is united in its opposites.

At this point I must recall as an analogy the mystery of the unique effect of the ancient stained-glass windows of Chartres Cathedral. There was that very same picture.

The first time I visited Chartres was on a gloomy day, and I did not understand anything.

I only perceived that part of the stained-glass windows of the cathedral related to the thirteenth century, and the other part − to the sixteenth century.

And besides that, in the system of the small, multicolored pieces of glass, out of which the first are composed, it is very difficult to make out the connected depiction; whereas the larger surfaces and much less intense color of the glass pieces composing the second, form, without any difficulty, into images of well-known characters in traditional scenes.

I could not calm down after I discovered this.

In pursuit of the solution to the mystery of the supernatural effect of the Chartres windows, which I had heard so much about, I set out for Chartres once again − and this time on a sunny day.

And what happened?

Almost the same thing, except the characters and the scenes on the stained-glass windows of the sixteenth century shone somewhat brighter.

But in regard to the legacy of the thirteenth − truly a miracle occurred.

And now I understood that what had seemed to be the technical weakness of the thirteenth-century masters, still unable to produce large colored-glass surfaces and to achieve refined nuances of coloration − was not weakness at all, but the wisdom of strikingly profound calculation.

The windows of the sixteenth century − are nothing more than a transparent picture, letting in sunlight, whereas the sheaf of sun rays passing through the field of colored pieces of glass, for which the subject and scene serve only as an external reason for existing together, suddenly undergoes the process of optical blending of separate rays cleverly arranged, suddenly merging into the unity of a single "immaterial" de-corated gold column sparkling with gold and white.

Probably the column of sun in the ecstatic vision of Katerina in *The Storm* was like this, a column along which a host of cherubim and seraphim descended and flew up again to heaven.[87]

And such, undoubtedly, is the ecstatic call of this miracle of flowing gold, which pours in, through the mysterious stained-glass windows, into the dark bowels of the ancient cathedral trembling with chorals, as the image of divine thanksgiving pouring out above the heads of the depressed sinners.

This dynamic optical fusion of rays − adorned in all separate nuances of the spectrum into one single gold-white, super-colored ray − is at the same time an image of a unity of opposites, and each nuance of the spectrum has its opposite antagonist ("complementary color"), which seems to be growing into an image of unity in variety as elevated as possible, into whose grandeur all the unities of opposites and contradictions merge.

Above, while touching on Whitman's method, I also introduced several examples of this type of *pathos* construction, taking for its basis this prototype, which apparently represents the next elevated stage within the method in relation to those cases we have analyzed.

Thus the multicolored spectrum of stained-glass windows merges in a gold unity.

But there is more.

The spectrum of the stained-glass windows in turn appears to be a synthesis of the whole colored diversity of what surrounds a Gothic cathedral,

the whole colored diversity of colored richness of eternally changing nature surrounding it, added to the group of pure, glittering tones.

And in the miracle of the sun's rays, not only the colors of the rainbow of stained glass merge into a whole but through them also the whole colored variety of all France [...]

Many centuries later these mines of precious colored riches surrounding France reveal to the world another generation of artists – the impressionists – and again force the walls of exhibit halls to blaze for a time (let us recall Claude Monet or van Gogh!) similarly to the stained-glass windows of medieval churches.

These same churches, catching up in turn the tendency of "flaming" ("the flamboyant") of late Gothic, with tongues of flame of the lancet arcs soaring up together with screens of stained-glass windows, flaming with color, are transported into the art of painting like real fire – let us recall the art of painting in fire by decorative fireworks displays, so strongly developed in the era of its particularly rich heyday.

Thus, even more persistently the element of active dynamics bursts into the realm of color.

At one end of it stands the slow, progressive overflow of the colored symphony through the body of the cathedral, to the extent that the sunlight penetrating around the church forces window after window to blaze in succession.

Here at sunrise the apse begins to burn.

Here in the middle of the day streams the colored light of the window of the nave.

Here at the end of the day blindingly burns the fiery wheel of the central round window over the main portal.

Light alternates with shadow.

The colored radiation – with artfully rhythmic and musically calculated interruption of darkness and with a melodic calculation of the change of one tonality for another, as the rays pass the artfully composed shift of these transparent screens of glass.

The miracle of the colored cascade, which, as with a time exposure, reflects the lively phases of the movement of the sun, extended for an entire day, from sunrise to sunset.

And at the other end – that same miracle of change, sparkle, and overflow of color pushed to the other extreme.

In those few moments of colored, fiery illumination in which – glittering and blinding – magnificent fireworks burn on the background of the night sky.

Here out of the darkness arose dragons and cascades merged into a general picture of furiously spinning, fiery wheels.

Blue. Green. Red. Orange.

Here for the last time they exploded with the blinding rain of Bengal fire.

And before dying out in the miracle of pyrotechnic wonder, in a few moments our imagination was drowned by the magic of the super-dynamic images of the fiery color painting...

And, of course, only the miracle of our century – color film, which occurs between the momentariness of fireworks and the slow movement of the sunlit day around the cathedral – will be able with equal fascination to bring to the viewer all the *pathos* of a color symphony, by whose rhythms, like the gallop of wild horses, subduing them to his will, the color painter of the new cinematography will be able to operate.

In merging the colored element with the audial element – in removing the opposition between the areas of hearing and vision – both he and his viewer will find the most inspired images of audiovisual exaltation as the best means capable of instilling into the viewer's consciousness and feeling that magnificent system of ideas that alone is able to engender a similar, truly effective symphony.

I experienced a premonition of the rapture possible here in the fragment of the audiovisual experiment with which I ended my production of Wagner's *The Valkyries* at the Bolshoi Academic Theater of the USSR in 1940.

And it is difficult to forget that enjoyment of *pathos* with which the blue flame grew to sound of the "Magic Fire" music in the last act, sometimes repeating it, then conflicting with it, then isolating it, then absorbing it; the blue flame grows, devouring the red, red subduing the blue, and both – rising out of the crimson ocean of fire to which the whole bronze wall of the backdrop returned, which became like this after first having turned its original silver into heavenly azure – at the moment of the culminating scene of Wotan and Brunhilde's farewell.

And how incomparably broader, richer, and overwhelming are the possibilities of this method for color film!

And now let us continue our investigation in another area, a new one. The field of the visual arts.

And the golden-white ray of Chartres Cathedral – is the most perfect way of approaching the deliberate ecstasy of El Greco, who, in my opinion, so unexpectedly corresponds to the titanic actor Frédérick.

Actually, the huge collection of self-portraits – clear and unclear, right up to the projection of states of his own soul into tangible forms of threatening landscapes,* and, finally, the constant picturesque repetitions, not only of the same motifs but of whole pictures perfect in their composition, in the course of the most varied stages of his life – somehow unintentionally force you to recall El Greco along with those who in act and deed every evening, from the theater stage, through these masks or others, or through endless variations of the performance of the very same role, reveal the ocean of their experiences and the *pathos* of their soul before the electrified crowd of spectators.

But here we won't let one's own body, soul, and voice, trembling through the movement of time and space of stage action, serve as material for the embodiment of these feelings.

Here we will let it be the figurative embodiment of one's own soul through subjects and colors that, after a hurricane of painterly acts, has been kept for centuries on the unmoving surface of painted canvas.

And yet nevertheless they tremble with no less vividness of holy emotion than if the bloodstained painter himself had hung alive on these crosses; in these prayerful ecstasies, the one who guided his brush along the canvas would twist and writhe, or, like an arrow, there would rise up into the sky before us the one before whom the miracle-working visions of *The Seventh Seal of the Apocalypse* soared.[88]

We stand electrified, in exactly the same way, before the creative miracles of the indefatigable brush of this indefatigable creator, as we would stand before the fact of the actual culmination of these same events in the performance of a great tragic actor.

The problem of the technical and painterly means of embodying the ecstasies of El Greco on his canvases – is, of course, an independent, vast, and fascinating theme.

I studied it in no less detail than in my analysis of the composition of Zola's novels. However, here I do not want to deal with this work in fragmented details.

But in a somewhat different, perhaps somewhat unusual, and, certainly, a quite uncanonical way, I would like to demonstrate here the method of a frenzied "being beside oneself," in material from two painted works of the great master, juxtaposed side by side. It is El Greco himself who leads to a similar method.

Doesn't the astonishing *Burial of Count Orgaz* (Toledo, Santo Tomé,

---

* I have in mind *Storm over Toledo*, which is discussed in detail later in a section of the last chapter, called Nonindifferent Nature.

1586) belong to his brush – this remarkable diptych, which seems to be cut in two by the horizontal line of the heads of the Spanish grandees in white collars?

Into two worlds.

Into above and below.

Into heaven and earth.

So that it bears the double portrait of the dying count – earthly and mortal in the lower region, and the one in the world beyond, coming alive near the throne of the most high, in the semicircle framing the top of the picture.

Here, on earth, in a setting of luxurious posthumous honors, his body in luxurious black armor, in the arms of high dignitaries of the church in shining gold vestments, whose roles the aged, holy Augustine and the young martyr St. Stephen do not disdain to take on.

And he is there – high above in the sky – naked and genuflecting before the throne of the high judge, naked, but alive again, having been transported out of his corruptive and mortal vestment, out of his black and shining armor, out of the luxurious environment of prelates and grandees – "being beside himself" and revived for a new life in an otherworld existence.

And how fascinating it is to recall here that this strikingly profound creation was made for a most...vulgar reason.

If one can believe Morris Barres,[89] then, in its initial conception, it was conceived as a kind of intimidating placard to frighten the peasants who did not want to pay quitrent to the monks of the monastery to which their villages had been bequeathed.

In its original theme this canvas was to have asserted threateningly and reproachfully to the disobedient peasants that even such rich cavaliers as Count Orgaz himself, in the world beyond the grave, will stand revealed and defenseless in all his nakedness before the terrible, punishing judge of the disobedient.

And it is even more fascinating to see how, in the sweep of creative elevation, the theme of the picture bursts the limits set for it and also, "going beside itself," through the images of luxury and self-destruction, gives us one of the most profoundly conceived creations of Spanish religious thought and painting.

So we should not go further along this same path and – just as the artist himself here juxtaposes along a vertical the two halves of one picture, as if the wandering of the human soul – why not juxtapose two whole, independent pictures, taken from different stages of the life of the same master on the way to that final transport "beside oneself," which brought years of ecstasy to the last years of the life of the great Toledoan, enveloped in a legend of madness?

And just as the two opposing worlds here are unified by the ascent into heaven of a single soul, so let the life path of El Greco himself establish in them that same organic unity in the process "of ecstasy as it were" from one canvas to another.

It is quite possible to find such a real instance of this kind.

[El Greco]

Speaking for myself, out of all of El Greco's works, there is only one I dislike.

This is – *The Expulsion of the Moneylenders from the Temple.*

Moreover, I am always irritated by the fact that, even in the most slender and pitiful monographs devoted to the artist, it is namely this picture that almost invariably figures among the reproductions of his most popular pictures.

Why does this picture irritate me so much?

This picture exists in four variants.[90]

The earliest variant is now in the collection of Sir Francis Cook; another variant very close to it is in Minneapolis. The most famous and most often reproduced is in the National Gallery in London. And a variant almost identical to it is in the Frick Collection.

And, finally, a very late variant is in the church of San Gínes in Madrid.

But this picture irritates me because, even in its most popular third variant, it on the whole continues to retain all the features characteristic of the *pre-ecstatic* period of El Greco's painting.

In the very last variant, the work is somewhat mollified by what has become more usual for the "remarkable" El Greco, the stretching of the figure of Christ upward.

But this is not all.

Because, even in the general composition, the picture is distinguished here from the other variants only because in the distance are painted quite "independent" columns stretching upward, a niche with a sepulchre and an antique, and – for some reason naked – figure with calf muscles so exuberantly presented that they seem to be slipping off the figure like pantaloons!

This group of characters seemed to have been automatically transported from another variant and, like a bas-relief, put in front of this background.*

And, insofar as this group is concerned, in the structure of the whole,

---

* This method of "transporting" an entire compositional group into a new combination with other elements is encountered quite often in El Greco. Just recall the two variants of *Prayer over a Chalice*, where the second – horizontal – is "made" from the first – the vertical – by transporting, without any changes, the entire group of sleeping apostles from the lower part of the first variant into the lateral part of the second.

in the inner composition, in the arrangement of the tiny groups and characters composing it, in the color (and for some reason they especially love to reproduce it in color!), in the general rhythm and dynamics (especially lacking!), this picture is totally conventional, traditional, quite in the manner of El Greco's contemporaries, out of whose milieu in other of his works he burst with such an inimitable explosion into the century ahead (*The Laocoon*, or *The Taking of the Fifth Seal*, or in pure painting – *The Concert of Angels in the Clouds*).[91]

Of course, even comparing the first variant of *The Expulsion* with the last, it is possible within the composition – in the treatment of the movement of the figures and even more in the painting technique itself – to trace the principle of "ecstasy" quite clearly.

Let us just compare the figure of the boy covering himself with his left hand, to the left of the figure of Christ.

Enriqueta Harris* considers one of the figures of Michelangelo's *Last Judgment* as its prototype. And in the comparison of this figure of Michelangelo, of its interpretation in the first variant of *The Expulsion* (from Cook's collection) and its last variant in the Church of San Gínes, it is quite clear how the expression of a separate figure changes, from Renaissance "cosmicness" through everyday drama to "ecstasy," on a canvas belonging to the "extravagant" style of the late El Greco.

But this is by no means a caprice of the artist, but a very precise reflection on the techniques and forms of his painting of that profound inner process of reconceiving the essence of the same scene, which he paints at different periods of his life.

On the early canvas, this scene is nothing more for El Greco than a painted embodiment of an everyday episode from the life of Christ.

In the last variant of the theme, El Greco completely departs from the everyday, narrative principles.

Here the scene becomes wholly symbolic, pushing into the foreground its inner significance of allegory and parable.

The National Gallery variant seems to serve as a connecting link between the two.

Here Enriqueta Harris very convincingly remarks:

...Before the Reformation, *The Purification of the Temple* was normally treated as one of a series of scenes from the Life, or from the Passion, of Christ. After the Reformation, however, the story acquired a new importance. Protestants compared it with their own reforming activities; and to the Catholics of the Counter-Reformation it symbolized the purging of the Church of heresy. El Greco's interest in the subject, and his interpretation of it, are certainly connected with these ecclesiastical controversies. In his earlist version he is mainly intent on telling the story as set out in the Gospel. In the National Gallery picture,

* See *El Greco, The Purification of the Temple*. Gallery Book n. 2, London.

(a) ↑   (b) ↓

Figure 4. Two versions of *The Purification of the Temple* by El Greco: (a) c. 1560–5 ([c. 1570] 1957.14.4 *Christ Cleansing the Temple*, El Greco; National Gallery of Art, Washington, D.C.; Samuel H. Kress Collection), (b) c. 1600–5 (Reproduced by courtesy of the Trustees, The National Gallery, London).

however, he is more preoccupied with its symbolical meaning. The two reliefs in the background are the Old Testament prototypes of Sin and Redemption; and the two groups on either side of Christ are clearly divided into the unredeemed, placed beneath the *Expulsion of Adam and Eve*, and the redeemed, placed beneath the *Sacrifice of Isaac*. Finally, in the last version of S. Gínes, the interest in the narrative is almost entirely subjugated to its symbolical interpretation. The emphasis on the atmosphere of the Temple, the unearthly figure of Christ sweeping through the crowd, and the divine apparition driving back the sinners with one hand and pointing to heaven with the other, combine to give the scene the quality of a mystic vision – a vision that evokes the fanatical spirit of the Counter-Reformation in the adopted country of El Greco...[op. cit., p. 11–12]

However, in spite of this, as I have already shown above, this inner leap from a narrative interpretation into a figurative interpretation (a familiar phenomenon!) in the given case is expressed only in an inner "reconstruction" of the elements of the picture. The picture as a whole does not undergo genuine "ecstasy," a genuine "explosion" in this process. To the very end El Greco remains in the captivity of general compositional "fetters," extending from the first variant that, both as a whole and in its details, is still completely subject to Renaissance conceptions.

And even an excursion into the history of the inner dynamics of *The Expulsion*, through its four variants, is insufficient to capture the power of the ecstatic explosion of the other works of El Greco. Even they cannot "reconcile" me to the picture, which is incapable of giving that strength of direct ecstatic experience that makes the other canvases of this man so remarkable, in whom the concepts of the East and West – the traditions of the Greek and the fanaticism of the Spaniard – experience such a striking unity.

And involuntarily, looking at the most popular middle variant of *The Expulsion* in the National Gallery, you begin to mentally estimate how one would "ecstaticize" it in the unique spirit and manner of El Greco.

Let us fantasize here in that direction!

It would follow that, out of the boring horizontal rectangular format of the picture, balanced and impersonal in its proportions (41.5 × 50.5 inches), you would make a rectangle that clearly flies vertically upward.

The miserable arch, carried off into the distance and squeezed by the mass of walls, after having exploded and been hurled forward, would have necessarily seized the entire canvas of the picture as a whole by its edge...

In the same way the setting of the boring material surroundings of the confined room would scatter into the immaterial heavenly and cloudy space of the exterior.

The figure of Christ angrily (not too angrily) threatening certainly could not remain on the same level as the other characters in this scene.

The figure would have to hang over them, like an arrow winding into the darkening clouds of the parting background.

The figure to the left of Christ, hardly expressing amazement through foreshortening – with his right elbow lifted up in defense from a blow – taken from the back, would undoubtedly become a figure turned over completely on his back, his legs up, resting on the ground with his shoulders, neck, and shoulder blade, and under the best conditions having bent one of his legs in the burst of amazement that overturned him.

The old man on the right, not very expressive, phlegmatic, having propped up his cheek, looking at what is occurring almost right next to him, would, of course, begin to expand to the height of the powerful figure of the youth. Forced to look, not at what is occurring on the same level with him and on the same plane, this figure would be hurled daringly forward into the strongly emphasized foreground that almost bursts out of the picture.

And that youth would begin to look at what is happening above and behind him, of course – by bending backwards!

Finally – "the masses" from the group of regularly placed mannequins would inevitably have to burst into a chaos of torsos, knees, elbows, forearms, and thighs, spread along the canvas of the picture and interwoven with each other.

And, as if expressing the idea of an ecstatic explosion to the extreme, a rapture of the "bond of time" upward and downward, two figures would burst from the center of the picture: one – the hero – head upward toward the sky, and the other – the figure of the opponent – also vertical, but "'mirror image" toward the earth, downward.

In addition, the figures would undoubtedly burst out of their clothes.

And the very theme, of course, would burst beyond the limits of the narrow everyday subject of *The Expulsion of the Moneylenders from the Temple* – despite the whole mysterious figurative and symbolic significance of this biblical tale – into something from the cycle of clearly wonder-working events from the pages of the biblical biography of the central character of the scene.

Something, well, let us say, like... *The Resurrection from the Grave*...

Stop!

Indeed, just what we sketched in this "desirable" picture is actually reflected in the immortal *Resurrection from the Grave* painted between 1597 and 1604 in the most complete ecstatic manner of El Greco!

At the feet of the *naked* Christ,

in a cloak *being torn*

and *flying*

into the sky's abstract, *swirling*, cloudy expanse

Figure 5. *The Resurrection* by El Greco, c. 1595–8 (Reprinted by permission, Museo del Prado, Madrid). [Alternatively dated c. 1600–5.]

– a *human jumble* of human bodies – shins, shoulders, chests, heads thrown back, and arms uplifted.

Out of this group two figures burst into the center of attention, into the foreground.

Into the foreground – *extremely stretched out, with glance thrown backward*, the *young man's* figure on the right.

And into the center of attention – amazed, completely *turned upside down* on his shoulders, *feet up* – the second – as if turned over "mirror image" in his stunned fall, in contrast to the amazing flight to heaven of the figure of Christ.

Christ, not with a pitiful lash, but with the unfurled triumphant banner in his hands!

Isn't it so?!

How was such a "trick" possible of juxtaposing two apparently randomly chosen pictures from the gallery of works of the great Spanish-Greek master of the past?

Two pictures, of which the second actually seemed like an explosion, into which the first burst along the line of all its basic features?

It turned out to be possible because each of these pictures – each in its own way – is truly a precise imprint of two different phases of the creative condition and development that relate to each other as an explosion and the static state preceding it.

These two phases, in the fate of the true artist, stand on either side of that moment when the dungeon of pitiful being is suddenly illuminated by the holy flame of a mission.

When yesterday's simple mortal burns with the creative flame of the preacher, seer, and prophet.

When on the path of every artist there occurs the same thing that happened to Pushkin's "Prophet," growing to the fullness of creative inspiration at his encounter with the "six-winged seraphim" who illuminated his consciousness with his unique creative mission:

...And with a sword he clove my breast,
Plucked out my palpitating heart
And deep into my gaping chest
A coal of fire did he implant.
I, corpselike, in the desert lay
And then the voice of God heard say:
"Rise up, Prophet, hear and see,
This my will fulfill and fend
And crossing over land and sea
Burn with words the hearts of men.*

* [My own translation – HM.]

Such is this leap within the same creative personality from a state like that of a corpse "rising up" in order to "burn with words the hearts of men."

And such is the expression of this state through all the means and characteristics of the palette, of the course of the brush, of the composition, of the manner of painting, and above all, of conceptions transported from the sphere of balanced and trivial structures done in the manner of numerous contemporaries, into the inimitable area of unique, individual, unrepeatable ecstatic painting, in the transition of El Greco from the epoch of youth to the epoch of creative perfection.

And therefore the "miracle" of a similar dynamic juxtaposition of two different works of his, from different stages of his creativity, turns out to be quite possible.

Actually, the source of both is the same creative individuality represented in two phases of his creative being – "on either side" of the watershed of ecstatic explosion, "enrapturing" the author, carrying his unique spirit up in ecstasy, like the path from one world to the other made by the soul through the two halves of the memorial picture on Count Orgaz's fate beyond the grave!

Is a similar experiment possible on the creation and works of any other artists?

If they turn out to be artists communicating *pathos*, then certainly.

And not only are such examples possible, but there is one more we simply must bring in here.

As a necessary third link, it supplements the complete triad of examples from an area of creativity that we began with Frédérick Lemaître and El Greco.

And these three examples are arranged as models from various spheres of art, beginning with the most subjective variant of it to the most objective.

Actually, in terms of the expression of one's self, the most subjective art is the actor's craft, where creativity flows "in and of itself," where the creator is simultaneously the subject and object of creation, where he himself is the material and the architect.

We observed this situation in Frédérick Lemaître.

The second step in this direction is the semiobjective art of the painter.

Here, also reincarnated in various images, the individuality of the artist plays through them; now a self-portrait moves into the foreground – as invariably happens in literature; for example, Lord Byron – then almost hiding behind images of his work, which exist independently and objectively, as if reflecting only objectively existing reality. With them are connected the almost invisible threads of the individual features of the vivid characters expressed in their fullness – so it is in the literature of

Gogol, where, from hints of certain features within the character, he engenders an immortal gallery of generalized types, so that in certain cases they seem to dissolve as a whole into objective pictures of the landscape. These landscapes seem to be totally free from the "visible," "concrete" subjectivity of the author, although in his best examples they are entirely woven from rebellious or appeasing rhythms of the state of the soul and character of the author.

Such was the second case analyzed – El Greco: The subjective, ecstatic dissolution of him in the apparently "objective" landscape – this is what makes his *Storm over Toledo* so striking and captivating.[92]

No less striking in this relation is Leonardo da Vinci.

The presence of his vivid self-portrait in his own works, which were apparently already quite abstract, is even more astonishing.

Emil Ludwig noted this very well:*

...Leonardo drew a stone-cutter, a crow-bar, a dredging machine – and though these were without landscape, sky, or people, their wood and iron, their stone, wire and plaster seem nothing less than living muscles, pulsing veins, and glowing flesh. The shadows play so musically along the cold and murderous edges of a cannon that no one who knows the madonnas of this master could fail to recognize the same hand here...

And if at this point we note that the Leonardo madonna is a type that permeates all his work, embracing both the *Mona Lisa* and *John the Baptist*, then we would not be surprised that here what reigns over the apparently totally abstract projects of practical objects is that same basic image standing before Leonardo's eyes, an image that through hundreds of variations, as though through hundreds of mirrors, looks at Leonardo looking at us in them, and through their generally recognized "mystery" he wishes to express certain inner depths of himself.

Andrea del Sarto[93] proceeded in a cruder and simpler way: Almost all his works – both *John the Baptist* and *The Madonna* – simply resemble him in face (compare them with his self-portrait).

And if Leonardo proceeds here in a more refined and elegant manner, carrying over into his work not his simple, "crude" appearance but the most complex flutter of inner conflicts of his own inner spiritual nature, passing with a strange smile through the images created by him, then we have no reason to speak of his works as being less of a self-portrait or self-expression.

This self-portrait quality does not impede the objectivity of his painted works, it does not remove the documentary aspect from his sketches of the turbulence of air waves and sea waves, it does not destroy the strictness of the technical invention of war machines, fortification

* *Genius and Character*, K. Burker; trans, Jonathan Cape, London, 1927, p. 176.

Figure 6. *Storm Over Toledo* by El Greco, c. 1595–1600 [also known as *View of Toledo*]. The Metropolitan Museum of Art, bequest of Mrs. H. O. Havemeyer, 1929. The H. O. Havemeyer Collections. [29.100.6]

constructions, the passion of his sculptured horses, or the projects of a system of sluice dams.

And the lyric melody of this subjective subtext is hardly less temperamental, less ecstatic than the boiling passion of El Greco thundering through *Storm over Toledo*...

And after what has been said, it will be easy to apply here directly a third example taken from a third area.

From an area where subjective experience has already been completely devoured by objective concreteness, through whose exterior depiction the artist's temperament and fantasy are quite unexpectedly and no less intensely aroused.

Architecture.

Having verified the norms of ecstatic construction discovered by us in examples from the first two areas, let us try to show how persuasive they are also in the area of architectural conception, fantasy, and imagery.

We could make this excursion on the principles of the Gothic that seem to explode the balance of the Romanesque style. And, within the Gothic itself, we could trace the stirring picture of movement of its lancet* world from the first almost indistinct steps toward the ardent models of the mature and postmature, "flamboyant" late Gothic.

We could, like Wölfflin, contrast the Renaissance and Baroque[94] and interpret the excited spirit of the second, winding like a spiral, as an ecstatically bursting temperament of a new epoch, exploding preceding forms of art in the enthusiasms for a new quality, responding to a new social phase of a single historical process.

We could show this clearly in a very concrete example of what was done with the "cosmically balanced" project of the plan of St. Peter's Cathedral in Rome [created by a man of the Renaissance, Bramante[95] (1506)], by Michelangelo, in whom the temperament of a man of the Baroque is exploding when this initial project finally falls to him forty years later for its final completion.†

But for clarity I would still prefer to trace this case as well – again within the limits of one biography – by juxtaposing two works of two different stages of the creativity of the same artist – the builder completing his path by a leap from the architect and archeologist into the image of the artist – and the visionary.

Such is the case of Giovanni Battista Piranesi:[96]

If El Greco is known by every youngster in his aspect of an ecstatic mystic, then perhaps it would do no harm for Piranesi if we introduced several "corroborations" of this from "authoritative sources" before rushing into a direct observation of his etchings, although they cry out most eloquently of this themselves!

A. Benois's *History of Painting* has discussed this exhaustively‡:[97]

...History knows few artists in whom the excitement of creativity would appear with such strength, in whom there would be such *ardor*...

...A remarkable ability to be at the same time both a *scholar* and a *poet* (no

---

* [Lancet arch: sharply pointed arch associated with the Gothic style – HM.]
† After Bramante, the project passes to Raphael. Raphael dies in 1521. The project is continued by Peruzzi and Antonio da Sangallo the longer. Sangallo dies in 1546 and the next year the work passes to Buonarotti.
‡ Issue 16, p. 486. In the quote I allowed myself to categorically choose those passages that have particularly direct relation to what is relevant to us.

one will say where Piranesi the *archaeologist* ends and where the *artist* begins,
where the *poet* passes over into the *scholar* and the *visionary* – into the strict
investigator)...

...Myopic minds reproached Piranesi for the fact that in proceeding from his
archaeological studies, he was not able to restrain his fantasies. However, one
may ask what is essentially more valuable: those grains of so-called knowledge,
which a true archaeologist may discover in his investigations, or that new fairy-
tale world which arose in Piranesi's imagination as the result of his *ecstasy*
before the power and beauty of Roman architecture?...

Even in this short, descriptive discussion, even in these traditional
turns of speech, which are always at the service of art critics and
historians of art ("...where the archaeologist ends and where the artist
begins, where the *poet* passes over into the *scholar* and the *visionary* –
into...the *investigator*"), even in them we can perceive what we already
know as the basis of the characteristic quality of ecstasy, of the ecstatic
personality!

Here what is taken, not as a series of rhetorical phrases but as a
biographical fact, gives us another broad example of a leap within the
biography itself.

We already saw Zola passing from a "novelist" into a "teacher of life";
we know that same evolution from the satirist to the utopianist in the
biography of Gogol; we know Leonardo da Vinci, transported from an
artist to a scholar. We also know this latter from Goethe's biography,
where the jump from poetry into the sphere of pure philosophy (even if it
be the second part of *Faust*) is even more striking...

However, in his biography Piranesi gives us transitions of a reverse
leap instead: from archeologist to artist, from scholar to poet, from
investigator to visionary.

Thus at least inner discovery moves through the sequence of a series of
etchings, through the etchings themselves, and, finally, through visibly
changing editions of the same series in intervals through a period of
fifteen to twenty years.

Let us recall something analogous in the regeneration of the pictorial
treatment of one and the same theme in El Greco.

And let us turn to this area in discussing the problems of the work of
Giovanni Battista Piranesi...

Piranesi or the flux of form[98]

I am sitting in a bright yellow room flooded by sunlight. It is the corner
room of my apartment on Potylikha and through one of its windows it
looks out at the village of Troitskoe-Golenishchevo. From here, beating
the French "in the rear," partisans at one time drove out the army of
Napoleon's invaders from Moscow.

(This gave the name to the whole region.)

The other window looks out at a bare field.

Once this field was an apple orchard.

The apple trees of the orchard – I dug up, in 1938.

I liberated this area of its orchard under a studio lot for "The Battle on the Ice."

Here in the summer, after transforming the lot into the ice-covered surface of Lake Chad, and after re-creating other hordes of invaders of the Russian land, I pursued for a month – the cur-knights of *Alexander Nevsky*.

Recently beyond my windows the limits of the city of Moscow terminated.

And the house where I lived was the last house within Moscow city limits.

Inadvertently dropping a cucumber out of the kitchen window, it would now drop into Moscow...Province.

But now the limits of the city have been extended, and the line of the watershed of both province and city go far out beyond my windows.

In 1941 the invader-Germans were not allowed up to this line and were held back somewhere, above the village of Troitskoe and the field of "The Battle of the Ice," not reaching my yellow room, which looked out through its windows in the direction of Mozhaisk and Minsk.

Between the windows – in the corner – a windowsill.

On the windowsill – it.

It – the object of many years of longing and searching.

I first saw it as a reproduction in a small – but actually quite thick – little book on the history of theater decoration: Guilio Ferrari, *La Scenografia* (Milano, 1902), from the library of the former theater of S. I. Zimin.

It is a sheet of a Piranesi etching.

It belongs to the series *Operie varie di Architettura* [*Various Works of Architecture*].

And it is called *Carcere oscura* [*Dark Dungeon* or *Dark Prison*].

It is assumed to have been created under the influence of the work *Prison d'Amadis* of Daniel Marot.[99] It far surpasses the prototype. And it is dated 1743.

Quite recently – just now – I was finally able to get it.

As always – by means both strange and inscrutable.

In the form of an exchange.

An exchange with one of the peripheral museums.

The museum was based on an extravagant and unsystematized collection of rarities of a certain merchant, who often traveled abroad.

In his private residence a stuffed bear got along quite peacefully with a dish, a terrible carved "blackamoor" with candlesticks, and beautiful items truly upper class: for example, several sheets of Piranesi.

Figure 7. *Dark Dungeon* [or *Dark Prison*] by G.B. Piranesi, 1743. From *Prima Parte di Architetturee Prospettive inventate ed incise da Gio. Batta. Piranesi architetto veneziano*..., Plate 2, drawing 6. Photograph © Ashmolean Museum, Oxford.

In exchange went – one Edelinck,[100] one Hogarth,[101] one Nanteuil,[102] and the charming Claude Mellan[103]...

Perhaps that was a lot.

But in return I finally got this one and one other sheet of Piranesi – my very own.

My very own, accurately framed, is distinguished from the canary-yellow walls by its expressive coffee-stained color of burnt sienna and white passe-partout.

I have been a long-time admirer of the architectural violence of Piranesi's *Dungeons*.

But more an enthusiast than a connoisseur.

Therefore I always related this sheet I liked so much to the series *Invenzioni capriccosi di carceri*,* well-known in two variants – 1745 and 1761–5 – not to the earlier *Opere varie*.[†]

I am looking at this sheet on the wall right now.

And at first I am struck by its complete perfection – the degree of its balanced...meekness.

Probably, because of the freshness of the first impression made by originals of the latest *Carceri*,[‡] it seems unexpectedly harmless, without much *pathos*.

Not ecstatic...

And now, looking at the sheet and mentally examining the means used in the method of "ecstaticizing" the material, I involuntarily begin to apply them to the given etching.

I ponder over what would happen with this etching if it had been brought to a state of ecstasy, of being beside itself.

Both as a whole. And in all of its features...

I admit that this experiment on Piranesi preceded what has been described above and applied to El Greco.

And both experiments are put here not in the "historical" sequence of their origin but with the aim of maintaining a progressive sequence (actor – painter – architect) according to the motives discussed above.

For a clarifying exposition of what I worked out in my thoughts, here is a reproduction of the etching and a diagrammatic breakdown. Let us enumerate the basic elements in the diagram and its distinctive features.

Now – step by step, element by element – let's "blow them up" one by one.

We already did this once with El Greco's picture.

Therefore now it is already simpler, habitual, demanding less time and space.

---

* *Fantasies on Dungeons.*
[†] Moreover this same mistake was made (with less justification than by a lonely dilletante) by the album published by the Academy of Architecture USSR *Piranesi* (1939), which, without any basis at all, also includes this sheet in the wrong series.
[‡] Dungeons.

A dozen explosions will be sufficient to ecstatically "transform" the diagram that is drawn before us.

However, it would be wrong to deny completely any quality of *pathos* in this initial sheet.

Otherwise – what would be this print's attraction for me, the sheet I knew before my encounter with the raging [*Dungeon*] of the basic series?

But here, in this sheet, if there is a degree of "being beside itself," then it is realized, not as an explosion, but as...dissolution.

And – not as form, but only as a system of means of expression.

And, therefore, instead of violence and strongly impressive uproar – a flowing lyricism of "mood."

Giesecke, in his work on Piranesi,* writes about this print in exactly this spirit:

The etching *Carcere oscura* is daring and yet still restrained (befangen im Vortrag [restrained in delivery]) in the presentation of the material...The bright and airy perspective here goes even further...(in comparison to other etchings of the series – SME) the soft silvery light, which the Venetians so love streams down from above into this airy chamber and loses itself in the gloomy distance; forms are softened, are quite indistinct, as if they were in the process of dissolution (Auflösung), and the drawing itself tenderly scatters like streams of separate lines...

To this I would add that the vaults rise and stretch upward so that the dark mass at the bottom, gradually growing light, overflows into the vaulted top flooded with light...

However, let us turn to the technique of the explosion.

In order to analyze this, let us enumerate the basic data of depiction in the etching.

A – the general arch confining the entire etching as a whole.

a_1 and a_2 – its side walls.

B and C – the arches carrying the basic support of the architectural composition of the whole.

D – the system of passing far into the depths of the lower corner arches, and in its depths resting against the wall with the grated window.

E – the ascending staircase, carried off into the depths, behind the columns.

F_1F_2 – the ropes, outlining the center of the composition (F), and underlining its movement into the depths (F_1)

G – the little round window over the "zavalinka." [†]

H – the firm base of the stone slabs of the floor.

J – the heavy masonry of the stone blocks of the severe vertical columns.

m_1m_2 – the little balcony to the right and left near the columns of the foreground.

* We will refer later to this work of Giesecke: *Meister der Grafik*, Band IV. *Giovanni Battista Piranesi von Albert Giesecke*, Klinghardt and Biermann, Leipzig, 1911.
[†] [A small mound of earth along the outer walls of a peasant's house – HM.]

Figure 8. Eisenstein's schematic outline of Piranesi's *Dark Dungeon* [*Dark Prison*].

Now let us try to give freedom to the ecstatic fury of the whole and let us observe what must occur – and would occur – with all these concrete elements of composition to achieve this.

First of all, arch *A*, which confines the etching, would explode.

The upper stone semicircle flies out beyond the limits of the sheet.

If you like – from being semicircular it will become...angular.

From stone – wooden.

The intersection of wooden rafters – instead of a stone arch – would allow it to "jump out" simultaneously from both the material and the form.

The columns a_1 and a_2 would appear to "burst" inside the sheet out of its borders, and the sheet, broadening out beyond their limits, "leaps over" from a vertical format – to a horizontal one (we may recall such a leap of the format into its opposite – but from horizontal to vertical – in the example of El Greco!).

But the arches *B* and B_1 would not submit to this tendency to explode.

As distinct from arches *A* and *C*, which flew apart completely, these arches may undergo an "explosion" *within their form*; that is, preserving the "idea" of the arch, they could change into something of an opposite character.

What would the qualitative jump inside the form of the arch in the given circumstances be like?

The jump from the semicircular arch – into a lancet arch:

Moreover – this can be another leap from a single-flying arch into an arch of the double-flying vertical type.

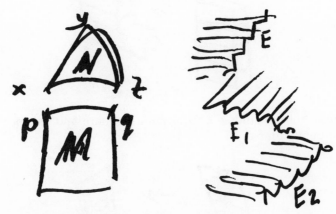

Such a form would be particularly appropriate, since its very outline bears the image of an upper lancet arch N exploding as if it were in flight out of the flat overhang M and with the two-cornered outline $p-q$ transported into the triangle $x-y-z$, thus keeping in this drawing a trace of that process that occurred with the whole arch A.

Rushing ahead and moving into the depths by column a_1 downward, the staircase in its growing explosion pushes down column a_1 standing in its path, dashes ahead, and not only by one flight of stairs E, but like a triple break in a flash of lightning – E, E_1, E_2 – it dashes in zigzag fashion ultimately forward. And this ultimate movement seems like a dash beyond the limits of the contours of the sheet. In exactly the same way the system of arches D, increasing their tendency into the depths, during which they change the angularity of the contour into a semicircle – knocks out by its pressure this confining wall with the grated window and dashes off somewhere in the direction of the general point of descent that, in turn, in contrast to the initial form, seems to already exist not between the upper and lower edge of the sheet, but somewhere beyond its limit; not only to the right, but also *below*, and with a rumble, repeating it, the firm base of the floor disappears, which is so distinctly visible in the first sheet and which in the second disappears somewhere in the framed depths of its new ecstatic appearance.

The little broken balconies m_1 and m_2 on the columns of the foreground a_1 and a_2 dash toward each other, become a single bridge, and this bridge remains not as balconies in front of the arch outlining D, but undoubtedly dashes beyond it – into the depths and, perhaps, upward.

The strict proportion of the stone breaks apart in the masonry.

The little round window c turns into a square and escapes into the plane perpendicular to it.

And finally, having broken away from the centerline (which is outlined so distinctly), the ropes and blocks explode into those parts of the etching that, in its vertical stage, were not even in the initial variant of the sheet!

And, as if catching their signal, all the other details seem to be caught up by a whirlwind;

and "everything is swept by a powerful tornado" – as if they would roar out from the sheet, which has lost its initial reticence and "cosiness" in the name of raging violence...

And here in the thoughts before us, in place of the modest, lyrically meek sheet of *Carcere oscura* – a whirlwind, aiming like a tornado at all sides: Ropes, scattering staircases, exploding arches, stone blocks torn apart from each other...

The scheme of this new ecstatic form of the etching emerges in our imagination before our very eyes.

The eyes themselves – glide along the yellow wall.

Here they slipped out beyond the limits of the edges of the first sheet.

Now they slipped by another model of violence hanging between the window and the door – *The Temptation of St. Anthony* by Callot.[104]

Figure 9. *Dungeon* by G.B. Piranesi, c. 1743. From *Carceri*, Plate XIV, 2nd state.
Photograph © Ashmolean Museum, Oxford.

And here they stopped unexpectedly on the second sheet of Piranesi,
which came to me from that same peripheral source, from under the
canopies of those same carved figures of blackamoors with candlesticks,
of a bear with a tray, and a second-rate Japanese bric-à-brac of bronze.

To where did the scheme that was just standing before our eyes
suddenly disappear?

I cannot catch it.

I think it – plunged into that second sheet of the incomparable
Giovanni Battista.

And so it is!

The "miracle" of El Greco – has been repeated.

The farfetched scheme – turns out to really exist.

Namely, it lies at the basis of Piranesi's second etching.

Indeed, it was necessary that in a bundle of all the other possible
Piranesi etchings besides the *Carcere oscura*, the late merchant Maecenas
should bring this very one from Italy.

That as an exchange for the second etching it was this very one that
fell into my hands.

That both of them, mounted, should hang on the yellow wall of that
same room of mine.

And that, having taken my eyes off one, they should stop with the imagined scheme before us; namely, on that sheet that cast, like invisible nets, this invisible scheme of transforming the first etching into the second!

Nevertheless, the second etching of Piranesi – is the first exploding in ecstatic flight.

Here it is.

Try to argue!

Let us quickly peruse its main features.

Down to the pettiest detail they are identical to what we approximately outlined above.

After this we have little need of general phrases of Benois on the ecstasy of Piranesi.

(By the way, we found these words many years after the direct "illumination" coming from the fusion of both etchings).

We are interested in the dates of the sheets.

The way they are linked in biographical succession.

The place of *Dungeons* in the general biography of Piranesi's work.

The stages of their creation.

The chorus of enthusiasm accompanying them.

The personalities of the enthusiasts.

The nature of the actual architectural fantasies, in which one system of visions grows into others; where certain planes, endlessly opening up behind others, push the eyes into unknown depths; and the staircases, ledge by ledge, grow into the heavens or, like a reverse cascade of these ledges, precipitate downward.

Indeed, the ecstatic image of the staircase, hurled from one world to another, from sky to earth, we already know from the biblical legend of Joseph's dream,[105] but the *pathos* image of the elemental down surge of human masses on the Odessa steps, reaching up to the heavens, we know from our own *opus* [*Potemkin*].

Carcere oscura as a restrained precursor of the most notorious *Carceri* just as famous [. . .]

Carcere oscura – still a distant peal of thunder from the depths of the series of 1743 is of quite a different ring.

Within two years this distant peal bursts out like a real blow. During these years in Piranesi's consciousness and feelings there occurred one of those explosions, one of those inner "cataclysms" shaking his spiritual constitution, worldview, and relation to reality that transform a man. One of those psychic leaps that "suddenly," "abruptly," unexpectedly, and unforeseen raise man from the class of those just like himself to the height of a true creator, capable of wresting from his soul images of unprecedented might, with unabated strength burning the hearts of men.

Some interpret the *Carceri* as the visions of an archeologist's delirium, who absorbed too deeply the terrible romanticism of the gigantic ruins of Rome's former greatness.

Others try to see in them the embodiment of the image of persecution mania from which at this moment the artist is beginning to suffer.

They also enumerate real causes for it, but give preference to imagined ones.

But I think that in the interval of these several years there occurs in Piranesi that same moment of illumination "of genius" that we noted above in Balzac, and that P. I. Tchaikovsky wrote so clearly about in discussing another musician of genius – Glinka.

June 27, 1888, Tchaikovsky notes down in his diary:

...An unprecedented amazing phenomenon in the sphere of art. A dilettante who played now the violin, now the piano; who composed rather colorless quadrilles, fantasies on fashionable Italian themes, who tried out serious forms as well (the quartet, sextet) and romances, but, except for banality reflecting the taste of the '30's, he had not written anything, when suddenly in his thirty-fourth year he composes an opera, which in genius, scale, novelty, and unapproachable technique stands on a level with the greatest and most profound works that exist in art?...At times I am alarmed to the point of madness by the question of how such a colossal artistic strength could be combined with such insignificance, and how, after having been a colorless dilettante for so long, Glinka in one step suddenly rose to the level (yes! to the level!) of Mozart, Beethoven, and whomever you please...

And actually there were no models at all; there were no antecedents* for Mozart, for Glinka, or for any of the masters. It is striking, amazing!...

Yes! *Glinka* is a real creative genius...[†]

It is necessary to assume that in this, "suddenly," abruptly, and instantaneously "there burst" everything that, as grainlike bits and pieces, accumulated and added up through the "banal," the insignificant and the "dilettantish," so that it could explode in *Ruslan* as a whole, organic unity of individual genius.

But what is particularly striking here is the complete "correspondence" to what happens to Piranesi between the series *Vedute varie*[‡] and *Carceri*.

Actually, *Carceri* stands almost at the beginning of the creative path of Piranesi.

Everything done before has almost no real, independent value (if you don't take into account two or three *Capricci*.[']

* That is, precedent – a case occurring earlier and serving as justification for subsequent cases of a similar type.
† *The Diary of P. I. Tchaikovsky*, GIZ, Moscow – Petrograd, Musical Sector, 1923, pp. 214–15.
‡ *Various Views*.
' *Fantasies*.

And even those different groups of etchings that Piranesi created before *Dungeons* do not constitute independent series, but later the majority of them became part of a suite of architectural views of 1750.

As we can see, "the divine word" of ecstasy concerns Piranesi at a rather early stage of his work.

And the blinding flash of *Dungeons* seems to retain its bright reflections and keep its sparkle, filling with its inspired poeticization not only the picturesqueness of the ruins of former Rome, which appear in such inspired profusion from under his burin, but also the more prosaic "vedutas" of the official buildings of the city contemporary to him.

This imperishable fervor through all his creativity is also apparent from the fact that, in fifteen to twenty years, from his hand there appears a new, more profound, even more perfect variant of these etchings, made stronger by the redrawing of the plates in their unrestrained elemental grandeur. (Let us recall how many times, continually perfecting its inner spirituality, El Greco repaints one and the same theme in several variants!)

Even here there is an echo in El Greco!

But there is even more in common with El Greco.

After the first hint of 1743, 1745 brings the series *Carceri* in its initial variant.

Giesecke names them – successfully, and in the tone of Goethe's "Ur-Faust" – "Ur-Carceri." (The first, original *Faust* is the first variant of *Faust; the "original" first Dungeons* – the first variant of the series *Dungeons.*)

Successfully and appropriately because, along with Goethe's *Faust*, replacing the first *Ur-Faust* (1770–75), comes *Faust* proper (1770–1806)

And in place of it, the second part of *Faust* (1773–1832).

Thus, in place of the first variant of *Dungeons*, in fifteen to twenty years the second variant appears – and, if it seems supplementary, retouched, and redrawn in terms of the etchings, then in terms of depictive, ecstatic "revelation" it is more profound and vivid. After this follows the third stage of the inner self-explosion of the *Dungeons*.

It is true – no longer within the work of Piranesi himself.

Beyond the limits of his biography.

Even beyond the limits of his country and epoch.

But a hundred-odd years ahead.

And not on the soil of Italy, but Spain.

But on one and the same line with it.

And with a step, beginning from there, to where the volume and space of his conceptions were quickly reached by the furious spirit of Piranesi.

Continuing to rise in the intensity of his plastic conceptions, these three phases seem to repeat the stimulating growth of the conception of Goethe's *Faust*, from a sketchy beginning to its apocalyptic concluding episode.

Carcere oscura plays a role here, similar to that which the *Faust* of the Middle Ages plays (which also served Christopher Marlowe in 1588), as a purely thematic herald of the future philosophical conceptions of Goethe.

They repeat "literally" that path made by El Greco's *Expulsion from the Temple*, from the stage of a depiction of an "everyday biblical scene" on a level that is still maintained by *Carcere oscura* – to the *pathos* dramatization of the middle variants of the composition – *Ur-Carceri* (1745) – to the ecstatic last variant *Carceri* (1760–66).

...Is it possible to gó even further?

And is it possible – after the comparatively short first stage with its dissolution of forms, through the second – already exploding the objects being depicted – and this in two jolts, strengthening the breaking up of forms and the pushing of the elements both into the depths as well as forward (by means of extensions of the foreground) – to foresee and find one more "jump," one more "explosion," one more "thrust" beyond the limits and dimensions and thus, it seemed, totally and completely to the limit of the exploded "norms" in the last variant of *Dungeons*?

Is such a subsequent jump possible?

And where, in what area of depiction should it be sought?

In *Carcere oscura* the concreteness was retained and the means of depiction "flew apart": Lines disintegrate into cascades of tiny strokes*; the density of form, softened by light, spreads into space, the clarity of edges plunges into the overflowing contours of form.

In *invenzioni capricciosi*, using those same means of expression (true, in somewhat heightened intensity), the concreteness has also "flown apart."

More precisely – objects as physical elements of the depiction itself flew apart.

But the representational concreteness of the elements in this case was not altered.

Stone "moved away" from stone, but kept its representational "stone" concreteness.

The stone vault was hurled into the angular wooden rafters, but the representational "concreteness" of both was kept untouched.

These were "in themselves" real stone arches, "in themselves" realistic wooden beams.

The piling up of perspective recessions coincides with the madness of narcotic visions (see below), but each link of these generally dizzy perspectives "in itself" is even naturalistic.

The concrete reality of perspective, the real depictive quality of the objects themselves, are not destroyed anywhere.

---

* Although they do not undergo that furious turbulence that governs the disintegrating (exploding) strokes, for example, in drawings by the pen of van Gogh.

Madness – is only in the piling up, in the juxtapositions, exploding the very basis of their everyday "possibility," the grouping of them into a system of arches consecutively being "beside themselves," erupting from the bowels of their new arches; staircases exploding into flights of new stair passages; vaults continuing the leaps out of each other into infinity.

Now it is already clear what will be (or should be) the next step.

What is left to explode – is the concreteness.

Stone no longer stone, but a system of intercrossing angles and planes, in whose play the geometrical basis of its forms explode.

Semicircles of their structural contour burst out of the semicircular outlines of vaults and arches.

Complex columns disintegrate into primary cubes and cylinders, from whose interdependence the concrete appearance of the elements of architecture and nature is constructed.

The play of chiaroscuro – the conflict of illuminated projections with areas of gaping darkness among them – becomes independent spots, no longer of light and dark, but concretely drawn dark and light colors (namely, colors, and not a range of "tones").

Can it be that this is everything that occurs in Piranesi's etchings?

No, not within the limits of the etchings.

But beyond them.

Not in the work of Piranesi.

But beyond their limits.

A leap beyond the limits of this opus.

And as a cannonade of directions and schools exploding out of each other.

And in the first place, beyond the limits of the canon of realism in the sense it is interpreted by popular understanding.

The first leap is beyond the limits of a precise outline of objects in the play of geometrical forms composing them – and we have before us Cézanne.

The connection with the object is still imperceptible.

Next – the young Picasso, Gleizes, Metzinger.[106]

A step further – and the blossoming of Picasso.

The object – the "cause" – is already disappearing.

It has already dissolved and disappeared.

It has exploded in general outlines and elements, as fragments and "stage wings" (the continuity of Piranesi), which build a world of new spaces, volumes, and their interrelationships.

Leftists of the arts and...ecstasy?

Picasso and ecstasy?

Picasso and...*pathos*?

Whoever has seen *Guernica* will be even less surprised by the possibility of such an assertion.

The Germans, looking at *Guernica*, asked the author:

"Did you do this?"

And proudly the painter answered:

"No – *you!*"[107]

And probably it is difficult to find – although one should include the *Destios* of Goya (*The Disasters of War*) – a fuller and more agonizing expression of the inner tragic dynamics of human annihilation.

But it is interesting that even on the paths leading here to the militant Spaniard's explosion of the *pathos* of social indignation could be seen the tie of Picasso with ecstasy, in relation to his actual method in earlier stages of his work.

There the ecstatic explosion did not coincide with the revolutionary essence of the theme.

And the explosion was not born from the theme.

There – like a unique elephant in a china shop – Picasso trampled and smashed any kind of merely "cosmically established order hateful to him" as such.

Not knowing where to lash out at those who were guilty in the social disorder of this "order of things," he lashed out at "things" and "order," before he suddenly "began to see clearly" in *Guernica* – where and in what lay discord and "initial causes."

Thus, curiously enough, Burger (*Cézanne and Hodler*), for example, includes Picasso before *Guernica* into the category of mystics.

And this is because of signs of – ecstasy.*

But in *Guernica* Picasso experiences a leap from an abstract ecstatic "protest" into the *pathos* of a revolutionary challenge to fascism trampling Spain.

And Picasso himself – into the ranks of the Communist Party.†

The fate of the majority of others – is different.

Internally they are not aware of ecstatic explosions.

For internally they do not burn with *pathos*.

They are not scorched by the flame of an enduring idea.

And with the most lofty of all possible ones – the idea of social protest.

With the fire of battle.

With the flame of the re-creation of the world.

They are not shaken by an inner peal of indignation.

In their souls the coiling lightning of wrath does not flash.

They do not blaze with white fire, in which service to an idea flares up with action.

And few are those who know ecstasy within their works.

The ideological impulse is lacking.

---

* This quote was cited by me on another occasion in the chapter *Nonindifferent Nature*.
† We will return to the problem of ecstasy in Picasso again in the chapter *Nonindifferent Nature*.

And there is no *pathos* of creation.

And they lie in the scheme of ecstasy like separate links of a single historical chain of the leaping movement of art as a whole, and in their personal biographies there are not those huge leaps and jumps, beyond the frame, of newer and newer limits, with which the life paths of El Greco and Piranesi overflow as well as Zola or Whitman, Pushkin, Gogol, Dostoyevsky, and Tolstoy.

Even if they do not burn with that hint of flame.

Even if the fires of their burning did not achieve the degree of the flame of social protest.

Nevertheless, they still are all devoured by ideas that are more valuable to them than life itself.

And only with such ideas.

Only with the obsession of such ideas.

Only with the self-dissolution and self-kindling of self in the service of those capable of giving birth to *pathos*.

Only with such a degree of incandescence of obsession is the ecstasy possible, shifting by continuous leaps through the expressive means of the artist enveloped by an idea, as by a flame; by images erupting like lava; by his heart nourishing his works with blood...

However, after this flight of personal *pathos*, which is somewhat unexpected on the pages of a research essay, let us turn back and look again at a series of features of the phenomenon that interests us – the work of that same Piranesi.

Perhaps here it would be most appropriate to linger slightly on the strange appearance of ecstasy, which for some reason is very often connected with visions of architectural images.

One of the greatest merits of architectural structures and ensembles is considered to be the harmonic transition of certain of their forms into others – like an "overflow" of some into others.

In completed examples of architecture this is discerned directly.

And the dynamics of these construction elements overflowing into each other promote that feeling of emotional seizure, that "abstract," "nonrepresentational" whole that the harmonic building truly represents for us.

The "abstract" and "nonrepresentational" quality in the given case in no way removes a very definitely expressed "imagistic" quality from such an ensemble.

And in this sense the architecture in different epochs is expressed in different ways, and, besides, it expresses a definite thought or idea in the most concrete sense of the word.

And this is why the "image" is always socially and historically conditioned and expresses a definite ideological content of a certain epoch.

The very rhythm (and melody) of forms harmoniously flowing over into each other is the reflection, through the interrelationship of volumes and space and the structure of materials, of a certain leading image of social concepts; and the completed building thus expresses and embodies the spiritual content of the nation-builder at a certain stage of its social and historical development.

[The mistake of the so-called leftist architecture – especially the constructivist – is in the rejection of the imagistic content of a building, which is totally reduced to utilitarian aims and the properties of building materials.

No less abominable in its architectural ideology is the substitution (in the imagistic content of the building) by an eclectic reconstruction "in parts" of elements of obsolete architectural epochs, reflecting in their forms ideologies of other nations and social and political conditions alien to us.]*

If one compares the perfect transitions of architectural forms into each other in such different examples as, let us say, the Hagia Sophia or Chartres Cathedral with a government building of the Nicholas epoch or a facade of the Pitti Palace, then one is clearly struck by the fundamental difference of the rhythmic characteristics both of the forms themselves and of the rhythmic course of their transition into each other, in the process of the composition of the organic architectural whole.

And each of these examples begins to speak with the strongest figurative rhetoric of its epoch: of its system or of its inner aspirations.

Typical is the expressive form of the palaces of sovereign feudal dukes, who built a fortress in the center of the city – a bulwark against the two independent communes of the townspeople.

The image of absolutism frozen in the invincibility of its principles – is the structure of buildings of the Nicholas epoch. The terrestrial emperor – the concrete "Tsar and God," leaning on the bureaucrat and policeman.

And on the other hand, the exalted "upward" flight of the Middle Ages in Gothic churches, directed toward the abstract, idealistic god of the mystics, whom the Roman high priest – the pope – had not yet succeeded in replacing.

However, in all the historical differentiation of architectural images in the composition of ensembles of different epochs, there lies the same basic principle – the principle of the transition of separate parts from one to the other, a principle of harmony resounding in different ways in different ages.

And it is on this second feature will will now focus our attention.

* [Here Eisenstein is clearly criticizing the so-called Stalinist style of eclectic architecture – HM.]

On the roads and crossroads of my path to cinematography I once had to study architecture as well (in the Institute of Civil Engineering).

I had just begun to work on a project when the whirlwind of the Civil War snatched me away and returned me not to the drawing boards of architectural projects, but transferred me to the stage of the theater, first as a set designer, then as a theater director, and then – as a film director.

The experience of an architect-designer and set designer for the theater did not last long.

But long enough to capture one – most fundamental – feature of the actual process of the "creation" of volume – space constructions.

Architecture is not called "frozen music" in vain ("Gefrorene Musik" – Goethe).

At the basis of the composition of its ensemble, at the basis of the harmony of its conglomerating masses, in the establishment of the melody of the future overflow of its forms, and in the execution of its rhythmic parts, giving harmony to the relief of its ensemble, lies that same "dance" that is also at the basis of the creation of music, painting, and cinematic montage.[108]

The massive and spatial caesuras between them, the spots of light and pits of darkness shading them, the conglomeration of details growing out of each other and then in scattering trills the outlines of the general contours – all this preceded by spots, lines, intersections, in the form of a rough draft, striving on paper to consolidate that flight of spatial visions, which is condemned to settle as stones or bricks, iron and concrete, glass and the prefabricated walls of a prepared structure.

At the basis of the architectural design is that same emotion that, from the level of inspired obsession, now overflows in a flame of ecstasy – and the dithyrambs of its visions consolidate the cathedral chorale frozen in stone, now by a magnificent marching step, whose image has been kept for centuries by the court and park structures of Versailles, now finally able to scatter through the artificial play of the pipes of porcelain shepherds and shepherdesses, which came to life through the coquettish play of the Trianonites...[109]

We are interested in the first case.

The case of maximum restraint.

A case when architecture is no longer an analogue to salon conversation by the fireplace but a unique stone "symbol of faith" – a passionate expression in stone of its ideological *credo*, whose ardor forces the stones to pile upon stone, and in their straining toward heaven, to forget their own gravity, to soar up in the lancet form of arches, hanging in the air and, piers unfolding between them, to return in them on the surfaces of stained-glass windows, burning like multicolored flames.

It is difficult to find structures more clearly representing the embodiment of ecstasy frozen in stone than Gothic churches.

It is difficult to find buildings capable by their structure alone to sequentially "turn on" to ecstatic harmony those entering beneath their vaults.

And to the degree that the structure and image of such a cathedral in all its features repeats that system of sequences of intensity bursting out of each other, those principles of being beside oneself and of passing into each other, and the final fusion together of all elements composing it, when the vaults tremble like an organ, and the sun streams through the stained-glass windows, etc., etc. – could serve as a separate chapter.

However, besides the social-historical validity of the image of the Gothic cathedral, of which much has been written, we are also interested in its inner prototype as an ecstatic vision.

And we have every right to suspect such a psychic basis for it.

If an ecstatic state had not been at the original source of this image, then the image, not having been born of such a state, would not have been in a position to be that "copybook sample," by which the experiencing viewer would have fallen into a state of ecstasy.

Thus Tolstoy wrote about music.

(The shortest path of direct transmission of the original state of the author – to the listener.)

Thus, the waltz tempo is a copy of that state in which Johann Strauss's "soul danced," repeating by its movements the structure of this tempo in the completed waltz. Those dancing join that same state in which its author was at the moment of the creation of the dance.

A rudimentary example of that phenomenon we know in the culture of ancient Mexico.

Here the examples are not as grandiose and systematically elaborated by a system of canons as in the culture of the Gothic cathedral. But just because of this, probably, they are clearer and more perceptible. The chimeras sit solemnly on these cathedrals like frightening visions of delirium.

Thousands of frightening figures, like a forest, covering the structures of their coeval Asiatic contemporaries – the Hindu "gopurams."[110]

But they (basically component images of separate natural phenomena: the head of an eagle above a woman's breast, a human body crowned by an elephant's head) in no way reach the level of horror of the ornamental monsters of ancient Mexico.

And here – the monstrosity and frightening unexpectedness derive not so much from the combination of various frightening details, actually belonging to various animals (the way in which Leonardo da Vinci created realistic models of unreal beings, and Barnum[111] demonstrated in the puppets at the beginning of his career), as much as in...the ornamental decomposition of visible objects of nature.

Your head literally whirls when you see the treatment of the corner of

 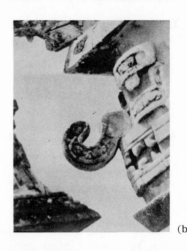

(a) (b)

Figure 10. (a, b) Sculptural decorations on the Mayan Pyramid, Yucatan. From Eisenstein's 1931 film *Que Viva Mexico*! (c) Detail from the frieze of the façade of the Governor's Palace, Uxmal, showing some of the two thousand sculptured stone elements comprising its decoration.

"Las Monjas Palace" in Uxmal[112] in the form of a decomposed human profile or in the serpent heads disintegrating into incredible disjointedness in the galleries behind the Teotihuacan pyramid.

How simply and clearly the stretched-out details compose "backwards" into "a bear": its face, eyes, claws, back on the light blue carpets of the tribes of the North American Indians.

How easily the whole is gathered together again "montagelike" from this ornamental distribution. And what real dizziness seizes you when the stone hook, protruding along a diagonal from the corner of the building, begins to be interpreted as a nose; you must look for deformed stone eyes through the system of carved stones going around both sides of the corner; and the teeth of the lower part of the treatment of the building suddenly appear as a system of monstrously transformed jaws.

Dizziness is the result of a constant slipping from the prototye face into this system of stretched-out details losing their human features, and again back to the face in a tormenting attempt to create the process through which one becomes the other, the original – a monstrous result – again – "backward" – to the original (without which it would be impossible "to interpret," to organize, to perceive, to include it into a system of representations comprehensible to us).

And...dizziness – is not simply a rhetorical phrase – it is what actually occurs.

For in the attempt to "enter" into the process of birth of these ecstatic –

(c)

Caption to Figure 10 (*cont.*)

actually "having become ecstatic" from the appearance given to them –
images of the ornamental decomposing of faces and heads, you enter a
system of the norms of that process, which gave birth to these images of
decomposed forms inaccessible to the normal state of consciousness [. . .]

. . .The visions of similar architectural images in states of exaltation
and ecstasy connected. . .with opium are described by De Quincy.[113]

(He calls his own devotion to opium a disease.)

. . .In the early stages of the malady, the splendours of my dreams were indeed
chiefly architectural; and I beheld such pomp of cities and palaces as never yet
was beheld by waking eye, unless in the clouds. . .

Later he quotes from Wordsworth[114] ". . .a passage which describes, as an appearance actually beheld in the clouds, what in many of its circumstances I saw frequently in sleep."*

In the same passage of poetry he clearly stops at the moment of the continuous fluctuation of architectural ensembles that piled up with threatening clouds:

"The sublime circumstances – 'that on their restless fronts bore stars,' – might have been copied from my own architectural dreams, so often did it occur..."

These quotations would be enough to compare Piranesi's amazing architectural visions flowing into each other, not only in the uniqueness of their system, but also in their figurative system, with the reflection in concrete forms of the fantastic architecture of these authors' ecstatic states.

However, this is also confirmed by the fact that De Quincy uses, namely, Piranesi's *Dungeons* as the most precise correspondence to those architectural visions that seize him in states of exaltation under the influence of opium:

Many years ago, when I was looking over Piranesi's *Antiquities of Rome*, Coleridge,[115] then standing by, described to me a set of plates from that artist, called his Fantasies, and which record the scenery of his own visions during the delirium of a fever. Some of these (I describe only from memory of Coleridge's account) represented vast Gothic halls, on the floor of which stood mighty engines and machinery, wheels, cables, catapults, etc., expressive of enormous power put forth, or resistance overcome. Creeping along the sides of the walls, you perceived a staircase; and upon this, groping his way upward, was Piranesi himself. Follow the stairs a little farther, and you perceive them reaching an abrupt termination, without any balustrade, and allowing no step onwards to him who should reach the extremity, except into the depths below. Whatever is to become of poor Piranesi, at least you suppose that his labors must now in some way terminate. But raise your eyes, and behold a second flight of stairs still higher, on which again Piranesi is perceived, by this time standing on the very brink of the abyss. Once again elevate your eye, and a still more aerial flight of stairs is described; and there, again, is the delirious Piranesi, busy on his aspiring labors: and so on, until the unfinished stairs and the hopeless Piranesi both are lost in the upper gloom of the hall. With the same power of the endless growth and self-reproduction did my architecture proceed in dreams. (pp. 249–50.

We must not be disturbed by the factual imprecision of his details.

This *Dungeons* is called *Fantasies*.

The movement of Piranesi down the stairs of his own fantasies is – inventions.

There is no sheet in the series *Dungeons* like the one described.

* [Thomas De Quincy, *Confessions of an English Opium-Eater*, Routledge, London, 1905, p. 250 – HM.]

But the fact that the flights of stairs reflected the inner flight of the author himself – is obvious.

And it is not accidental that the combined memories of two poets – one about the etchings and the other of a story about them – embodied this thought into a real image of the author of the etchings running along the staircase passages.

There is also no evidence of visions of allegedly feverish delirium engraved on these sheets. And the reflection in them of states of real exaltation – is nothing more than a conjecture without any real basis. But an even more basic mistake is the designation of the hall as – Gothic.

This is not so much a mistake as the ecstasy of Piranesi caught quite precisely, an ecstasy expressed through an architectural image, particularly fully expressed in Gothic halls and cathedrals.

The scheme, device, formula, or method is particularly apparent when you see them applied not only in pure form, but also in parody.

Parody can be of two types.

Either both the theme and manner of its application are parodied – "made fun of" – and then parody is something attacking from the side.

Or a parody of the method (device, formula, scheme) arises when it is not the "manner" but the "theme" that is subjected to mockery. Then these means are in the hands of the author, and he uses them when, for example, to achieve persiflage [banter], "the insignificant" is raised to the height of *pathos.*

The application to the "insignificant" of the means of treating what is "valuable and significant" – in the incongruity of the story's content and form – by itself produces a mocking, comic result.

(Thus, for example, the comic "catalog" of Rabelais sounds as if it were a parody of Whitman, in its "patheticizing" the trifles of everyday life from the details of the childhood of the giant Gargantua.)

A similar case has arisen in my own experience.

It is interesting to note that it wedged itself into the middle of the shooting of *The Old and the New* (during suspended production) – that is, in the middle of shooting that very film in which the problems of *pathos* were refined.

This "case" is one of the scenes of the film *October* (produced in 1927).

This scene is the ascent of the head of the pre-October Provisional Government, Kerensky, up the Jordan Staircase of the Winter Palace, treated as an ironic symbol of his ascent to the peak of high power.

The "trick" of this scene (and its ironic effect) consisted in the fact that the same piece of the ascent of the chief up the marble staircase of the Winter Palace was joined together one after the other "without end." Of course, not really without end, but in the length of four or five retakes in which this scene was shot. During the shooting of what was a simple everyday "domestic" episode, it was conceived as being extremely...

ironic in behavior – after his ascent up the staircase, Kerensky "democratically" shakes hands with the former tsar's janitor, standing on the top landing of the staircase.

Already in the course of editing emerged the concept of a *pathos*-parody solution with the repeated shot of ascending the stairs.

Thus the exact same ascent piece is repeated four or five times.

Besides the "insignificance" of the object, an ironic effect is achieved by the fact that in the scheme of *pathos* construction – where a move (jump) from dimension to dimension, from piece to piece, is obligatory in the design of ecstasy – here not only were there no "jumps" of quality, but even no change in the piece itself.

From below Kerensky went up in one shot.

From below – up that same staircase – in the second.

From below up – in the third.

In the fourth.

In the fifth.

This absence of qualitative crescendo from piece to piece is emphasized by the fact that a crescendo of captions went into the cuts between these pieces and carried ranks of increasing importance, with which this pre-October toady of the bourgeoisie obligingly decorated himself.

"The minister of this," "the minister of that," "the president of the council of ministers," "the commander-in-chief."

And the repetition of the same method of depiction, in its turn, "invalidated" the crescendo of callings and ranks – reducing them to the level of that absurd ascent "to nowhere," which the feet of the commander-in-chief, fettered by English-type leggings, tramped out on the marble stairs.

As we can see, by an essentially insignificant system of displacement, the *pathos*-filled ascent of Piranesi merges from the visions of De Quincy and Coleridge into the ironic marking time of Alexander Fedorovich Kerensky.

"From the sublime to the ridiculous – is one step."

In the essence of the phenomenon as well as in the principles of its compositional embodiment!

Thus, this example throws light on our basic principle from yet one more angle of scrutiny.

From the position of ironic parody construction.

The "significance" and meaning of those very forms flowing into each other – architectural forms that belong to a system of more stable objects of nature organized by man, has already been discussed by us above.

[...] However, let us go back even further, back for just a moment, and again compare what Piranesi does in his classical *Carceri* with what Giesecke calls the *Ur-Carceri*.

The merging of these two variants is extremely remarkable. One and the same technical compositional device is in them absolutely everywhere.

For the already existing variant (see, for example, in Giesecke the reproductions of both variants of the title page or the page with the powerful monumental staircase with armor, helmets, and flags at its foot), Piranesi definitely draws new foregrounds.

These new foregrounds are hurled one more step into the depths by planes of the deepening conglomeration of forms.

Even without this, the very composition of the architectural ensembles is built on the continuously diminishing and contracting repetitions of one and the same architectural motif, which (in terms of perspective) appear to thrust themselves out of each other.

Literally stretching lengthwise, reduced to the diameter of a single telescope tube, these diminishing arches, engendered by the arches of a plane brought closer, these flights of stairs, these progressively diminishing new stair landings bursting upward, plunge into the depths. Bridges engender new bridges. Columns – new columns. Vaults – vaults. And so on – ad infinitum. As far as the eye will allow you to follow.

Raising the intensity of the engravings from variant to variant, Piranesi, while adding new foregrounds, seems to push even more into the depths, yet one more stage deeper, the whole fugue created by him of volumes and spaces consecutively plunging deeper, joined and inter-sected by the stairs.

Plane bursts out of plane and like a system of explosions, plunges into the depths.

Or, through a system of continuously arising new foregrounds replacing them, it thrusts forward from the sheet of the etching advancing on to the viewer.

Forward or into the depths? – Isn't it all the same here? And in this simultaneity of opposing thrusts – forward or into the depths – one more pair – a pair of opposites – is again triumphantly shot in ecstasy!

As we can see, not only in a scheme of finished construction, but even in the method of the process of construction itself, "pushing out" from plane to plane.

It is necessary to stop here for a moment and say a few words about the significance of perspective reduction.

Its role in Piranesi is twofold.

First of all, the common one – illusion-spatial perspective, that is – "drawing" the eye into the imagined depth of space, which is represented according to the rules of how it was used to seeing receding distances in actual reality.

But there is something else – "second."

In Piranesi perspectives are constructed in a very unique way.

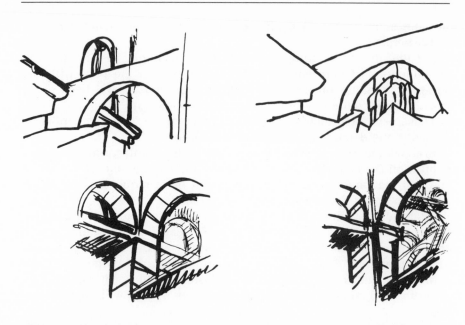

Figure 11. Four sketches by Eisenstein analyzing Piranesi's *Dungeon*.

And their basic uniqueness lies in their inherent interruptions and leaps.

Nowhere in *Dungeons* do we find an uninterrupted perspective view into the depths.

But everywhere an initial movement of plunging into the depths through perspective is interrupted by a bridge, column, arch, or passage.

Each time the perspective movement is caught up again behind a similar column or semicircular arch.

But it is not in this perspective key, but in a new one – usually in a considerably reduced scale of representation than you would expect or wish to suggest.

This gives a double effect.

A direct one, which is manifested in the fact that such a reduced representation through a break in an arch, or from under a bridge, or between two columns, gives the illusion of the extremely great remoteness of what is represented in the distance.

But even stronger is the second effect.

We have already said that the scale of these new pieces of architectural space seem to be different from what the eye "would expect" to see.

In other words: The size and movement of the architectural elements striving, let us say, to meet an arch, finish by drawing their scale behind the arch in a natural way, that is, the eye expects to see behind the arch a continuation of the architectural theme in front of the arch, reduced in a normal way through perspective.

Instead of this, another architectural motif looks through the arch at it, but moreover – this motif, in terms of perspective reduction, is approximately twice as large as the eye would suppose.

And as a result there is the feeling that the suggested arched structure seems to "explode" out of the naturally suggested scale into a qualitatively different scale – into a scale of heightened intensity (in the given case – exploding "out of itself" from the normally presumed spatial recession).

From this arises the unexpected qualitative leap in scale and space.

And the series of spatial depths, cut off from each other by columns and arches, are constructed as disconnected links of independent spaces, strung together not according to the quality of uninterrupted perspective, but as a sequential collision of spaces with different qualitative intensities of depths.

(This effect is built on the ability of our eye to continue by inertia a motion that has once been set up. The collision of this "presumed" path of motion with the other path substituted for it gives the effect of a jolt. The phenomenon of cinematographic movement is also constructed on an analogous ability to retain the imprint of the viewer's impression.)

It is very curious that in certain features of this method, Piranesi corresponds to the "vertical" landscapes...of Chinese and Japanese painting (*kakemono*).

This is its scheme [see Figure 12].

Here also an amazing feeling of ascension is achieved.

But the nature of this "ascension" is very different from the examples of Piranesi.

If in Piranesi everything is – dynamics, whirlwind, the furious tempo of drawing one into the depths and into the interior, then here everything – is a calm and solemn ascent to the illuminated heights.

Both this and the other model in their emotional effect go beyond the limits of the usual realistic effect.

The first – by passionate intensity.

The second – by lucidity.

In them it seems the active aggressiveness of Western ecstasy was imprinted (Spanish, Italian) in contrast to the ecstatic quietism[116] of the East (India, China).

It is interesting to compare the different means by which these effects were achieved, different in nature but similarly ecstatic in relation to the "normal" course of effect on things.

The attempts of the Italian are directed with full force to making out of the flat surface of the engraving a truly captivating three-dimensional body.

Figure 12. Eisenstein's schematic analysis of "vertical" landscape in Chinese art.

The attempt of the Chinese – to make out of three-dimensional reality – a two-dimensional image of contemplation.

This is the source of the representational canons – the extreme perspective of one and – the reverse perspective in the other.

Common to both – is the interruption of the continuity of representation done in an identical sequential manner.

In Piranesi the continuity of perspective is broken by columns, arches, and bridges.

In Choko and Yosa Buson[117] the fusion of representation is simply interrupted or "motivated" by streaks of clouds.

After each such interruption or layer of clouds that slipped through, the next representational element of landscape (a mountain mass) is again not given in the scale dictated by an effect of real recession.

But, in contrast to Piranesi, here the new element turns out to have been unexpectedly decreased, but also unexpectedly increased (also exactly twice as much!):

not:

but:

The volume of the object (the mountain ridge) also is "beside itself" in relation to the presumed scale.

But this is a leap not in an increase of the range between the normal size of details in perspective, but on the contrary – in a decrease of this range.

In the diagram below it is apparent what is happening in both cases.

Let the real perspective reduction of the object AB at the point A_1 be expressed through A_1B_1.

Piranesi at this point depicts it in measure A_1C (i.e., $A_1C < A_1B_1$.)

Consequently the "jump is more powerful, and the illusory sense of depth is greater, and the eye, carrying point A_1 to A_2, plunges into the depths.

The Chinese at the same point A_1 represent the object in the dimension of A_1D (where $A_1D > A_1B_1$).

The jump between AB and A_1D is *less* than the normal perspective interval $AB - A_1B_1$, and the eye, bringing point A_1 to A_3, stretches it forward into the plane.

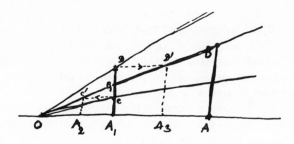

As a result both cases have an ecstatic effect, going beyond the limits of a simple true reflection of the appearance of phenomena.

But they are characterized in a different (opposite) way: One serves as the expression of the pantheistic quietism, characteristic of the ecstatic contemplation of the East; the other expresses the "explosiveness" typical of "active" ecstasy – one of the proclivities of "Western" ecstasy. (This certainly does not mean that the East is unaware of the fanatic ecstasy of the dervishes or of Shakhsy-Bakhsy, and Spain – of the mystical ecstasies of St. John of the Cross[118]; or that the works of Fra Beato Angelico[119] do not correspond to the Bodhisattva[120] of India or the Mongol demons with the works of El Greco. This division, of course, is quite "conventional."

Quietism tries to bring opposites together by *dissolving them into each other*. Hence the reduced scope of the difference in size repeats this, returning and bringing the explosive jumps to a single smooth flow.

The other type of ecstasy acts in a different way: Maximally intensifying each of the opposites, it tries at the highest point of this intensification to force them to *penetrate each other*, thereby raising their shattering dynamism to the highest pitch.

The present section of this work is basically devoted to this type. Attention is given to quietism in another chapter in this collection – in Nonindifferent Nature.

This method of capturing the depths of space is close to me because of my own work on the shot.

It is interesting that this method has been most distinctly formulated in *The Old and the New*, and its most extensive application occurs in the set designs for *Ivan the Terrible*, promoting the effect of the "giganticness" of the interiors. I wrote about the significance of the different scales in relation to the theme of Ivan in *Izvestiva* (Feb. 14, 1945) in connection with the premiere of the first series of the film. And it was probably not accidental that I referred to their size not by a static term, but by a term reflecting the dynamic conception of "growing size," "rising" vaults, etc. The feeling put into them of the obsession and exaltation of the theme achieved by the author appears through the terminology.

This method consists of the fact that the "set design proper" for my shots never in itself exhausts the real "place of action."

Most often this set design proper seems to be a "spot in the background," which appears through a system of foregrounds placed like "wings" attached endlessly in front of it, driving this set design proper further and further into the distance.

In my work set designs are inevitably accompanied by the unlimited surface of the floor *in front* of it, allowing the bringing forward of unlimited separate foreground details; and a collection of just such details: portable columns, parts of vaults, stoves, piers, or objects of everyday use.

The last point in this method is the close-up of the actor carried beyond all thinkable limits. Over the actor's shoulder is put the whole space in which can be outlined the set design with all its substructures, and the back of whose neck covers that part of the studio that can no longer be fettered by the insufferable details of the "place of action."

This "ecstatic" method of construction of set designs according to a scheme... based on the telescope, is not limited in my work to the area of the visual and plastic.

As in all other "schemes" of ecstatic construction, this also occurs in my work in the dramatization.

If in respect to *Potemkin* and *The General Line*[121] we touched on a "transference into the opposite" within the course of the drama itself, and in *The Old and the New* the very pivot of the action consisted in such a transference from the "old" to the "new," then in another epic-drama case we are dealing with a pure scheme of phases of a developing historical subject that consecutively – "like a crossbow" – eject each other.

It is in just this way that the scheme of the film about the Fergansky Canal was constructed, which we planned with P. A. Pavlenko[122] right after *Alexander Nevsky*, but, unfortunately, it was not realized.

I conceived it as a triptych of the struggle of man for water.

Three phases:

Tamerlane,*

    Tsarism,

        The kolkhoz [collective farm] system.

How should one connect in a dynamic unity three similar epochs standing apart from each other by centuries and decades?

Here the device turns out to be the "triple crossbow" separated in the tempo of narration – the double transference beyond oneself arranged in retrospective sequence.

The first link.

The epic-lay deployment of Tamerlane's campaigns and Urcheng's sieges passed by.

And its tragic finale flowed together into an image of an old man, the narrator Tokhtasyn, singing about these times of yore.

The figure of the old man closed the first link.

And the singing old man opened

the second link.

It narrated – no longer in primordial forms but in common, everyday forms – the tone of battle for a centimeter of an irrigation ditch of Central Asia impoverished under the tsars, a battle, replacing the scope of the campaigns of medieval titans, that drove hundreds of thousands of soldiers against each other, draining rivers from besieged cities, fighting each other by depletions and by the influx of water that drowned the besieging armies.

In the unequal battle with the bey [Turkish governor] and the tsarist official, the old singer abandoned his native Central Asia after having begun the mournful page of this story with his song.

The daughter was taken away by a merchant and bey "for a debt."

Along with the father, the meditator and nonresistor to evil, the young son broke away, leaving for the liberation movement.

And the old man dragged himself into the Iranian foothills, far away from the people.

But even this episode turned out to be a narrative: not a song of the past, but a tale around a campfire.

---

* ["In 1395 Moscow barely escaped invasion by the army of one of the greatest conquerors of history, Tamerlane, who had spread his rule through the Middle East and the Caucasus... Tamerlane's forces actually devastated Riazan and advanced upon Moscow, only to turn back to the steppe before reaching the Oka River" (N. Riazanovsky, *A History of Russia*, Oxford University Press, New York, 1970, p. 11) – HM.]

The tale of an engineer-builder, one of the participants of the unprecedented construction of the Fergansky Canal.

The engineer was that same young man – the son of Tokhtasyn, who had left his father – but the "second link" of the film was the story of how, passing through the revolution, he came to the Fergansky construction.

And his story opened

the third link of the epic narration.

The third link, beginning with his tale, unfolded a new monumental fresco of new campaigns by masses in the thousands, but no longer in the form of a battle against each other, but in that unique battle that remains the lot of a man freed from exploitation, freed from the chains of slavery, a man creating Communist society* – a battle with the elements, a victory over nature, a subjection of the natural forces to the creative genius of free man.

In the fury of this construction, the lively Tokhtasyn returned from the Iranian foothills and met his son in the joyful moment when the water begins to flow...

In the epic structure of this film, as if in slow motion, that same telescopic structure slowly unfolds that, in its springlike, instantaneous leap from phase to phase, we saw in the action of the ecstatic effect in preceding examples.

[Examples of ecstasy]

At this point I remember an amusing incident that may serve as a transition to the next section of examples of ecstasy.

My general conception of the *pathos* composition, as it has been discussed here, had been developed long before.

And even if it had not been worked out at once in all its aspects, still its basic elements had been studied in such detail that even thirty years later I included it in a course of lectures on how a director composes a film of *pathos*.

I remember how, after one of those lectures – I think it was in 1933 – concerning the ecstatic leap within a composition of *pathos*, one of my audience came up to me, Comrade D., and with a sly grin mysteriously communicated to me: "Sergei Mikhailovich, I bet you couldn't guess what inventions your lecture made me think of?"

He shook his head even more mysteriously at a question about the details of this improbable invention (as to the shape of his head, it was

---

* [I read these words now with tragic irony, for the Fergansky Canal, along with the White Sea Canal and other "socialist" constructions of the Five Year Plans, were in the main built with slave labor from Gulag, as documented by A. Solzhenitsyn. Perhaps that was the real reason Stalin forbade the making of yet another Eisenstein film – HM.]

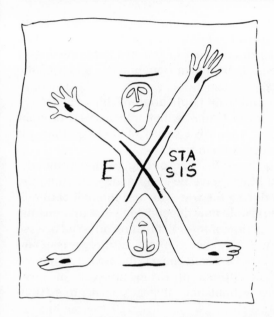

Figure 13. Eisenstein's drawing (Mexico, c. 1930) showing
ex stasis (=*pathos*).

somewhere in between the head of a tapir and a dolphin, and the profile
seemed to resemble the beak of a parrot, if such a beak could
impetuously puff up from a terrible attack of a cold; add a small,
extremely lively black eye to this...though what does his appearance
matter to you?!)

Comrade D. refused to divulge his secret to me, but promised to
confess his ideas in a few days.

In several days he really did come up to me again, but with an
embarrassed look rather than a mysterious one.

The invention turned out to be a fiasco.

It turns out that the contents of my lecture on ecstasy made him think
of...a rocket missile system of consecutive ejections of one rocket out of
another.

He rushed over with this idea to someone in the military department.

However, there they calmed him down, saying that something of the
sort had already been investigated there and was well known.

What it was exactly and to what degree – is unknown.

Later something of the sort really seemed to have been adopted in the
Finnish campaign, judging by a chance tale, somewhat confused, of one
of the participants of the battles in Finland.

In general, rocket missiles of the "chain" type seemed to have been
adopted for practice even in World War II.

It is quite probable that the principle of the rocket missile is actually
quite ancient, and there is an opinion that even in 1232 the Chinese used

such missiles against the attacking Mongols. Since the fourteenth century this missile was widespread in Europe. But definitely since 1850 – when the perfection of precise aim increases – the missiles of the rocket type being imprecise in this regard, disappear from practice and from the area of any theoretical interest.

The honor of a new revival and wide application of this principle in World War II belongs to the Soviet Union, which, since 1941, brought down on the German invaders a massive series of rockets from our multirocket projector (nicknamed Katusha).

The Germans are building their "V-2" according to this principle. England and later the United States have been diligently studying the discoveries made in this area during the war. The new intensification of interest in the idea of a rocket missile now depends on what this missile would be like if freed from the action of the so-called recoil – the reverse push that unavoidably is produced by each common artillery missile on the weapon ejecting it. This lack of recoil makes the rocket principle particularly valuable under conditions of firing missiles of great destructive power from relatively light and unsteady structures (light airplanes or small sea units).

But I have no particular interest in the "simple" rocket missile – or if I have, it is only because the "beautiful" here is in the initial active principle being taken in reverse or the "impeding" principle of the "normal" type of artillery. The principle of recoil is what should be taken as the active basis, transported from the area of counteraction into the principle of action itself; the power impetus is directed totally to the side, and, figuratively speaking, "the cannon" is reversed with its back to the opponent and strikes at him by means of the infinitely increased power of recoil aimed in his direction.

Thus the significance of the common expression, "cannon go to battle backwards,"* is reversed from the image of where to strike the enemy, into a new phase more shattering in its blow! This almost recalls a similar paradox in the area of agricultural industry.

It is well known what a scourge the locust is.

But it is also well known what a great bearer of fatty tissue is this pest, which utterly devours the crops, grain, and earthly vegetation.

This fat forces steam engines to skid helplessly on the rails covered with the squashed little bodies of locusts.

And during my stay in Mexico they told me about an incident that took place in South America, where it turns out in certain districts it was more profitable to process the fatty substance of the locust (which was not allowed to develop to the stage of being able to fly) than to try to save the carelessly sown and unsown fields.

* ["*Pushki k boyu stali zadom,*" a Russian idiomatic expression – HM.]

A comparison of a military-technical incident with an incident from the biological-zoological field (where else could you find a similar use of locusts?!) is quite normal at this point, when spheres of principles previously rigidly opposing each other are closely connected, spheres that lie at the basis of physics and biology, the treatment of inorganic phenomena of nature, which merge with the norms of the organic kingdom of nature, etc.

This will be discussed below.

But even now it is curious to note that the rocket movement of missiles whose application clearly has a broad future has as its most profound "prototype" a phenomenon that is purely biological and, one might add, in its earliest stages of development.

Doesn't it seem that this principle is completely "copied" from the characteristics of the first steps on the path of independently moving *shifts* of the so-called Brownian movement in colloids?

This is how John Yerbury Dent describes the scheme of how molecules of living protoplasm shift:

Now let us imagine this catalyst as a compound with a big molecule: It has the attributes and behaviour of a colloid – that is, it is big enough to be comparatively stable in an environment of vibrating smaller molecules, yet small enough to be jostled by them. It exhibits what is called Brownian movement. We also must picture this molecule as being able to absorb and combine with certain molecules which we may consider its food, and able to break down at the other end of its molecular chain, giving out molecules as its waste products. This large molecule is impinged upon on all sides by other molecules but, it is able to absorb some of them. It is not displaced by the molecules it absorbs, and it suffers some recoil from the molecules it discharges; in other words, it moves towards its food and away from its waste products. It has developed another of the attributes of life. It is quite possible to picture all movement of protoplasmic molecules in this way. The direction is governed by the absorption of some molecules and the discharge of others.*

However, let us return to the type of rocket missile my lecture on "the formula of ecstasy" inspired Comrade D.

It is quite apparent that such a "formula" applied to the treatment of increasing speed of the missiles (or flying machines) must definitely take into account the normal limits of speed, just as the flight of ecstasy must regard the conditions of normal emotion, and as *pathos* must regard – simple uplift.

And it cannot be that technical thought – so skillfully using the "ecstasy" of transferring certain forms of energy into others, provoking "explosions" by a definite form of composed mixtures, which are

* John Yerbury Dent, *The Human Machine*, Alfred A. Knopf, New York, 1937, p. 7.

transferred into the gaseous state, etc. – would not use such a construction so distinctly ecstatic, increasing the speed of flight.

It is curious that this idea was not applied in the prewar period, that it also was not used during the war; the first (in any case, published) data on a serious introduction of a similar idea into new technology appears only at the height of the period of postwar existence, when the world, hardly yet reestablished, already has begun what devilishly looks like preparations for a new war.

Thus, only by June 1948, – judging by the information from the mid-year congress of members of the American Society of Engineers and Mechanics in Chicago – similar experiments and a practical treatment of the application of this principle became a reality.[123]

It is interesting that the data in this direction go from the more crude and superficial applications of the ecstatic formula to the most refined areas, connected not only with constructions of new flying devices, but with a revision of the conception of the actual physical structure of matter, giving practical results that force you to observe "in a new aspect" a whole series of positions of theoretical physics that had appeared to be stable and indestructible.

Thus, Colonel Philip B. Klein, a staff member of Major Air Command of American aviation (the Air Material Command), describes the simplest possible of these aspects – the rocket plane, which is ejected from a "flying" airwomb rushing at full speed. According to his statements, such an experimental rocket plane (XS-1), ejected from the "womb" of a B-29, as shown in the test in California, is close to achieving the speed of sound.

Up until now, still not having tested to the full capacity of the power available to it, this rocket plane XS-1 and the model following it apparently confront one major difficulty – the inability of the pilot's reflexes to function in similar circumstances. This forces Colonel Klein to direct the attention of engineers and designers to the fact that in the future they must invent "something of a type" that would completely free the work of controlling similar apparatus, by means going far beyond the limits of functions conceivable for man.

More interesting and precise in construction – and, I might add, solved inwardly completely according to the "ecstatic prescription" – are the so-called space rockets on which M. J. Zucrow, professor at Purdue University, reported.

Part of the problem concerns the realization of flights, totally beyond the limits of the atmosphere, encircling the earth, and into regions free from the earth's gravity. In order to launch similar rockets, it turns out that it is not necessary to wait ages for man to master the control of atomic energy. It is possible to solve this problem by means of that same fuel (liquid oxygen is a component) on which the rocket planes

XS-1 work, if at the basis of the construction principle one puts the "multistep" principle, according to which a system of tandem rocket motors acts like a consecutive "chain," ejecting the "head one" forward – into space. The difficulty in its practical realization is still the high temperature (5,000 or more degrees Fahrenheit) to which the chamber of the inner structure is subjected. If this difficulty is finally overcome, then the given construction completely ensures the possibility of passengers flying beyond the limits of the space directly surrounding our planet...*

The third "deepening" of the principle – from an airplane ejected from an airplane, through a rocket ejected by a rocket, ejected by a rocket, ejected by a rocket, etc.[†] – to a fraction of the material ejected in an endless series of chain reactions of new particles flying out – carries us beyond the limits of the Chicago conference of the practitioners of rocket construction – into areas of the practical application of the atom, which is now so much obsessing the imagination of nations after the destructive action of the atom bombs dropped on Japan.

The Gothic

Already several times in the course of this work the sharp profile of Gogol protruded through its colorful variety, as a shadow slipping through its separate sections. [...][125]

It would be too simple and too easy to flood these pages with another sea of quotes, taken from well-known pages of *pathos* in his works, in which digressions "rear up" once in awhile in his poems, stories, or tales.

The "ecstatic" structure of them is distinct and clear everywhere.

And we will relate Gogol to our theme in more detail at this point.

In an area with which he wouldn't usually be associated.

Let us consider Gogol alongside of Piranesi...

In regards to...architecture.

This would appear to be strange and unexpected only if one forgets how many months Gogol spent in that same Rome that put Giovanni Battista's imagination in a fever.

Forgetting about those spiritual "prisons" through which Gogol drove his reader in "The Inferno" and "Purgatory" of the final parts of *Dead Souls*,[126] out of which he himself so desperately sought an escape into the light, like the figure of Piranesi conceived by Coleridge, rushing along the precipices of the passages and staircases of his own etchings.

---

* I am describing these data according to a report on a conference in *Newsweek* of June 30, 1947.
† I treat this formula here in the manner of the "translanguage" of Gertrude Stein[124] because in the next section this will help us establish the "correspondence" between the material of this chapter and the next.

And having quite forgotten Gogol's wonderfully passionate enthusiasm for architecture.

And how Gogol perceives architecture and how he writes about it – probably the closest approximation of how Piranesi forces it to live and tremble in his etchings.

Namely, the way Gogol writes about architecture as a form of being beside oneself and as a form of transition of one form into another; in the *pathos* of his descriptions he reveals the ecstatic character of his nature, as well as a reflection in the very principles of architecture of those basic necessary strivings of our nature, which find their expression in architecture.

There are probably few who now reread the *Arabesques*. Even fewer readers linger over the article "On the Architecture of Our Time." Yes, and even I would have hardly glanced at it if it had not been put next to the article "A Few Words on Pushkin," which I needed for another, quite special occasion.

Therefore, this article should be discussed in detailed excerpts.

It is particularly characteristic that, of all the various types of architecture, the kind that is most attractive to Gogol is the architecture that is the most ecstatic – the Gothic.

Not in vain, Coleridge (and after him De Quincy), in defining the actual style of Piranesi's visions, turned to the term "Gothic hall." Incorrect in defining the true style of these halls, but quite correct in defining what Piranesi (ecstatically) does with these halls!

...No matter which kind of architecture it be – the smooth, monumental Egyptian, the huge and colorful architecture of the Hindus, the luxurious architecture of the Moors, the inspired and gloomy Gothic, the graceful Greek – all are good if they are suited to the specified construction; they will all be magnificent only when they are truly comprehended.

. . . If, however, one must give a definite preference to one of these architectural styles, then I would always give it to the Gothic...

. . . But it disappeared, this beautiful architecture! As soon as the enthusiasm of the Middle Ages was extinguished, the thought of man was dismembered and strove for a multiplicity of different aims; as soon as the unity and wholeness of the one disappeared, so did the grandeur as well. Its forces, once having been dismembered, became small: it suddenly produced a multiplicity of wonderful things in all shades and varieties, but no longer something grand, something gigantic....

. . . They passed – those centuries when faith, strong, ardent faith, directed all thoughts, all minds, all actions to one end; when the artist strove to raise his consciousness higher and higher toward heaven, to it alone he strained, and before it, almost in sight of it, he reverentially raised his praying hands. His building flew toward heaven; narrow windows, columns, vaults stretched infinitely toward the heights; transparent, almost lace-like spires like smoke appeared over them, and the magnificent temple was as great before the common dwellings of the people as the demands of the soul were great before the demands of the body....

...Gothic architecture, that Gothic architecture which was formed before the end of the Middle Ages, is a phenomenon which the taste and imagination of man has never again produced...In it everything is unified together: this forest of vaults rising harmoniously high over your head, windows, huge and narrow, with numberless variations and intertwining, joined to this terrifying, colossal mass of the tiniest, most colorful decorations, this light web of carving, entangling it with its net, winding around it from the foot to the top of the spire and flying with it to the heavens; grandeur as well as beauty, luxury and simplicity, heaviness and lightness – these are the virtues which never, except for this period, were contained in architecture. Entering into the sacred darkness of this temple, through which the windows multicolored light peers fantastically, and raising your eyes upward, where lancet vaults lose themselves and intersect one over another, one over another, endlessly – it is quite natural to feel an involuntary terror in your soul at the presence of a female saint, whom the insolent mind of man dare not touch...

...Look more often at the famous Cologne Cathedral – there is all of its [Gothic – SME] perfection and grandeur. A finer monument was never produced by ancient or modern epochs. I prefer Gothic architecture because it allows the artist to engage in more revelry. The imagination strives more vividly and more ardently to height rather than breadth. And therefore one must use Gothic architecture only in churches and in high rising buildings. Lines and Gothic pilasters without cornices, close to each other, must fly through the whole structure. It is sad if they stand far apart from each other, if the building does not rise up to at least twice its height, if not triple! It then destroys itself. Raise it as it should be: so that its walls rise higher, higher, as high as possible,* so that their numerous corner columns surround them more densely like arrows, like poplars, like pines! Let there be no cut, no break or cornice that would give another direction or would diminish the size of the building! So that they be equal from the foundations to the very summit! Huge windows, varied in form, more colossal than their height! More ethereal, lighter spires! So that the more everything rises upward the more it flies and penetrates. And remember the most important thing: there is no comparison of height and breadth. The word breath must disappear. Here there is one principle idea – height. †

Magnificent pages!
Magnificent in the feeling of the *pathos* of Gothic architecture.

---

* Wasn't the cry of Plevako, so famous for its – pathetic quality, taken from here, which had resounded in the trial of the Mother Superior Mitrofanya,[127] which, as is well-known, lay at the basis of the subject of A. N. Ostrovsky's *Wolves and Sheep?*

† N. V. Gogol, *On the Architecture of Our Time*, collected works in 6 volumes, vol. 6, Goslitizdat, Moscow, 1959, pp. 40–61. This article is cited later. [Victor Hugo, "*Preface to Cromwell*," also sees contrast as a mark of modern genius: "...it is of the fruitful union of the grotesque and the sublime types that modern genius is born – so complex, so diverse in its forms, so inexhaustible in its creations; and therein directly opposed to the uniform simplicity of the genius of the ancients." In G. Anderson and Robert Warnock, eds., Scott Foresman, *Tradition and Revolt*, Chicago, 1951, p. 356 – HM.]

And wonderful examples of the feeling for the characteristic features of *pathos* construction.

A basic significance that, in the given case, has the ardor of an idea.

The flowing of all variety into the problem of expressing the unity of this idea.

The unity of opposites as a factor of its expression ("grandeur as well as beauty," "luxury and simplicity," "heaviness and lightness." At another place in his article Gogol writes: "The true effect is contained in sharp antitheses").

Repetition leading to infinity ("lancet vaults one over another... without end").

The leap from dimension to dimension ("so that their numerous corner columns surround them densely like arrows, like poplars, like pines"; "lace-like spires," coming out of the stone substance and, "like some," appeared over the building).

And in the statement itself about the features of the Gothic – there is a jump from description to direct authorial address to the reader: "Raise it...higher, as high as possible..." From an address to the reader – to direct command to the phenomena: "Let there be no break...So that they be equal...Huge windows...A more ethereal, lighter spire! So that everything would...fly and penetrate!"

And now, as if in ecstasy, we scan that same scale of gradations ejecting each other by which Gogol many years later achieved the description of the *pathos* flight of the "bird-troika" in *Dead Souls*.

But other pages of the article are variegated with that same type of dynamic exposition of the vivid movement of architectural forms.

Sometimes the exposition is ecstatically explosive, and the image of it resounds like a well-known figure (I will emphasize it in the text):

...A portico with columns...we also have lost: it did not occur to him to give it a colossal size, *to push apart the whole width of the building, to raise it to its full height*...Is it surprising that buildings, which they demanded be huge, seemed empty, because the pediments with columns were sculpted only over their porches...

...New cities have no form at all: they are so correct, so smooth, so monotonous that, after crossing one street and feeling bored, you reject any desire to look at another. These are a series of walls, and nothing more. Useless to try to find a viewpoint from which one of these continuous walls would at some point suddenly grow and *explode into the air* like a bold broken vault or would *be ejected* like some kind of tower-giant.

Sometimes the very form of the description slips into another system – a metaphoric system.

And then these descriptions take on a particular sensual charm, for the comparisons themselves are chosen by the marks of those external prototypes of imitation or inner dynamic stimulants (the dance) that to a great extent determine the forms and rhythms, harmony and nature of architecture constructions:

In Gothic architecture what is most notable is the imprint, although somewhat unclear, of a tightly woven forest, gloomy, grand, where an axe has not rung out for centuries. These decorations, surging in interminable lines, and the nets of filigree carving, are nothing but a dark recollection of the trunk, branches and leaves of a tree...

And the building went beyond its stone limits, and the temple turned into a forest. But there is more – this is how the image of "the kingdom of Asiatic luxury" is drawn:

A huge Eastern dome – either totally round or curving like a delightful vase turned upside down, or in the shape of a sphere, or loaded, sculpted with carving and ornaments, like a rich mitre – reigns patriarchically over the entire building; below, at the very foot of the building, small domes go around its vast walls like a whole fence, and resemble obedient slaves. Slender minarets fly out on all sides, presenting the most charming contrast between its light, cheerful towers and the solemn, majestic appearance of the whole building. Thus a grand Mohammedan, in a wide robe decorated with gold and precious stones, reclines among the houris, slender, nude, and blinding in their whiteness...

The forms of the building come to life when combined with people.

Below it obedient slaves walk around it, its light minarets cluster around it like houris, and reposing in the center, its dome turned like the grand Mohammedan in a gold robe...

But even these transformations are not enough for the author.

By his will the architecture is forced to fuse into all possible variety of forms pouring into each other (he is discussing architectural cities):

Here the architecture must be as capricious as possible: it must take on a stern appearance, show a cheerful expression, breathe with antiquity, shine with novelty, spill over with fear, sparkle with beauty, be at one moment gloomy as a day seized by a storm full of thunderclouds, at the next as clear as a morning full of sunshine...

...Architecture is also the chronicle of the world, writes Gogol later, "it speaks when songs and legends have already become silent and when nothing speaks any longer of the nation which perished..."

And probably the most dynamic picture of the constant transition of architectural forms into each other, which his imagination draws for him, can be found in...a footnote to the same article:

...A very strange thought occurred to me earlier: I thought it would not be a bad idea to have one street in a city which would contain an architectural chronicle, so that it would begin with heavy, gloomy gates, and on passing through them the viewer would see on both sides grand buildings rising high of a wild, primeval taste common to pre-historic peoples, and then a gradual shift of it into different forms: a great metamorphosis into the colossal, full of simplicity, the Egyptian, then into great beauty – the Greek, then into the sensual Alexandrian and Byzantine with low domes, then into the Roman, with several rows of arches; later descending again to wild periods and then suddenly rising to unusual luxury – in the Arabic; then to wild Gothic, then Gothic-Arabic, then pure Gothic, the crown of art breathing in Cologne Cathedral, then a terrible confusion of architecture, proceeding from a return to the Byzantine, then the ancient Greek in new costume, and, finally, the whole street would terminate in gates which would contain elements of a new style...

The perception of this formation of new types of architecture as a single stream of different varieties flowing into each other is manifested the whole time in the words in which this strange vision is described ("a gradual shift...into different forms," "a metamorphosis...into the Egyptian," "then into great beauty – the Greek," "then into the sensual Alexandrian," "descending again to wild periods," "then suddenly rising," etc. – all this characterizes these changes as a single stream, as single forms "metamorphosizing" into others, "descending" from some to others and "rising" from some to others.*

However, what is probably most striking in this whole article is how Gogol, with the true insight of a seer, "distills" from a conglomeration of models of past architecture and contemporary architecture – a rough sketch of models of future architecture.

Meanwhile, he seems to have "guessed"...the skyscraper (although of medium height) when he drops remarks about houses placed on city hills ("One should observe that houses show their height one behind the other, so that it would seem to one standing at the foot that a twenty-story mass was looking at him.").

Sighing very reasonably:

"Surely it isn't impossible to create (even for the sake of originality) completely original and new architecture, by-passing former conventions?..."

No less justly – even for our day! – he grieved:

"...Isn't it possible for us...to turn shattered bits of art into something grand? Must everything we meet in nature necessarily be only a column, a dome or an arch? How many other forms have still not been touched by us at all!... How many of these which not a single architect has yet entered into his codex!..."

In anticipation, Gogol mischievously throws in a concrete example at the end of the article:

* At another point in the book I will bring in (for another reason) a description of a similar type of picture composed of the movement of changes in the appearance of women's fashion. It was written (in an ironic manner) by Jean Cocteau.[128] As we have seen, our Gogol, a good hundred years earlier, "outgalloped" the French wit of our time.

Let us take, for example, those hanging decorations which have recently begun to appear. So far, the hanging architecture only appears in theater boxes, balconies, and in small bridges.

But if whole storeys hang out,

if daring arches are hurled one after another,

if whole masses instead of heavy columns find themselves on castiron supports,

if a house is hung over from top to bottom with balconies decorated with castiron rinceau banisters,

and in thousands of different forms, castiron decorations hanging from them envelop it with their light net,

and it will look through them, as through a transparent veil,

when these castiron rinceau decorations, twined around a pretty, circular tower, fly with it to the sky,

what lightness, what aesthetic etherealness would our homes acquire then!

Once Andrey Bely struck his readers by a quote from *Nevsky Prospect* that anticipates Picasso.[129]

But somehow even Bely saw that Gogol had anticipated Le Corbusier's ideas about a house on tree trunks;[130] and if his idea of "the transparency" of architecture was solved, not by his castiron "transparent veils," but by...glass, then – it was the glass of the American (Frank Lloyd Wright), "father of transparent houses,"[131] and the conception of his "beautiful tower" – is Tatlin's tower.[132]

It is also interesting how, here in Gogol, a separate tiny detail (hanging theater boxes, balconies, small bridges) develops into a new form of an unprecedented whole.

And how he has become aware by himself of this feature and potential.

And now he considers this feature and potential to be inherent in the creator and poet:

"But what a multitude of hints about everything exist, capable of engendering an extremely unusual and vivid idea in the head of an architect, if only this architect be a creator and poet."

And this was all written in – 1831!

Superconcreteness

[...] We discovered a certain "formula" according to which works of *pathos* are constructed.

We found an extremely clearcut condition for that state, in which all elements and features of a given work must be or appear, in order that the *pathos* effect of the whole be achieved (this condition was the ecstatic state of all its elements – a state that presumes the continuous spasmodic transition from quantity to quality as well as a series of other features).

We tried to verify the generality and universality of this "condition of a certain state," and following this, the characteristics of the compositional structure in the most varied areas and branches of art. We selected our examples so that they are as colorful and varied as possible, without taking into account time, place, nationality, or theme of the works chosen [. . .]

And we discovered everywhere that one and the same formula by which, without regard to person, epoch, or field, the fundamental ecstatic explosion is achieved, which lies at the basis of the *pathos* effect of the whole.

The question naturally arises – what is this extrahistorical, extranational, extrasocial "panacea" with certain "immanent" features "outside of time and space"?

And how can it be that with the greatly varied and incompatible *contents* in these most diverse examples of the principle of "*pathosization*," the principle of their *pathos* exposition, the conditions of the *pathos* quality of their sound – they suddenly turn out to be exactly the same?

If I did not think I had an answer to this question, I would hardly emphasize it so much, but, on the contrary, like a circus juggler performing his tricks, would detract attention in every way possible from posing such a question. But I really think that it is perfectly possible to reply to such a perplexing question.

For this we must pose very clearly and effectively the question of what occurs in the course of creating a work of *pathos*, what task the author has set himself, under what psychic and psychological conditions it has been created. [. . .]

Let us first look at the most rudimentarily understood intentions concerning the employment of *pathos*, with which consciously or unconsciously, intentionally or without control, the inspired author of a work of *pathos* operates. In short, such a description would sound something like this: this is a certain psychic, or even nonpsychological state, that the author wants to tie to his theme to make an indelible impression on the audience.

He either does this consciously or it comes to him involuntarily in the form of inspiration (see above how I "came" to this type of solution).

And if a very precise definition is proper, then it is, namely, in cases of genuine *pathos* and in the very production of such a work that consciousness of will and inspired immediacy are so inseparable and flow in a single process of creative achievement, serving as a necessary condition of the state of all elements of the work, when it finally achieves the effect of *pathos*.

One way or the other, examples of *pathos* construction manifest their final results in exactly such a form.

If any production, from any area of the arts, turns out not to have been treated according to the discovered "formula" *pathos*, then that special psychic state cannot arise (I repeat: not a psychological, but a psychic state beyond its limits) that, coloring the theme, was the reason for the creation of the work, forcing it to vibrate with what we call *pathos*.

What at first glance seems to be so "daring" an assertion turns out on close inspection to be "impudent" only in terms of size, volume, scope, and variety of the enormous compositional edifices, which are based on a single universal principle: No matter what, these are the most overwhelming examples in the creative works of the most varied countries, nations, epochs, and periods.

Essentially this mark of "universality" is characteristic of all more or less basic, stable methods, which in a certain way impregnates the means of artistic expression.

The content of Homer's and Mayakovsky's metaphors are different, incompatible, incommensurable, and often can be compared only with great difficulty.

And it cannot be otherwise through the abyss of the ages and the diapason of different social systems that gave birth to both giants.

But "the principle of the metaphor" – its structure, its psychic effect, and the norms of its appearance and presence in a definite degree of thematically necessary impressionableness – is identical.

The waltz "cannot occur" until a system of images, exciting equally (and in an equally colored emotional state) composers of such different nationalities and epochs as Johann Strauss and S. S. Prokofiev, "kicks" the "given" waltz into the canonical structure.

(And now, of course, any historical changes are possible, but if the "Viennese waltz" is not the "Boston waltz," still – they both remain "waltzes" and as such they are not confused with the mazurka or "turkey trot"!)

There is probably nothing that, on a par with theme and content, is modified so sensitively in step with the change of the times and the social systems as the multitude of rhythmic signs of works of different periods and epochs – from the hexameters of the galleys of antiquity[133] to the helicopters of the "chopped line"[134] of the twentieth century, from the structure of the Gregorian chants sung in unison[135] to the rhythmic zigzags of the musical palette of Gershwin.[136]

But the principle of the necessity of rhythm, without which a work would simply not exist, has remained true to itself through the centuries, just as the thesis of theme and content begins to turn into the flesh and blood of a genuine, artistically impressionable work only from the moment when it begins to pulsate through the material with an animated and vital *independent rhythm.**

We must add to the category of such phenomena what we have

---

* See "How to Make Verse" by V. Mayakovsky, Curbstone Press, Willimantic, Conn., 1976.

allowed ourselves to call "the formula of *pathos*," discreetly putting this term in quotation marks so as not to hide the fact that even to our ears this term sounds somewhat unusual.

Having put it in quotation marks, we should note that this term should not be understood primitively, vulgarly, statically, or mechanically, but in that dynamic sense in which we have tried to show it in practice through all the pages of this work.

"Technique, technique, technique."

We are interested in the technique of the creation and the technique of the composition of works of *pathos*.

And, turning to the nature of the act of the actual achievement of the work of *pathos*, one inadvertently recalls – from another aspect – those words Schopenhauer[137] spoke on the freedom of the will: "Man, of course, is capable of achieving what his will pushes him toward, but outside of his will he is capable of determining what it is his will is pushing him toward – to what he wants."

Here is that "unmanageable" prerequisite for positive "creative willing" in the artist, and that obsession with the theme, outside of which it is impossible to create not only genuine works of *pathos* but also any other kind of work of a less exalted temperature.

The rest – is a question of a purposeful (conscious and unconscious) creative "willing" and technique.

By posing the question in this way, "the theme" engendering the necessary "obsession" is equally protected from the extreme of "getting carried away with the theme – the rest will fall into place" – as well as from the extreme of underestimating its historical significance and its constantly changing basic social significance for creations of unsurpassed value.

The phases of the details of the actual course of the process of creation repeat exactly the outline of this general theme.

The definite degree of obsession, charm, and absorption of the theme engenders that "special" psychic state in which described norms of perception, vision, expression, and performance operate in the vivid images of that given material of the theme that appear in the finished work.

This state is possible only at that same "precise degree" of a psychic state ("of inspiration") as the transition of liquid to a gaseous state is possible, only at a precise degree of temperature, and as the stormy and unrestrained leap of mass into energy is possible only at a precise degree of the state of necessary physical conditions, the leap that, according to Einstein's formula, "liberated" the unprecedented supply of natural forces in the explosion of the atom bomb.[138]

This psychic state was characaterized by us above (quite early – in the first article on *pathos*) as the sense of participation in the laws governing the course of natural phenomena (from which also comes the scheme of the composition of works of *pathos* as a copy of the dialectic laws, according to which the continuous process of the formation and development of the universe occurs, second by second).

As such, by its very nature, it is "objectless" to a certain extent — ecstatic in relation to those psychological guides that lead to this psychic state. But the obsession with this state does not spread to some kind of abstract, timeless, spaceless, formless, and objectless state: Through conscious willing, its whole force "electrifyingly" makes its way into material* through whose essential qualities this very state arose, so that it forces this material to take shape according to the law of copying precisely that psychic state in which ("inspired") the artist found himself.

The norms of this state, as we have already said, are known to us. They are single and unchanging.

These are those basic laws according to which the formation of everything that exists flows.

The "obsession" relates to them.

The structure of its psychic state is tuned in unison to it.

And through it this system becomes the basic structure of the work and "the formation of its material."

And in a vivid experience, those perceiving this structure, through the system of images of the work, participate in the operating of the norms of motion of the whole existing order of things and, experiencing it in dizzy ecstasy, participate in the state of being possessed by *pathos*.

Now it is clear why, independent of the material and the figurative execution of the content, all examples of art of genuine *pathos* of different periods and nations — by the mark of nonconcreteness — by the mark of the structure of itself — unavoidably and inevitably correspond and must correspond.

For this structure is a copy of the structure of those norms of general movement and development, according to which, changing geological eras and historical epochs and succeeding social systems, the cosmos and history and the development of human society move.

If you allow yourself "to vulgarize" and somewhat mechanize and debase the picture of the process discussed here, then the following phases apparently result:

1. The inspiration of the subject (idea) of the theme.
2. The ecstatic state evoked by the intensity of the inspired experience of the

---

* ["...and the earth was without form, and void" (Genesis 1:2). "There was not nonexistent nor existent...All that existed then was void and formless" (*The Rigveda Song of Creation*, Book X, Hymn 129, R. T. H. Griffith, trans., Motilal, Banarsidass, Delhi, 1973 – HM.]

theme, in the form of going beyond the limits of concreteness and figurativeness into a sense of pure participation with the principles and the actual process of the course and movement of the "order of things."

3. The participation in this "order of things" with its theme and created work by reconstructing this process of movement through the material of its theme.

At this point one would like to bring in data and illustrations proving that the process really and truly flows in this way.

Let us limit ourselves now to only one "illustration" — the inspired coloring and refined experience in the "psychotechnique" method of a "witness" who is quite convincing. In addition, it will be taken from an area that, in terms of ecstasy, is close to the ecstasy and *pathos* created in the area of art.

From the area of religious ecstasy.*

The aims and problems of religious ecstasy, of course, are different from the aims the art of *pathos* set for itself.

But in the method of achieving "rapture" they use a psychotechnique quite close to it.

Strictly speaking, "demarcation" occurs at the third juncture. At the stage of material "embodiment" into a system of concrete images of that ecstatic experience that the "second phase" produced.

In the process of creation of an artistic work, everything is directed toward compelling these discovered laws of the movement of the cosmos to resound and act through the most complete, clear, and varied presentation of the richness of real objects and concrete images of the created work, intended for the widest field of social distribution, contact, and influence.

In religious ecstasy, the process is also directed toward getting the formlessness and objectlessness at the highest point of the psychic state of phase two — "to turn" into a concrete objective image in the third phase.

But only one.

Confined introspectively[139] in itself. Way inside. Asocially and agnostically. Outside of his conclusion not only as to the needs of his fellow man but even outside the sphere of dim experience into the stage of concrete contemplation, perhaps in the clear forms of a conscious mental process.

By its nature this "image" is totally abstract. And therefore it is very diligently "objectivized" into concrete objectivity.

---

* It is quite impossible here to probe into the details of the whole picture of psychological ecstasy – this is really the theme of a separate book. It is also inconceivable here to go into the aims, problems, and nature of religious ecstasy in general. Therefore we will discuss only that feature from both of these areas that interests us here directly.

The formless "beginning" – the course of the laws in which the ecstatic takes part – is quickly dressed up in the image of a materially objective, "personified" god.

The participation just experienced (the experience) in the movement of the universe, which the ecstatic has just shared, is stubbornly and foresightedly connected in it – in all the refinement of the mechanics of forming a conditioned reflex – with the image of an apparently really existing god, with all the objective attributes depending on which of the Olympuses it belongs, through whose ecstasy he is approached, out of what shades of religion and in whose interest this personification is called from the religions to serve, this creation in the image and likeness of man, a personification of the basic principles and laws of the movement of the universal elements!

Can one find in the positions discussed here any objective testimonial confirmation?

Just imagine, there is!

And what is most surprising – according to just that religiously colored branch of image making.

It would appear that, namely, here would have to be hidden forever every smallest detail that is capable of shedding light on the genuine psychological features of the mechanics of that psychic process that, not only for art, metaphorically signified as "a holy sacrifice to Apollo," but also for religion, is exhibited here as a certain mysterious, holy, hermetic, theurgic,[140] and mystical, and, in any case, "divine act."

What kind of practical "analysis" of genuine psychic states at such moments can take place here?

At best it is possible to expect numerous and endless authentic poetic effusions on the theme of their experience at these moments from Saint Theresa, Saint Angelo, Saint Catherine, etc., etc.

And meanwhile, from the very bowels of the mysterious Manresa[141] – this cradle of the most refined methods of ecstatic psychotechnics – and from the hand of the very creator of this most perfect method of achieving ecstasy, from the hand of Saint Ignatius Loyola,[142] we have a most interesting psychological observation on the most refined and delicate phase of the ecstatic state – on that very phase we are particularly interested in here.

However, strictly speaking, in whom would we look for similar data than in a man devoting his staggering energy not only to the creation of one of the most powerful organizations of the world (for his time and the periods following it) but who, with similar persistence, delved into the refinement of the tiniest bend of the human psyche, so that it, as well as the earthly sphere and the universe, would obey his merciless direction in fear and obedience to Rome!

However, the scientific honesty, scholarly objectivity, and psychological perspicacity nevertheless strike with that boldness of the record of the "materialistic" result of this ruthless observation.

And all this in the epoch of boundless spiritual fanaticism, of the blossoming of mysticism and the insurmountable *veto* placed on the smallest attempt at gnostic scrutiny[143] concerning questions of truth, religion, or canons established once and for all!

It is true that this material has been taken from a little notebook of personal notes not intended for anyone's eyes.

This notebook – is singular.

And what a miracle that it has been kept up till now in contrast to a whole series of its sisters ruthlessly burnt by St. Ignatius.

And not without reason.

Into these notebooks were noted down the data from the observation of ecstatic states and "trances" into which Loyola himself plunged, not omitting here the most penetrating analysis of his own psychic state in the aims of the most refined treatment of the principles of the unconditional and shattering "plunge into ecstasy" of his followers, novices, and flock.

At what moment of careless indiscretion did the Révérent Père Poulain allow a passage from this little notebook to slip into his weighty tome of exhaustive research and methodological guidance to the "spiritual exorcism" of Saint Ignatius (*Des Graces d'oraison*)?

At what moment of a tragic dimming of reason did a chapter of the Order of Jesuits decide to print (although in small print) this unprecedented and improbable assertion of the first general of the Society of Jesus Christ ("de la compagnie de Jesus")?

In any case, these lines were brought to my attention by this very book.

Describing for himself – considering that no one ever would see this note – Saint Ignatius defines his experiences at the culminating moment of ecstasy in this way:

St. Ignace eut de ces visions à Manrèse. Il a décrit de semblables dans un petit journal spirituel qu'il avait oublié de brûler et qui comprend quatre mois de sa vie. Parfois une image symbolique telle que celle d'un soleil, accompagnait cette vision; mais ce n'etait evidemment qu'un accessoire. Tantôt il apercevait "non point d'une manière obscure, mais dans une vive et très lumineuse clarte l'Être divin ou l'Essence divine" "sans la distinction des personnes," tantot dans cette vision il voyait le Père seul, "sans les deux áutres person."*

---

* Saint Ignatius had these visions in Manresa. He described their appearance in a small spiritual journal he forgot to burn and that encompassed four months of his life. Sometimes a symbolic image accompanies his vision, for example, the image of the sun, but it is evidently only an accessory. At times he perceived "not obscurely, but in a clear, glittering light, the divine Being or divine Essence" "without distinction of person," sometimes in these visions he saw only the Father, "without the two other persons."

And it is here that Saint Ignatius makes his remarkable observation: "Il voyait l'Etre du Père, mais de maniére que 'je voyais d'abord l'Etre et ensuite le Père, et ma dévotion se terminait à l'Essence avant d'arriver au Père'"* (that is, "participating in the principle," and *then the image* of the father).

I think everything we need has been expressed here openly, directly, and without beating around the bush.

The shattering effect of this assertion for the whole system of religious concepts, the unconditional atheism at the basis of the system of a religious "treatment" of believers, etc., does not move me right now.

Something else moves me.

What moves me is the testimony of the most experienced past master of psychotechnics as to the real image of representations and states through which the consciousness passes and in which it is found when it is in a state of ecstasy.

And if the situation in religion is like this, and the testimony comes from the hand of the most experienced "technician" of this practice in the interests of religion, then it is quite obvious that we were totally correct when we observed, in an analogous section, the process of how it proceeds in the creation of works of *pathos* and ensures the *pathos* of similar creations.

From the evolutionary point of view, this path is entirely organic. Assuming the state of ecstasy to be an "ascent toward origins," that is, a consecutive transition from a phase of development to a phase considered in a form contrary to evolutionary development – it is, namely, that picture that must occur in an ecstatic phenomenon.

The formation of the most divine concepts and the appearance of personified gods proceeds in a historical and evolutionary way along just such a path as this.

It is exactly identical for the majority of pre-Christian beliefs of antiquity.

On the lower (earliest) stage – it is no more than the feeling of a certain force, a certain principle – formless and objectless.

At a higher stage – the personified divinity reflects the characteristics being established at this moment of an earlier social formation of society.

...In the process of ecstasy, as we have said, the ecstatic person "ascends" to the earliest phases – therefore he also inevitably must find himself experiencing "Essence" and "Etre"[†] [being] – becoming and the principle of becoming, and the image of "the personified god" also appears in him "afterwards," when he returns, "enriched" by the object-less and formless experience of ecstasy, to the stage of a normal state.

---

* "He saw the Being of the Father, but in a manner that 'at first I saw the Being and then the Father, and my prayer ended with the Essence before arriving at the Father.'"
[†] [Footnotes here in the original translated these terms into Russian – HM.]

In art he introduces a composite of this experience, not in the image of a god who is "spiritualized" or "filled" with this feeling, but into a system of those images that are constructed and formed from the material and theme of his production. And these are those same themes and material that served him as the original elements for his inspiration, as the contemplation of religious "subjects" served the same purpose for the ecstatic person.

Here, by the way, is a clear picture of the sequence of stages from religious inspiration to inspired art.

One should equally note here both the connection between them, of proceeding in stages, as well as the qualitative gulf between these two varieties of human "activity."

(It is approximately the same between the concept of "cult" and "culture," in which historical sequences are also both connected to each other and opposed to each other in approximately the same way, in approximately the same degree.)

At this point a categorical refinement of descriptive terminology is necessary so no mistaken concepts may arise.

This is particularly applicable to the term "participation."

As in the circle of the usual associations accompanying it, in the descriptions of ecstatics as well – this expression always evokes concepts of a process of establishing links or contact with something outside of us: "participation in someone's experiences," "participation in someone's activity," "participation in some kind of ritual action," "participation in some kind of process."

For religious ecstatics the significance of this statement is thereby exhausted.

God exists.

He exists outside of us.

Through ecstatic manipulation we participate with him who is outside of us (he settles within us, we in him, etc., etc.).

This term has quite a different interpretation in the application we give it.

In the first place, we are not dealing with God, but with the principles of those laws by which the Universe, Nature, etc. exist and function – that is, by which the manifestations of matter function.

Thus we "participate" in the feeling of the laws of being, of matter as a continuous process of becoming.

But what is the nature of the participation?

Is this the establishment of a connection with certain matter, existing outside of us – something like a divinity, existing outside of us somewhere, in individualized form?

No. No. And, of course, no.

We ourselves – are part of that very matter.

One of the particular manifestations of this matter.

And as such a particular manifestation of it, those same laws function in us as in any other manifestations of matter.

Thus, theoretically speaking, we should be able to discover and feel the laws of the movement of matter by "knowing ourselves."

Is this possible to any extent?

To be more precise: Is this possible as an objectively formulated presentation of these laws?

It seems not.

An objective "presentation" may be realized only when the phenomenon can be objectively "presented" to itself, that is, when it is possible to put it in front of itself, that is, having separated it from itself, that is, having put the phenomenon separated from itself, and itself as an observer of itself – opposite each other.

Actually, even in the most common phenomenon, for example, a totally "objective" relation to it is possible only under conditions of the removal of any "subjective coloring" in relation to it, that is, any personal connection with it except for a scholarly, unprejudiced interest as to an object or exterior phenomenon.

We certainly cannot put ourselves into these conditions that are necessary for an objective discernment of the laws of the movement of matter, in respect to that matter that we compose (and that composes us!).

An orientation of our interest to an awareness of this movement through that part of matter, which we ourselves are, which each one of us is, is inevitably predestined to be inseparable from the subjectivity here completely dominating us.

Therefore such an orientation to ourselves (into ourselves) cannot produce objective knowledge.

However, what does such a striving toward oneself give to someone turning his thoughts in this direction?

It does not give objective knowledge (as we have already said), but . . .the subjective experience of these laws.

Such a man contemplating may experience the laws of the movement of matter; he may feel them subjectively, but he will be incapable not only of objectively knowing them but he will even be incapable of drawing and describing them clearly and articulately.

This will be a very curious state.

We are aware of it in less improbable situations and circumstances.

"The common mortal," for example, "cannot find the words" to describe the feeling that seizes him, for example, in a burst of love or in ecstasy before a sunset. His subjectively lyrical state cannot be arranged by him into objectively registered rhythms, images, or features of that "state" he experiences.

Being in the area of subjective experience, he cannot "become higher than himself" and objectively observe what is happening to him, and in the proper way, through reproduction by words and speech to give a concrete, objective presentation of it.

But here comes the poet, who knows how to "experience" not less (but probably more!) strongly the subjective emotional state and, *besides that*, can also convey it in objectified form through description, structure, images, and the *recreated law* of the process of the analogous experience (Pushkin, Tolstoy, or Dostoyevsky from the point of view of the "feelings" of their heroes).

What condition lies at the basis here?

What necessary prerequisite is operating here? What provides the possibility to the writer to "objectively" (and, in addition, as sensitively and subjectively colored as you please) state through the individual "particular" experiences of his heroes the very essence of those feelings, the truth of their nature according to given norms?

Why does "the word seize" him where, in someone incapable of becoming more subjectively enslaved by his feelings, "speech is paralyzed" and he is capable of "burning with experience," but incapable of leaving a nonephemeral trace of it in concrete images or precise concepts and ideas about these feelings? First of all, because such a truly great artist is never limited to introspection alone.

Parallel to "knowing *oneself*" and as a necessary condition for this awareness – he knows *others*: He knows the manifestations of those same feelings in others that are analogous and exist objectively around him.

(This includes that knowledge of reality without which a creator and artist cannot exist.)

In this process he stands at the opposite extreme: Here – in a conflict with someone else's feelings – he is completely separated from them, he is completely opposite to them – he is in a condition of complete separation, complete objectivity.

But such a position, of course, can occur only in a mathematically abstract situation. And if one follows such a concept of the existing order of things, unintentionally and unavoidably the artist must arrive at the principle of the unknowability of the nature of things, the unknowability of things "in themselves" (Kant, Berkeley, etc.).

Actually, of course, this is not the case.

And here the community of norms, basically identical and identically governing both "me" and "them," provides the possibility of knowing "them" through "oneself," but...only through "them" can one understand "oneself."

And this is not only true in respect to oneself and those very similar to oneself, but in a significantly broader range.

[...] If such is the position with mastering the nature of one's own emotions and the possibilities of their objective representation, then this occurs to an even greater extent when one's attention is directed to an objective awareness of nature, the laws of the movement of matter.

In introspection, not analytic but sensuously lyrical – as occurs in the self-absorption and self-contemplation of mystics – one really participates in this course of the laws of the movement of matter. But, as we have said, it is not known objectively but only in the form of experience.

In one's feelings there is that "omniscience," "knowledge of the principle of everything," "laws of the movement of worlds," etc., etc. (which the testimony of mystics is absolutely full of), those laws that – to the extent they are universal and basic – permeate everything.

But it is impossible to bring an awareness of them "to the surface." They are not separate from the subjective state and therefore are not objectively formulated, not objectively formed.

One can bring oneself to these states of exaltation or ecstasy by different means.

This can be direct, unforeseen, and unenvisaged shock. Or special means by which one can "bring" oneself to this state.

There are three methods that are most effective here. Crude forms of ecstasy – the type of ecstasy of the Dervish – built on purely physical, basically rhythmic, pulsating principles of special gymnastics.

"Spiritual exercises" – the most developed in the system of the particular psychic gymnastics of St. Ignatius (repeating almost entirely those very same principles in the psychic realm that Dervishes put at the basis of their physical manipulations).

Finally, the same thing can be achieved also by means of narcotics, various nuances of which can evoke any shades of the psychic states, which can be evoked by means of the physical and psychic-psychological exercises we have mentioned.

But I am asked if it is obviously impossible to recognize these laws inside oneself, then is the sensation of them in oneself possible?

Isn't this fantasy?

As an answer to this, let us look once again at examples that are simpler, closer, and more accessible.

Let us take the simplest cases from the area of subjective feeling, like the feeling of one's own muscles or the registration in one's sensations of the pulsating movement of blood.

It is a common saying that "you don't feel your teeth until they ache."

You do not feel your legs under you until you get tired, when you begin to register their "heaviness" and you can barely "drag" them.

Finally, you begin to register and feel the process of blood circulation only when it is extremely high (for external or internal, physical or psychic reasons), when the degree of this state is such that "your temples begin to throb," "your heart begins to pound."

You begin "to notice" your breathing apparatus only when your "breathing stops" or there is "shortness of breath."

And finally, there is an immense collection of so-called subsensory phenomena, i.e., those that act on us not only without being noticed in the field of consciousness but without being registered in our sensations.

The change of usual *habitus* [moods], the introduction of additional irritation, etc., can lower or raise this threshold of sensory perception; that is, it can translate into a state of sensation those effects that in normal circumstances are not registered in our centers of sensibility.

After everything has been said, it is clear that in the area of sensation it is possible to penetrate, more than is usually thought, those laws of movement in which our "material essence" manifests itself, that is, we as "bundles" of thinking material.

For this there needs to be a certain release from the generally accepted psychic state – a certain degree of liberation from superstructural layers of figurative representations and ideas; that is, that primeval, purely sensual state into which a "patient" is plunged by the whole invented system of "exercises" leading to a state of ecstasy.

The pantheistic "self-dissolution of self in a universal feeling," in nature, "the sensation of self as one with the heavens, the grasses, and the insects" (on this see, for example, the words of George Sand,[144] which we will write about elsewhere in this volume, in the chapter Nonindifferent Nature) is absolutely relevant here.

It is a "picturesque" description of the same feeling that everything "is governed" by a single system of laws to which even my own littleness is subordinated through a sense of "participation" in this structure.

Participation is understood as a feeling of general unison, as leading to a "reality of feeling" of these same permeating and universal laws in oneself, within oneself, as well. [. . .]

On the question of suprahistory

The excerpt from Loyola's notebook cited above is extremely remarkable.

A whole system of cunningly invented technical devices in the "patient" evokes a definite state of exaltation, nervous excitement, and ecstatic state – however, you wish to call it.

This state in and of itself, according to its psychological nature, is formless.

To be more precise, this state is – preformed.

If there is a stage in the state of thinking when there is still no real understanding, and the only means of expression is the image, it is a much earlier state that is limited only to sensation, still not having found any means for expressing itself except by simple signs of the state itself.

Ecstasy is exactly like this in its final peaks: a transport out of understanding – a transport out of conceptualization – a transport out of imagery – a transport out of the sphere of any rudiments of consciousness whatever into the sphere of "pure" effect, feeling, sensation, "state."

In a comic aspect this is – the notorious bear that Munchausen forces with blows of a whip to jump out of. . .its own skin and to run off naked into the forest, abandoning its "fur coat."

This naked bear – this objectless, formless, "contentless" psychic "state" – of course most passionately and ardently seeks a concreteness into which it must be embodied "materially," seeks material through which it must become tangibly real.

And now by a new maneuver of the system of "St. Ignatius," anticipating the method of the intentional formation of "new" bonds on the basis of a conditioned reflex – this "amazing psychic state" combines with images and concepts connected to a cult, to a religion.

For the person having fallen (been brought) into this state – the uncommonness of it is connected with the image of the Lord God.

They explain to him that this is the "fusion with the essence of God," the state itself combined with the image or a reference to divinity, etc.

As a result, this strongest psychic state receives divine coloring post-factum.

And always from then on, when the divine is mentioned, by a very simple scheme of the mechanism of the formation of conditioned reflexes, there definitely arises in the emotions of the believer the sensation of this "extranatural" psychic state – and extraordinary state of nature – that, under the influence of those spiritual mentors, he is ready to assume to be. . .a "supernatural" state.

Here at a very particular point that same technique of inculcating religion takes place that, independent of the "systems" of cult (that is, the variety of religious beliefs), always maintains that religion is attached to all the basic, fundamentally impressive or fundamentally essential moments of a secular career.

Religion always fastens itself both to birth (the "exercise" of the shamans around this "mystery of mysteries" and baptism with such – to this very day! – "blowing and spitting on Satan" in the text of the rite of baptism!), and to adolescence ("the ritual of initiation" among savages and "confirmation," not differing from it in any way), to marriage, to holy unction for the sick, to the last rites and wakes (it is all the same whether it is a pagan "funeral feast" of the ancient Slavs or the "requiem" of the Orthodox Slavs).

A cult keeps a hypnotic force over a free consciousness, being connected by reflexes to all the essential moments of physical human existence.

(I will not discuss the fact here that the cult itself "grows" out of concepts at lower stages of development connected with those same "events." Right now I am interested in the "second phase" when the cult no longer lets the reflex apparatus out of its clutches, continuing to rivet religious concepts to consciousness by means of a "reflex arc"!)

How all-embracing and appropriate this technique is can be seen from the experience of war.

A son returned safe from the front. Or a husband. Or a father. Joy.

And the servant of the cult drops by the house apparently by chance. Even more accidentally he drops the phrase.

"And we prayed for the health of your son (husband, father)."

The heightened, intensified emotional state is ready and willing to color any phenomenon falling into its orbit (the desire to "share" joy) and is unusually receptive to receiving such an irrelevant communication, almost as if it were the prime cause!

And the trap for the establishment of the first reflexive or associative tie of religion and well-being has already been set; this is particularly convincing for a consciousness that is not too steadfast or predisposed, and in a state of joy; that is, of heightened effect less controlled by reason or analysis, and therefore quite compliant to this type of influence at a given moment.

This same technique also works in a state of "grief."

The father has been killed. The son. The brother. The husband.

Again – a poignant effect.

And sometimes a mournful sigh of sympathy is sufficient: "Oh, why didn't you pray to God to watch over your father (son, brother, husband)" in order to connect the concept of the possibility of avoiding sorrow with the name of the Lord God!

One can read about this "technique" in literature also, and not only in artistic literature, but even in Marxist literature.

And in the latter – because of a touching description of a scene of similar technique, described in the form of the spiritual good deed of a pastor-mentor, from whom Marx angrily and damningly tears off the mask of falsehood and hypocrisy, thus revealing the "mechanics."

The description belongs to Eugène Sue and is taken from the touching pages of *The Mysteries of Paris*, devoted to how Madame George and the priest Laforte are taking care of the spiritual salvation of Fleur-de-Marie.

And the exposure of Marx and Engels taken from the pages of criticism in *The Holy Family* (III), devastating for this novel:

Let us follow Fleur-de-Marie on her evening walk with Laforte, whom she is accompanying home.

"Look, my child," he begins his unctuous speech, "at the boundless horizon, whose limits are invisible to the eye" (it was in the evening). "I think the stillness and boundlessness almost inspire us with the idea of eternity...I am saying this to you, Marie, because you are susceptible to the beauty of the universe...I have often been touched by that religious ecstasy which they evoked in you...in you, who have so long been without religious feeling."

The priest had already succeeded in turning the spontaneous, naive, joyful enthusiasm of Marie for the beauties of nature into *religious* enthusiasm. *Nature* has been depreciated to the bigotry of *Christianized* nature. It has been brought down to the level of *creation*. The transparent ethereal ocean has been dethroned and turned into a symbol of motionless *eternity*. Maria already perceived that all human manifestations of her being were of an "earthly" nature, that they are without religion, true holiness, that they are anti-religious, godless...

That is, again we see that this special psychic state of "rapture" – under the influence of the infinitude of the heavenly vault at twilight, a state having no definite "address," no definite "direction," no definite content – is skillfully captured by Father Laforte and "turns into" forms of "religious" rapture because of its capacity to be linked with images of religious conceptions.

And, if we remember that for a whole series of figures of particularly sensitive, emotional inclination, the contemplation of the magnificence of a landscape is enough for them to fall into exaltation or a state of ecstasy, then the case discussed above is completely appropriate both from the nature of the observation of Ignatius Loyola and from the "technique" of the use of the given circumstance in the interests of religion. (Let us recall the "ecstasy" of Pierre Bezukhov in *War and Peace*.)

And the conclusions of Marx and Engels put a final dot on the "i" in this matter!

However, right now I am interested in something different.

Namely, that it follows that such a state of rapture – whether under the influence of contemplating evening nature, or as a result of the psychic "exercises" of St. Ignatius's system – can also be coupled with images that are totally unreligious.

It is quite obvious that, if it is not Fleur-de-Marie who will be looking at this evening sky, whose rapture the crafty Father Laforte links with the system of religious images, then it will be a poet reveling in the landscape, pining for a beautiful lady, or a social reformer – then the rapture of the first will merge in him with the image of the lady of his heart, and the second's rapture at the infinite scope of the heavens will "stick to" the breadth of those good deeds that he intends to shower on humanity.

Thus it turns out that one and the same evening sky, having evoked a definite, particular psychic state (rapture-exaltation) in three different cases adds exalted rapturous coloring to three quite different objects: God, a pretty lady, and a utopian plan of social reform.

The state itself – is vague and neutral, objectless, and only in combination with an object of interest, on the one hand, does it take on material objectivity of the content of experience and, on the other hand, "raises" the very experience of each of these themes to the "unreachable height" of uplifting, exalted effect.

Thus, before us is an example of such a "particular" state, whose characteristic mark is, on the one hand, its transport beyond the bounds of the concept-image of an object, and on the other – of the ability to add its dynamic intensity to any image acting in connection with it.

The sensation, "first of being."

And "then – God."

And, therefore, there is nothing surprising in the fact that these states of "ecstasy," "exaltation, " "frenzy," and "being beside oneself" are similar both in their distinctive features and in the method of their psychological "bringing into being."

They are brought into being through a definite psychic "distillation" of perception through distinctly arranged phases of the work, copied from the structure of the phenomenon itself. (We defined this structure and phases as a system of qualitative jumps, marking a continuous transition from quantity to quality.)

Therefore we should not be at all surprised at the fact that, in extremely different authors or anonymous authors, this basic structure turns out to be identical in terms of its overwhelming feature.

An accusation of the "suprahistoricity" or "ahistoricity" of this condition is not appropriate here.

In the first place, according to the actual material of the analysis, this condition is demonstrated quite clearly.

But, in the second place, also in terms of the interpretation of the real cause for this condition, to which we have devoted so much space.

And finally, because, outside of a concrete connection with a definite system of images, this "special" feeling cannot really be "materialized," cannot be embodied in any way.

But this is really an object of historical change and variability, and above all – social conditioning.

Alexander Borgia[145] and Shakespeare, Count Benckendorff[146] or Hafiz[147] all burn with an identical feeling of hunger in exactly the same way.

But one satisfies it with Eastern fruits, another – with Renaissance viands, a third – with the substantial food of the time of Queen Elizabeth, a fourth – with the refinements of French cooking.

Dante, Pushkin, Simonov,[148] or Mayakovsky in the final analysis, all burn with lust in exactly the same way. [...]

And in the same way, "I love"* is similar to "Wait for Me" † and stanzas of Dante to "I Remember the Wonderful Moment."‡

---

* [See Herbert Marshall, *Vladimir Mayakovsky*, Dobson, London, 1977, p. 122 – HM.]
† [By Constantine Simonov – HM.]
‡ [By Alexander Pushkin, – HM.] Walter Arndt, *Pushkin Threefold*, Dutton, New York, 1972, p. 18 – HM.

And, in addition, in all of them there is one and the same general state
– the same state of being in love, penetrating through its various
nuances, a different stage of realization, a different system of socially
defined concepts, reflected not only in the nature of the feelings but also
in the structure of the works. And this general state, present in
everything, forces Simonov to understand Dante, and Mayakovsky –
Pushkin, just as Dante would have understood Mayakovsky, and
Pushkin, and probably Simonov, if they had lived in a reverse sequence.

Such a dynamic generality of "the formula of ecstasy" also passes
through ecstatic works of *pathos*, which are both extremely different in
subject, aim, idea, theme, time, and place, and are from different
countries and peoples appearing at times as a quite unexpected echo.

The last consideration relating to it, however, concerns the condition
that the "formula," according to which the very movement and origin of
natural phenomena occur, be taken as the structural prototype of the
construction of *pathos*.

These laws, meanwhile, have endured from the beginning of the vital
functioning of our planet's system until this very day as penetrating and
unchanging.

The degree of the distinctness of their interpretation changes according to the extent higher forms of social reality are approached, and the
highest of them – the reality of the classless society in the Soviet Union –
and the broadening of our means of scientific knowledge. [. . .]

The kangaroo

I once had to write somewhere, but perhaps not – about the fact that
everything I once thought absolutely necessary to examine in separate
areas of art – I always first encountered as an object of direct passionate
enthusiasm.

I became intoxicated with Daumier much earlier than I was able to
realize the significance he later had for the development of the principles
of expressive human movement.

I was enthusiastic about China much earlier than when its hieroglyphics helped me master and understand the system of montage
speech.[149]

And the enthusiasm for primitives long preceded an understanding of
the norms of their sensuous thinking, which, like Pandora's box, hides
the whole syntax of the language of the forms of art.[150]

It is striking that the chain-rocket method of ecstatic writing first
began to occur in conceptions that were quite irrelevant and figurative.

Moreover! – as a comic picture...

And in two aspects.

As a memory of a comic tale.

And as a thick black vignette illustrating it in the whole length and breadth of the white pages of the *Strand Magazine* of one of those years preceding the Imperialistic War of 1914.

I am a respectable hoarder and love to hang on to any material I found striking. I keep it to remember. It might come in handy.

And quite recently in a bunch of archives appeared before me this very page of the tale that had once captivated me, torn out of the English monthly *Strand Magazine*. (And the same magazine was among my household goods because it had once published short stories of Conan Doyle about...Sherlock Holmes!)

I must say with pride that the memory of it arose much earlier, in the form of a direct association with a possible aspect that the formula of ecstasy would have had to take in the case of a comic interpretation.

Like black spots on the margins of the English magazine, there jump one after another increasingly smaller – kangaroos.

Not one after another!

But one out of the other!

Out of the "pouch" of the biggest arc flies out the second in size. Out of the pouch of the second – the somewhat smaller third.

Out of the third – the fourth!

Out of the fourth – the fifth.

And it seems that it won't end until the sixth, until the twelfth!

What is going on?

What is the source of this chain of kangaroos, scared to death, ejected "rocketlike" from each other?!

They are illustrations to the short (second) comic story of tricks invented by smugglers.

In the first story the dodger smuggles dozens of...alarm clocks across the border, having them swallowed beforehand by...an ostrich, for which he does pay duty.

They play a wicked joke on him.

An offended partner winds all the alarm clocks to go off at exactly the minute when the ostrich will have to pass solemnly through the customhouse.

The alarm clocks begin to shake inopportunely, due to the panic in the ostrich who, it turns out, was "unpacked" a bit too early.

The second story is about kangaroos.

And of someone who wanted to bring twelve pieces of merchandise over the border, after having paid duty for only one.

Twelve kangaroos are carefully put one after the other successively into the "pouches"...

But then at the critical moment the largest of the kangaroos... sneezes! And...what happens is that they run like black spots across the white margins bordering the story. Like a catapult, all twelve kangaroos shoot out of each other!

I am not trying to assert that the lively potpourri (settling somewhere into the layers of the subconscious) of the customhouse fate of the kangaroo family definitely helped me in interpreting the ecstatic scheme of the construction of *pathos*!

Although, of course, it is very suspicious why somewhere between Piranesi and Frederick Lemaître, just behind the corner from El Greco and the *Battleship Potemkin*, just these twelve playful surviving inhabitants of the Australian plains had to intrude, in the form of an "accidental" association, with silly tricks of an absolutely identical formula.

Nevertheless, it is they who, in the form of an association, emerged from the stock of impressions that had once attracted my attention.

And once having appeared, they loudly – as "friends of childhood" – demanded the rights of residence here in the environment of serious effective images,

making claims to an island of comic interpretation of material according to the canons of ecstatic writing.

One must agree with this. [. . .]

The adventure of the family of kangaroos, of course, is an extremely clear example of a comic interpretation of the formula of ecstasy.

And, in addition, according to the ancient scheme of creating a comic effect through "taking something literally." Thus, even in the comic theater of the ancients, those who were the host's spies, they say, appeared in masks that depicted nothing but one eye or one ear. [. . .]

It is difficult to conceive of a more "literal" interpretation (i.e., a reverse transposition from a metaphoric concept to a nonmetaphoric) of the formula "being beside oneself" than a kangaroo jumping out of the "pouch" of another kangaroo – absolutely identical to it (and actually only somewhat larger in size!).

Many, many years later – after the end of World War II – I again remembered my contemporaries: the kangaroos from an epoch preceding World War I.

What provoked my memory was the very well-known, popular drawings of Saul Steinberg.*

The simplicity of his drawing is striking, not only in the purity of its line but also in its theme.

What seems even more striking is the exceptionally strong attraction of this, apparently not only vapid, but simply trivial drawing.

Meanwhile, its effect is almost hypnotic.

And this drawing consists of – all in all – a hand with a pen drawing

* Saul Steinberg is a Romanian engineer who, with the arrival of the Germans, emigrated to America and exchanged the curves and T-square of the architect for the sharpened drawing pen of some of the nastiest caricatures during the war. His anti-German and anti-Italian series are wonderful, as are his impressions from the front in Italy, China, Morocco, and India.

the figure of a man up to the waist, who draws (the exact same) figure of a man to the waist, who draws (the exact same) figure of a man to the waist, who draws (the exact same) figure of a man to the waist, who...

The graphic equivalent of the well-known "endless" verses memorized from childhood:

A priest had a dog	And he loved it.
And he loved it.	It swiped a piece of meat,
It swiped a piece of meat,	And he killed it.
And he killed it.	And into the earth he dug,
And into the earth he dug,	And an inscription he wrote,
And an inscription he wrote,	That – a priest had a dog,
That – a priest had a dog,	And he loved it,
	etc., etc.

The attraction of this irrelevant, innocent, and apparently vapid drawing is built on many elements.

Not only on that hypnotic effect, which has a constant monotonous repetition, inevitably inserting "automatism" into the viewer's perception and from here on his visual behavior, evoking a temporary inhibition of gray matter in the brain.

And especially in the thematic side of it.

Actually here that same thing that was represented in our kangaroos is depicted in black and white: Here step by step a man comes out of a man, comes out of a man, comes out of a man.

But each person is identical to the other, and thus the man continuously – is being beside himself!

Here the difference in size is not even distracting.

That is, before us there seems to be an extreme version of the formally observed condition of ecstatic construction.

We are already aware of its profound ties with the structure of the most profound life processes, and therefore we should not surprised by the uniquely fascinating effect proceeding from here, of the unprecedented chain reaction of the drawing created by such a prescription.

However, why is there no effect of an explosion here?

First of all, the dynamics of any drawing are, of course, conventional, and a genuine explosion in the conventions of a drawing has to be conventional, although by certain means it can lead to very ecstatically explosive effects, less completely, perhaps, than painting or etching (we did after all analyze El Greco and Piranesi!), but still powerful in its own terms.

However, in this drawing – secondly, even basically – the most important condition of evoking an ecstatic effect of being beside oneself is not observed – this leap is not accompanied by a leap into a new quality.

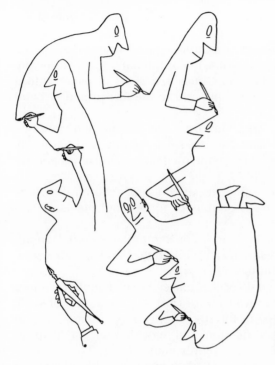

Figure 14. Cartoon by Saul Steinberg: © 1945, 1973 The New Yorker Magazine, Inc.

A person is beside himself, is beside himself, is beside himself, but he does not leap into a new quality [even in the sense of a simple change in size, which, for example, was done by the kangaroos diminishing in size, and through this, realizing a leap (of self) out of self and a leap to a new quality of new size], but remain themselves, themselves, themselves.

This is the source, on the one hand, of the chain-reaction force of organic prescription remaining in effect (plus its continuously increasing automatism) but – on the other hand – the lack of a qualitative leap, i.e., like an "explosion," photographed in slow motion, where the frenzy of the material is presented smoothly – like circles on water – like a concentration of waves being dispersed.

The jolting flood of a chain of depictions issuing out of each other – This is like the straightening into a chain of mono planar ornament of a multiplanar knot of a simultaneous spatial complex of illumination or the instantaneousness of a chord played by a sequence of notes. [The mysterious tie (of elements of ornament and a chord) is preserved in both cases, for the sequence, in order not to be perceived as one whole, must be psychologically collected into one; the chord is perceived not simply as one sound when it is felt as a multisound unit of both a definite sound "composition" and its interrelationships].

However, this same Steinberg also often uses the exact scheme of the kangaroos: He forces the scale to diminish step by step.

Such is the sketch of the interior of a Chinese junk* where again in the foreground is a "self-portrait" – this time not only a hand that is drawing, but also the knees of the author, on which is a sheet of paper with a drawing of the inside of that same junk and in the foreground, a hand that is drawing, etc.

More often the drawing is separated from the "originating" author's hand, and the drawing represents, let us say – simply and endlessly series of figures shaking each other's hand on the principle of proportion "small, smaller, smallest."

Here it is interesting to note that the direction of reading drawings done according to this scheme is double, or to be more precise – two directional.

On the one hand, if one reads them according to the formula "small, smaller, smallest," we have before us a rush into the depths, backwards, into a cell, and within the limits – "into zero."

On the other hand – with equal success one can read a similar column as an image of "progressive" movement forward – in the aspect of scale in reverse; that is, of spatial perfectability – from "zero," from a "cell" to an increasingly enriched modification and growth that, in a spiral motion, becomes qualitatively more complicated.

Over the "entrance" to this type of drawing one would like to place a "double-entendre" sign of a double arrow, pointing the way simultaneously both "there" and "back." Both these principles are also strong in Steinberg: leading off into the depths and dictating to him the unexpected features of figurative uniqueness taken from there – and leading out forward and upward, forcing him to function in the very thick of militant satire, in a skirmish with the fascists by means of his pen, in this skirmish sharpened into a sharply attacking bayonet!

The mutual presence of both these principles cannot but find plastic expression in the work of the master. (And, of course, in comic form, the comic pointedness so characteristic of him).

And...doesn't this lie at the basis of yet another of its outer appearances, stunning in its simplicity and in the profundity of the conception of the drawing lying behind it? Where is the path toward the exit drawn [as in Fig. 15]?:

For the uninitiated – this is the point of stopping dead in place.

For the initiated – this is the formula of that double path by which a truly effective work is constructed – equally descending by its roots into the subsoil depths of the accumulation of the past experience of

---

* Junk: a Chinese flat-bottomed ship with battened sails – Webster's.

Figure 15. Cartoon by Saul Steinberg (exit sign). Reprinted by permission of Saul Steinberg.

humanity, and by its crown, growing into infinity of heavenly perspectives of the future social and spiritual progress of humanity.

Here given statistically in a comic scheme, it contains within itself that same figurative embodiment of this thought as those systems of drawings read "from any end" that we lingered over above.

The "materialization" of this process, the "literal" representation in them of the "principle" of being beside oneself makes them humorous in form, but the actual principle provides them with that effective content that, in these drawings, is not the decreasing or increasing figures or pairs themselves, but the actual principle and process of the endless formation of phenomena of nature and its inhabitants – by cycles or generations immutably one from the other.

The principle discussed above lies somewhat less literally emphasized in another favorite theme of Steinberg's as well – to show a half-opened door through which the next half-opened door is visible, through which – the next, then the next, etc.

Finally, there is the fascinating example of a deviation so remote from the basic scheme that one can recognize it only by "renouncing" the everyday motivation on which it is based.

This is – surprised passers-by looking at a gigantic profile by which a little boy with charcoal in hand, crawling along the sidewalk, outlines them.

The "perspective" intersection of the figures of the passers-by by the outline of the large profile drawn on the ground, if read "flatly," that is, to the exclusion of spatial associations – simply as a two-dimensional drawing – would be read as a smaller human figure "flying out" of the contour.

In this form of a larger human being (a human face), the direct connection of this drawing with the basic scheme we have traced by which Steinberg works, is apparent.

Equally comprehensible is the attractive force of this drawing as well –

Figure 16. Cartoon by Saul Steinberg (Hitler invading Russia). Copyright ©
1943, Saul Steinberg; originally appeared in *PM*, 1943.

even more attractive in its own way, since here the basic "attracting"
image is given not directly, but as penetrating through the everyday
subject. The "attracting" scheme of the transport of the small figure out
of a large one is present simultaneously "in two interpretations,"
depending on whether you interpret the drawing two dimensionally or,
three dimensionally, or simultaneously "thus and thus" – a condition in
which the maximum inner tension of the movement of the drawing is
created as well as its quite shattering attractive force.

However, let us now look more intently at the reason why these
drawings are so effective.

On our path to this it is perhaps appropriate to mention that "verbal
equivalents" of the construction of the first drawing are not limited to the
"ballad" of the priest and his dog.

This is the style – usually of a triple repetition – that the late poetess of
trans-English and trans-French letters used to love to write in – Gertrude
Stein, whom I was fortunate enough to meet in Paris in 1929.[151]

The "mechanisms" at the basis of Steinberg's drawings and Gertrude
Stein's "verses" are exactly the same.

The witty and ironic application of these mechanisms by Steinberg to
often satirical drawings differentiates them (see, for example, the
traditional application of it that has been analyzed in being applied to a
caricature of Hitler and his satellites, which are continually decreasing
in significance), at the time when the late poetess drummed them "in
herself," formlessly and pointlessly, which might have a strong shock
of surprise "once," but not as a device "done to death" by being
applied both opportunely and inopportunely (and most often it was
inopportunely).

Still, what, besides the features we have indicated, is the basis of the uniquely comic effect of constructions done according to this formula?

Of course, as usual, what lies at the basis of the comic composition is a concept that was once taken seriously, but then rejected by a more advanced and developed understanding of that phenomenon [laughing, we take leave of our past which has been overcome].[152]

It is interesting that a case of such identical figures proceeding "telescopically" into each other has beneath it just such a conception that has been outlived.

Such a reservoir of all future generations of all future people formed out of each other! – in the Middle Ages was considered to be. . . the proto-mother Eve.

(Something of this conception is included in the actual ancient Judaic literal meaning of the name of Eve.)

Swedenborg[153] drew the structure of a man as a system of "persons plunged into persons." (Thus, according to Swedenborg, a head is like an independent "little person" heaped on the shoulders of the figure as a whole, etc.)

A whole paradoxical direction in biology – the so-called animal cultists – saw the human organism in exactly the same way – as a composite colony of separate, independently existing animal units grouped into larger, again independent, animal units (organs), in their turn forming the entire person.

(A trace of a similar conception – also in a comic aspect – was preserved in a very popular type of composite portraits; for example, the profile of Napoleon III composed of the naked bodies of court ladies of the Second Empire, etc. In its purest form – with the preservation of the basic motif of repetition of the tiniest link, which is completely identical to the whole – this "idea" was preserved in the Japanese variety of these pictures. There the gigantic face of a cat is composed of separate cats. A masculine face – of analogous masculine figures and faces, etc.)

The theosophic "trisubstantial" man is also drawn as if he were in a triple encasement – an "astral" body in the "mental," the "mental" in the "material."[154]

The obsessiveness of this image pursuing human imagination has been preserved in the early ritual of the "seven veils" even now in a metaphoric-colloquial meaning (recently the English brought to the world the picture called *The Seventh Veil*,[155] where, by means of psychoanalysis, the original trauma is gradually laid bare from under superficial layers of later impressions in the heroine).

We find traces also of a definite cult basis now in the putting of numerous boxes packed into each other as a form of amusement.

A purely playful variant can be found in the *matrëshkas* of the former

Sergey suburb, where into a conventionally depicted human figure – mostly female (let us remember Eve!) – are stuck in succession those same "small, smaller, smallest" female figures. (Of course, even here somewhere along the way there probably was a cult ritual stage that has been lost and probably the transitional "crosspiece" leading from it to the *matrëshkas*.) Nevertheless, another toy, in principle if not in appearance, is connected with the *matrëshkas*.

It is remarkable that in its dynamics it corresponds to what the basic drawing of Steinberg showed us in the form of consecutive static drawings of beings besides themselves and little figures drawing themselves, with which conversation about it began.

This toy – is the system of sticks attached by hinges and arranged crosswise that instantaneously (pay attention: instantaneously!) fly out lengthwise, as soon as the ends of the sticks at one of the extremeties of the system are pressed (see the drawing).

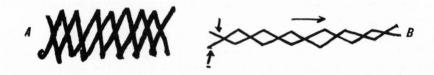

Here also each new pair of sticks comes out (is thrown out) of each preceding pair. The sticks are equal in size, but they are charged by speed, and this occurs at one and the same moment, magnificently growing from the beginning sticks to the sticks at the end, which are capable at that interval of time of being hurled an incomparably greater distance.

From here the free end of the system flies out instantaneously, so swiftly and incommensurably, with a quantity of the spent energy.

If you could imagine this system still exploding – flying to pieces – then I think that in this toy you could find a model of the instantaneous effect of a huge explosion, as in the simultaneous mutual ejection of a whole chain of separate links; that is to a certain extent what occurs in a "chain reaction" of the fission of uranium, observed only from the point of view of the accumulation of the dynamic energy of an explosion.

This toy is also good because it clearly demonstrates plastically what we had in mind when we spoke about a spatial complex of illumination, "straightened" into "chains" of ornament or presented in a sequence of sounds.

The first will be drawing *A*, the second – drawing *B*, the "culmination" – the dynamics of the *moment* of transition from one to the other.

In the case of Steinberg – a chain of little figures drawing and growing out of each other will be *B* – the "result" is drawn in the sketch.

According to this result, perception "collects" them back into A. This occurs at the moment of the recognition of their identity; the recognition of a similar identity can generally also be realized only through speculatively putting separate depictions on top of each other, which thus give a precise flattened scheme of the state A in contrast to the "extended" – B.

Speculatively the next phase also flows as – an "explosion" from state A to state B.

A trace of the dynamics of such a speculative process is included in the actual literal meaning, that one figure *comes out* of another, that one figure *draws* (that is, actively – really – calls to life and being) another.

On the other hand, the system of continually decreasing boxes going into each other – a toy especially popular in the East – is answered "mirror image" by. . .the pyramids of peoples, which grow into mammoth size. The invasions of these peoples swept earlier cultures away, erecting new pyramids over the existing pyramids, swallowing them into the core by their incomparably huge size.

Thus one on top of another kind of "coverup" hangs strata of Mexican pyramids placed one on top of the other. Whether they are in far-off Chichén Itzá – Yucatan, where that is done with palaces; or in central Mexico – near the Pyramid of the Sun and the Moon in San Juan de Teotihuacán. Incidentally, this method of "entombing" more ancient pyramids under the strata of new pyramids ensures complete protection for monuments of an earlier stage of culture, in strata going deep, one under the other.

Excavations in Mexico are carried out by cutting such "stratified" constructions section by section, and the lower stratum is revealed in an almost perfect, untouched state of preservation.

The Spanish conquerors continued the process by erecting on the pyramids. . .Catholic cathedrals.

It is interesting to note how seemingly, right up to the fifteenth and sixteenth centuries instinctively in this process – in the reverse direction! – the scheme of the "ejection of the next out of self" has been preserved.

It is natural that the scheme of the most obvious embodiment of the image of a "liquidation of the preceding" had to use the directly opposite scheme of "coverup."

We should not forget what an extremely decisive role their figurative structure had in all early rituals. The image of a similar structure in these periods is at the same time an actual fact, and not a figurative reflection of it in ceremonial forms. And in this situation the outer form, by means of which the liquidation of the subjugated previous culture occurred, had a definite "practical" significance. It is not accidental that such a method of cover up of one pyramid by another exists everywhere in Mexico.*

In this device we probably have a multilevel metaphor of earth and stone of approximately the same sound as what is preserved in the literary metaphor "to cover."

Until now one says of an orator who has beat the argument of his opponent that he has "covered him with a higher card." (i.e., trumped him)

And a map with a great number of points on all corners of the earthly sphere, for some reason, until now has been considered as "covering" a smaller map, which it destroys or subdues (especially *when, in the form of a "trick," it brings the smaller "trumped"* one to itself...into captivity!).†

The actual act of the coverup by placing the new pyramid onto the old one includes the conscious act of destruction in its plastic form, naturally "reverse" to the act that responds to the entry of the new God into the world: Out of the womb (the middle) the arising one mingles in the middle (in the womb) with the imprisoned one.

Of course, only a structure effect of this sort can completely provide satisfaction to the figurative demands of thought, for which the visible image prevails by its significance over the substance of the act.

Thus, in these external reflections of conceptions in objects we have analyzed (apparently quite unmotivated), as in all the enumerated interpretations, fantastic in form, we see an awkward attempt to include in a tangible, imagistic form, in a new aspect, the vague feeling of the "spiral" repetition of features and characteristics of phenomena according to the degree of evolutionary movement and quantitative leaps from generation to generation (the actual transition from self into those similar to oneself), from type to type, from form to form. And such soaring repetitions, from the smallest particles to the whole, which we observed above in the structural laws of natural development, correspond to formulas of logarithmic spirals and the golden section.

---

* [Many Mexican cultures practiced this among themselves. Pierre Ivanov says, "The discovery of one edifice inside another is not exceptional, for the Maya of the classical period often demolished their temples in order to build new ones in the same place. The Aztecs also, like the Toltecs, followed this procedure in obedience to a ritual 'edict' that required the destruction of all temples at the beginning of every fifty-two-year cycle. As a sign of new life, new sanctuaries sprang up on the enlarged pyramids" (Pierre Ivanov, *Monuments of Civilization: Maya*, Grosset & Dunlop, New York, 1973, p. 102) – HM.]
†The correspondence to the cattle breeding connotations of this term does not contradict this in any way. Just the opposite – we should not forget that the very first form of subduing oneself was realized by this method, and among men at the dawn of the formation of human society – at the stage of couples getting married – where the first enslavement was introduced at the same time as this act. As is well known, Marx and Engels see in this the principle of the enslavement of women by man, which they consider the "kernal" of the next exploitative principles of class society (see *The Origin of the Family, Private Property and Government*) [by F. Engels, International Publishers, New York, 1972].

The "trouble" with all these concepts – and the reason they excite our curiosity – lies, of course, in the fact that they are all trying to present the dynamic principle, the norm, concretely and figuratively.

In addition, the law is taken not as the structural principle of their constructions (which, in such a case, even takes on the actual corresponding reality – which the given work has discussed at length), but as the content of concrete representation.

It is quite clear that this was apparent in the *principle* of "being beside oneself" presented *concretely* through a phalanx of kangaroos.

Thus, through a comic structure there operates that same basic generalization of the law that underlies serious structures (partly also at the basis of structures of *pathos*, where they are presented and act in the most complete and pure form), thus ensuring the efficiency of the construction.

The comic "accent" on them presents the conflict of a similar early conception face to face with a contemporary conception, which has already overcome a former one, connected with an earlier structure of ideas, in its turn also overcome by today's stage of the development of consciousness.

A comic effect is always achieved by the juxtaposition (the conflict, from which the explosion results) of presentations, responding to different levels, when in a corresponding situation they are presented as equally correct and equally significant.

It is interesting that it is not the more progressive that are necessarily funny, but the more backward ones turn out to be in the comic position; for example – the chivalrous, romantic Don Quixote who has "overstayed" beyond the limits of his epoch.

I was definitely convinced of this, in a very remote area of Mexico, for mentioning the second story of a house. The Mexicans in this area – never having learned about two-story structures – really burst out laughing since, according to their ideas, "people do not live on top of other people." And, on the other hand, it is difficult to name even one innovative idea, concept, or invention that was not only greeted with skepticism, but didn't escape being laughed at.

Be it the orchestration of Wagner, the "eccentric" assertion that people can fly in the air, or the first discoveries of the Curies or Pasteur.[156]

(The dean of one of the colleges of Cambridge University, J. J. Thomson,[157] in 1929 told me that when he was young, a special Commission of Great Britain's War Ministry, of which he was a member, was amusing itself by testing the assertion of a similar crank, who said he could be lowered to the bottom of a pond in a covered boat and would swim back up again. Of course, he didn't emerge at the top: He sank in the mud, and they had to pull out the "ill-fated" inventor with hooks, and this in the space of only one incomplete human life, from two world wars which raged with the cruelest underwater battles!)

Besides which, it wouldn't hurt to remember that a comic effect also discharges and discharges...like an explosion. Let it be a burst of laughter. But the burst – is a leap from dimension to dimension – which also lies at the basis here as well. [...]

Without plunging into the most essential aspect of this question – the problem of the main compositional difference in an identical external appearance between structures of *pathos* and comedy (this is a problem for a separate work) – let us only point out the remarkable similarity (identity!) of the method of constructing one and the other.

For this we will bring in several examples where the "formula of the kangaroos," taken not really figuratively but as a structural principle, is employed in the interest of very different effects – effects of *pathos*.

One of the most exalted pictures in conception and composition on the theme of the Madonna in world art is *Saint Anne, the Madonna, and the Infant Jesus with Saint John* by Leonardo da Vinci.[158]

There is an opinion that this picture, quite uncommon in both theme and composition, owes its unusual quality to purely biographical data on the childhood of Leonardo da Vinci, which reflect in it their singularity.

They suggest that a group represented in this way bears the figurative imprint of those special family conditions in which the child Leonardo grew up.[159]

Whether this is the genesis of this original composition or not, nevertheless, what resulted was a group of three figures, each growing out of the bosom of the preceding, and, in addition, distributed so that each of the subsequent figures appears to grow out of the preceding.

This "play of characters" is motivated by the fact that the Infant Jesus reaches from his mother's knee toward the boy John, and the mother, trying not to drop him from her arms, bursts forward from the knees of Saint Anne, on which she is placed.

From the purely physical aspect, we have three figures here – representatives of three generations – from which each bursts out of an embrace – from the bosom (*Schoss*) (in German, *Schoss* means both "in the arms" and "bosom" in the direct sense of "womb") of the older one and appears to continue it (the older) externally. It is interesting to note that, if one compares the finished picture with the magnificent sketch for it, the distinctness of this dynamics is achieved only in the finished creation.

This concept even comes through in the name by which this picture is known among German art historians: *Heilige Anna Selbdritt* – something like our Russian "three-yield." It is interesting that a similar term, inapplicable in Russian examples of art, preserves its applicability where it is a matter of pure reproduction of self in the next generation – for example, in agriculture, where the identity of the descendant is

Figure 17. *St. Anne, the Virgin, and Child* by Leonardo da Vinci, c. 1470/1490 (Louvre, Paris) [Cliché des Musées Nationaux 87EN3764].

particularly emphasized in relation to the ancestor who produced the grain: "six-yield," "eight-yield," in evaluating the productivity of grain!

The difference here, of course, is in the fact that the German *Selbdritt* is not based on the principle of the wheel, that is, radially, but is stepped – like a tandem – not "one into three" but "one – into the second – into the third."

Thus, Leonardo's picture seems to have an unusually dynamic image of growth: Saint Anne seems to grow without restraint, continuing herself through the Virgin Mary even further, into one more generation [...]

And usually only that figurative quality "teases" the imagination at whose basis – in whose structure – lies one of the profoundly natural laws, which is the *embodiment into an object* of a certain profoundly natural *process*. We have already seen this condition in action – both in ecstatic structures and in comic structures, which required for its effect only certain compositional corrections [...]

Such are the features of a "figurative" representation of growth, the connection of the generations, the passage of the generations, into each other.

As any "figurative" representation, under conditions of scientific exposition, it will always, and here as well, be called "naive." [...] However [...] – it can burn with real tragic *pathos* when it falls into the orbit of the creative inspiration of a genuine poet [...]

I do not want to say as a development of all that has been said above that the ecstatic structure in works of art is constructed according to the formula of the fission of the atomic nucleus of uranium or that a rocket missile is built according to "the form and similarity" to a poem of *pathos*!

This would only be silly and stupid.

But I will also stubbornly refrain from considering these phenomena "analogous" to each other or "corresponding" with each other in appearance.

What do I want to say? That in these areas so far apart from each other – each in its own way – the same laws are operating at those moments when in each of these areas it is necessary that extreme (and not only extreme, but superextreme) versions of phenomena be realized, phenomena of the highest – but still "accessible" – manifestations of the content of these areas.

The law of construction of such processes – the basis of their form – in these cases will be identical. The effectiveness of the results in the norms of each area is equally "transported beyond the limits" of these norms and the areas themselves as well. The actual processes – according to the same formula of exstasis – is "being beside oneself." And this formula is nothing but the moment (instant) of the culmination of the dialectic law of transition of quantity into quality.

The ability to force the process to move according to the "programming" of this law, to momentarily culminate in it, gives both the maximum (for the time being) effect of a physically possible manifestation of explosive strength – in the atom bomb, and the maximum effect of a psychologically conceivable physical state of a man – the ecstatic possession of man by the power of *pathos*.

The areas of application are different.

But the stages are identical.

The nature of the effects achieved is different.

But the "formulas" at the basis of these highest stages of manifestation, independent of the areas themselves, are identical.

For at their basis lie the fundamental laws of nature, and the power of the results of those processes that, through reproduction, unite with the power of nature. This seems to be another new aspect of the wise image of the ancients about Anteus, who acquired invincible indestructibility by the closest connection with the source of all strength – according to the ancients – with the earth. According to us – a connection with the essence of the laws of the movement and formation of the universe.

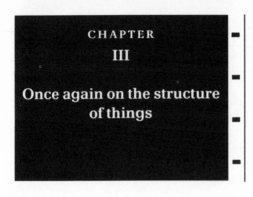

CHAPTER

III

Once again on the structure
of things

In a book on directing I have been writing now for many years,[1] among various other problems I noticed one interesting fact, which was the way the general dialectic position on the unity of opposites is applicable to the area of composition.

A definition of it is that, under any given compositional conditions, both the direct solution and its direct opposite are equally valid and effective.

This phenomenon also occurs in the treasure house of expressive manifestations of man — in nature itself.

Thus, for example, in a moment of terror a man not only backs away from what inspires fear in him, but, just as often, as if bewitched, he is drawn and comes closer to what inspired this fear.

Thus, the edge of an abyss "draws" you toward it. Thus, the criminal is "drawn" to the scene of the committed crime instead of rushing away from it. Etc., etc.

So in a composition, deriving its experience from the material of reality, these circumstances can be immediately revealed even in the most trivial examples.

If, for example, it was decided that at a certain moment in playing a role one had to utter a frenzied scream, then one could also certainly say that a barely heard whisper would be just as powerful at this point. If rage is resolved in maximum movement, then a complete "petrified" stillness would be no less effective.

If Lear is powerful in the storm surrounding his madness, then the directly opposite solution — madness in the environment of the complete calm of "indifferent nature" — will be no less powerful.

Of two opposites, one is usually more "marketable" and common-place. And therefore you think of it first. The second acts more unexpectedly and more sharply; it is fresh because it is unusual. Let us just recall the dizzy effect of the Negro syncopated movement of jazz, where the principle of accentuation, the same for all music, is solved in

200

an opposite way from that which the European ear is accustomed to. The "King of Jazz," Paul Whiteman, writes in his autobiography:*

Today, however, jazz is a method of saying the old things with a twist, with a bang, with a rhythm that makes them seem new. Strictly speaking, it is instrumental effects. A large part of its technique consists of mutes being put in the brass. The first beat in any bar, which normally is accented, is passed over, and the second, third or even fourth beats are accented.

This can be roughly illustrated with a familiar bar of music. Suppose we take "Home, Sweet Home."[2] Here it is in its original form:

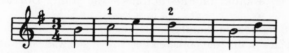

Now let's "Jazz" it up:

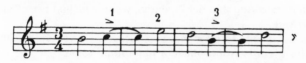

It is interesting that later – when jazz and the fox-trot had become common forms – cases of the opposite arise...the "unjazzing" of melodies.

This occurs in the fine film *Going My Way* with Bing Crosby[3] in the main role of the priest (it won an Oscar in Hollywood in 1944).

Here the "sinner" plays a seductive fox-trot for the young priest. The priest is upset that such a pretty melody is being played in such an undignified form, when it is basically – a prayer. He sits down at the instrument and turns the fox-trot into the prayer leitmotif of the whole film.

Here, what is most interesting is that, in the given case, the "reverse" of the form is provoked and really caused by the concrete *ideological premise* of the overall religious *tendentious* essence of the film.

It is also interesting that the actual reverse is applied, with the perfectly conscious aim of creating *pathos*, and, moreover, this is done brilliantly and successfully!

In regard to jazz itself, it very quickly became very popular; although very often the introduction of a similarly "unusual" opposite was not easy.

For example, how nastily Dumas-père attacks the Théâtre Française, just because the concept of the poetry of immobility ("La poesie de l'Immobilité") is completely incomprehensible to this theater.

* Paul Whiteman and Mary Margaret McBride, *Jazz*, J. H. Sears, New York, 1926, p. 119.

And Dumas-père himself introduces one of the most eloquent examples of the effectiveness of direct and reverse solutions in the composition of the actor's performance. This example has been noted down in his charming *Memoirs* (*Souvenirs dramatiques et littérares*).

In Dumas's new play *Antony*, the leading lady was to be the famous Mme. Mars.[4] Dumas did not get along with her or the theater, which did not understand the drama, and when the rehearsal was in full swing he took away his play.

He handed the play over to another theater, where the role of Adelé was played by another famous actress – the young Dorval.[5]

...She played the role brilliantly.

Only one place in the role bothered her, which she was never able to perform properly.

"But I am lost!" ("Mais je suis perdu moi!") – she was supposed to have shouted, on discovering that her husband, whom she had betrayed with Antony, had just arrived...

She was never able to utter this sentence...And yet she felt that, if uttered correctly, these words would make a huge impression.

And suddenly it was as if she had a revelation.

"Are you here, my good author?" she asked, approaching the footlights so she could see into the orchestra stalls.

"Yes...what's wrong?" I answered.

"How did Mme. Mars pronounce the words: 'But I am lost'?"

"She was sitting and with these words jumped up."

"So," Dorval said, returning to her place. "I will stand, and with these words I will sit down."

In the intoxication of the success of the premiere, her partner Bocage[6] forgets to return the armchair that was necessary for this scene. But Dorval, seized by passion, does not notice this.

...Instead of falling on the cushion of the armchair, she fell on its arm, but with such a shout of despair, in which there resounded such pain of a wounded, rent and beaten soul, that the entire auditorium jumped out of its seats.

The reverse solution was no less justified than the "direct."

Of course, a purely mechanical construction of opposition, not growing out of a genuine sense of opposition within the phenomenon or, more precisely, not growing out of a possible contradiction within the very relationship to the phenomenon, will never be sufficiently convincing.

It remains a superficial play of contrasts in relation to what is conventional, and is never raised to the point of being embodied in a single theme, presented in the less common of two equally possible and valid oppositions.

Actually the construction "in reverse" made by Mme. Dorval, which at first glance looks like a "formal" device, is only apparently so. One might discover in this single small example of two treatments of one and the same movement essentially the whole conflict of opposites of the two styles of acting, the conflict of the remnants of classicism with the romanticism sweeping them away, a conflict reflecting the complex social processes at the beginning of the nineteenth century.

The contrasting solutions in our example are only reflections of the contrasting traditions with which the "classical" actress Mme. Mars departed and with which the "romantic" actress Mme. Dorval entered.

It is easy to "arithmetically" enumerate a third solution that, in spite of its unexpectedness, may appear opposite to *both* preceding solutions simultaneously.

Perform this scene, not using a range of movements (upward or downward – it is all the same) but in restrained movement or purely by intonation.

But even in this case, within this "arithmetic" there lies the most complicated complex social process, which was reflected in that style of acting, about which one of the first figures of this new theater would write to another:

"...It is necessary to express suffering just as it is expressed in real life, that is, not with your hands and feet, but by tone of voice, by glance; not by gesture, but by grace" (Letter of A. P. Chekhov to O. L. Knipper)...*

Is it not surprising that what for us now appears as possible variations of different stage solutions was once one of the only possible stylistic types of solution? Solutions that artists arrived at through complex conflict, accompanying the assimilation of a new artistic ideology.

But this is not at all surprising.

We are the heirs of the whole incredible treasure of the culture of the human past.

Our art in its nuances, in stylistic features, in genres, and simply in its individual characteristic, include the experience of what was, for the presynthetic stage of the history of the arts, the foremost sign of whole epochs, of whole styles, of whole stages of artistic ideology.

And, what once took shape in art on the springboard of a change in style now becomes the means for variations and nuances within our single style of socialist realism, which, besides all that is new and unprecedented in it, can in the great variety of its particular productions be inspired with any nuance of what was once obligatory and predestined to be the only possible exhaustive color.

However, the condition of the inner validity of selection of one or another nuance, or one or another opposition within it, remains in force

---

* A. P. Chekhov, *Collected Works in 12 Volumes*, vol. 12, Moscow, Goslitizdat, 1957, pp. 382–3. Letter of January 2, 1900, from Yalta.

to this very day. Also one replaces the other. Thus the example of Mme. Mars and Mme. Dorval is quite appropriate and not only in conditions of historical development and change of styles.

There are many similar cases that could be quoted. Indeed, one need not go very far for analogous examples. Probably the most prominent case, which caused a fairly big reaction, was one occurring on our Soviet screen.

This concerned the stylistic characteristics of the films *Strike* and that same *Potemkin*.

How well I now remember the period when I conceived the stylistic aspects of the cycle "To Dictatorship" from which only the first film was realized. I even remember the place when it was discussed.

The place was the curve in the wall of the now demolished Strastnoy Monastery.* Right by it went the road from the once famous movie theater, *"Kino Malaya Dmitrovka, 6"* which celebrated the "performance" of the most dizzy films of American production. *Robin Hood* and *The Thief of Baghdad, The Gray Shadow*, and *The House of Envy* played here.[7]

How could one surpass these "giants" of the scope of American cinema, by the first timid steps of our own cinematography?

How could one force our young cinema to resound with its own voice through the chaotic thunder of American–European productions, mastering all the refinements of craft and production? Where could one find plots that could outdo American plots in their ingenuity?

Where could one find native "stars" capable of eclipsing with their radiation the "constellation" of American and European luminaries of cinema?

Where to find a hero who by his personality, could at once put the *coryphaeus*[†] of bourgeois cinema "on their backs"?

The problem was not simply to make a good picture. The problem in this area as well – in the area of culture – was to inflict a blow on the bourgeoisie, to oppose it in both culture and art. To force it to listen and respect what was coming from the young land of the Soviets, which was enigmatic and unknown to the Europe and America of those years.

An impetuous twenty-six-year-old saw all this as a personal Promethean task.

And the solution arose almost "mathematically."

A plot more ingenious than an American one.

But what if one rejected a plot all together?

"Stars" surpassing the American and European ones.

But what if one made something unprecedented for that time – a film without "stars."

---

* Once in Pushkin Square, Gorky Street, Moscow.
† [Leader of the chorus in Greek drama – HM.]

An individuality more significant than the individuality of conventional film heroes.

And what if one denied isolated individuality in general and built it on something quite different?

What if one did "everything in reverse": Abolish the plot, throw out the "stars," and into the center of the drama move the masses as the basic "dramatis personae," that same mass on whose background individual actors conventionally played.

Thus, almost by means of the formal reverse course, the solution "in reverse," those stylistic features of our cinema were formulated, which remained for years as its defining uniqueness.

Of course, it would be naive to suggest that "mathematics" just by itself could engender what was characteristic and extremely expressive for its time.

The emancipation of consciousness from that whole system of ideas that are connected with the bourgeois system. A new world revealed with the victorious entrance of a new class onto the arena of world history. Victorious October and the victorious entrance of the ideology of the victorious proletariat.

These are the prerequisites from which one overheard the possibilities of new speech in culture and in the arts.

And just as opposite and mutually exclusive as the ideologies of these two classes were, so those stylistic features in art, with which these classes expressed themselves at the moment of sharpest conflict, could not but turn out to be opposite.

It would be impossible to find and discover deeper inner roots for solutions that are opposite from the "formal" point of view.

It is true that many authors also try to expound the history of the creation of one or another set of works, while trying to fit them into certain canonic formulas.

Too little has been written honestly and frankly about how these things were conceived, and created.

Anecdotal details, unexpectedness or seeming haphazardness, by no means removes all the well-known basic laws of the origin of works of art.

But these original details of creative biographies give a living tangibility to the process of creativity, and not an abstract scheme, which corresponds least of all to such a full-blooded process as creativity.

Here is one more example of a similarly frank page of creative autobiography that is very close to what we cited above:

This season I put on *The Cost of Life*. In Moscow for a benefit of Lensky[8]; in Petersburg for a benefit of Savina.[9] In both places it was successful from the very first act and turned into an ovation.

...The value of life, the question of suicide, double suicide – naturally suggests that the author was burning with this huge moral problem, that he was seized by the phenomenon of general suicides, etc., etc. Actually this was not the case at all. The author was sitting during summer in his village and said to himself that now he had to write a play. For various everyday consideration it was necessary. Which play he still did not know himself; he still had to find a theme ...And then once he had put this question to himself: contemporary dramas usually end with a suicide, and what would happen if I would start the play with a suicide? The play begins with a suicide – is that not amusing?

And then somehow the author set himself another task: playwrites always write so that the third act would be the most bellicose, the most effective...a big ensemble scene – But what if the most important act were built as a duet? That the whole act, let us say would be carried by Ermolo and Lensky, and that the interest would be exciting...

And even when the plot had already been conceived, the suicide was still only a stimulus for dramatic situations. Remember, two acts had already been outlined, and the author still had not worked out the moral essence of the "value of life"; this question in and of itself had still not risen over the images, scenes, snatches of observations, as fog rises over the swamp, hills and bushes...

The Griboyedov Prize for the best play of the season was awarded *The Cost of Life.**

Here in conclusion I would like to bring in one more example of construction in reverse used as a means to pass as the original. It concerns a term that it would not be a bad idea to bring into circulation. The term is "a platitude in reverse."

This is how the conversation went about Dostoyevsky. As everyone knows, Turgenev did not like Dostoyevsky. As far as I can remember, he said this about him:

You know what a reverse platitude is? When a man is in love, his heart beats, when he is angry, he turns red, etc. These are all platitudes. But in Dostoyevsky everything is done in reverse. For example, a man meets a lion. What does he do? He naturally turns pale and tries to turn away and hide. In any simple story, in Jules Verne for example, it would be told like this. But Dostoyevsky tells things in reverse. The man blushed and stood still. This would be a reverse platitude. This is a cheap way of passing for an original writer. †

I would not like to argue or agree with Turgenev. But I know that in cinema sometimes they turn to this very method in order to pass for the original. Thus, for example, the lion's share of the "enigmatic quality" of Marlene Dietrich[10] is constructed by Sternberg[11] by exactly this principle of the reverse platitude. In such pictures as, for example, *Morocco*, all the mystery of her figure is built on the simple device of her continuing to give an affirmative response...with a questioning intonation. "Have you eaten already?" – and the answer is drawn out "Ye-es" with a question

* Vl. I. Nemirovich-Danchenko, *Out of the Past*, Academia, Moscow, 1936, pp. 68–72.
† S. Tolstoy, "Turgenev at Yasnaya Polyana," *Voices of the Past*, Moscow, 1919, No. 1–4, p. 233.

mark at the end. And the public immediately supposed heaven knows what kind of secret connection with a whole series of enigmatic motifs. And all in all what is present is only her reverse platitude.

However, besides similar examples, we know more than a few cases when "reverse solutions" were accomplished in a purely "formal" way, that is, without *inner necessity* or without historical substantiation for a similar reconsideration, but "contrary to the traditions" no matter what.

Thus in the memory of us old theatergoers, along with brilliant instances of a fruitful revision of traditions (which at times stood models of moss-covered tradition on their heads examples were also preserved of groundless arbitrary performances in "reverse," without any apparent necessity it turned the traditional old man Josip into a young man, the chatter of Bobchinsky and Dobchinsky* into slow and leisurely tirades, and the unique volleyball response during the dances in *Woe from Wit*,[†] into response rolling the whole length of a table stretched to the full breadth of the footlights – the full width of the open stage.[12]

Moreover, this mise-en-scène of dinner in the Famusov home probably calls up associations with the *Last Supper* of Leonardo da Vinci, which also would turn out to have its distinctive raison d'être – its distinctive substantiation.

In both, unexpected news rolls from one end of the table to the other, plunging into alarm the gathering of friends and like-minded people dining peacefully.

Thus the appropriateness of compositional laws noted by us are justified in different cases in different ways. We will not plunge into all the depths that lie beneath this phenomenon, but we will try to trace it in one more area of its application. The law of the appropriateness of an opposite solution, while the conditions pointed out above are observed, is not only true for particular solutions. It is justified also within a whole system of principles connected with a definite compositional structure.

Therefore the general picture drawn by us earlier, of principles of *pathos* construction, would not have been complete if we had not brought in another example of an *opposite type of construction* leading, however, to a *pathos* effect of the same force.

The *pathos* of the theme can also be solved through two opposites, by which the possibilities of compositional construction are always arranged.

An example of a straight course in constructing a *pathos* effect was shown by us in *Potemkin*.

---

* [From Gogol's *The Inspector General* – HM.]
[†] [Play by Griboyedov at the beginning of the 19th century, satirizing contemporary Russian nobility, as produced by Meyerhold – HM.]

There we showed that the basic indication of *pathos* composition consists in the fact that for each element of a work, the condition of "being beside oneself" and a transition to a new quality must be observed.

We brought in observations on man's behavior in this state.

"...Sitting, he stood up. Standing, he jumped. Motionless – he moved. Silent – he shouted. Lusterless – they gleamed (eyes). Dry – they became moist (tears)," etc.

About his speech we wrote:

"Nonorderly in its usual flow, the structure, imbued with *pathos*, quickly takes on the imprint of a growing rhythmic quality...prosaic in its forms, it soon begins to sparkle with forms and turns of speech that are characteristic of poetry," etc.*

Finally, using the "Odessa Steps" we analyzed this position in detail in terms of composition.

All these were examples of the "direct course" in the construction of a *pathos* effect.

We will reveal the reverse construction giving a similar effect in another example.

Such an example will be another film of strong social *pathos* – *Chapayev.*†

The *pathos* effect of *Chapayev* is undoubted and verified in the many millions of spectators carried away by it.

However, if anyone who read the first half of this work tries to apply directly to *Chapayev* the data of the research on *Potemkin*, he will find himself in an extremely difficult position.

"Formulas" will not work.

And either one must accept formulas "with grave doubts,"

or...deny the fact that *Chapayev* – is filled with *pathos*.

Both of these are incorrect.

And the secret here is that *Chapayev* is built on the principle of a second opposition, through which the principle of *pathos* construction, the same in both cases, is operating.

For such a perfect work as *Chapayev* we truly should expect inside it a "key" scene, where one of the decisive inner technical and stylistic conditions definitely "bursts through" into the action, or into the dialogue, or into the situation.

This will be certainly most true for a film remembered for its most "characteristic" scene or phrase.

In such a scene the key to the basis of the theme must necessarily emerge, the key that, at the same time, will be able to function as the key

---

* See "On the Structure of Things" p. 3.
† Directed by Vasilyev brothers, Mosfilm Studios, 1934.

to a correct understanding of composition as the embodiment of a given theme.

It is in this aspect that the "Odessa Steps" sequence in *Potemkin* is justified: As the maximum high spot of the film's drama, it turned out to contain the most critical passages of the composition, providing the possibility of revealing their "secret" and leading them right up to revealing the method itself.

I think that the episode that is *least* dramatic will be characteristic of the "method" of *Chapayev* in all the richess of its dramatic effect.

This is, without any doubt, the episode "Where Should the Commander Be?"

For this is the episode that introduced into Soviet film practice something new in principle, style, and quality.

Actually one of the most significant features of *pathos* in *Chapayev* was that here *the hero was not raised onto a pedestal.*

That here the hero is shown as not distinct from the human milieu, not standing *above other people*, not jumping *ahead of other people*.

Here the hero is shown as flesh from the flesh of his class; inside it; with it; not only leading, but also listening – as a real national hero.

As it were, an "ecstatic" image of the ordinary person, *for whom there is a place in the ranks*, who as a hero forged ahead.

Equally "ecstatic" is the image of the hero who though "by rank" *has a place ahead of the ranks*, is shown *inside the ranks*, flesh of their flesh and they, like him.

When the hero is presented so that you feel that he – is us; that he – is each one of us, rank and file; that he – is "you and I."

This is achieved not by a lowering of the hero nor by a leveling of him.

This shows that the ranks that gave birth to him stand in a row on a level with the hero.

By this the whole nation that gave birth to him raises the hero to a certain level.

There is a remarkable scene in *Napoleon* of Abel Gance.[13]

Napoleon – although still only General Bonaparte, is nevertheless already Napoleon.

He takes a look at the army after a certain battle in Italy.

In the first row of soldiers is a private, a former friend of Napoleon's (the actor Colin plays him well). He brags among his neighbors of his closeness to Napoleon.

He will prove it: He will break discipline, he will take one step forward from the ranks and nothing will happen to him.

He takes this step forward.

On a galloping horse Bonaparte approaches.

Bonaparte sees the transgressor.

The horse stops as if petrified.

Bonaparte recognizes the transgressor.

A dead pause.

A harsh command.

And...the whole row of soldiers take a step forward.

Sparing his friend's self-esteem, Bonaparte did not force him to take a step back into the ranks, but ordered the ranks to take a step forward – toward him.

The horse turns sharply. Napoleon gallops on.

Colin falls in a faint into the arms of his comrades...

And the treatment that forces Chapayev to appear to step backwards, to go back into a single row with the others is, essentially, a step by which he forces everyone to heroically resound in key equally with him.

For in *Chapayev* there is no division between the generals – and the ranks.

In him – is a unity that can be found only in the army of conquering socialism.

We did not find the key scene of the drama in a dramatic scene.

And the fact that what is characteristic of the *drama* about Chapayev is not a situation *dramatic* in action is notable in itself from the point of view of those suppositions we stated about the "reverse" solution of the *pathos* effect in this film.

Let us look at this situation at greater length. In order to do this, let us look at the same episode.

The argument is about where the commander must be. Everything is based on the fact that the place of the commander is *ahead*, with saber drawn.

But *Chapayev's* military wisdom alone says it is *not always* like this, that there is a case when the commander is to be *behind* so that at the moment of pursuit of the enemy, however, he will again forge ahead.

This is the lesson of the dialectics of battle.

And researchers into the effect of *pathos*, who would like to mechanically disseminate theses on *pathos*, as they are revealed in *Potemkin* and in *Chapayev*, could be given the same lesson on questions of the dialectics of composition by the film *Chapayev* itself.

Under *certain conditions* of the unfolding picture of battle, the commander, who should be *ahead* must be *behind*. And both these contrasts in his location, penetrating each other in his actions, equally form into a unity – into the perfect behavior of a commander in battle.

In exactly the same way under *certain conditions of the inner content of the theme*, the structure of *pathos* also must not "rush ahead with saber drawn," but "take his place behind," that is not going through the opposite revealed in the case of *Potemkin*, but by way of a reverse contrast.

In addition, both, while penetrating each other, merge into a unity of that general method of *pathos* composition, which we revealed in the preceding part of the work and which remains true, no matter by which of two possible opposites the *pathos* construction of one thing or another will move.

Actually, in a suitable place we brought in earlier examples of the behavior of a person in ecstasy, a person seized by *pathos*.

We spoke of eyes, from which tears flowed. We spoke of silence, broken by a shout. We spoke of immobility, thrust into applause.

We spoke of common prose unexpectedly passing over into the structure of poetry.

But won't the *reverse picture* of these phenomena correspond to that same formula of "being beside oneself"? Moist eyes, suddenly turning dry. The paroxysm of shouts, suddenly becoming silent. Applause, suddenly stopping. *Totally appropriate exalted poetic speech suddenly beginning to sound. . .like common conversational prose.*

But is this not the unexpected effect of the Russian female name on the pages of novels used to names such as Eloise, Clarissa, Alina, Pauline, and Selina:

Her sister was named Tatiana. . .
For the first time with such a name
Do we willingly sanctify
The tender pages of a novel. . .*

There is basically, of course, no analogy here whatsoever.

The discussion is about something historically quite different.

In regard to the best examples of the first type films of *pathos*, you cannot say that our cinema acted like Tatiana's mother:

. . .Her name was Paulina Praskovya
And she spoke in a sing-song voice. . .

It would have been just as untrue and insulting to our cinema to say that with the arrival of *Chapayev* our cinematography

. . .began to call
The former Akulka Selina.

However, if one removes the ironic "Selina" *from the poetic language* of our cinema, and from *its lofty prose* – the humiliating "Akulka," then we are coming close to what took place in *Chapayev*.

Actually, in *Chapayev what is conventionally spoken in the structure of a hymn, elevated speech, or verse was said in simple conversational speech.*

---

* [Pushkin's verse-novel: *Eugene Onegin* – HM.]

The heroic quality of the subject seems "in itself" already to resound with kettledrums; but the composition demands an exposition of this subject, from forms of "lofty writing" that are totally natural and appropriate, to be incessantly transported into a new and unexpected quality – into the construction of everyday prose.

Engels popularized the memory of Monsieur Jourdain,[14] who mentioned that he did not know that he was conversing in prose.

One might say of the subject of *Chapayev* that, without knowing it, "by nature" it speaks in verse.

Verse for such an exciting subject is just as common and ordinary as the prose construction of speech for an unexcited person.

And the change from naturally expected exaltation of style into conscious prosaicness – is the same *leap from quality to quality, as the leap from conversational prose into measured speech – in the opposite case.* . .

The style of the *pathos* effect of conquering October was reflected in the compositioned structure of *Chapayev.*

And the method of construction of the *pathos* effect of *Potemkin* and *Chapayev* are just as identical as the methods of the victories of Bolshevism up to October and after.

We have almost exhausted the material that we were interested in; but as they say, "something remains to be noted."

That is, even *Chapayev*, which was "basically" made in the second *pathos* "manner," solves its problems at three crucial points by the direct method of *pathos.*

This is the attack of the *Kappelevtsev.**

This is the scene with the shooting of Chapayev in the garret.

And this is the explosion at the end of the film.

Constructed according to the first method, they prove to be those places that directly correspond in composition to *Potemkin*, although strict *pathos* composition is not observed in them everywhere to the same degree as in the *Battleship.*

However, another interesting thing occurs at these three points: the fact of the *leap of pathos composition into composition of opposites, which is basic and characteristic of the entire film.*

For here there is a leap from one opposite to another *within the very method of pathos composition*, arranged according to these opposites.

This then, is the second method, by which *Chapayev* enriches the experience of *pathos* composition and its available images.

All this as a whole reflects the fact that the method of *pathos* composition, as we discovered above, is *unified in its opposites and equally true, no matter from which opposite we might take up mastering this unified method.*

---

* [The White Guard forces that were opposing the Red Army and *Chapayev* – HM.]

In addition, however, it is necessary again to firmly remind you that the chosen opposite – is not the author's whim. It is always historically conditioned, produced by the epoch, by the moment.

At one time I was very much abused because I divided the fifteen years of Soviet film into three "stylistic five-year periods," having distinct features and physiognomies quite different from each other.[15]

Whether I am correct or incorrect, of course, only a detailed analysis of the history of our cinema will decide.

But the unity of the stylistic principles for a whole group of films, which were "progressive" for a certain period, is undoubted and evident even now.

So it is also with those indications of *pathos* composition we have just analyzed in two articles.

Strike, Potemkin, Mother, Arsenal, etc. – are films of the first type of *pathos*.

Chapayev, the trilogy about *Maxim, the Deputy of the Baltic* – are clear examples of the other opposite type of *pathos* composition.

In addition it is interesting to note to what degree these or other films are connected to one or the other method of composition.

Thus, for example, the lovely *Deputy of the Baltic*, as soon as it tries to go beyond the limits of the manner of *pathos* composition characteristic of it – immediately turns out to be compositionally weak.

Thus, the end of the film – leaving for the front – which is not solved by the "second method," turns out to be incomparably inferior to the whole rest of the film.

The same thing can be discovered in *We from Kronstadt.** Here the same thing occurred in the scene of the sea landing, so well conceived in the scenario, which was not capable of rising to the necessary power of *pathos* composition of the "first type."

However, one would like to say of this film as a whole that, paradoxically, according to the scenario, it undoubtedly belongs to the first method, whereas according to the director's sympathies it undoubtedly is closer to the second.

In connection with all these considerations, it is extremely curious to note that the fourth five-year period of our film (1935–40), which initially produced fine examples of *pathos* composition of the second type – in *Lenin in October* and *Lenin in 1918*[†] also returns to the rich experience of the first type of *pathos* composition.

Then appear *Alexander Nevsky* (1938) and *Shchors* (1939), which are undoubtedly connected with the new aspect of the tradition of *pathos* writing of the pre-*Chapayev* epoch of the *Battleship* and *Arsenal* (1929).[‡]

---

* [Directed by E. Dzigan, script by V. Vishnevsky, 1936 – HM.]
† [Both, in Krushchev's day, being condemned as a falsification of history and reedited, cutting out the *pathos* of Stalin – HM.]
‡ [Directed by A. Dovzhenko – HM.]

This kind of historical "regularity" of "pulsating" changes perhaps will one day be deciphered or solved.

But the historically determined stylistic originality of both these films, as such, is now already clear.

Both these pictures, in the greatest creative period of their production, coincide with the great patriotic uplift of our whole country.

That brilliant uplift of national patriotism, which remains in one's memory, is inextricably connected with the heroic battle on Lake Hasan.*

This flaming militant *pathos*, enveloping all the peoples of the USSR in 1938–39, was what determined the methodological bent in which the *pathos* composition of both films was embodied.

Borne on the shoulders of the many-million nation's patriotic uplift, these two films – *Nevsky* and *Shchors* – became like the pylons of a gate, through which films with great turns of *pathos* of the first type, again surged toward us in a broad wave during the next five years.

And by their style, they were by no means simply a return to the first type, but an "apparent" return to the preceding one, in accordance with a genuine dialectic progressive movement and development, without losing in their progressive movement anything that could enrich this movement with experience, wisdom, and progressiveness – in the interests of the workers of the whole world.

In regard to the method of *pathos* construction in general, in taking leave of this theme I would like the reader to remember in the depths of his soul what has been said above, that the structure of this *pathos* method is so just because it is a copy of the structure of the grandest moments in the developing fate of the History of the World and Humanity – moments of the *dialectic culmination* of this fate.

I think I first must do a detailed analysis of the methodology and practice of *pathos* composition.

This is understandable.

Never did anyone, who had been working in art until now, have before him a similar real piece of *pathos* history so exciting and so consistently scientific in those methods by which the greatest explosion of human history had been achieved, destroying the barriers of class society and establishing a classless state at one sweep in one-sixth of the earthly sphere. And if only our epoch, especially now, crowned by the victories of our Red Army, emerging victorious and leading nations óut of world massacre, will be able to master scientifically all the secrets of the structure of things – for which the positions developed in this work are first attempts – then we have a right to search into the material of the past, if not for a methodological development of this feeling of unity of

* [On the Soviet–Chinese border, against the Japanese – HM.]

action with nature and history through concrete methods of composition – then, in any case, for illustration *about this feeling as the basis of the actual pathos of experience.*

And where does one seek such illustrations if not in the epoch of the French Revolution, when *pathos,* in the words of Marx, seemed to have flooded into all the secluded corners of everyday life.[16]

And so it was.

And the sought-for expression of the past was found by the united forces of two ecstatics in the words and speeches of one of the great figures of *pathos* of the French Revolution: [Saint-Just].[17] Jaures[18] and Rolland[19] – the vehicles and masters of *pathos* – found a similar idea in his words.

In the epilogue to *Robespierre,* in the article "History has a Word," Romain Rolland on January 1, 1939, writes about Saint-Just*:

He was inspired by the enthusiastic consciousness of his identity –

with the power of things, which leads us, perhaps, to results of which we would not dream. His identity with the laws, guiding the history of humanity.[†]

With his wonderful insight he was moved by a profound feeling for nature, which Jaures noted in his speech of 23 Ventuse (March 13, 1794) – by a romanticism of intuition, which tore like lightning through his otherwise lackluster speech...

---

* How curious! – the same day I finished the first section of this work, a separate article was printed under the name "On the Structure of Things" in the journal *Iskusstvo Kino (The Art of Film),* No. 6, 1939.
[†] These are the words of Saint-Just. See Romain Rolland, *The Theater of the Revolution.* Khudozh. Lit., Moscow, 1939, p. 360.

CHAPTER

IV

Nonindifferent nature

The music of landscape and the fate of montage counterpoint at a new stage

And by the graveyard's gateway
young let life play unconfined,
awhile indifferent nature
with eternal beauty shines!*
　　　　　　　　　　– Pushkin

In the preceding article,[1] we treated in detail the majority of cases where the elements of *Potemkin*, as a construction of *pathos*, "were beside themselves."

There is another area of "being beside oneself" by which, in general, *Potemkin*, with a light hand, came into fashion, although not always into methodology.

This is the passage of representation into music.

This is that inner "plastic music" that, in the various stages of silent film, bore within itself the actual plastic composition of film. This task fell most to the lot of landscape. And a similar emotional landscape, functioning in the film as a musical component, is what I call "nonindifferent nature."

The following pages will be devoted to an analysis of this phenomenon and various phases of its development. This theme passes naturally into general questions of plastic sound, into problems of the development of these principles with the arrival of sound and audio-visual cinematography, and finally it studies the clarification of general changes within the theory and practice of montage at a new stage, twenty years later, after they had been established in this form in *Potemkin*.

Thus, silent film wrote music for itself.

Plastic music.

* [My translation – HM.]

And this also was a peculiar form of "being beside itself," an escape into another dimension. The *plastic art* of silent film also had to *produce sound.*

The musical course of a scene in those days was decided by the structure and montage of representation.

Out of montage pieces, not only was the course of a scene composed but its music as well.

Just as a silent figure "spoke" from the screen, so representation "sounded" from the screen.

The greatest share in "making sound" fell to landscape. For landscape is the freest element of film, the least burdened with servile, narrative tasks, and the most flexible in conveying moods, emotional states, and spiritual experiences. In a word, *all that*, in its exhaustive total, is accessible only to music, with its hazily perceptible, flowing imagery.

At this point the question might arise: "And...generally why, as a matter of fact, is music so necessary? Why is music spoken of here as of something *generally* necessary, a priori, and taken for granted in film?"

I think the answer is quite clear. It is not so much a question of strengthening the effect (although to a great extent, it is), *as in emotionally expressing what is inexpressible by other means.*

The interrelationship between representation and music here can probably be characterized by the same words that Wagner found when comparing *spoken* speech and *tonal* speech:

"Tonal speech as the purest organ of feeling, expresses only what spoken speech is not able to express, that is, essentially – the inexpressible."*

Another composer, Arnold Schönberg,[2] writes the same thing on the pages of the collection *Der Blaue Reiter*† about the songs of Schubert:

"But when I read the poems I found that I had gained nothing in the understanding of the *lieder*, that they did not in the least influence my opinion of the musical statement. On the contrary, I had quite obviously grasped the content, the real content, perhaps even better than if I had clung to the surface of the actual verbal ideas."

Saint-Saëns uses the same expressions when he writes:[3]

Music begins where the word ends; it expresses the unutterable; it forces us to find in ourselves unknown depths; it conveys moods and "states of the soul" which no words can convey. And we note in passing that this is why dramatic music so often uses a mediocre text – or something even worse. The point is that in certain moments music becomes speech, it expresses anything; the text becomes secondary and almost unnecessary.

---

* Richard Wagner, *Opera i Drama*, Vol. IV, p. 218 [Russian translation].
† *The Blaue Reiter Almanac*, published Munich, 1912, p. 31.

On the various paths approaching the embodiment of this sphere of *pure emotionality* from all the elements of plastic art, as we have said above, *landscape lies closest to music.* Given the conditions of silent film, it is landscape that has the problem of expressing emotionally what only music is able to express completely.

This was realized by the interweaving of "landscape sequences" into the general course of the film, where they acted exactly the way the printed title did in a more compressed form of what appeared to be spoken text, inscribed between the moving lips of close-ups.

Here was also an attempt to make the continuity of such musical "passages," inevitable in silent film, approach the feeling of synchronic *simultaneity* with the remaining parts of the film.

Most often this was achieved by an introductory musical-landscape "prelude" that, after having created the necessary emotional state and mood, by its rhythmic elements slips into the further course of the same scene, thematically resounding in the same key: The introductory part revealed this sound in pure form, and in the course of all the scenes, built according to the same rhythmic and audiomelodic structure, this inner music continued to resound in the feelings of the spectator.

In this connection *Potemkin* was destined to include one of the most polished and developed models of the musical solution of landscape, in spite of the fact that at the time it was one of the first films that had solved musical problems plastically.

Much later we see more than a few abuses in this direction, even, for example, among the masters of the so-called French avant-garde who, in the works of Man Ray or Cavalcanti, after having removed the *concrete trend* of emotions[4] from the landscape symphonies, inevitably dissolved the possibility of their definite effect into a purely impressionistic *play of abstract, hazy experiences.*

The fate of landscape in Soviet cinematography was different.

If *Potemkin* somewhat surpassed other films in the method of organically including the emotional landscape, nevertheless it basically expressed a general direction that became characteristic around 1925 for the major part of our cinematography as a whole.

The cameraman Golovnya[5] writes correctly about this in one of his articles:

In 1925–26 three films appeared almost simultaneously: *The Battleship Potemkin, Mother,*[6] and *The Overcoat.*[7]

In these pictures the landscape functioned in a completely new way. It was included as an expressive component into the dramatic composition of the film, and the *pictorial* form of the landscape became something different, something cinematographic.

In *The Battleship Potemkin* before the culminating scene, mourning over the body of Vakulinchuk, the celebrated "mist" was inserted – a series of shots where in the slow motion of the heavy mist over the water, in the black silhouettes of the ships jutting out of the mist, a feeling of stillness and anxiety is born, and in the shots where the sun's rays begin to penetrate through the shroud of the mist – expectation and hope.

In *Mother* the episode of the murder in the tavern ended with a shot – where the weeping willows with lightly rustling silver leaves are translucent in the soft morning sun. Thus the emotional "resolution" of the tragic scene is conveyed by landscape.

And this same prison alternated with "shots of spring." The bright sunshine of spring brooks and little light clouds in the sky are dissonant with the gloom of the prison, and this contrast helped express the state of the hero.

In *The Overcoat*, Gogol's Petersburg is presented to us visually. The landscape in this film was not edited in as separate shots, no – the action of the film unwound on the background of landscape. But this was an active background, it characterized the epoch clearly while determining the style of the whole film. . . .

Later Golovnya writes:

. . .I think that in the contemporary artistic film the landscape functions more in a literary than in a pictorial way.

Sometimes the landscape is edited into the film as an insert, sometimes – as the introduction to one episode or other – but mostly it is included in the direct development of the action, fulfilling simultaneously a function both pictorial and dramatic.

This "literary" treatment of landscape in the composition of a film – is one of the stylistic marks of Soviet film. . .

Here, of course, we are somewhat surprised that with the mention of the "literary" treatment of landscape and its dramatic role there is still no mention first of all of its *musical function*, which is actually the *basic means of solving the problems mentioned*.

Moreover, this is really not accidental, because the *musical line of landscape* begun by *Potemkin* was certainly not continued by all Soviet cinematography, having limited the musical line in its best examples to *only the emotional landscape.**

Our research will concern itself with the musical landscape in particular.

In *Potemkin* I have in mind the introductory part of the episode of the mourning over the body of Vakulinchuk – the symphony of the mist in the port of Odessa.

This scene is by no means the only one concerned with plastic music.

The "night full of anxiety" in expectation of the encounter with the squadron is also structured in this way. Carrying within it the high point of development and growth of the theme of the murdered Vakulinchuk,

---

* See below on the difference between the two.

it corresponds – both plastically and rhythmically – to the scenes of mourning over Vakulinchuk.

The increasing dramatic effect forces the gray mist of dawn in the Odessa port to thicken here to the blackness of twilight and night. The gray silver surface of the water in the mist scenes here become black with reflections of strong highlights abruptly scattered through it. The gray seems to divide into a black surface and a white gleam. The silhouettes of the details of the port from the misty scenes become first statuary figures of sailors freezing on the watch, only to come to life, at the approach of the admiral's squadron, as numerous separate actions, into which preparation of the battleship for battle was broken down, connecting separate parts of the battleship (gangways, cannons, machines), as well as the people, into one whole surge to battle. The built-up energy is released here also as an explosion, but not as the expected thunder of weapons, but as the shout "Brothers!" and the flight of the sailors' caps into the air, catching up the theme of the protest meeting over the body and its culminating point – the raising of the red flag over the battleship.

In a very different type of structure – and, I would say, in a different type of orchestration – other scenes are solved; for example, the *shooting on the Odessa steps*, built on the basic theme of the drumroll of feet and the salvos of the soldiers shooting the peaceful inhabitants of Odessa, of the symphony of machines at *meeting the squadron*, whose plastic thunder and rhythmic pulsation seem to lead in an opposite direction that same theme of the "soldiers' feet" from the preceding scene.

However, in both scenes the situations are first of all loaded with the dramatic effect of the unwinding events, and therefore, for the sake of analysis, it would be better to look closely at an example of a musical mood created purely by means of landscape.

Therefore, we will select *the scene at dawn at the Odessa port* for analysis.

The tradition of similar compositional solutions in general has certainly not been curtailed with the departure of silent film from the screen; on the contrary, in its *progressive* beginnings, the audiovisual film broadened immeasurably similar stylistic and expressive possibilities, synthesizing all the means of expression available to it.

And, therefore, one should concentrate on this episode not *as if it were a relic of the past*, but as a definite stage of the development of a completely distinct area of expression of the film in general.

The "Odessa Mist" is like a connecting link between *pure painting* and the *music of audiovisual combinations* of the new cinematography.

The suite of the mist is still painting, but a distinct type of painting that through montage already perceives the rhythm of the change of *real spans of time* and the tangible sequence of repetitions in time, that is, the elements of what in pure form is only accessible to music.

This is a type of "postpainting" passing into a distinctive type of "premusic (protomusic)."

Therefore it is quite normal and reasonable at this point to look at *traditions of the past* of a similar stylistic manner – "music for the eyes" – before drawing the path along which the development of this manner and method moves ahead within the richest possibilities of audiovisual film.

The "music of the eye"* flourished fully in the art of the Far East – in China and Japan.

And very richly in landscape painting.

We should not be surprised that we can find the most polished models of this in China.

For it is in China that even in literature this phenomenon exists not as *the poetry of sound*, but – *the poetry of graphics alone*!

"The character of the Chinese language, which *represents* a phenomenon unique of its kind, forces one to distinguish poetry uttered aloud from written poetry, words, composing a poetic work, from the signs which represent them. Everyone should be made aware that in calligraphy, drawn signs, corresponding to a certain word, do not have any relationship to the sounds composing this word."†

Hans Bethe writes even more powerfully about this aspect of poetry in an epilogue to the collection of translations of Chinese lyrics.‡

Chinese prosody is extremely complicated. From a combination of the most complicated pictorial features of Chinese calligraphy and of the particular sound system of Chinese speech a particular rhythm is created, which dictates both the pictorial and musical standards to an equal degree.

There is nothing in common here with European poetry if you do not consider the exterior sign of the presence of rhyme.

"Here everything abides by a profoundly developed parallelism of great refinement, which in the form of an antithesis rests, not only on words, thoughts or verbal images, but also penetrates into refined details of syntactic constructions and spreads further into the innermost features, into the so tastefully developed ornamental expressiveness of the designs of calligraphy. And all this is interwoven very tightly with the concept of Chinese poetry. This poetry appeals equally to both the ear and the eye..."¶

But the *matter* is even broader.

In Chinese poetry there is no blank verse, and all poetry is built on rhyme. The *Odes* collected and published by Confucius[11] are like an "encyclopedia of rhymes." Any words shown rhyming in this collection

---

* "Music of the eyes" – a term of the great set designer Pietro Gonzago.[8]
† V. Markov, Preface, *The Chinese Flute*, Insel-Verlag, Leipzig, 1919.
‡ Hans Bethe, *Die Chinesische Flöte*, Insel-Verlag, Leipzig, 1919.
¶ We can discover an interesting "rebirth" of all this at the end of the nineteenth century in the play with different scrips and typography in Marinetti,[9] the dadaists (Tristan Tzara),[10] and among our early futurists!

can be used in a rhyme wherever convenient, but it is impossible to use other words or other rhymes. As a result, all the groups of possible rhymes came to 106. Moreover – it is understandable that words that rhymed around 500 years before the birth of Christ, in many cases no longer being pronounced as they were pronounced earlier, lost this feature of rhyming harmony long ago. Nevertheless, only the once-established set of rhymes was allowed to be used, just as before. H. A. Gilles, who introduces these interesting data in his little book *China and the Chinese**, illustrates the latter position by an analogous example from Chaucer.[12]

Two lines from the *Canterbury Tales*, read as they are pronounced today, do not rhyme at all:

When that April with his showers sweet,
The drought of March hath pierced to the root...

Today it would not occur to any one to rhyme:
"sweet" and "root." But the main thing is that in Chaucer's time the words were pronounced differently – and "soote" and "roote" *were rhymed.*

This is a literal application to the area of literature of what occurs in the plastic "rhyming" of visual depiction and lines in a drawing or painting.

The words ("sweet and root") are written quite differently from the way they were rhymed in ancient *pronounciation* ("soote–roote").

Here this is unexpected and unusual.

In the art of plastic composition this occurs at every step.

Actually, two objects different in form in terms of "plastic pronunciation" – that is, according to the *graphic manner of their design* – appearing as lines corresponding and repeating each other, are found in conditions of what could be called *"elastic rhyme."*

Thus the line of a mountain avalanche repeats the line of the bent back of an old man.

the hem of a dress repeats the lines of the flow of a river

or scattered curls – the flight of clouds, etc.

And it is just such a "rhyming" of lines that is so characteristic of Chinese and Japanese drawing.

As we can see, the devices lying *within oral literature* and the devices *within painting* are combined by interesting features from the area lying between them, *written literature*, that diverges from spoken literature and *that applies more to the standards of plastic visual depiction.*

The distinctive character of Chinese writing, and especially – of Chinese prosody, strikes us by their unusual nature.

We think this is all very distant from us, and we supposedly have nothing similar in our artistic practice.

* Cambridge University Press, New York, 1902.

The imprint of the "child's stage" of poetry undoubtedly lies in similarly undifferentiated prosody, which is the mark of the infantile stage.

And if we would look for analogous examples in the "infantile" areas of our poetics, then we will find as many examples as we wish.

Especially, of course, in the area of children's books and verses.

I myself remember verses from childhood where the design of words harmonious in sound are given by different means: The words themselves are given in letter designs, and the rhymes for them – in drawings.

Chtoby gvozdi zabivat'   [In order to hammer in nails
ikh vnov' vytaskivat'   And pull them out again
nuzhny nam dve veshchi: We need two things:
(molotok i kleshchi)   (hammer and tongs)]

If such are the forms of edifying entertainment for little children, then young children and older children are amused...by rebuses, where the same thing occurs.

The "standard" rebus is built on the fact that the sound designation of the object corresponds phonetically to several meanings.

The solution of a rebus usually is based on the pictures' being read in their second sense based on sound, just as the components of Chinese hieroglyphics are read.

The most popular form of the rebus is the comic rebus, which is built on a phonetic change of two corresponding words that do not coincide orthographically.

(In poetry this device is quite frequent and adds a certain sharpness to the language of rhyme.)

Pogodi, tovarišč *Gofman,**   Wait, Comrade Hofmann,
Ne dovol'no li stikhov *nam.*   Verses are not enough man.
Net li zdes' u vas *Izvestii.*   Don't you have Izvestia here,
Očen' khočetsja pro*čest'.*   We'd like to digest it here.
...Ne dumal, ne gadal,   ...I never guessed, never thought that
Čob mogla, kak V. Kačhalov,   I could, like V. Kachalov –
Deklamirovat' voda...   be reciting water...
        Kirsanov,   Kirsanov
    (Moya imeninnaya)   (My name day)

* [Abnormal rhymes italicized; my translation – HM.]

An example of a comic rebus is this witty sign, apparently a billboard:

According to the conception of the anonymous author of the rebus, it means:

"Doroga razdvoyaetsa" (doroga raz-dva-yaitsa) [The road divides (a road one-two-eggs).]

This example immediately brings to mind examples where an independent, concrete visual interpretation is added to the silhouette of the visual design of letters.

We know that both the earlier, purely pictographic hieroglyph[13] as well as the earlier, purely representational letters proceeded from schematic pictures.

This is why the return of these former representational silhouettes into representations inside pictures functions so powerfully, and often comically.

This occurs quite often, of course, in the East, where the hieroglyph lost its tie with its representational past to a much lesser degree than the design of letters in our alphabet.

Thus, there is an amusing moralizing print of Hokusai[14] appealing for greater purity in a son's piety toward his parents. The little picture depicts this directly: A cloud of small funny people diligently carves, washes, and cleans a huge hieroglyph meaning "child's respect for parents."

I remember a similar play on words in another example:

in a very virulently anti-Semitic postcard, which was circulated in 1905 and directed against the consolidation of international Jewish capital. On the postcard were depicted the words "Union of European States." To the letters "O" and "P" in the word "evropeisky" [European] ropes were attached, which representatives of international Jewish capital were hanging onto with all their strength. The letters crawled out of the word "evropeisky [European]," turning it into the word "evreisky" [Jewish] and adding a new meaning to the saying on the postcard.

An analogous example of the play of representation and meaning of letters, used this time in an advertisement, appeared in the journal *Die Reklame* for September 1925.

Here the figure of a little person with head attached was made out of the letters of the word *WER* [who]. This is the trademark of one of the Frankfurt advertising firms.

Again, in each advertisement this figure functions *both as* a word in a sentence composed of it with other words *and as* a comic personage, whose action illustrates the content of the sentence ("*who* thinks for you," "*who* will bring you a profit," "*who* will show you your mistakes," "*who* will always hit the mark," etc.).

A very popular device from the field of athletics also applies here – when letters or national emblems are formed from constructions made out of masses of figures.

Sometimes more than a small share of unintentional irony is hidden in such constructions.

I remember how I was amused once in Mexico when I was filming, from the top of the freedom column, the emblem of liberated Mexico composed of figures of policemen, participating in the sports parade...[...]

I hope that after all the above examples of the particular nature of Chinese prosody,[15] they have become significantly closer, more comprehensible, and more perceptible to us.

But, if this is not enough, let them recall *Tristam Shandy*[16] at this point; in this collection of ironic examples of literary writing, one of "my Uncle Toby's" tirades passes over into rhetorical gesture, and the author introduces it not as verbal description but places on that same page after the colon – a graphic stroke of this very gesture!

It is also interesting that the variety of plastic motifs from which one can compose a drawing or picture seems so limited in number, as if here, there was also a similar canon, regulating their quantity and quality – a canon similar to the canon of Confucius' *Ode* for literature.

In any case, the number of elements of this set of representational motifs, existing in all mutual combinations, is not very large.

Variety is achieved by a refinement of compositional methods rather than by increasing the number of objects; they are usually confined to a river, lake, cliffs, mountain chains, waterfalls, trees of a certain type, thatched-roof cottages, and details of monasteries.

I will return to Chinese landscape again because I am interested not only in the *emotional effect* of landscape but especially in its *musical effect*, that is, that variety of "nonindifferent nature" when the emotional effect is achieved not only by a *set of representational elements* of nature but especially and mainly by the *musical development and composition* of what is represented.

It is in this direction that the musical landscape of the period of silent film is working; there is a direct development from this method into the musical work at further stages of the development of film, and a single tradition and methodology of this work is *preserved* – from *silent* film through *sound* film to *audiovisual* cinematography.

I think the division of cinematography into three such stages is essentially correct.

By *sound* film I mean the cinematography of the *inorganic synchronization of sound and of representation*.

Such, from a theoretical standpoint, is the earlier sound *cinema*, but from a practical standpoint, unfortunately, a large number of contemporary *films*. These films are characterized by the prevailing role of sound of *the basically verbal spoken type*.

The next stage of audiovisual cinematography is *the cinematography of the organic fusion of sound and representation* as commensurate and equivalent elements composing the film as a whole.

It is interesting that the main responsibility of the culminating creative act in respect to the film in all three stages moves further and further toward *new phases at the end*!

If in *silent* film the *"montage"* (editing) phase is this part, and in sound film – the *"sound recording,"* then now in audiovisual film the most complex work in "vertical montage" occurs in the process of . . . re-recording.

It is interesting to note how organically the first and third stages continue each other – in their tendencies toward the fusion of different spheres of effect into one *unity* – and how opposing them is the middle phase of film, which is the least cinematographic, consisting mainly of "dialogue," this is that same median stage for which (in order to achieve the correct movement toward what was needed), I as well as Pudovkin and Alexandrov, recommended in *Manifesto*, 1928,[17] a *strong explosion, divergence*, and *counterpoint opposition* of the elements of sound and the elements of representation.

In respect of our basic theme, it is quite obvious that emotion can be evoked not only by a musically structured landscape but often, of course, by the *concreteness* of the landscape.

I have not spoken of blasted houses or smoking ruins, which have an identical effect in the shots of a newsreel or in the lithographs of Daumier (especially in the series of prints connected with the Franco-Prussian War), but every "desolate" landscape of bare earth and a solitary tree always has a chance on its own – *by the compositional arrangement of the objects* – to evoke a gloomy mood and gloomy emotions. Let us just recall such background landscapes of Daumier from other series of his lithographs, or let us bring in for the sake of variety W. M. Thackeray's description[18] devoted to a landscape of George Cruikshank.[19]

We must not forget to mention *Oliver Twist*, and Mr. Cruikshank's famous designs to that work...Syke's farewell to the dog; what a fine touching picture of melancholy desolation is that of Sykes and the dog! The poor cur is not too well drawn, the landscape is stiff and formal; but in this case the faults, if faults they be, of execution rather add to than diminish the effect of the picture: it has a strange, wild, dreary, broken-hearted look; we fancy we see the landscape as it must have appeared to Sykes, when ghastly and with bloodshot eyes he looked at it.*

Speaking just among ourselves, Thackeray, in my opinion, somewhat exaggerates the degree of the actual emotional resonance of this landscape. Therefore, we will limit ourselves to only one description of the picture, without a reproduction. And moreover, perhaps for the forties of the past century, this was enough!

The end of the sixteenth century was more demanding; it is sufficient to recall what was considered, I think, almost the first independent landscape in the whole history of painting, *Storm over Toledo* from the brush of El Greco – simultaneously remaining the almost unsurpassed example of a stormily emotional landscape!

Here, however, I repeat, I am interested in landscape that is not only emotional but above all musical.

What is most interesting is to trace the basic features of musical landscape to the sources of the genre, where it also achieved the highest degree of perfection. It is here that, in the features of its *youth*, it naturally corresponds to *the stage of the origin* of a similar phenomenon, in the first stages of development of cinematography as an independent art.

The landscape suites that the Chinese use, one might add, are extremely close in their method to the symphony, for they are built out of the *sequence* of a whole series of *landscape* shots, which silent film used when creating its "music."

Let us not forget that a separate landscape shot "pasted" into the action like a postage stamp never achieved a similar effect, and inevitably acted only as limited geographical information (such "information" is almost always the lot of a shot taken separately, and most of all of the *first* shot of a sequential series. The shots of "crashing waves" at the beginning of *Potemkin* is of this type).

* William Makepeace Thackeray, "George Cruikshank," June 1840, in *Westminster Review*, Henry Hooper, London, 1841.

The latest methods of development of what was found in the "Odessa Mist" lie beyond the *limits* of silent film.

The audiovisual solutions in *Alexander Nevsky* continue their tradition in the same direction (the "dawn" before the "Battle of the Ice")[20] and, to an even greater degree, separate scenes in *Ivan the Terrible*.

However, before turning to the *pictorial past* and the *audiovisual future* of the "Odessa Mist"; let us try to discover briefly, how and with what the impressionable performance has been structured.

Here the black mass of a buoy, like a massive chord of "Solidity," bursts out into the elemental water and calmly rolls on the silvery surface of the sea.

And here the black mass of the hulks of ships swallows the whole expanse of the screen and slowly floats past the camera...

The general combination of motifs moves from the airiness of the mist through the barely perceptible outline of objects – through the lead-gray surface of the water and gray sails – the velvety black hulks of the ships and the hard rock of the embankment.

The dynamic combination of separate lines of these elements flows together into a final static chord.

They merge together into a motionless shot, where the gray sail becomes a tent, the black hulks of the ships – the crêpe of the mourning bow, the water – the tears of women's bowed heads, the mist – the softness of the outlines of the – out of focus – shot, and the hard rock becomes the corpse lying prostrate on the paved, cobblestone embankment.

And now – almost inaudibly – the theme of fire enters.

It enters as the flickering candle in the hands of Vakulinchuk, so it may grow into the flaming wrath of the meeting held over the corpse, and it flares up with the scarlet flame of the red flag on the mast of the mutinying battleship.

The movement goes from hazy, almost ethereal moods of sorrow and mourning in general to a real victim, who perished for the cause of freedom, from the gloomy surface of the sea to the ocean of human sorrow, from the trembling candle in the hands of the murdered fighter through the mourning of the grieving masses to the uprising, seizing the whole city.

Thus, interweaving, the separate lines of these "elements" move into the opening part, now floating into the foreground, now giving place to others and becoming lost in the depths of the background, now emphasizing each other, now setting each other off, now opposing each other.

In addition, each line passes along its own path of movement.

Thus the mist thins out from shot to shot:

concreteness becomes more and more transparent.

And on the contrary, before our eye the hard rock thickens and grows heavier: At first this is a black haze merging with the mist, then it is the bony skeletons of the masts and yard arms or silhouettes of cranes, resembling huge insects.

Later these bows and masts, jutting out of the shroud of the mist, grow before our eyes into whole launches and schooners.

The impact of the *Vorschlag*[21] of the black buoy – and now the massive hulks of large ships enter.

And the theme of the water turning silver passes into the white sail, dreamily rolling on the sea's smooth surface...

I have touched here only on the mutual play of *concrete* principles, that is, the actual "elements" – water, air, and earth.

But they are all also strictly echoed by the mutual play of purely *tonal* and *textural* combinations: dull gray, the mellow atmosphere of the mist, the silvery gray smoothness of the glittering surface of the water, the velvety sides of the black masses of concrete details.

All this is rhythmically echoed by the *measured length of duration of the pieces* and the barely caught *"melodic" rocking of photographed objects*.

The sea gull in the air – seems to be part of the mist and sky.

The sea gull, alighting down like a black silhouette on the buoy – is an element of solid earth.

And among them – as if the sea gull's wing grew enormously – the whiteness of the sail of a yacht slumbering on the water.*

And it seems that the textures of the separate elements, just as the elements among themselves, form the same combination as an orchestra does, unifying into the *simultaneity* and the *sequence* of the action – the winds and strings, wood and brass!

Let us now look at the past and we will be convinced that the "mist" in *Potemkin* continues the tradition of the most ancient examples of Chinese landscape painting, as China cultivated it, and whose traditions were later adopted by Japan.

In the general discussion I will purposely use a comparison of quotations from various types of investigation so that the *identical nature* of the principle is presented distinctly and objectively. I will try to introduce additional material only when other statements relevant to the theme I am interested in are not at hand.

One of the most ancient forms of visual depiction of landscape is the

---

* It is interesting to recall the early perception by man of a bird as *part of the sky*.

And moreover: N. Ya. Marr[22] proved that, in the original meaning of the roots of ancient languages, birds are called..."skylings," that is, "fledglings of the sky"!

As we can see, plastic "poetry" also invariably corresponds to the original concept of how humanity perceived the world at the dawn of its development!

Chinese picture scroll – an endless ribbon (almost a film reel!) of the panorama of landscape unwinding horizontally.

"Panorama" in the narrow sense of the word, as cinema uses it in those cases when the camera on tracks slides by the changing chain of events and scenes.

And "panorama" also in the sense that the whole picture cannot be grasped entirely by the eye *all at once*, but in *sequence*, as if pouring out of one independent subject into another, out of one fragment into the next; that is, it appears before the eye as a stream of separate depictions (shots!) merging into one.

It seems that the landscape has been copied from the movement along the river, from the deck of a junk, slowly floating along the shore.

And almost always the calm flow of the river leads the eye along the changing curves of the unwinding Chinese picture.*

"Around 750 AD the emperor was seized with longing and the desire to see the surrounding area of the river [*Tsalmtsan*] Yangtze in the province of Szechwan, and he sent Wu Ch'ao-ch'u[23] to represent them in a picture. Wu Ch'ao-ch'u returned without a single drawing. When the emperor demanded an explanation, Wu answered: 'I have everything drawn in my heart.' Then he went to one of the chambers of the palace and in the course of one day painted a hundred miles of landscapes." This is the way H. A. Gilles conveys the ancient tale in *An Introduction to the History of Chinese Pictorial Art*[†] where the historical moment is given of the transition from the old type of picture scroll – which is *informational and narrative* above all – to a new type: poetic and musical. (The origin of the new type is *connected with the name Wu Ch'ao-ch'u*.)

The lack of drawings and sketches, which so struck the emperor, makes it quite clear that the painter was attracted above all by the *emotional resonance* and *change of moods* of the river landscape and not the *documentation* of river banks.

In the same way the camera caught separate details of the misty morning, penetrated by the faded sun in the Odessa port, in search of a mood that would harmonize with the theme of mourning, so as to weave from them not a topographical presentation of the port structures of the city of Odessa but the introductory part of the scene of mourning on its shore.

What does a similar emotional landscape scroll represent?

Apparently there is not a single author who, while describing the Chinese landscapes, would not resort to a musical interpretation of them, to a musical reading of them, to musical terminology.

* This device of an actual film panorama, floating along the shore, was applied with great talent by A. Dovzhenko when, in the introductory part of *Ivan* (1932), he wanted to create a distinctive film equivalent to the famous passage from Gogol's *Terrible Vengeance*: "How wonderful is the Dnieper in quiet weather..."
† Kelloy and Walsh, Shanghai, 1905.

And in the transmission of the general sensations they evoke.

And in the musical realization of their rhythmic and melodic structure.

And in a comparison with certain names of composers, with whose works they would correspond.

And in a direct comparison of their horizontal and vertical divisions with the classical form of a polyphonic score.

Curt Glaser wrote*:

These pictures of pure mood, freed from anything concrete, are difficult to interpret without resorting to concepts which Europeans have only in other areas of art – in lyric poetry and music...

...This musical character of the painting of Eastern Asia is easy to discover, if you open an album of landscapes belonging to the brush of one of the greatest masters such as Sesshū.[24] A very small number of invariably identical motifs and elements of form and constantly repeated in them – a hint of mountains, a clump of trees, the roof of a hut, a fisherman's boat. Only the juxtaposition of economic dabs of the brush each time different, and each time their common resonance gives a new note to one and the same basic mood. One theme is touched, and it goes through numerous variations. You are unintentionally forced to make a comparison with the fugue in music....

(Fisher also compares Sesshū's plastic fugue with Bach.)[†]

This is even more vivid in the group of what are called scrolls.

...The old scroll, built on the principle of sequential phases of a story, was more representational and informative. In the new one we experience a changing sequence of moods. And here the painting also proves to be a temporal art, but not according to a type of epic narration, but according to the principles of music. The unwinding sequence of elements of the landscape became a symphonic sketch. Steep cliffs change into expansive lakes; a quiet fishing village huddles on the shores of a bay, and a little village swarming with people – high in the mountains; wide rice fields disappear in the mist, and in the distance stretch extensive walls which enclose a monastery.

One is interwoven with the other. One theme quietens down and introduces a new one; the deep chord of the leit-motif of the mountain peaks is echoed by the tender melting tones of the mists, hovering over the watery expanse, from which in the distance emerges but a single sail.

Sonorously the motif of the steep cliffs enters and with triumphant chords the mountain chain playfully intertwines with the business of the human ant-heap. Snowy mountain heights emerge from the depths, with alternating sharp rises and quick descents and a wonderful linear cadenza of depicted trees completes the multi-voiced song of this landscape poem...

...A later scroll of a river landscape attributed to Kuo Hsi[25] (around 1068)

---

* Curt Glaser, *Die Kunst Ostasiens. Der Umkreis ihres Denkens und Gestaltens*, Insel-Verlag, Leipzig, 1922.
[†] Otto Fisher, *Chinesische Landschaftsmalerei, Vorwort von Alfred Salmony*, Neff, Vienna, 1943.

already unites the mountains and valleys in whole compact masses of form, and at the same time as Siu-jan[26] (second half of the tenth century) was limited by the fact that the planes went deep into his picture like scenery wings, here contrasts of space dominate the compositions, here the foreground and increasing distance are in opposition, the break of a ravine – to the mountain mass abruptly forging ahead, and thus the former compositional limitation of lines and planes are replaced – by a new variety of play: the play of volume and space, all done according to those same basic rhythmic norms. Just as before there was an opposition between high and low or angular and smooth, in rhythmic play the near and the far are now interwoven...

...Soon a new element appeared which takes the place of the former line of movement. This is the pulsating growth and fall of elements of the range of dark tunes.

As early as the epoch of T'ang (618–906), painting developed from an original schematic shading of details into a rich and tonally differentiated treatment of planes. But in the first periods they were still severely limited by contours of separate planes arranged like stage wings. At a new stage a unique emancipation occurs, and the pictures are enlivened by the play of mutual contrasts of light and dark as well, and their overflowing into each other. For movement occurs even here: darkness arises from a mass of light, the light appears through the dim and heavy darkness, and barely perceptibly, it again creeps into the night; the outlines of the objects appear out of the mist and flow back into the general atmosphere, softly the general tonality unfolds, and a strong rush of darkness suddenly and unexpectedly develops in the picture. The landscape of Siu-jan[27]* is constructed in this way, as a system of motifs of severely outlined dark planes continually arising and repeating and engendered by a lighter flickering in the background. And it is impossible not to note the same thing in the works of Kuo Hsi where tonal changes – smoother and more flowing – arising and becoming pale in exactly the same way, break up the general flow of the picture by the variety of their changes...

...And they have every justification for comparing this singular manner of plastic composition with the structure of sound patterns of our greatest musicians: Lu Ssu-hsün (651–720)[28] and Wang Wei (699–759)[29] with Beethoven and Mozart; masters of the Sung Epoch (907–1270)[30] with Schumann or Grieg; artists of the Ming Epoch (1280–1643)[31] with Mendelssohn and Meyerbeer, with Weber and Lizst. The symphonic harmony of the unit with the whole, the rising and falling flow of images, the presence of a basic theme, invariably caught up into this general flow and permeating the whole, and, finally, the birth of the picture out of a strictly rhythmic division into parts and of the melodic variety of the play of tonalities – testify to the truly justified relation of the structure of these two areas of composition – landscape and music...

Ernst Dietz writes:

Here on the surface the same harmonization is achieved as in music – through time, and in the same way, rhythm and melody are its means...

* [See Wm. Cohn, *Chinese Painting*, Oxford University Press, New York, 1948, p. 64 – HM.]

...Rhythm is created by grouping material; the melody – through the linear unification of motifs and elements corresponding to each other...*

And passing on to the description of landscape as a whole, Dietz successfully compares the *elements of landscape, floating on the surface of the unwinding scroll of the picture, with the designs characteristic of a score*:

We cannot capture in one glance the visual depiction unwinding on the surface of *emakimono* (the Japanese term for a scroll picture), as we have become used to doing with usual pictures; we can only capture seperate impressions of it, as far as the picture slips by our eyes. We are able to perceive it in time, like music, and from this it follows that the composition of landscape must be subjected to formal laws, similar to the laws of music.

The most important formal device of music is repetition. The same motifs in different tonality and in performance by different instruments, in different timbres, return and are varied again and again. Symphonic phrases are repeated. The same method is adapted to landscape scroll pictures, where the unity of the whole is achieved not by the spatial perspective of its combination, but by the musical method just described. Thus, for example, in the panorama of Yangtze by the brush of Siu-jan, we can see six or seven mountain chains arranged directly over each other, like a set of wind and string instruments in a score; and the same linear motives arise, alternating above or below – now in a thick bass flourish, then in the refined height of descant...

Two schemes applying this can clarify what is being discussed in all these excerpts, and what cannot but be caught by the highly sensitive eye of every lover of beauty.

Here is the scheme of Siu-jan's landscape.

Here are several variations of similar motifs that alternately are repeated in a different tonality.

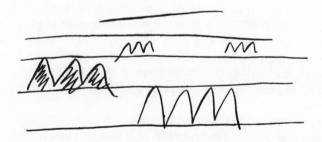

And here is another type of landscape, where the theme is introduced by the inclusion of a consecutive combination of the sounds of aspects of the various "natural elements" composing it. Now the water of the river

* *Einfuhrung in die Kunst des Ostens*, Hellerau, Wien, 1922.

plays the theme of the landscape, then the river and clouds together, now a mountain chain, then the combination of mountains, water, and mist, etc.

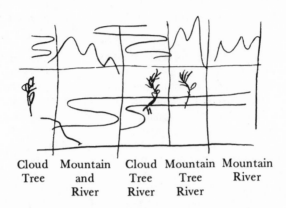

| Cloud Tree | Mountain and River | Cloud Tree River | Mountain Tree River | Mountain River |

Here it might be interesting to note that, when the painting has the task not only of *a musical-emotional interpretation of a piece of visible nature*, but the solution of a *purely musical problem*, then the "score" type of composition inevitably arises.

In these "abstract" cases it is even clearer, since under these conditions the author is not tied to any strict representational logic, and is completely free to perform a purely musical play of separate representational motifs.

The once-so-thundering Churlyanis[32] is particularly characteristic here. Among his pictorial "sonatas," the "allegro" from the sonata *The Pyramids* is particularly illustrative in this respect.

The repeated motifs of pyramids and palms repeated in various planes and in various vertical and horizontal divisions seem to give a picture of those plastic excesses in the area of abstract art, toward which the system of the composition of Chinese landscapes might have gone if their authors had taken one step further, and in the name of music, would have broken with the representational logic of their natural landscapes.

The surprising ability to combine real landscape representation with a musical and emotional interpretation of it through composition, and the pungency of its musicality, which surpasses the symphonic abstractions of Churlyanis by many times – is one of the particularly striking aspects of the Chinese masters.

This becomes very obvious in a comparison of Chinese landscapes, with their mutual interweaving of clouds, mountains, and water expanses, with the "allegros" of Churlyanis from the sonata *Chaos*.

This is the nature of the aesthetic canons of the structure of Chinese and Japanese landscape.

Naturally, like all canons, these aesthetic canons grow out of the concepts based on one's worldview. Or, more precisely – grow out of those same social premises as do philosophical conceptions.

Therefore, philosophical conceptions, which are connected historically to certain stages of development, are extremely helpful in clarifying aesthetic problems connected to those epochs and nations.

Thus we used our basic philosophical and theoretical premises – the nature of the properties of the dialectic – in order to investigate the problems of the *pathos* effect.

One must seek philosophical premises, both as the basis of the particular features of Chinese aesthetic thought and of the canons proceeding therefrom.

In contrast to the Elizabethan perception of the world as a system of "the four elements" (which has been mentioned above), the Chinese picture of the world is based not only on these same elements (which among the Chinese are five)* but above all on the mutual interaction of "*two principles*" – the notorious opposite principles of yin and yang.

According to this Chinese conception, which on a rudimentary level is similar to the principles of the dialectic (as we know it even among the ancient Greeks), the world is built, maintained, and moves through the interaction of two opposite principles, permeating the whole universe.

All phenomena is classified into a series of corresponding opposites that, in their interaction and conflict, create all the phenomena of reality out of themselves.

These principles are represented in different forms in different areas, but the essence of their interaction remains identical.

According to the teaching of the Chinese, this is the female principle and the male principle. And all phenomena can be classified according to them. Some correspond to the female series, others – to the male.

For example: light and dark, soft and hard, flexible and harsh, flowing and motionless, loud and soft, vague and distinct, etc.

The play of interaction, change, and mutual penetration of these opposite principles (by which, according to Chinese teaching, all universal phenomena are preserved) also lies at the basis of the dynamics of the structuring of the visual music on which landscape is built.

It is this principle that dictates the features of those inner laws of the weaving and unweaving of elements of landscape, separating naturally into groups, according to the same subordination of certain elements to the principle of yang, and others – to the principle of yin.

---

* The Chinese number wood among these elements.

And this principle is revealed especially in the bases of composition – the raw nerves of the artistic intention, thought, and ideology.

If we focus on this small part, even within the limits of a purely concrete comparison of the elements of landscape, we will certainly discover that

the *flowing* of water is opposed to the *immobility* of the shore,

the *softness* of the mist and the *transparency* of air – to the *firmness* of the cliffs and mountains,

the *bare surface* of mountain slopes – to the *vegetation* of trees and the *thickness* of reeds, etc.

And A. Salmony is correct when he closely connects the nature of the play of similar elements in a landscape score and the principles of yin and yang:

The masters of the T'ang era had already created rules, leading to a type of language of forms, which showed how the smallest motif – no matter how small it might be – was forced again and again to embody first principles (*Grundprinzipien*); and these principles are those same ancient Taoist symbols[33] of the male and female principle, from whose mutual penetration arises the whole essence and all the processes of the visible world. In this play of principles through both the images of mountain and fog, the moisture penetrates the solid, an artery of water penetrates a cliff and the earth. All of visible nature unrolls before us in the forms of a living organism. To capture and embody its characteristic features was the inevitable task of the great masters of the past...*

The famous waterfall attributed to Wang Wei was subjected to this law:

In this landscape of the great master of the T'ang dynasty the struggle of the only two primordial natural principles is captured – flowing and hardening.

Probably it is in the *musicality of the structure* of this painting that the secret lies, of how effectively the painting succeeded in conveying the feeling of purely sound phenomena and sounds by purely plastic means.

Salmony also introduces a landscape called *The Evening Chimes of a Distant Temple* (the name probably came later), where by plastic means an almost concrete feeling of the distant dull chiming of the gongs is achieved; the repeated appearance through the misty atmosphere of similar landscape details of temples and villages, repeating each other through various intervals and in various scales gives a total illusion of the feeling of the chiming of gongs, by various voices resounding in answer to the basic sound.

I think the repetition of motifs can be read as an *echo* and as *chiming*,

* *Die Chinesische Landschaftsmalerei mit einem Vorwort von Alfred Salmony*, Orbis Pictus, Bd. 4, Neff, Vienna, 1943.

just because the chiming and the reflection of sound as echo also lie at the basis of direct external impressions, which *help* to form into a method the general rhythmic feelings ("beats") that lie at the basis of the pulsating *repetition*, characteristic of the structure of rhythm in general.

Using the term "chiming" instead of the term "repetition," we discover in the actual nature of these terms the *dynamic premise of a really tangible phenomenon of nature – a resonance that, hardening into a device*, becomes *repetition*.

In the methods of its composition, the Chinese landscape is probably closer to the initial phenomenon – the chime – than to the stage when this phenomenon develops into a *device*: *chiming* – into *repetition*.

On the other hand, our common European types of composition are typical structures formed according to a *repetition of motifs* – whereas Chinese structures are perceived as the *chiming of motifs*.

I do not know how far one could differentiate, in more detail, the difference by accumulating additional arguments. I am afraid you won't be able to manage here without the help of a vivid and direct sensual perception of the difference of both these terms!

Here there is the same "abyss" of difference as between the title of the play, *Vishnyévy Sad* (*The Cherry Orchard*) instead of the original *Víshnyevy Sad* (*The Cherry Orchard*) (just recall the description of Chekhov's excitement described in Stanislavsky's book when, after changing the accent and the intonation in the name of the title, he achieved complete *harmony of this name with the actual mood of the play*).[34]

A similar nuance of difference lies in whether we will begin to read and designate the structure of the Chinese landscape as a *repetition* of a motif or the *chiming* of motifs.

The different nature of these two methods is revealed most clearly if we compare the examples of chiming in Chinese landscape with the most distinct examples of repetition – and purely geometric ones as well – in the form we might encounter it, for example, in the weaving of serrations, shapes, angles, and intersections typical of Moorish patterns.

In any case, this plastic phenomenon, which appears to have been born from the resonance of sound, is probably for this very reason so flexible, not only in the plastic transmission of sounds or in its own independent plastic resonance, but even in those cases when it is not concerned with solving audiovisual problems.

The visual depiction born of music inevitably strives to resound.

It is interesting that the most "resonant" examples of landscape turn out to be landscapes connected to mist.

This is also characteristic of the pictures of chiming from a distant monastery, discussed above, where the stillness and distant chimes of the gongs stream through the plastic details, protruding out of the misty nonexistence of a monotone background; but this is true as well of the misty symphonies of Whistler[35] – who copied much from the Japanese – which are certainly appropriate to mention here.

And the "mists" of *Potemkin* with which, as a matter of fact, the whole conversation began.

And this is not accidental.

This is the most obvious case, and most easily understood, for the effect of a plastic transmission of sound here is strongly aided by another feature of sound caught by plastic means – the washing away of outlines of certain elements of the depiction: This is like a sound becoming lost in the distance (*Ausklang* of sounds).

It is not in vain that by its own means the suite of lyrical mourning of the "eye" music of "Potemkin mists" seeks that same thing, while working within the possibilities of film photography. Here a whole set of devices passes through the skillful hands of the cameraman Tisse:

The natural tulle of real mist is aided by tulle and muslin filters placed in front of the lens for washing away depth, and it is repeated by the optic washing away of the edges of visual depiction by using a soft-focus lens.

However, before going further, we must note one more compositional canon of the Chinese and Japanese, which proceeds totally from those same ancient principles of Taoism – from the principles of yin and yang.

The point is that these principles govern not only the arts but also the basic first premises of the sciences. The system of Chinese numbering is also partly subject to them. This system is based not on the fact that one number is larger than the one standing next to it in a single unit. For the Chinese the essence of the difference between numbers standing next to each other (unavoidably odd and even) is not at all in the fact that they are quantitatively different or that one can be divided into two without anything left over, and the other cannot.

For the Chinese, the decisive difference between similar numbers is that one of them belongs to one series or clan – *to the family of evens*, and the other to the other clan or type – *to the family of odds*.

And one of these clans is subject to the principle of yang, and the other type to the principle of yin, and the mutual interweaving of both through each subsequent unit of the normal series of numbers builds the unity of the whole series that here – as everywhere – is maintained on that same principle of the *mutual penetration of those two opposite principles!*

Marcel Granet, in his magnificent book,* writes about this interesting phenomenon:

* Marcel Granet, *La Pensee Chinoise*, Paris, 1934.

The concept of quantity plays essentially no role in the philosophical conceptions of the Chinese.

However, numbers as such held a passionate interest for the sages of Ancient China...

...One of the basic features of Chinese thought is the unusual respect for numerical symbols at the same time as a striking disregard of quantitative concepts... (p. 149)

In China numerical classification governs all details of thought and life. By the combination and interweaving* of them among themselves, the Chinese erected a whole varied system of numerical correspondences... (p. 241)

This engenders highly unusual principles of mathematics and mathematical operations.

But we are basically interested in something else here, namely, the supposition that this conception must inevitably also reflect the principles of plastic composition, where the Chinese artist is dealing with numbers and quantitative elements.

And actually, we see that the mutual play of "odd–even" in plastic composition is widespread, and gives here just such a singular effect of "chiming" and the same sense of *original organics* as in all the other similar cases, where structure and composition arise from the same *basic principle* of yin and yang.

What I am writing here is not simply to renumerate Chinese and Japanese methods of composition under the rubric of "curiosities."

Nor because this principle is found far beyond the bounds of composition in the East (more on that later), but above all because the compositional structure of the odd–even type (whether in length, in quantity of figures, in rhythm or grouping of shots) has a very important significance also *in the laws of montage combinations.*

In a supplement to the article on *Potemkin*'s structure, which analyzes the principle of the sequence of editing pieces in the scene of the battleship meeting the yawls,[36] we referred to this "golden rule" of alternating odd–even in groups, within the sequence of close-ups of this scene.

We are very interested in the principle of odd–even because it is one of the most effective means used when a purely *landscape paysage*† grows into what we may call a "human landscape," that is, when a group of human figures become the center of attention in the picture.

Till that moment a group of people, spread through the landscape, are completely subordinated to the general principles of plastic chiming and repetition.

---

* Granet here uses the term *"Imbriquement,"* which literally means combining them according to the principles of bricklaying. Of that later.
† [Eisenstein uses the words *"landschaft paysage"* – HM.]

At the same time, in a subject where there are many figures, they are distributed along the same lines of the score, as also are elements of landscape.

This is because, just as in Egypt, there existed in the art of the Far East a stage in which they were unable to place figures *one behind the other.*

And here, as in Egypt, they are placed instead *on top of each other.*

If in the landscape the analogy with a page of a musical score is based on the elements placed there *according to the height they are drawn in nature* (mountain ranges – above, rivers – below, trees and cliffs – between them)

then in combination of many figures this occurs as a result of the necessity of putting a row of figures over a row of figures, since they still do not have the ability to put some figures behind others!

It is interesting in this respect to trace a certain evolution. Between the period when they simply draw row over row in an almost "Egyptian-like" way and the period when the distribution of groups behind each other *in depth* like "wings" on a stage is reached, there is a long period when figures remain distributed as rows over each other, but this distribution attempts to find some motivation.

This can be noted to a certain extent in one of the oldest examples of Chinese plastic art that has come down to us – in the bas relief of the work of the second century A.D., from the tomb of Wu-kung-tse,[37] depicting the famous *Battle on the Bridge.* In certain parts of this relief the distribution of figures – in horizontal rows – is motivated by the fact that some of the people and a chariot are moving along the bridge (that is, *above*) and the other part of the people are active on the river (this is, *below*).

In the remaining portions, the horizontal arrangement of separate "lines" of the details of battle no longer have any motivation, and it is very fascinating, as one runs one's eye along them, to establish the rhythmic repetition of isolated details along the different lines: Sometimes they are simply identical, sometimes they are presented in the form of reverse "mirror image," sometimes in modifications and in variations of one and the same motif, etc.

Stephen W. Bushell, in his book on Chinese art,* brings in examples of similar relief depictions from Mt. Tse-Yun-chan belonging to the first century B.C. The subject here is a large hunting expedition, but the type of arrangement of the figures is exactly the same: the same rhythmic repetitions of identical figures, interweaving with rhythmic repetitions of others. It is interesting that these reliefs have not only been preserved but the poetic descriptions of this hunt as well.

And in comparing the type of poetic description of this event with the

* *L'Art Chinois*, Laurens, Paris, 1910.

plastic composition of its graphic exposition, you will be struck by *the identical nature of the structure of both*.

Just as there are separate plastic depictions here, there the separate verbal elements alternate repeatedly.

Our chariots were heavy and strong
Our harness – well-coupled galloping horses.
Our chariots gleamed and shone,
Our steeds flashing and powerful...

All the lines begin with the same word ("our").

The beginning of the first and third lines are relatively identical ("our chariots").

The beginning of the second and third are not identical but thematically resemble each other and the other lines ("harnesses," "horses," "chariots").

The second line speaks of "galloping horses." In the fourth they are called "steeds" (as if the same "horses" had been foreshortened).

In the second line they speak of "coupled" ("steeds").

In the three other lines we have two coupled designations in each ("heavy and strong," "gleamed and shone," "flashing and powerful").

When we begin to examine a reproduction of *The Battle on the Bridge* from this point of view, we see that the repetitions and variations of separate figures repeat the same verse harmony here, that is, the musical movement as it occurs in the verse passage we have introduced.

In later examples, this primitive manner of distributing figures "in rows" on top of each other now becomes motivated by a specific type of "perspective" (the axonometric type, that is, without a vanishing point and a corresponding contraction of figures). This produces a very remarkable impression of spatial "timelessness." The vanishing point seems to be the goal of space rushing off somewhere. These spatial compositions, without any vanishing point, seem to be free of the bustle of worldly goals and plunged into pure contemplation and timeless existence. This is also assisted by the liberation of these depictions from casual "transient" elements of chiaroscuro; and, in terms of color relationship, they seem equally free of the eternal change of the worldly vale, like the mind of a sage plunged into the contemplation of the eternity of the basic principles of the universe. [...]

When we are concerned with the usual type of scroll picture, but one with human figures, then the compositional juxtaposition of such groups of people echo precisely the same deployment we unfolded in the analysis of landscape.

An example of this type is the thirteenth-century painting depicting Minister Sugavarano Michi-tsan shooting a bow. Here is a particularly fascinating repetition of the "triads" – three seated figures at the lower edge and their "chiming" with three figures placed at the top.

But the most fascinating, of course, is *The Moonlit Night in the Emperor's Palace* – this is a genuine "Moonlight Sonata" of Eastern painting. It belongs to the eleventh century, is attributed to the brush of Fujiwara Takayoshi,[38] and composes part of a large number of painted scrolls illustrating the classic novel of *The Tale of Genji* written by the princess Murasaki Shikibu.

I only know a fragment of this picture found in *Propylaen Kunstgeschichte.** But even in this separate fragment its striking "melodiousness" is visible. It seems that the sound of the flute, on which one of the figures is playing, streams along the slanting lines of the balcony rising toward the moon. The rare verticals of the columns rhythmically intersect the pale green strips of the diagonal of the carpets; the dark blankets, thrown across the banisters, repeat the motif of the verticals in the soft folds; groups of transparent lines of sitting figures contrast with the dry imprint of the lines of the buildings; the silver shimmering of their clothing (in the original they are strewn with silver dust, the so-called mica), and dark spots of headdresses, inclining in different directions – taken all together create the amazing lyrical, but also plaintive, atmosphere of this perfect model of "eye music."

The analysis of how the principles of musical composition of pure landscape develop into a similar composition of human groups and figures is very relevant here, for we see the same thing occurring in the scene of the mist in *Potemkin* where it begins with "nonindifferent nature" in pure form and gradually passes into the silence of mourning of city inhabitants who had come to visit the body of Vakulinchuk, where separate groups and separate close-ups are combined according to the same musical principles by which the beginning of the scene was constructed.

In the analysis of the scene mentioned above of the encounter between the battleship and the yawls, we showed clearly that very "golden rule" of odd–even alternation as an example of genuine cinematographic composition.

In this example of the yawls scene, more than just the interweaving of numerical elements is apparent.

There we also traced the interaction of the *rectangular and circular*, as well as the type of movement of motifs within them.

However, the most important thing one must always keep in mind is that it is not so much a matter of the alternation of odd and even as the

---

* Otto Fischer, *Die Kunst Indiens, Chinas und Japans*, Propylaen-Verlag, Berlin, vol. IV, 1928.

feeling of an *apparent mutual penetration* of two complexes belonging to two opposite principles of phenomena.

And this "entering into each other," in its turn, is a means of the plastic method that approximately conveys the sensation of the process of their *transition into* each other, that is, the sensation of the basic dynamics of the process of becoming, which occurs in the transition of opposites into each other.

In the finished montage this transition from even groups to odd is never perceived as a jolt or alternation, but is actually felt as *a transition of one numerical quantity into another.*

In terms of the actual type of picture scroll and the peripateia of its development, it turns out that it is much more related to cinematography than might be thought.

The tradition of the picture scroll has largely been preserved for a long period in Japanese engraving, especially since this engraving is not limited at all by the edges of a single sheet, but very often consists of several sheets – diptychs and triptychs – that can exist completely separately, but the full picture of the mood and subject are produced only when they are placed next to each other.

In this sense the montage method of cinematography, where, in the process of shooting, one *stream of events* is broken up into separate shots and by the will of the film editor is again collected into a whole montage sequence, repeats completely this stage of the general evolutionary course of the history of painting.

It is very distinct in examples of Eastern art. And although in the thematic sequence of the engravings of, let us say, Hogarth[39] (*Marriage á la Mode* or *The Rake's Progress*) it is possible to catch such tendencies – the East remains much closer to the nature of film in purely thematic montage, where such paradoxical suites as *One Hundred Views of Fujiama* by Hokusai are possible, which appear to be similar to the multiview perception of the *Eiffel Tower* in Delaunay's[40] painting (at the dawn of cinema), or even more so, a series of shots, from which, on being looked through, arises that same many-sided sensation of Fujiama mountain, which grows out of the combination of shots merging into a monumental montage image of phenomena.

In terms of the principles of composition, in these small parts, on these separate sheets, the general laws of composition remain the same.

The picture scroll type is illustrative and interesting because in it the chiming and arrangement of motif are *clearly tangible*, since it *stretches out horizontally*, and it is easy to trace the line of each element in all subsequent modulations through which it passes.

The picture of the *interweaving and correspondence* of separate plastic motifs and lines is just as graphic in this case.

As we have noted above, normally separate pictures of usual views are born from this type of picture by disintegration – the breakup of the general flowing continuity into separate motifs, snatched out of the general flow.

The continuous flow of glissando, characteristic of voice and strings, is broken up in exactly the same way, passing, for example, into the *tempered* construction of the piano.

But what is even more interesting is the other method of approaching the canonized conventional type of rectangular picture.

The ribbon of the scroll is "swung around" into a rectangle! *But it is not swung around itself*, as ribbon into scroll; but *on its surface* (on the flatness of the picture) *the visual representation is swung around.*

The depiction on the ribbon of the scroll is "swung around" into a rectangle!

And this is not a metaphor, not a play of words, but an actual fact.

It turns out that there is an *intermediate stage* lying between the canonical form of the picture scroll – where the lines of the plastic score are very clearly run side by side – and those rectangular sheets, no less canonical, where there is a strict score of interconnected separate motifs, but where they no longer run side by side, but are placed *on top of each other*. This endlessly complicates the possibility of "reading" and "tracing" the course of separate motifs, which no longer rush *parallel* to each other, but *through* each other!

The scheme of this transitional stage from *makimono* stretching endlessly to the limited rectangle – in the case of this "swinging around" – suggests, and looks almost like, a graphic "play of words" with an inherent ironic aftertaste.

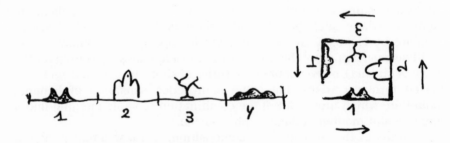

I do not know whether one could find many similar examples, but I have come across several similar cases.

One of them belongs to the brush of an anonymous artist of the eighth (!) century. It is reproduced in Fischer (and, in addition, without any commentary!) right next to and on a level with certain "normal" examples of Chinese painting.

Figure 18. *The Day of Death*, woodcut by José Guadalupe Posada (1853–1911).

The other case refers also to a certain early variety. But this time to an early prenewspaper period...of journalism.

In the East, as in the whole world, the appearance of newspapers was preceded by a stage of illustrated leaflets, usually in the verse form of a ballad, singing of some sensational event (an earthquake, murder, punishment of a bandit, etc.).

Usually such a leaflet is also supplied with a little engraving.

Similar leaflets have been in circulation in Mexico even until today (especially in those parts where newspapers are normally in less circulation).

In addition, the sales person sings the ballads and sells sheets, where, with most heartrending expressions, there is a description of how a criminal repents just before being punished, or how in such-and-such a year such-and-such a popular general perished. There is good reason for their often being called "lamentos" – laments.

In Mexico I happened to meet an old lady – the widow of the famous Venegas Arroio, the late publisher of these "coridos" (little songs). For a long time, I rummaged in her tiny shop, searching for little prints of the incomparable José Guadalupe Posada,[41] one of their most prolific illustrators at the beginning of our century.

However, the example I have in mind belongs to the seventeenth century.

It is one of the few of the first sheets that have been preserved, and it is devoted to the seige of the city of Osaka in 1615.

I happened to see it in a certain book devoted to the history of Japanese journalism, but in such a bad reproduction that it is impossible to reproduce it here.

And, therefore, I will limit myself to the scheme of the print depicted on it.

In the center is Osaka. Around are figures of marching soldiers. On four sides are the upper parts of lances and flags of the troops beseiging Osaka. On the upper edge – the sun going down behind the mountains (and not descending out of the clouds, as might appear at first glance).

What is also interesting is that the tendency to "swing around" here is aided by the theme itself: – the seige – is an encirclement.

However, the seige, like the theme, is broadly spread out and is in unfolded *makimono.*

Thus there is no base for concluding that the circular principle of composition is derived only from the subject.

One must also not conclude this out of purely practical considerations, for example, when this occurs in a "four-sided" picture...by Holbein[42] (now restored): In this there is a *fresco painting...of the top of a table*, a fresco painting, part of which was swung around naturally toward the four edges of the table – "face to face" with what was set around it!

However, the first example most consistent in principle remains the most interesting, and this is because more than 1,000 years later, approaching the moment when painting, after having stiffened in the rectangle of a frame, again leaps over to movement along a moving ribbon – this time a real running ribbon of film tape – we will again find an analogous transitional stage, where elements of landscape are again distributed in exactly the same way as in the eighth-century anonymous painter just mentioned.

Between painting and cinema, amid a huge legion of "-isms," there is one that has given over all its qualities of visual depiction to the embodiment of what cannot be captured on canvas, the basic element of art – movement.

This intermediate stage, *this* very distinct connecting link between painting and cinema – is futurism, in its initial, very original experiments, which are grouped around the "six-legged figures of people" as attempts to convey by such a method . . . the sensation of the dynamics of running, etc.

To the brush of our copatriot David Burliuk[43] belong the painted landscape and a series of pen drawings where the normal flow of the subject depicted in the picture in one case is arranged along an unwinding spiral, and in the other – just as in the anonymous eighth-century painter – along all four sides of the rectangular canvas.

What was left was to "smash" the frame and extend the elements into a row of divisions of a continuously running ribbon.

Then – to cut this ribbon into separate subjects.

And then in rapid succession – subject after subject – they would be shown to the viewer, thus achieving not a static morphological unity of the picture but a dynamic unity.

And this is exactly what cinema did as the *highest stage of painting*. And as such, its features force it to come into unavoidable conflict with the original stages of painting: as if again reproducing the form of the early picture scroll on the screen, but this time in the form of the *real movement* of ribbon that really *runs*, divided not into separate frames of sheets but growing out of separate rectangles – the visual depictions of shots forming the actual reality of its course.

At first this movement is born from the system of dynamic change of frames that, in its course, engenders the basic cinematographic phenomenon of movement of visual representation so that from a similar comparison of new magnitudes – no longer of frames, but of montage elements – of shots – it will give birth to a whole variety of physical phenomena – the tempo and psychophysical sensation of dynamics.

In regard to the actual principle of *continuous flow*, here movies – as the most perfect representation of the art of *moving dynamics* – unavoidably, as always at the highest stage of development, repeat in a new quality the initial forms of the continuity of the flow of events, as it occurred in the earliest stages of the development of any area of narration or story.

This does not only occur among the Chinese and Japanese.

The North American Indians expressed their narration in the same pictorial manner, that is, in the form of semirepresentational writing. Yielding to the East in the level of technique and possibilities available to him, deprived of paper and ink (paper was invented around 105 A.D. by the Chinese minister Ts'ai- Lun), the Indian did not have the possibility of creating his own type of *makimono*.

However, despite this, even here the basic tendency remains the same – and we can see that the notation of the Indian, who was limited by the number of buffalo hides, nevertheless was also stretched consecutively into one continuous line – into a pictographic story that, beginning in the center, swings around in the form of a *spiral*.

A similar principle of continuity is seen in the old way of drawing used by the ancient Greeks – the notorious *boustrophēdon*, where the text also flows continuously, passing from line to line; for this reason it goes

 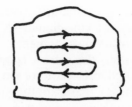

from line to line by alternating now from right to left, then from left to right (the very term preserved the memory of the original image, which was the term for this type of writing – "following the ox furrow").

The transition from examples of the arrangement of visual representation to examples concerning the direction in writing systems is quite appropriate: in the first place because they belong to a single evolutionary series (and in the example of raw pictographic writing this is clearly obvious); and second, because at the basis of both lies that same tendency toward continuity*; and in the third place, finally, because the process of breakdown in them is identical – into separate sentences and lines in one case and into independent pictures in the other.

As an example of the "rebirth" of flowing continuity, with the rather sharp effect of the paradoxical novelty of the "device," we can introduce an example from one more area – not from the history of *drawing* but from the history of *literary exposition*.

Literature also has its "tempered" structure and division by paragraphs and punctuation marks. A solid "flow" without division by sentences and punctuation marks is written only by illiterates (more than once I have had to read such writing aloud to my old domestic servant – Auntie Pasha – from her relatives, who live in various villages in the Soviet Union).

However, an instance of this rebirth can be seen as a *literary device* using this compact "flow" of writing; this is the case of the famous last chapter of James Joyce's *Ulysses*.[44] This is the chapter in which Mrs. Bloom, while falling asleep, remembers by a unique multivoice polyphony, the images of her former lovers as she awaits the arrival of her legal spouse while lying on the marriage bed.

This chapter, as we know, is written without a single punctuation mark, and reproduces very precisely the presleep flow of thoughts of someone falling asleep.

One of the secrets of the effect of this chapter (and of the presence of this device) is, of course, that here one of the profound aspects of the very first stage of human consciousness is captured: the undivided whole-

---

* The continuity of general flow is perhaps the simplest and most primitive method of the realization of the *unity of the whole* – the only means accessible in these early stages of development.

ness and flow of undifferentiated representations of the stage preceding the stage of consciousness that actively "makes divisions" at higher stages of its development.

However, the correct combination of both tendencies: both the *continuity* (characteristic of early thinking) and division (developed consciousness), that is, of the independence of the *single* and the generality of the *whole* was, of course, able to be realized only by cinematography – cinema that *begins from where* the remaining variety of arts "roll downhill," at the cost of destroying and decomposing the very bases of their art, when they try to capture areas that are only completely accessible to cinematography (futurism, surrealism, Joyce, etc.).

For only here – in cinema – is the embodiment of all these expectations and tendencies of the other arts possible – *without rejecting realism* – which the other arts were forced to take into account (Joyce, surrealism, futurism); moreover – here they were realized not only without detrimental results, but even with very brilliant realistic results.

Perhaps this is exactly the point where I should discuss why, in the majority of my analyses concerning the elements and nature of cinema over so many years, I often introduce a parallel analysis of the characteristics of Far Eastern art.

This is because in China, art, as with other forms of human activity, its worldview, science, and language as well, while reaching certain stages of development (not too far in terms of progress), *stopped at these stages.*

Having achieved this limit, it moved not *forward* but *in breadth.*

I will not discuss the historical and social conditions that affected these phenomena – this would lead us too far astray. But this very fact thus gives us the possibility of looking at certain phases characteristic of the early development of thought and art. These phases seem to be artificially preserved in such "childish" and "adolescent" stages that it is possible to discover them in our arts only in examples of the very archaic and primitive.

In China and Japan we encounter examples of such archaic canons side by side, but with their richest elaboration in breath – in all the richness of means and possibilities provided by an epoch of higher development.

The canon remains inviolable.

Thus, for example, in the incomparable mastery of acting and the theater by Mei Lan-Fang[45] there has come to us in pure and untouched form, the basic original *principles of all early theater* (of course, with a correction of purely national elements).

In the majority of other cases, these principles have to be restored almost by conjectures or intuitive means, worthy of Cuiveau![46]

Theater historians find an affinity between the theatrical constructions of Mei Lan-Fang and early Greek forms of theater. This affinity is not fortuitous, observing how the director Mei, in actual performance, returns to the canon of continuity; we can observe in a vivid example how the established and stable "canon" can simultaneously be the source of the most vivid pleasure in creatively overcoming it within the limits once set. Let us recall the liturgical canonic quality of the medieval spectacles and miracle plays,[47] canonized conventions of the drama and performance of pre-Shakespearean Elizabethan theater – and how *all this* was given new life by the genius of Shakespeare. Living examples of this period have long ago disappeared in the West, and we can imagine only by hints (and even then not very concretely) what this was all like. Where ancient examples have remained as survivals, they usually remain in such a primitive form that it would be very difficult to discover directly from them the embryo of future, more perfectly evolved forms.

An example is the theatrical presentations of the Basques, who in the little villages in the Pyrenees preserved features of the earliest theater in its purest form (I know of this only from the literature: *Etudes sur le Théâtre Basque, La Représentation des pastorales à sujets tragiques* by Georges Hérelle, Paris, 1923).

Another example is the religious festival presentations of the Mexicans.

I had occasion to see an example of the latter spectacle myself.

And in order to decipher the striking features of these "embryos" of theatrical forms, one must have, of course, more than a small experience of examples more richly developed in *breath*.

And such are the examples of Chinese culture.

And no matter what area of culture we might touch on here – whether it be the principles of writing or early pictography, the structure of the language and rhetorical tropes or the technique of theater, the principle of the composition of painting or the system of counting and numeration, etc., etc. – everywhere we will see the principles worked out with great richness, with great variety and in great detail, which is peculiar to the *initial phases of the development of separate branches of culture in general*.

And now it happens that it is to our lot, the lot of Soviet film directors, that the task has fallen not only of making films, but also of realizing, constructing, and forming the very first principles of film culture and aesthetics in general.*

---

* The pioneers in this direction, who were first of all pioneer-practitioneers, were, of course, the Americans – and especially D. W. Griffith; however, even they have written that with the appearance of Soviet films "a new era of film aesthetics has begun," which absorbed the experience of everything that had been done earlier, and were the first to formulate the distinctive principles of film art and composition (see Lewis Jacobs, *The Rise of the American Film*, Harcourt Brace, New York, 1939, p. 312; and my article, "Dickens, Griffith and Us," *Film Form*, J. Leyda, ed. and trans., Harcourt, Brace and World, New York, 1949, p. 195.

This art is young, having been born before our very eyes, but it is closely tied to the cultural traditions of all the separate arts, which seem to have merged into a whole within it.

The main problem was the clarification of the specific nature of the essence of this young art, that is, an essence that would be free of slavish borrowing and copying of examples and features of the other arts that cinematography synthetically unites within it.

And in this instance, of course, an acquaintance with those beginning phases through which all the other arts have passed does help, for in the history of the development of its particular distinctive quality, cinema aesthetics inevitably must pass through those same phases that stage by stage, the development of the other arts had passed through.

The culture of the East is particularly valuable at this point.

And especially the most ancient culture and cultural traditions coming from China.

What is also characteristic in this respect is that in my personal research during the course of all these years I moved from the more *superficial* and *mechanical* conceptions, characteristic of the *Japanese* treatment of a heritage received from China, to the *organic essence of the conceptions of the Chinese themselves.*

This is a very natural process in the investigation of an object, inevitably going from *appearance* to *essence*, from *sign* to *principle*, from *device* to *method*.

This method passed from the more popular and simplified sphere of Eastern culture – from the Japanese – to the profound feeling for principles of China. From the *"Romans" of the East – the Japanese – to the Eastern "Hellenism" of Ancient China.*

We saw that the principles of construction of the musical, emotional, "nonindifferent" landscape of the Chinese corresponds in a very particular way to those methods by which the landscape of the "mist suite" of *Potemkin* was built, as described above.

Can one speak here of stylization or borrowing or direct influence?

Knowing the author of *Potemkin* fairly well, I can assert that this had no place here at all: I became interested in the nature of the composition of Chinese landscape much later. Before becoming interested in Eastern art in general, the East attracted me in other ways, partially by the hieroglyphic writing that at certain initial stages helped me form concepts about the principles of montage.[48]

I became interested in Chinese landscape much later – in the period when I was analyzing how landscape is used in my pictures, and not the other way around.

In general, landscape plays a very large role in all my films: the city night landscape of Petrograd in *October*, the four seasons of the Russian landscape in *The Old and the New*, and *Que Viva Mexico!* – unwound completely on the landscapes of Mexico, etc. In addition, everywhere the role of landscape is above all invariably musical and emotional.

However, we are limited here only to an analysis of the "founder" of the genre of "nonindifferent nature" – *Potemkin.*

The landscape suite of *Potemkin* was born youthfully and directly from the means available to the youthful art of cinema and, naturally, overflowed into "youthful forms" of expression, for the *tangibility of the counterpoint structure* in my view is one of the typical forms of a similar *youth.*

At a more mature age such *thick knitting* of the texture and *motifs* occurs that the *direct tangibility* of them is lost.

And I think that for this very reason of the "feeling of youth" the invariable effect of eternally popular forms... rough homespun rugs and fabrics (for example, English homespun)... are so *vitalizing.* On the general background of other fabrics, which increasingly lose the tangibility of the course of the threads and fibers composing them, they always act and impress one by their freshness; at a time when the charm of other fabrics is no longer based on this, but on the perfection of the play of the modulations of the *even and smooth surface of the material.*

The limits in this respect were reached by fabrics made out of... glass threads – fabrics that have penetrated American life more and more. [...]

The pattern of the fabrics is formed here no longer out of the *natural course of the threads composing it* but passes over *as a pattern on the smooth surface* composing it. This is somewhat like what occurred with the picture scrolls described above, where a moment occurs in the history of their development when not only is the ribbon of scroll swung and turned around but the *representation itself* is swung around on the surface of the scroll (and from a continuous ribbon it becomes a self-contained rectangle).

Something of the sort also occurs in ceramics, and it is especially evident, for example, in Peru. Here in the early periods there is not yet a division of the *functions of form* into *utilitarian and artistic.* Here the form still serves both functions inseparably.

The vessel by designation is first of all utilitarian.

This determines its form.

However, this form at the same time is a *rudiment of visual representation* because this earliest primitive also *reflects* the original "leading" image – *man* – as all aspects of art will do in the course of their entire history.

Of course, this earliest "portrait" of man "reflects" only one feature of the original – his ability to contain food and liquid.

This connection between the vessel and the human stomach was retained for a long time in language: If the Middle Ages call man "the vessel of sin," then until this very day we talk about "potbellied" stoves and bottles.

Therefore in the first stages the vessel was formed like a man by the crudest primitive, when the form of the pot captures *only the image of the stomach*, before the vessel begins to take shape in the form of a potbellied man.

But very soon the problem of *putting in liquid* and the problem of *depicting a man* became separated.

The vessel (at least in the Peruvian example) *was topped no longer by a face* or the head of a man or animal but by the whole figure of a man, of people, or animals: They "crawl out" in the form of independent sculptural representations on the top of the vessel, and the function of *the form of the vessel* is now *only* purely *utilitarian*, now freed from the function of reflection, representation, and depiction.

In other cases the representational line is not captured and continued by sculptured figures on top (usually an amazing work), but *by a flat representation on the walls of the vessel*.

In this way the very first "hollow" sculptured "portrait" of a person is distinguished from the utilitarian form of the vessel and becomes an independent representation.

Here it seems to "become differentiated" into two areas of the conventional view of the representational arts: into sculpture (the figures above) and into flat painting (the drawing on the walls).

As we can see, the *reflection of man in art* was realized significantly earlier than the *representation* of him appeared in art!

Samples of all these subsequent stages can be easily traced in Peruvian ceramics.

Strictly speaking, the early Peruvian continued to perceive the unity of vessel and figure in indivisible form even *after* this division. After the actual unity, they are now found in a "hieroglyphic" unity, that is, while standing side by side, they are still read as one whole. In Chinese hieroglyphics as well, "sack" and "man" stand next to each other, and this means "woman" ("man with womb"). Besides, this is also preserved in the English language, where "woman" is "womb + man," that is, it literally designates the same thing.

The same process also occurs repeatedly on the surface where patterns subsequently are formed from the interweaving of separate elements of pure representation.

And the tangible vitality of the constructive "supports" are based on the tangibility of *the course of the structural line* or the *brushstroke in painting*, which corresponds to the *perceptibility of the unpolished trace of the course of the chisel in sculpture* or the "unnoticed" course of the brush on the canvas of a picture.

In terms of structural elements, we experienced a certain reductio ad absurdum of this phenomenon in constructivism.

But we have experienced this same feeling of vivid counterpoint when observing the peripeteia of the exciting course of van Gogh's brushstroke or when looking at the rough surface of figures, for example, in a series of Michelangelo's works.

The sculptural group "Youth Conquering Old Age ("The Conqueror")," for example, is like this, or the head of his "Brutus," where all traces of the chisel of his creation have been preserved.

And it is the "nonsmearing" course of the brush on van Gogh's canvases – one of the particularly refined charms of the art of its author – that explains the seemingly strange accusation against him that Herbert Read mentions:

It has been said in depreciation of van Gogh that he remained all his life a draughtsman – that he painted his pictures as other men draw their sketches, that his ideas were only black-and-white ideas.*(!)

We have allowed ourselves to dwell in greater detail on these examples intentionally. Later we will have to analyze the questions of what courses the *evolution of forms of montage* took, and all these considerations and examples will help us solve this problem.

We should note one more thing, that we can find an interesting analogy to the example concerning Peruvian ceramics in Chinese and Japnese theater.

Here in the theater it is often not necessary to give *the form of a man to a vessel*, but *to form the man himself into the image of something else* – into something often extremely fantastic. Among the stage characters of China and Japan one encounters "spirits," for example: the spirit of a frog, the spirit of a bat, the spirit of an oyster, and even the spirit...of a stone.

Here in *stage make up* we encounter literally the same thing according to the method employed.

A small carved image sits on the upper part of the Peruvian vessel or there is a drawing on its walls, and this "means" that the vessel as a whole *is* exactly what the carved image depicts.

A Chinese or Japanese proceeds in exactly the same way with makeup; he draws a bat or fold of an oyster on his face, and this means that the *whole* person is the *spirit* of the oyster, the bat, or the frog.

One should also not forget that many Chinese clothes and the kimonos of the Japanese are usually representational: white herons, rose-colored branches of blossoming cherries, or green needles of ancient pines, cypresses rising upward like waterfalls, or a sunset.

* Herbert Read, *The Meaning of Art*, Faber & Faber, London, 1931, p. 187, 203.

If, in the area of makeup, knowing the key to the conventions, we can catch the intention hidden in it, we can no longer consciously keep up with it in the depths of the earliest pantheistic fusion of man and nature through the magic of representational clothes, and what remains for us is only to admire them. And perhaps in this admiration we participate, even if only partially, in the experiences of what completely dominated the thoughts and feelings of those who first put the patterns of real nature and landscape onto clothes.

And it seems that here before us is the *third phase* of the general theme of "man within the landscape:"

here he is – *living and undepictable* – materially invested in clothes in-wrought with landscapes;

in pictures his *pictorial depiction* is surrounded by the details of painted landscape; and finally, in lyric stanzas, he *simply exists invisibly*, for in the most ancient lyric "a cherry branch," "a chrysanthemum," "moonlight," "a butterfly," or "a nightingale's trill" often designate not only what they speak about openly and obviously – actually they are all essentially *metaphors* engendered by the comparison with "tenderness," "the color of the face," or "the sound of the voice," of the beloved.

Here, in this "third phase," a similar enumeration of such apparently irrelevant "elements of nature" are at the same time allegories about the beloved, who often bears a similar metaphor or simile in the form of her name (this even applies to Puccini's *Madame Butterfly*)[49].

Perhaps this is why Chinese poetry is so lyrical, for it speaks by means of landscape about the beloved, and vivid, trembling human feelings that penetrate every element of nature, that are woven into the pattern of lyric poetry or into the concealed meaning of a pictorial detail flung on silk or drawing paper; it is, above all, *a living image of man* conveyed by poetic allegory through a detail or element of the landscape.

Such an "anthropomorphization" of nature, essentially an allegory about man by means of the elements of nature, is characteristic of the poetry of any nation.

And in this respect what is extremely interesting is not the fact itself, but those "individual" nuances by which the poetry of different nations solve the same problem, proceeding from the distinctive aspects of their worldview or world perception.

At this point it would be interesting to compare the Chinese, whose images and themes are full of unuttered, flowing, flickering nuances and modulations with the clean-cut efficiency of the Greek, practical and concrete in spite of his lyricism, his mythopaeicism and his mysticism of Pythagorean numbers.[50]

To the Chinese, a strong puff is sufficient: In the branch of a cherry tree or flower, he captures the breathing of his beloved's image; he does not even need comparisons – blossoming petals are in themselves capable of including a swarm of lyric visions and representations, vaguely outlined, and the more poetic they are, the less are they grounded in actual concreteness.

And how is this "metaphoric" theme drawn in the consciousness and poetics of the Greek?

Ovid brought to us the Greeks' legacy of the mutual embodiment of man and nature in each other. And here there are no longer any nuances or hints.

There are no strokes or transcience.

No lyrical outpourings, guiding over the changing scales or semi-concrete metaphors.

Here there are no lyrical stances, but romantic stories.

The cypress, narcissus, or hyacinth are not a charming fragment or detail of the landscape to which the muse runs in search of poetic comparisons; but, of course, even here at the basis is – a comparison.

But the comparison is now efficiently recorded as story, the transient nature of the metaphor – as metamorphosis, scrupulously and "concretely" stating the "process" of a "fact," which is fantastic and unthinkable in itself.

And it seems that in these "fairy stories," there is a premonition of the future clear representation of "the origin of the species" (which no doubt subconsciously always nourishes a similar species of poetry, as does the teaching about the "transmigration of souls"), which is more than a direct desire to find plastic expression for its lyrical aspiration.

It is not enough for the Greek to focus on the transient similarity of a hyacinth and a young man, or a young man and a hyacinth. And he is not limited to contemplating the fact that one of them would engender a vaguely experienced image of the other, so that one would signify the other in a poetic allegory, and at the mention of one you would think of the other.

No. The Greek will conceive a story where one is *concretely* turned into the other.

And in his own words, in the *Metamorphoses* Ovid also resurrects before us the scene of how the god and the young man compete in throwing the discus.

He illuminates in detail the situation where the young Hyacinth is wounded and killed by the force of the "ricochet."

He has Phoebus mournfully moan and sob over the body of his partner killed so tragically.

And finally he establishes in detail and very precisely the decisive sign of the similarity of the perishing youth with the sad flower, into which the despairing god turned him – the crimson wound across the lily-white figure that had turned pale:

...The blood that filled the grasses at his feet
Turned to a brighter dye than Tyrian purple,
And from its lips there came a lily flower,
And yet, unlike the silver-white of lilies,
Its colour was a tinted, pinkish blue.*

In this case the "thematic" interpretation of the strange black designs of the pattern on the white petals of the hyacinth will not be forgotten:

...Nor was this miracle enough for Phoebus;
He wrote the words "Ai, Ai" across its petals,
The sign of his own grief, his signature.†

In other cases the description will be given as a reproduction in documentary detail of the "process of reincarnation," which any "naturalist" would envy! Thus, for example, in the case when the punishment of Phoebe comes down upon the wild Edonian women tearing apart Orpheus:

...Lyaeus could not let the killing of Orpheus
Pass without revenge on his mad murderers.
Angered by loss, he captured Thracian women
Who saw him die, trussed them with roots,
And thrust their feet, toes downward, into earth.
As birds are trapped by clever fowlers in a net,
Then flutter to get free, drawing the net still tighter
Round wings and claws, so each woman fought,
Held by quick roots entangling feet and fingers,
Toenails in earth, she felt bark creeping up her legs,
And when she tried to slap her thighs, her hands struck oak;
Her neck, her shoulders, breasts were oak-wood carving;
You'd think her arms were branches – you're not wrong.‡

The lyrics of the Chinese and the lyricism of Ovid's tales are equally poetic.

They grow out of identical premises.

And they embody similar aspirations.

But the structure, their character and method, as we can see, are profoundly different, although each is lovely in its own way.

And above all because they both equally grow out of the national and cultural distinctiveness of their nations.

Is there an equivalent to this in the composition of *Potemkin*?

There is! And most interesting is that here this does not concern so

---

* Ovid, *The Metamorphoses*, H. Gregory, trans., Viking Press, New York, 1958, p. 280.
† Ibid., p. 280.
‡ Book XI, 69–84, p. 301.

much man and his emotions, which are veiled only in images of the lyrical landscape.

It is interesting that here the film as a whole – which made such a great fuss about abolishing the system of individual hero-protagonists and overcoming the fetters of the indescribable "triangle" in a canonic subject – seems to a certain extent to be a gigantic allegory, a monumental metaphor of such a triangle.

Only one critic* in his time guessed that the fifth act of *Potemkin*, by the skeleton of its dynamic construction, in a modified way grows out of the traditional scene of liberating the hero from the claws of the villain – right out of the womb of the classical tradition of the chase.

In exactly the same way – for the "pretty word" and in the form of a well-made metaphor – only one other critic (I no longer remember where) in passing dropped the remark that the "Odessa Steps" is essentially the traditional triangle, raised here into mass action.

The "Steps" rush toward "The Battleship." But barring the way is the villain – "The Feet of the Tsarist Soldiers."

It is interesting to note in passing that here is a completely consciously preconceived sequence.

I accidentally found among my old notes one relating to a work conceived between *Strike* and *Potemkin*.

At that time, I wanted to make an epic about the First Cavalry.[†]

And in the notes relating to the proposed dramatic structure of this film, I find this observation: "to build the fates and interaction of the collectives and social groups according to the type of peripateia inside...a triangle!"

The Cavalry was never realized.

but the method slipped over into *Potemkin*.

And probably the "humanity" of this film, without any human individual protagonists, is maintained to a great extent by the fact that vivid human prototypes with their vital peripateias live under the collective images.

In the same way the beating of the *Potemkin's* engines is interpreted almost everywhere both as the beating of the anxious collective heart of the battleship and of the living sailor collective.

It is interesting that this same imprint lies on all my "personless" films.

In *October* this same interrelationship is presented between the leading center and the workers' district. In the episode of the July days of the "villain" – the Provisional Government – they become disconnected;

---

* Apparently it was the young Asquith[51] in the journal *Film Classic*.
[†] [Based on Isaac Babel's book – HM.]

this is presented in the picture concretely by the raising of the Giant Palace Bridge. The episodes of October 25 begin with the closing of the bridge, along which the masses are moving into the victorious storming of the Winter Palace.

(There is also a parody episode when a comic procession of old men led by the city Mayor Schreider move along the tiny Bankovsky (!) Bridge "to the aid of the Winter Palace.")

And if you "unveil" *The Old and the New* according to this principle, then here the structure goes far beyond the frame of a "lyric" treatment of the "triangle" – in many cases in generalized forms reaching such a degree of naked eroticism that on the "personal level" would be worthy of more than a few pages of Zola's *Earth or Les Liaisons Dangereuses!*[52]

However, returning to the problem of counterpoint, one must say that not only does the *tangibility* of counterpoint, arise in the stages of youth – but secondarily, also in the epoch of decay and withering away.

"Ends" and "beginnings" resemble each other externally.

In the morning glow of the dawn of the arts, colored spots of separate tesserae of mosaics run together into a general picture with a tendency to grow together into one whole; in the sunset of the art of Central Europe – on the eve of its fall – the flatness of the picture again bursts into flame with colored spots, but this time these spots – are the precursors of a fall: The repeated "mosaic" of pointilism[53] signifies the beginning of disintegration.

Several years more and the body of painting will break down into a variety of "-isms" from which each will carry a certain component aspect of painting as a whole – and will raise this *component* into *an end in itself* – will put down the part in place of the whole.

For cinematography this encounter of *the counterpoint of breakdown* and the *counterpoint of rebirth* is particularly interesting: What serves as a sign of extinction for the "preceding" arts passes directly into the originating forms of a new kind of art – cinema!

Perhaps it would be interesting to illustrate the beginning of these two counterpoints – at the *beginning* phase and at the *closing* phase – with an example from the history of literature in the period of its stormiest development during the nineteenth century with the rise of realism.

At the threshold of the new realistic literature in the eighteenth century stands the epistolary counterpoint of the novel of Choderlos de Laclos.

Laclos having used the dry traditional form of written exchange of discourse, was able to discern the potential dynamic possibilities of this form.

He poured new life and pulsating dynamics into this scholastic form and achieved incomparable success. Criticized and misunderstood by contemporaries, he paved the road, however, for the great masters of the nineteenth century – Stendahl, Dostoyevsky.

In the preface to *Les Liaisons Dangereuses** A. Efros writes:

Stendahl learned to write no less from the code of Laclos than from the code of Napoleon, whom he proclaimed to be the source of his stylistic inspiration. The counterpoint, in which the whole epistolary variety of *Les Liaisons Dangereuses* is constructed, is remarkable. These leitmotifs of manner and turn of speech, accompanying the letters of each of Laclos's heroes, are exciting in their vividness and precision even until this every day. They lose nothing of their significance even after half a century of cultivated experiences of the same sort, even after *Poor Folk* of our Dostoyevsky...

...Early contemporaries of Laclos saw in this polyphonic writing manner only "un grand defaut" (a great failing).

Count de Tilly – one of the brilliant corrupters of morals, whom Laclos might have taken and, perhaps, did take as the prototype of Valmont, says in his *Memoirs*:

It is a great failing – to try to give each person his own style. As a result we encounter side by side with a page written brilliantly, unnecessary naïveté or unpardonable carelessness, which seem to be not so much contrasts, as spots.[†]

Later these original distinctive and independent currents within the counterpoint knit into a single compact mass of minutely interknit fabric of literary material.

The course of the characteristic drawing of the *thread* is preserved in it, but this is now a combination of *drawings of separate threads*, and not a clearly tangible tie between the *threads themselves* as independent elements of construction.

The heroes of Balzac or Dostoyevsky, Gogol or Stendahl, their ties and relationships among themselves are no less complex or sophisticated than the actions of Choderlos de Laclos's heroes, but the tangible course of the epistolary counterpoint long gave place to a much more refined literary ligature (let us not forget that it is the *young* Dostoyevsky of *White Nights* who is epistolary. And when mature – as in the complex *fugue* of *Brothers Karamazov* – such is the complexity of the plaited fabric of interconnections, that only with great difficulty can one break it down into its simplest "constituent parts").

But with the publication of the monumental literature of high realism of the nineteenth and twentieth centuries we again encounter the most interesting examples of what we have called "contrapuntal decay."

Typical, for example, is the *tour de force* of Lee Masters[54] in his *Spoon River Anthology* or in Faulkner's[55] structure of novels and tales, which is many times more complex.

In Lee Masters, people do not exchange letters, but – gravestone

---

* Russian edition, *Izd Academia*, Leningrad–Moscow, 1932.
† [Text translated from the Russian as it appears in Eisenstein's text. This count himself (Johan Tserclass) was Flemish – HM.]

inscriptions. Here epistles are replaced by epitaphs! And how characteristic this is for a poet, contemplating the downfall of a whole world of
illusions and concepts, nourished by the stage of capitalistic prosperity
of America following the end of the Civil War, the battle of the North and
the South!

Here the subject is the history of a city and its inhabitants – which
grows out of the interweaving of short epitaphs decorating the grave-
stones of the dead inhabitants of a small American town.

From these short biographic verses, written in the first person of
whomever the gravestone is covering, there is gradually interwoven
tangled balls of the tragic and grotesque, sentimental and criminal,
terrible and cheerful relations, with which apparently the peaceful and
Godsaving town was swarming inside.

All this does not mean, however, that the contrapuntal method of
literary writing (here taken in the narrow sense, from the point of view
of plot construction) completely disappears from literature in the course
of the nineteenth century. However, here it is no longer the characteristic
or illustrative stylistic "sign of the epoch" as, let us say, the epistolary
style of the eighteenth century or – as a "clinical symptom" in the period
of the decay of literary forms at the turn of the twentieth century.

And if it does occur, then its application becomes so organically
subservient and inobtrusively "tactful" in its application that it is almost
not felt as *an independent means of effect*.

Its bare application, calculated for a tangible and *noticeably perceptible effect as such*, departs from the high road of "demonstrative" signs
of the works of the epoch.

The two-voice construction of the themes of "war" and "peace" and the
complex counterpoint of Tolstoy's novel is arranged in one's perception
as comprehensible in itself, almost as an otherwise inconceivable exposition of events, and not as one of the independent means of compositional effect.

The *tangible effect* of similar constructions must be sought either in
such striking and extravagant compositional marvels as *Moby-Dick* by
Herman Melville[56] (1851), in technique running far ahead into the
devices of twentieth-century writing, or in the specific area of the literary
genre to which, for example, *The Woman in White* of Wilkie Collins[57]
belongs, whose *The Moonstone* is considered one of the cornerstones of
the history of the detective genre.

Here we are not only "shaken" by the subject but also by the very
method of exposition of this work, which resorts to the most unexpected
forms of "instruments" in the orchestration of the exposition of this
subject.

It is just in this way, on the principle of polyphony – according to
"polyphonic storytelling," – that the exposition of all the events of his
The Woman in White (1860) is built.

In the first chapter Collins discusses the nature of this method:

As the Judge might once have heard it, so the Reader shall hear it now. No circumstance of importance, from the beginning to the end of the disclosure, shall be related on hearsay evidence. When the writer of these introductory lines (Walter Hartright by name) happens to be more closely connected than others with the incidents to be recorded, he will describe them in his own person. When his experience fails, he will retire from the position of narrator; and his task will be continued, from the point at which he has left it off, by other persons who can speak to the circumstances under notice from their own knowledge, just as clearly and positively as he has spoken before them.

Thus, the story here presented will be told by more than one pen, as the story of an offence against the laws is told in Court by more than one witness – with the same object in both cases, to present the truth always in its most direct and most intelligible aspect; and to trace the course of one complete series of events, by making the persons who have been most closely connected with them, at each successive stage, relate their own experience, word for word.

Let Walter Hartright, teacher of drawing, aged twenty-eight years, be heard first.*

This style of exposition is maintained in the course of the whole novel. And it is interesting to note that the nature of this construction in itself repeats the exposition of the story: Thus with the approach of the end of the "second epoch" in the novel, that is, with the approach of the climax – the culmination of the novel – when the late Laura, Lady Clyde, appears near her own gravestone – pieces of conversation are not only shortened in volume, and because of this naturally quicken the tempo, but also the actual vehicles of the story suddenly begin to be modified: It is no longer narrators, but "evidence" and documents that figure in the story.

After the title on p. 673:

"The Story Continued in Several Narratives" – there follows:

"1. The Narrative of Hester Pinhorn, Cook in the Service of Count Fosco. [Taken down from her own statement.]"

Five and one-half pages of text concerning the conditions of the death of Lady Clyde, signed with a cross (apparently because of the illiteracy of Ms. Pinhorn).

"2. The Narrative of the Doctor."

Seven lines according to all the rules of a composed and signed certificate on the death of Lady Glyde on Thursday, June 25, 1850.

"3. The Narrative of Jane Gould."

Twelve lines signed by her on how she was invited to prepare the body of the late lady.

"4. The Narrative of the Tombstone (!)"

Five lines of the grave epitaph of Lady Clyde.

---

* Wilkie Collins, *The Moonstone* and *The Woman in White*, Modern Library, New York, 1937, p. 383.

"5. The Narrative of Walter Hartright."

Five pages of the concluding part of the subject of the second section of the novel with a coup de théâtre [theatrical effect] of the last line in which, according to all the data introduced – the dead lady stands before Walter Hartright, "looking at me over the grave" (p. 681).

In this case it is important to emphasize not only the fact that the action unfolds by a grouping of the "evidence" of separate characters – the eavesdropping on the evidence (an indispensable attribute *inside* any detective novel), but in this work this occurs within the narration, that is, not in forms of *bare polyphony*, as it takes place here.

Here it is interesting that the principles of polyphony and counterpoint are introduced into the structure of this work as a whole.

We also focused on this example in such detail because here in literature, in extensive "pieces" of the subject and event, we can see that same principle of a "many-pointed" exposition – "from different points of view" – that is, what in the art of film later became one of the basic methods of montage shooting (of the objects, milieu, performance, and dramatic scenes as a whole).

Moreover, literature also has a sufficient number of fine examples of this type of montage cinematic *change of points of description*, even within the limits of a scene taken separately.

Let us just recall such a detail of realism from Tolstoyan descriptions such as in the scene of Vronsky's suicide where the objects are described *from below*, that is, from the point of view of the fallen man!

On the other hand, the type of literary story telling described above is also encountered in film – thus this device resounded with paradoxical freshness and novelty, for example, in the beautiful film of Orson Welles,[58] *Citizen Kane*, where whole fragments of the biography of the hero are expounded by different characters who had known him in his lifetime. The sharpness of the device also grew out of the fact that these "pointers" were presented not in successive chronological order, but *were shuffled* among themselves. Because of this Kane appeared in different scenes not in the form of how one age follows another in a man's biography, but old before young, etc. This sharp effect is also achieved by the fact that the stylistics of montage shooting construction in each story were treated according to the character of the narrator (to what degree this actually occurred and to what degree it was the fruit of my own "creative conjecture" – is difficult to say; I saw the picture quite a while ago, but in any case, if this did occur, it would have been completely consistent and would have responded to the stylistics of the ancestor of this type of structure – Choderlos de Laclos mentioned above.)

In general in its structure *Citizen Kane* is probably closer to *Kater Murr* of E. T. A. Hoffman,[59] where the reflections of the wise cat alternate with the episodes entangled in their sequence from the life of Kapel-meister Kreisler.

The very terms: "counterpoint," "polyphonic writing," "fugue" – have slipped through and interwoven during the entire course of our analysis, and this is because the actual development of the montage form vibrates according to the degree of tangibility in it of such features, devices, and methods.

And it is natural to ask oneself at this point on what is built the attraction (not in the sense of "pretty to look at" but in the sense of "the ability to attract and have an effect") of these methods, methods related to the *repetition* of motifs, to the *pursuit* of it through other motifs, to the *interweaving* and *unweaving* of different voices, working as a branching out of *a single whole*?

I think counterpoint at a high (or the highest?) stage in its basic features repeats two instinctive principles, lying at the very initial stage of human activity.

Here they generate for man two great spheres of art – although art that is still not truly "fine" but meanwhile wholly practical, the applied arts. But, therefore, both these arts in terms of their instinctive aspect are accessible not only to man but also to his early forebearers.

I have in mind two very early activities of man – the occupation of *hunting* and the ability *to weave baskets*, of which the latter precedes by far the ability to weave fibers into fabric (that is, into an elastic basket clothing a body!) – and is also accessible to birds who know how to "weave" their nests.*

In respect to hunting, who in the animal kingdom did not hunt for someone or who was not saved in flight?!

The attraction of counterpoint constructions is undoubtedly based on the fact they seem to resurrect those instincts deeply set in us and, acting on them, they therefore achieve such a *profound* power.

One of them defines and nourishes the attraction of the weaving of separate motifs into one whole, the other – the hunt for lines of separate motifs through the thicket of voices interweaving into one.

---

* Ernst Gross in his book *Die Anfange der Kunst*, 1894, writes about how woven baskets greatly preceded in time even such an ancient object of houseware as the clay pot:

"The clay pot is the usurper that occupied both the place and the decoration of its woven predecessor."

It is convenient to use this circumstance to explain the primitive ornamental develop-ment of the clay vessel that, in its drawing, reproduced the woven form of the very first woven basket and dish. At the same time, the woven dish can actually be encountered even now in Africa, America, and among our Kazakhstan Nomads; however, with the liquidation of the Nomad stage of existence, the Kazakh examples of the woven dish can be more often seen now not in everyday surroundings, but in ethnographic museums.

There is something just as "eternal" in this as in the eternal charm of weaving and unweaving riddles.

It is interesting that one of the most inflamed enthusiasts and consistent theoreticians of this principle of multilinear unity of composition – William Hogarth – on the exact same basis of the hunting instinct expresses his suppositions on the reasons for the attraction of what he calls *the principle of weaving* (intricacy).

One should note that in Hogarth's discussion of this theme, which is introduced in the second volume of *Masters of Art on Art,** apart from the inaccurate method of conveying Hogarth's thoughts, this part of his discussion is simply left out!

This principle is given more accurately and in full context in the fifth chapter of his *The Analysis of Beauty*:

CHAPTER V: OF INTRICACY

...The active mind is ever bent to be employed. Pursuing is the business of our lives; and even abstracted from any other view, gives pleasure. Every arising difficulty, that for a while attends and interrupts the pursuit, gives a sort of spring to the mind, enhances the pleasure, and makes what would else be toil and labor become sport and recreation.

Wherein would consist the joys of hunting, shooting, fishing, and many other favorite diversions, without the frequent turns and difficulties, and disappointments, that are daily met with in the pursuit? How joyless does the sportsman return when the hare has not had fair play! How lively, and in spirits, even when an old cunning one has baffled, and out-run the dogs!

This love of pursuit, merely as pursuit, is implanted in our natures, and designed, no doubt, for necessary and useful purposes. Animals have it evidently by instinct. The hound dislikes the game he so eagerly pursues; and even cats will risk the losing of their prey to chase it over again. It is a pleasing labor of the mind to solve the most difficult problems; allegories and riddles, trifling as they are, afford the mind amusement: and with what delight does it follow the well-connected thread of a play, or novel, which ever increases as the plot thickens, and ends most pleased, when that is most distinctly unravelled!

The eye has this sort of enjoyment in winding walks, and serpentine rivers, and all sorts of objects, whose forms, as we shall see hereafter, are composed principally of what, I call, the *waving* and *serpentine* lines.

Intricacy in form, therefore, I shall define to be that peculiarity in the lines, which compose it, that *leads the eye a wanton kind of chase*, and from the pleasure that gives the mind, intitles it to the name of beautiful... †

Almost literally the same thing is written about 100 years later by one of the classic writers of the detective novel, Mary Roberts Rinehart,[60] in the name of the heroine of *The Circular Staircase* (1908) – an old maid attracted... by the pursuit of criminals:

* Soviet publication by *Academia*, Moscow–Leningrad, 1975.
† William Hogarth, *The Analysis of Beauty*, Done at the Silver Lotus Shop, Pittsfield, Mass., 1909, pp. 49–50.

...If the series of catastrophes there did nothing else, it taught me one thing – that somehow, somewhere, from perhaps a half-civilized ancestor who wore a sheepskin garment and trailed his food or his prey, I have in me the instinct of the chase. Were I a man I should be a trapper of criminals, trailing them as relentlessly as no doubt my sheepskin ancestor did his wild boar.*

And this leads us directly to the fact that the shattering success of detective novels built on pursuit and chase appeals, of course, to those same vestiges of the hunting instinct about which Ms. Rinehart writes, conforming to the morals of her heroine. This is confirmed also by a fact that is probably not sufficiently known, that novels about a hunt by detectives for criminals to a great extent are indebted by its origin and genre construction to novels about genuine pathfinders, pursuing wild beasts in virgin forests, novels belonging to the pen of the greatest master of this type of literature – Fenimore Cooper.[61]

Balzac refers to Cooper in *The Glitter and Poverty of a Courtesan* where the theme of the pursuit of the police after Carlos Herrera occupies the central part of the work.

On the first pages of *The Mysteries of Paris*, Eugène Sue writes about Cooper:

Everyone has read those excellent pages in which Cooper, this American Walter Scott, reproduced the cruel morals of the savages, their figurative and poetic language, thousands of stratagems which helped them pursue or evade the enemy...We will try to suggest to the reader several episodes from the life of other barbarians, also existing outside of civilization, such as the wild people so wonderfully described by Cooper...

Victor Hugo also writes about this.

And Paul Feval[62] and Dumas[63] continue this line of transferring the morals of the virgin forests into the setting of the criminality of the labyrinths of large cities.†

In this connection it is interesting to note that the "hunt" is attractive from both ends! If there is the romance of the hunter, then, as it turns out, there is the romance of escaping from the hunter! If there is the romance of pursuit along a zigzag line of tracks left behind, then there is the romance of sketching similar zigzags and, while escaping, to cover up one's tracks.

In contrast to the French, the hero of one of our Russian novelists – V.V. Krestovsky – speaks eloquently about this[64]:

Many times I scurried all over Siberia practically every spring, you might say. Once I reached Tomsk and once Perm, and now in my old age the Lord has allowed me to come to the place of white-stones; Yes, to rot with you in Petersburg. Damned be Peter! It seems that I did my best to hide, and yet they

---

* This is the closest passage I could find to match the Russian translation – HM.
† About this, see Regis Messac, *Le detective novel et l'influence de la pensee scientifique*, Champion, Paris, 1929.

caught the big beast, the gray experienced wolf! That's how it is, brothers!...

"Why did the devil push you to run off like that? You could have lived quietly in the labor camp!" said Kuzma Oblako with sympathy.

"Well, dear man, how can I tell you what I don't know myself!" he shrugged his shoulders, "all my life, you might say, is on the run, because I love it...love it to death – the hunger, the cold, and the fear, too, that they will catch me at the wrong time, and then with cunning, just like a fox, I'll wag my tail – I just like it, and that's all."

However, the most interesting thing in Hogarth's statement is, of course, that he sees the appearance of that same hunting instinct *not only* in the development of plot and intrigue but in *the development of the construction of the form* in those cases when neither plot nor theme have anything in common in their content with the hunt or the chase. This seems to be a second, higher stage of the use of instinctive grounds with the aim of influencing the form of the work.

It is interesting that such a general genre development in the art of writing is often repeated in the cycles of individual biographies of different writers.

The idea of a similar "phaselike nature" between cleverly woven intrigue and strictly structured form can be read into one of the profoundly truthful notes of Sherwood Anderson:[65]

...There was a notion that ran through all story-telling in America, that stories must be built about a plot...The magazines were filled with these plot stories and most of the plays on our stage were plot plays. "The Poison Plot," I called it in conversation with my friends, as the plot notion did seem to me to poison all story-telling. What was wanted I thought was form, not plot, an altogether more elusive and difficult thing to come at.*

From the time of Sherwood Anderson, American literature has moved far ahead on this path, outlined in many ways by his stories. Such works, which are as charming as Saroyan's[66] *The Human Comedy* (the novel and the film) are completely free not only of intrigue but even of a normally unfolding plot: They seem to be independent episodes all strung out one after another – often without beginning or end; in fact, they represent the most refined interweaving of the fabric of a single thematic picture, which is maintained strictly by one *inner* system of lyrical leitmotifs, just as a play of Scribe[67] or a detective novel maintains *external* peripeteias of dizzy intrigue in a single unified tension.

Maupassant, in the preface to his story "Pierre and Jean," also writes in the same way about this phaselike nature of relations between intrigue and the refined structure of the form of literary fabric:

* Sherwood Anderson, *A Story Teller's Story*, Viking Press, New York, 1922, p. 352.

It is understandable that a similar manner of composition, so distinct from the old obvious method, accessible to every eye, often eludes the critics, and they often do not discover all the most refined threads, concealed and often invisible, which are used by several contemporary writers instead of the formed single thread whose name is: intrigue...

At this point, of course, it is impossible not to mention pictures that were very popular in their time, and that were also created by the flight of a single natural thread – the line of a stroke.

For example, I saw the mounted figure of Count Galvez (1796) drawn in a similar way in one of the Mexican museums. This is the result of the joint work of two monks – Father Pablo de Xesus, who drew the count's face and hands realistically, and Father San Xeronimo, who with one stroke and one continuous line calligraphically depicted the horse and the figure mounted on it.

In the museum of the city of Alençon (which for good reason is the center of the art of French lace weaving) I saw a cross similarly calligraphically depicted.

Finally, there is a very famous, seventeenth-century, engraving of Claude Mellan[68] in which the representation of the face of Christ on the veil of Saint Veronica is achieved by the fact that, along a continuous spiral, revolving out of the center of the face, the nuances and shades of the modeled image arise by means of pressures along this uninterrupted line.

This, probably, is the clearest example of how interest in the actual course and flight of the continuous line disappears, and the interest shifts to the drawing depicting its course.

We have already seen this in the case of the course of the thread inside the fabric, yielding to the drawing on its surface.

Here that same process seems to serve as a graphic illustration of that evolution in literature that I noted in the example of Maupassant and Sherwood Anderson.

It is interesting to focus on another instinctive inclination mentioned above, namely: the inclination for weaving and unweaving, which has flourished no less richly and even in *pure form* through the course of centuries. Let us point to two examples.

This "passion" in Dürer[69] has been noted by his biographer Waetzoldt:*

The sources of Dürer's passionate inclination for line drawing must be sought even deeper: they are an ancient Germanic heritage. In this inclination the later Gothic variation was again reborn of the initial satisfaction which Nordic man experienced in the play of the interweaving and mutual devouring of forms, of the

* Wilhelm Waetzoldt, *Dürer und seine Zeit*, Phaidon-Verlag, Vienna, 1935.

winding and unwinding of ribbons, and of the eternal melody of freely moving lines...(p. 283).

In this excerpt one thing only is unclear: why this inclination and this bent was interpreted as the exclusive prerogative of "Nordic man." On that very same page, the author points out that the prints known under the name "Six Knots" are made in imitation of the famous woven patterns of Leonardo da Vinci (engraved emblems known under the name *Academia Leonardi Vinci*).

Does this not speak of the fact that similar inclinations are characteristic of the "Italian man of the South"?

And we have even more eloquent proof of the presence of similar inclinations in the "American branch of the Anglo-Saxon race."

In 1941, the following book was published in America: *The Encyclopedia of Knots and Fancy Rope Work* by Graumont and Hensel (Cornell Maritime Press, New York). The American Institute of Graphic Arts included it on the list *The Fifty Best Books Published in 1941*. In it on 332 pages are 3,524 (!) depictions of existing varieties of knots, with a detailed catalogue and explanation of each knot.

The publication of such a book in general (and still so expensive – five dollars!) clearly shows it is read by a fairly solid circle of readers, attracted by questions of weaving and unweaving of artful designs in their most simple "rope" forms, no way less attractive than another contingent of readers interested in the same thing, but at the stage of and in the form of the mystery novel!

However – the imprint of this sign does not only lie in pure examples of the genre of the "mystery novel."

In the construction of any novel, where the technique applied is not of a consecutive tale, that is, one progressing chronologically, we are dealing essentially with both these same instincts.

Moreover – here we seem to be dealing with the fusion of the two.

Here "to overtake" means – to arrange in one straight progressive line those events of the story, which in it are not given in order.

But in the given case this is at the same time also...the unraveling of a knot. For actually, if one draws graphically the path of a narration, which does not move consecutively, then this path, full of twists and turns, produces a line that, having become a cord, seems to constitute a "potential" knot.

I will call this track line a "potential knot" because it becomes a knot when you pull at both ends of a cord arranged in this way.

I will explain everything by diagrams.

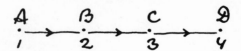

The consecutive course of the exposition of an event could be expressed by a diagram. Here the sequence of events is designated by letters and the order of their description — by numbers. In this case both rows coincide.

An example of the nonsequential course of exposition of a subject would be the case when the narration is carried on by a course not coinciding with the order of the events themselves.

For example, this is the simplest case. Having begun with event *A*, the story passes directly to *C*, from where it returns to *B*, after which it again moves ahead to *D*.

Let us imagine this line...as a cord, and we will see that the "pretzel" that results is actually one of the simplest arrangements of a cord, which provides the possibility of pulling it into a knot.

On the other hand, the pulled knot is always the "potential" course of the artfully woven line of the cord drawn tight into one point. That is, the *knot*, while unraveling, is what provides the complex course of inter-crossing and interweaving that demands a complex *process* in order to pull the cord into one straight line — to "untie the knot."

If we add that in order to pull an artfully arranged "loop" into a knot, it is necessary to apply, to its ends, two forces *moving in different directions*,

then we will see that the harmless, almost verbal metaphor in the term "dramatic knot" is absolutely precise in all its interpretations.

A truly dramatic knot is fraught with the possibilities of a complicated raveling and unraveling of the path of artfully woven action.

The more tightly the knot is tied, the more intense the conflicting forces within it act.

And, with the exception of Gordian means – of cutting the knot[70] – it is only possible to unravel it by a complicated process.

Most often this is achieved by the intervention of a "third force," overcoming the direction of the two basic forces.

Such a necessary "third force" in the subject can be extremely varied.

This can be literal intervention from outside.

An example of this is a device not unfamiliar to us, the "deus ex machina" of Greek tragedy.

Here the intervention of a divinity who solves the unravelable knot of conflict is simultaneously the most literal embodiment both of the "knot" and the "hand untying the knot."

But the third force can just as well be an external event or situation.

In this case, due to constitutive circumstances, it can *purely mechanically* force the people to act, in spite of the aims and goals chosen by them!

And this is the way the knot of relationships, otherwise tied "unto death," is unraveled (the uncontrolled nerves of Lady Macbeth and of Macbeth himself in conflict with the apparitions of fate: Birnam Wood and the very unusual details of the birth of Macduff, or Boris* in conflict with the tale of the patriarch about the murder of Dmitry).

But, of course, the most interesting case is when a similar external phenomenon (a situation) forces the heroes themselves to change inwardly the direction of the course of their character, and in this way the mortal loop of the knot of human conflicts is unraveled.

(The regeneration of Scrooge[71] in Dickens or a hint of the possibility of a satisfactory unraveling of the knots in the second act of *The Deluge*.[72])

The example of our knot, of course, is the simplest.

But let us not forget that the American book mentioned above has...3,524 varieties of knots.

And let us also not forget that we were concerned with "one cord" – with one line of action, and it is easy to imagine what a boundless quantity of possibilities arise here from the moment when the lines themselves are many!

The classic Russian examples of such a discontinuous story might be Pushkin's *The Shot*, beginning the story in the middle, or Bunin's *Gentle Breath*, and a numerous quantity of other examples.

Tristram Shandy generally remains the classic example, where in one of the chapters Sterne draws a diagram of the threads being knotted, with which he weaves the action of the novel.

* [Tsar Boris Godunov in Pushkin's play].

But Joseph Conrad[73] is particularly interesting in this respect. He consciously resurrects this method of narration at the end of the epoch of the Victorian novel.*

A colleague of Conrad, Ford, writes about this in the name of Conrad and in his own name (see Ford Madox Ford, *Joseph Conrad: A Personal Remembrance*):

For it became very early evident to us that what was the matter with the novel, and the British novel in particular, was that it went straight forward, whereas in your gradual making acquaintanceship with your fellows you never do go straight forward. You meet an English gentleman at your golf club. He is beefy, full of health, the morale of the boy from an English Public School of the finest type. You discover, gradually, that he is hopelessly neurasthenic, dishonest in matters of small change, but unexpectedly self-sacrificing, a dreadful liar but a most painfully careful student of lepidoptera and, finally, from the public prints, a bigamist who was once, under another name, hammered on the Stock Exchange...Still, there he is, the beefy, full-fed fellow, morale of an English Public School product. *To get such a man in fiction you could not begin at his beginning and work his life chronologically to the end. You must first get him in with a strong impression, and then work backwards and forwards over his past*...That theory at least we gradually evolved.[†]

And here is a short paraphrase of the order of events of the first half as they unwind in the novel *Lord Jim* [...]

The story begins when Jim is working in various Eastern ports after the conflict and trial. Then the story returns to a description of Jim's life from the beginning to the moment of the conflict. In the fourth chapter we are present at the trial of officers of the *Patna* for having abandoned the vessel, where Marlowe becomes acquainted with Jim. Then the description is given in the words of Marlowe, of the view that these dishonorable officers had at their first appearance in the port where they were being tried, and of the meeting he had much earlier with the German skipper before the departure of the *Patna* for sailing. Later we return again to the court scene and prepare for a future scene of the suicide of Braierly, the president of the court. Then in the course of several chapters Jim begins to tell Marlowe about what had occurred on the *Patna*, and after this Marlowe's answer follows about his conversation with the French lieutenant who took the vessel by boarding it after the conflict, etc., etc. [...]

However, the most interesting thing in this is that this Conrad–Ford method is calculated apparently mainly to overcome the boring grayness of the eternally boring and gray English novels, that is, the apparently

---

* In addition he also writes this with the narrative manner coming from different persons, which alongside of Wilkie Collins makes him one of the direct precursors of *Citizen Kane*.
† Ford Madox Ford, *Joseph Conrad*, Duckworth, London, 1924, p. 129.

purely "formal" intention, which is at the same time an extremely realistic "justified" device as well.

In this same book of reminiscences Ford speaks also of this:

We agreed that the general effect of a novel must be the general effect that life makes on mankind. A novel must therefore not be a narration, a report. Life does not say to you: In 1914 my next door neighbour, Mr. Slack, erected a greenhouse and painted it with Cox's green aluminium paint. . . If you think about the matter you will remember, in various unordered pictures, how one day Mr. Slack appeared in his garden and contemplated the wall of his house. You will then try to remember the year of that occurrence and you will fix it as August, 1914, because having had the foresight to bear the municipal stock of the city of Liege you were able to afford a first-class season ticket for the first time in your life. You will remember Mr. Slack – then much thinner because it was before he found out where to buy cheap Burgundy; . . . But we accepted the name [Impressionists] because Life appearing to us much as the building of Mr. Slack's greenhouse comes back to you, we saw that *Life did not narrate, but made impressions on our brains.* [p. 192]

And again we are convinced that the truly vital methods in art are those that, according to their prototype, follow the course of the thought and behavior of man, and also not just from the aspect of plot and representation, but in no less degree in the area of structure, composition, and the laws of construction of form in general.

Let us focus in somewhat more detail on this type of construction because, given certain of its symptoms, it seems this type of story has all the data to become very fashionable in the area of the scenic composition of our films.

Several references from the past prove to be useful here. On the other hand, this keeps authors from being too conceited.

With this in mind, we can refer to two other examples of theater drama.

These are J. B. Priestley's *Time and the Conways*[74] and Lillian Hellman's *The Searching Wind.*[75]

In the first case, the events are arranged in the order *A, B, C,* for an extremely dramatic effect.

In the second case – according to the diagram where both returns [from the situation in a Washington apartment in 1914 – to the fascist revolution in Rome (1922) and the Nazi revolution in Berlin (1933)] provide the necessary dramatic accents at the proper moment, both as to the social line of the unwinding drama as well as the intensification of the conflict of personal relationships, lying at the basis of the conflicts between the play's characters.

What remains is only to render homage to an author whose statement led me to think of combining the instinct of the hunt and the raveling of knots in one phenomenon – in the method of nonsequential narration in novels.

And it is not surprising – this author is... Dante.

And his statement – is one that at first glance is a dark passage out of his *Convivio*.[76] It concerns the origin of the word "author."

In exactly the same spirit of the figurative-associative-"physiognomic" manner of the Middle Ages, which had just been overcome, Dante ascribes it an etymological origin from the following of a series of possible roots.

One of these roots "... is a word almost completely out of usage in Latin and meaning 'to tie words among themselves' – *aveio*. And whoever looks with great attention at this word in its initial form will be convinced that it clearly reveals its unique meaning, for this word is composed of nothing but the connections among words, that is, the five vowels that are the soul and coupling inside each word. And it is formed from them in such a way that it takes the form of a knot. For, having begun with 'A', it is repeated in 'U',* and then goes directly through 'E' to 'I', from whence it returns back again to 'O', since it really represents a knot. And insofar as the word 'author' is produced and proceeds from this word, it is understandable only by poets, who connect their words by the art of music..."

It is possible, of course, to etymologically dispute this picture of the origin of the word "author," but it is difficult to argue about the beauty of the image by which the method of the poet's activity is drawn here.

However, I was even more surprised by something else in this passage.

What basis did Dante have for saying that the path from "A" to "U" – "returns," it runs "straight" again from "U" to "I", and from "I" to "O" it again "returns back"?

In addition it is these very passages back and forward that form the bowtie, which is also a plastic image of the tying of sounds by means of music that, according to Dante, is the fate of certain poets.

Apparently, Dante has in mind a certain standard sequence in which vowels must be arranged in succession "according to nature" (or something like that).

In Western European languages there is the custom of arranging the vowels in the order "A," "E," "I," "O," "U."

However, this is definitely not the order Dante has in mind. In this movement from letter to letter, which he is pointing out, a knot is not the result. Moreover, it is impossible that a path among them proceed according to his instructions. Here the path from "U" to "I" goes "backwards," and from "E" to "O" – forward, which is contrary to Alighieri's instructions.

---

* The consonant "V" in the noun "aveio" is here considered as being converted into the vowel "U."

In order to clarify what is going on here, one thing remained – to find such a sequence of arranging these five letters that, in proceeding along the path shown by Dante, a similar knot or bowtie is actually the result.

The order "I," "E," "A," "O," "U" proves to be such an arrangement.

Actually, in this arrangement of vowels the path of the sequence pointed out by Dante gives us a graphic image of the knot he writes about:

Thus, what is considered the organic sequence of the vowels according to Dante is the order: "I," "E," "A," "O," "U."

What is so remarkable here? And why is this order more organic than "A," "E," "I," "O," "U," accepted as the order of the sequence of vowels in all Western European languages?

And here, of course, is the most striking thing in the musical sensitivity of Dante.

If we take a table of the frequency of waves corresponding to each separate vowel, then it turns out that the sequence of vowels according to this sign proves to be just what Dante had in mind.

Let us, for example, just look at the table on p. 17 of Liddell's book* and we will be convinced of this.

Vowel	Pronunciation	Frequency
$\overline{oo}$	gloom	326
$\overline{o}$	no	461
aw	raw	732
ä	father	900
ă	mat	1,840
ĕ	pet	1,958
ey (ā)	they	2,461
i	be	3,100

Thus, it turns out that the sequence Dante drew "by instinct" as being normal and natural – actually turns out to be normal and organic according to the precise data of physical science.

* Mark H. Liddell, *Physical Characteristics of Speech Sound*, Purdue University, Lafayette, Ind. 1924–7.

We know about the masters of the Renaissance, that they also drew the curved domes by eye and "by instinct," proceeding from the position that the most organically beautiful under the given conventions of line proves to be the most normal in terms of construction.

The domes of Bramante[77] and Michelangelo[78] are typical, and much later mathematical verification of their curvature confirmed their absolute constructive faultlessness.

Now we can see that the sharpness of hearing among great Italians in no way yielded to the sharpness of sight.

And the ear of Dante Alighieri could systemize the harmonious organic sequence of the sound of vowels even without resorting to acoustic measuring instruments.

Something of this longing of each knot to be unraveled, corresponding to the yearning to tie knots, as we have seen, sits deeply in the psyche of man.

And the course along elements of a shuffled sequence, just so we can then recreate a true order from their parts, is therefore constant and gives us satisfaction.

It is all the same, whether it occurs in the graphic knots of Leonardo and Dürer,

in the frequencies of vibrations of vowels that wind into the phonetic knots of Dante,

or in the peripeteias of the arrangement of the sequence of scenes that attract equally Pushkin, Joseph Conrad, and Orson Welles!

Finally, in order to end with examples on the theme of the attraction of the process of tying, raveling, and unraveling, one should mention a mysteriously attractive case of their application.

This is the invariable attraction of the music hall number in which the actor of this particular genre is tied with ropes and chains, from which he breaks out almost instantaneously.

The king of this genre was the now-deceased great master of this art, Houdini.

Now it seems that there was not a single variation of chaining and imprisonment that was not included in the program of his wonderful self-liberations.

They hung him upside down in a straitjacket from a skyscraper over New York City.

Chained in shackles, they put him into a coffin and buried the coffin at the bottom of a swimming pool.

They locked him, entangled in chains, into chambers and cells in apparently all the prisons of the world – including the Russian tsarist prisons, of which he has the nastiest memories – which appear in his memoirs,* etc., etc.

---

* See Harold Kellock, *Houdini, His Life Story*, Harcourt Brace, New York, 1928.

He liberates himself from all these improbable incarcerations with a greater or lesser degree of ease.

And in the same way from the most intricate system of loops and knots by which they bound him hand and foot.

And, actually, his very effective and entertaining number is really only a more complicated form of that same basic situation of a man untying the knots by which he is fettered.

And the president of the American Association of Jugglers and Magicians, Walter B. Gibson, in his book on Houdini, writes about the mastery of Houdini in unraveling knots:

...Houdini could untie the most intricate knots with his hands, ordinary knots with his teeth, and some knots with his feet...*

I think what is attractive about Houdini's raveling and unraveling for the public applies directly to what we have been speaking of here.

Here the case is only a more intense identification with the actor than in those cases when "knots" have a figurative sense, and the "hopelessness of the position" is created by the psychological elements of the plot, and not by the bag or box where the actor is locked in, after having first been bound hand and foot either by shackles or chains!†

However, one thing is certain, and this is that in both these "instinctive" inclinations for weaving and for the hunt there is also preserved the age-long attraction of the fugue – whether it be spatial in the etchings of, let us say, Giovanni Battista Piranesi, or musical in the works of Johann Sebastian Bach.

The very etymology of the term "fugue" is characteristic, coming from the Latin "fuga, fugere": *flight, to run away, to be saved from pursuit.*

In this respect what is very characteristic – in connection with Piranesi's staircases in the cycle of his Dungeons – is the fact that in English the staircase is often called "a flight of stairs."

We also sometimes speak of stairs "racing upward," but with us this is rather – although trite – still a semifigurative expression, while with the English this early became simply a concrete term.

What can be a more appropriate term than the term "fugue" for a staircase in Piranesi's prints – eternally "racing" upward, into the

---

* Walter Gibson, *Houdini's Escapes*, Harcourt Brace, New York, 1930, p. 23.
† The psychoanalytic school has its own interpretation on this point. Otto Rank (in his book *Das Trauma des Geburt* [Internationale Psycho-Analitische Verlag, Leipzig, 1924] sees in this vaudeville number an apparently figurative reproduction of the "appearance into the world" – the birth of man. It is characteristic that in German, "family" is called *Entbindung* – literally "unraveling" or "disentangling."

The attraction of ways out of garden labyrinths and corridors of laughter, as well as the original myth about the Minotaur[79] and the Cretan labyrinth where he apparently lived, is explained in the same way. To subject these premises to a detailed critique unfortunately cannot be done here. I only note them for informational purposes.

depths, to the side – eternally varying and repeating itself! They are repeated by columns, arches, and stairwells. Combining with each other, these architectural elements engender that inexhaustible stream of the "flight" of architectural forms into the depths of the etching, which serves as the object of the continuous chase and pursuit of a bewitched eye!

However, the fugue and the principle of polyphony, as we have understood them here, both strive to give the most complete expression to one of the main basic principles lying at the basis of the phenomena of reality in general.

They try (as, moreover, the entire basis of the aesthetics of many-pointed montage) to realize in a work of art that *principle of unity in variety* that in nature permeates not only phenomena of the same order but also connects all the variety of phenomena in general among themselves.

In terms of the refinement with which this principle premeates the realm of aesthetics, it is frequently presented there in such a filigree fashion that at first glance it is sometimes difficult to guess that we are dealing with that same basic principle.

In the light of our considerations about the increasingly refined fabric of the construction of the elements of polyphony, what is particularly interesting, for example, is the position mentioned by Guyau:[80] "...Every figurative style essentially belongs to a style made rhythmic, for the verbal image by its very nature is the repetition of a basic idea in another form and each time in new material...and each repetition is attractive because it embodies *unity in variety*..."*

At first glance it might not occur to one to extend the features of repetition, so characteristic of rhythm, to the area of the verbal image as well. However, what Guyau is saying here is certainly correct. And moreover – the feeling of this *single* principle in *different* areas – in the given case in the areas of *rhythm and image* – in itself has its charm – for this position is a particular case of the application of that very same principle of *unity in variety*!

We could pull another example of this type from the thick of the production practices of *Ivan the Terrible*.

This is the unity of the developing figure of the tsar as he passes through the picture as a whole.

Here there are two separate areas of work. The concrete – the prescreen development of the figure of the tsar in the great mastery of the makeup artist V. V. Goryunov.[81]

And the lighting – that is, the screen interpretation of this figure from shot to shot in the magical hands of the cameraman, A. N. Moskvin.[82]

---

* Jean M. Guyau, *Problèmes Esthétiques Contemporaines,* 6th ed., Lacan, Paris, 1921.

Part of the problem of the first area was to make the type of figure once established – the countenance and plastic image of Tsar Ivan – pass whole and indivisible through all the various nuances of the changes in age: from the boy on the grand princely throne – to the young man crowned as tsar in the Uspensky Cathedral; from the maturing warrior under the walls of Kazan – to the emaciated, fiery, and feverish mourner for the unity of the Russian land; from locks turning gray on the head of a widower, bent over the body of a poisoned wife – to the strained features of the Terrible Tsar who had turned gray in conflict with the Metropolitan Philip over the mystery play *The Fiery Furnace*; from the tormented old man in a bloody sweat grieving over the necessary bloodshed in Novgorod – to the victor over Lithuania, whose eaglelike fiery glance tames the waves of the Baltic Sea, which has finally been attained.

The search for this "suite" of makeup was long and exhausting.

In the national consciousness there lives a certain image of the representative of Ivan in old age. There is a certain established tradition. Many have seen the figure of Chaliapin in *The Man from Pskov*, many remember the pictures of Repin* and Vasnetstov, many are familiar with the seated Ivan the Terrible of Antokolsky.[†]

To depart too far from these representations – would be inappropriate.

But no one knows either from original portraits (of which there simply are none) or by fantasy of painters or sculptors of later epochs, what Ivan was like in middle age, in adolescence, or in childhood.

And it was necessary in the unique process of "reverse development" to represent the childhood, adolescent, and mature face of a man from which could arise that image of an old man, which arises before us whenever we recall the name of the Terrible (although he did live, nevertheless, until fifty-four).

The indefatigability, talent, and selfless devotion of the work of V. V. Goryunov, our makeup artist, helped us very much to overcome these difficulties with honor.

Sometime, perhaps, one will also succeed in tracing how and from what associations this figure was composed, within a tradition that has been able to make its own voice heard.

Sometime we will be able to guess for ourselves which of the Deisises[‡] of ancient painting prompted the slit of the eyes and the drawing of the curls; in what peripeteias of flight away from the resemblance to Mephistopholes or Tsarevich Aleksey was the curve of the brows discovered; where, in trying to avoid a resemblance to Christ, Uriel

---

* [Repin's painting, *Ivan the Terrible and His Son Ivan*, 1885, depicts the psychological moment after Ivan has killed his son, his heir – HM.]

[†] [Marc Antokolsky (1845–1902) a Russian Jewish Sculptor of world renown – HM.]

[‡] [*Deisises*: configuration of Christ with Mary and John the Baptist on either side, often depicted in Russian medieval art – HM.]

Acosta, or Judas, we caught the outline of nostrils, the break in the contour of the nose, and the contour of the skull.

And this is all repeated by a long search for camera angles of the head and face in which the Terrible – is Terrible: A centimeter downward destroys the oblong interrelationship of the forehead and the lower part of the face; a half centimeter to the side – and the penetrating point of the second eye disappears behind the curve of the nose, etc., etc.

Mentally fixing, as it were, a "card index" of the suitable angles for Ivan, the shooting must pass strictly through these camera setups, quickly slipping by and not falling into those "danger zones" where the figure departs from the plastic canon once established for the film.*

Above we cited the words of Saint-Saëns on the relationship of music and the word, and how music tonally expresses what is inexpressible in words.

In the same way the changing figure of Ivan is expressed tonally through the film by the play of the actor's contour, the framing of the shot, and above all by the miracle of tonal photography of the cameraman Moskvin.

Here on a higher level the very same thing is repeated.

For a long time a penetrating *formula of light* for the figure was sought; a certain persistent shadow in the eye socket from which the pupil, caught by the light, begins to burn; somewhere the emphasized line of the skull; somewhere filled in and somewhere brought out the asymmetry of the eyes; the highlight of a protruding angle of the brow; the white of the neck softened by light filters.

But that is not all! The main thing lies ahead.

For into this basic light gamma – I would define it as "modeling with light" – from scene to scene we no longer just made "light corrections" relative to the changing appearance of the personage, but mainly introduced all those nuances of light that must echo, from episode to episode, both the emotional mood of a scene and the emotional state of the tsar-protagonist.

Here it is not sculptured modeling of an image with light that is demanded, not only the changing *pictorial interpretation of it* under conditions of a changing situation and environment (night, day, semidarkness, flat background, or depth), but the most refined *tonal nuances* of what I would call *intonations of light*, which Andrey Moskvin controls with such perfection.

Here is the same very refined *musical quality of light in a portrait* as in the most refined lyric of a landscape of Eduard Tisse – whether it be in

---

* In *Ivan* the suitable camera angles include about 75% of the natural figure of Cherkasov. In *Alexander Nevsky*, we arranged only 25%, and it turns out just those that were not suitable to Tsar Ivan!

the mist of *Potemkin*, in the city night ensemble of Petrograd (*October*), or in the whiteness of the icy expanses of *Nevsky* under the severe hanging vault of the ominous clouds.

Above we cited the words of Hogarth on the instinctive prerequisites of the attraction of the fugue and polyphonic writing.

But, of course, certain "instinctive" prerequisites would still be insufficient to explain the power of the effect of the means of counter-point and the fugue.

And one must add that the greatest intersocial changes proceeding in phases are also reflected here, in these structures.

In addition, it is interesting that these are the phenomena and norms that are invariably repeated both *in the early stages* of the birth of society and on *the highest stages of its development*.

And this is because these norms are characteristic of every aspect of development in general.

I think in the given case both the principle and all separate stylistic fluctuations within it repeat precisely in phases, and reflect fully within the basic historical stages, the interrelationships between society and the individual, between the collective and the personality, now devouring and dissolving the single in the whole, now providing the possibility for the particular to trample the general with their feet.

The aesthetics of all systems of art, of variations within it, and of the separate phases inside these separate variations, inevitably passes through those same stages of development, invariably reflecting the course of the social formations undergoing modification.

This is typical, for example, of the nondifferentiated quality of art passing into separate independent aspects in the early stage of its development.

Or, on the contrary, the complete isolation of the varieties of certain arts from each other. The denial of their commensurability. Moreover, the individualization of separate elements of art in a system of separate "-isms," idolizing a separate particularity.

Or the attempt, arising periodically, to unify the arts in a certain synthesis.

(And the Greeks, the theories of Diderot and Wagner, the prewar aesthetics of the Soviet land, and audiovisual film, etc. – in different ways and at different times, and with a differing degree of success!)

In another place – in a work investigating the history of the *close-up* understood filmically through the past *history of the arts* – I was interested in the historical process of the transition from "individualiza-tion" to "individualism."

Here I am attracted by the reverse – now before our eyes is the clearly developing stage of *the unity and harmony of expressive means*.

I do not know if this is occurring in the other arts, but in the aesthetics of montage we, apparently, are standing today at the threshhold of a *third phase* of the history of its development.

The *first* stage of this development was the amorphous undifferentiated stage of "prehistorical" montage: the cinematography of shooting from one setup (this stage was repeated and is often repeated very "magnificently" even today by the first stage of sound film!).

Then came the stage of the constantly increasing tendency to greater and greater *separation of separate elements* banging their heads together in montage (almost under the aegis of Anatole France: "Make the epithets bang their heads together").

On the various stages of the development of sound film, this also resounded in our manifesto of 1928* where, on the path to future counterpoint, we called for *sharp divergence and opposition of sound and visual image.*

At this stage of silent film, which directly preceded sound, the subsequent application of this principle led to such excesses of montage filmmaking *as the combination of unrelated pieces*, which in *their combination* gave the illusion of fused action or movement. *October* (1927) is full of examples of this, but the first experience in a similar direction again belongs to *Potemkin* – and to those same roaring lions from the staircase of the Vorontsov Palace in Alupka† (1925).

Here three independent phases of movement presented in three independent figures of three marble lions were combined, creating the illusion of one jumping lion [...]

About this time, several years earlier, I dreamt of composing consecutive phases of the gestures of the immortal French actor Frédérick Lemaître from *the hundred and one poses on the hundred and one pages* of the adventures of Robert Macaire. He [Lemaître] played Macaire on the stage in the famous play *L'Auberge des Adrets* [*The Inn in Adrets*], and the inimitable nature of his performance was imprinted on the hundred and one lithographs of Honoré Daumier – the series *Caricaturana* (*Les Robert Macaire*) (1836).

Such is the recent past of the montage form, of montage efforts, and montage quests.

In contrast, the new stage of audiovisual montage, I believe, entered with the sign of an increasing fusion and harmony of montage and polyphony.‡

This type of new "harmonious" counterpoint – beyond any paradoxes

---

* Signed by me and Pudovkin and Alexandrov.

† [A palace built at the beginning of the nineteenth century in the Crimea near Yalta by Count Vorontsov. It is the "Strawberry Hill" of Russia, full of Gothic and Oriental features – HM.]

‡ Perhaps the evolutionary change was realized here that occurred in the history of music when harmonic composition replaced the principles of polyphony?

and excesses – I think most fully expresses the picture of the activity of separate individuals inside the collective.

When a single social problem is taken up by the whole host of separate units, composing this society,

when each unit within it knows its personal independent path inside the solution of the general problem,

when these paths cross and recross, combine and interweave – and move ahead all together to the realization of the goal once projected.

From where did the vivid tangible impressions of a similar picture come from? Where and when did I happen to see graphically a similar picture in action?

When and where was I first intoxicated with the mania of counterpoint and the attraction of Bach, a mania that has afflicted me my whole life?

It was not soccer – this game is so attractive, probably, just because the symbol of joint battle and cooperation is embodied in it very strongly and magnificently, which forces one to pass on personal initiative along with the ball from participant to participant of the general event.

Probably for that reason the spectacle of one form of contest called "catch-as-catch-can" is so repulsive, in which any blow and any device are allowed: that particular combat when four men come from all four corners of the ring to fight simultaneously.

But here – not as in dominoes or in other games – two against two – but *each against each*, and the task is to beat all the other three, leaving the single victor in the ring.

And so we see that suddenly not just two but three hurl themselves onto one and, having overthrown him, begin to throw themselves on each other, and as two are finishing off the staggering third one, the fourth, regaining consciousness, knocks them off their feet, and the third one, saved by this maneuver, hurls himself, in a wild rage, onto the one who has just saved him!

This gladiatorial spectacle of each against each and all against all – not only without white gloves but even without leather gloves to soften the blows of bony fists – is no doubt so repulsive because it offends to the very depths what can be called social instinct.

However, my interest in counterpoint was not born from the vivid impressions of soccer. In favor of which the circumstances give evidence that the imprint of *a bifurcated equal-sided struggle* hardly ever lies on my style of films.

More often than not there is a strengthening unity under the blows of external assault – be they the strides of tsarist soldiers down the Odessa steps, the gallop of the German knights' cavalry wedge, or the serried ranks of the boyar opposition, rushing into battle against the works of Ivan the Terrible.

And stemming therefrom not so much a struggle of equal powers as an active conflict of contradictions within a single theme.

And therefore not so much Beethoven as Bach.

One way or the other, it is clear, that the course of my passion was not a picture of the clash of two inner harmonious collectives in an aggressive assault on each other but more likely the solidifying of a united collective for the fulfillment of certain constructive tasks.

And so it was.

And I remember this impression as if it had just occurred.

The Izhor Station.

The Neva River...

The year 1917.

The School of Ensigns of the Engineer Corps.

The camp.

Studies.

The pontoon bridge!

I remember the heat as if it were right now.

The fresh air.

The sandy shore of the river.

The anthill of newly recruited young men!

They move with measured steps.

With rehearsed steps and coordinated movements they construct the constantly growing bridge, eagerly crossing the river.

Somewhere amid the ant heap I also am moving.

On my shoulders are square leather pillows.

The edges of planking rest on the square pillows.

And in the leading machine fleeting figures,

approaching pontoons,

from pontoon to pontoon heavy transverse beams

or light railings, sprouting ropes,

are carried easily and cheerfully like a "perpetuum mobile"

from the shore left behind to the end of the ever-receding bridge!

The strictly set time of construction is divided into seconds of separate operations,

slow and fast, weaving and unweaving,

and, linked to them, delineated running lines of imprints in space, as it were, of their rhythmic flight in time.

These separate operations merge into a single general production,

and taken all together, are combined in an amazing orchestra counterpoint experience of the process of collective work and creation.

And the bridge grows and grows.

Eagerly it presses the river down beneath it.

It stretches to the opposite shore.

People scurry.

Pontoons scurry.

Commands ring out.

The second hand is running.

Damn it, how wonderful it is!

No, it was not in examples of classical performances, not in notes taken on leading shows, not in the complicated orchestra score, not in the complicated evolution of the corps de ballet, and not on the soccer field – that I first felt intoxicated with the charm of the movement of bodies, scurrying in different tempos along a diagram of divided space, the play of their crossing orbits, the constantly changing dynamic form of the combination of these paths – running together into momentary fanciful patterns so that they then can again scatter into distant rows that never meet.

The pontoon bridge, growing out of the sandy shores into the boundless expanse of the Neva River, revealed to me for the first time all the charm of this enthusiasm, which has never left me.

Here it was presented to me for the first time in forms that engendered my enthusiasm for mise-en-scène.*

Mise-en-scène even to this very day was to remain my favorite expressive means in the theater.

And mise-en-scène is also the first clear and perceptible example of spatial-temporal counterpoint!

Out of it, out of its initial combination of the play of space, time, and sound – which later became more complex – grow all the principles of audiovisual montage.

A gesture becomes the shot, and the intonation of a word – sound and music.

In general the charm of contrapuntal composition is also based on the fact that, in the form of its construction, it reflects and again compels one to relive a most wonderful stage on the path of the history of thought.

This is the period when the initial stage of undifferentiated consciousness has been left behind.

A period when the following stage of diffuse separation and isolation of each distinct phenomenon of the world in it has been accomplished.

(These periods, endlessly varying and increasingly complex, are again repeated at the highest stage of development: Thus, agnosticism corresponds to the first, no matter in which epoch or in what form it arose, which is a denial of differentiated cognition, and what corresponds to the second – can be Kant's metaphysics, in its own way repeating more ancient analogous theoretical positions.)

Thus montage counterpoint as a form seems to correspond to that fascinating stage of the evolution of consciousness, when both preceding stages have been overcome, and the universe, dissected by analyses, is recreated once again into a single whole, revives by means of the

---

* [In America called *blocking* – the planning of the stage movements of characters in a theatrical performance – HM.]

connections and interactions of separate parts, and appears as an excited perception of the fullness of the world perceived synthetically.

Just as in a mature person the first "discoveries" on the paths of his biography are imbued with particular warmth, with special enthusiasm and excitement – the first time he conquered a printed text (I can read!), the first arousal of emotions (I can love!), the first philosophical data available that helped him perceive the system of other worlds (I can know!),

in the same way we are invariably most excited in art by those constructions that, in their features, repeat the traits of the various stages of the evolution of our consciousness.

Thus, in the system of the tangible contrapuntal principle, living feeling has been preserved of the stage when consciousness – whether it be of nations achieving a definite level of development, or of a child who in the course of his development repeats those same stages – for the first time establishes the interrelationship between separate pheno-mena of reality simultaneously with the sensation of it as one great whole.

This, of course, is the guarantee of the excitement of polyphony and counterpoint, and the inevitable intensity of their characteristic features in the stages of youth.

The youth of any kind.

The youth of a social formation or class – and then they become the basic style of a particular epoch.

The youth of the most diverse forms of art, and then, beneath their symbols, it formulates the basic starting positions of its methodology for the future.

The youth of an author – then this inevitably arises in the manner and style of his writing and dominates his creativity.

In the period of the creation of *Potemkin* all three "youths" coincided.

The young (eight-year-old) Soviet power.

The young (thirteen-year-old) art of film, feverishly seeking the principles of its own self-determination.

The young (twenty-seven-year-old) author who, after a short five-year running start, was now caught up for the first time by a large theme.

And this totality could not but determine the structure of *Potemkin* as being contrapuntal above all.

But in its application to film (and especially in its application to silent film) the means of realizing counterpoint and polyphony was montage.

And thus *Potemkin* cannot but become the standard bearer of the montage-counterpoint principle in artistic cinematography.

The pulsation of the life of the montage form within art is the index of its vital energy. I wrote about this in the preface to the English edition of my book *Film Sense*, published in 1943 in England after it came out in America in 1942.

The preface never reached the book because of the blockade, and it did not reach England; therefore I will introduce the necessary excerpt from it here:

PREFACE TO THE ENGLISH EDITION
Exactly a year ago in the middle of October, around midnight, we received instructions to pack. During this night the Germans for some incomprehensible reason did not bomb Moscow. Each of us was able to pack his two suitcases peacefully.

In the morning we were at the railway station.

Twelve days – like a new Noah's ark – our carriage floated through the storm of the raging war.

We – meaning the basic group of moviemakers evacuated out of Moscow at the moment of the German attack on the capital of the Soviet government in late autumn of 1941.

The Germans were repulsed.

We were left to work in the heart of Central Asia.

Pass your finger from India going upward.

You will find the intersection of this line with the Southern Asian border of the Soviet Union.

Stop your finger on the point having the fantastic name of Alma-Ata.

This is where we are now.

* * *

It would have been unthinkable to live.

It would have been impossible to exist.

It would have been shameful and insulting to create and work at such a distant rear front –

if we had not known that two things had been entrusted to us:

first of all, to discharge film after film, just like missile after missile, with which to beat the Germans just as devastatingly as with a tank or plane,

second of all, to preserve the achieved culture of film from that whirlwind of destruction with which the fascist* interventionists were passing along the broad field of our Homeland.

In Pskov and Novgorod inimitable frescoes of the thirteenth and fourteenth centuries perished.

Near Leningrad – palaces and fountains of the eighteenth century.

Near Moscow – cathedrals and museums of the nineteenth century.

On the Dnieper – the miracle of the twentieth century – Dneproges Dam.[†]

Every European part of Russia is covered by ruins and ashes...

Cinema as an industry, cinema as cadres of people, as a great tradition of

---

* [Note that Soviet censors insist on the use of the Italian word "fascist" instead of the German "nazi" (i.e., National Socialists), which would be correct. They wish to avoid any comparison with Russian socialism, which is also nationalist – HM.]

[†] [The Great Dnieprostroy Dam, in its day the largest in the world, built under American planning and supervision – HM.]

Soviet art, as the custodian of the achievements of Soviet culture and scientific thought – has been preserved.

* * *

Before our eyes the gigantic snow mountains rest against the blue sky.

Behind these chains are others – on the other side of the border – in China.

The mountains are arranged for meditation.

Chinese sages have been gazing for centuries at our mountain chains from the other side.

The mountains are arranged for reflection.

And involuntarily, looking at the eternal snow of the mountains, one's thought arises out of the everyday chaos of madness and bloodshed to what will be on the morrow after these years' madness of war.

You will think about the tomorrow of culture and the arts.

The horrible shock of World War I turned the world upside down: Out of its chaos was born such an unprecedented phenomenon as the Soviet Union.

What will bring us hundred times more inconceivable cataclysm into which today's world is crashing to destruction?

It is not for us to foretell and foresee the paths of art, along which humanity will go, once resurrected out of the filth and death of these years, washed by the unfading heroism of its finest sons – the fighters against fascist darkness.

Along with a new social era, the end of World War I brought a new unprecedented rise and blossoming of culture.

And the culture of the most advanced of the arts – cinematography.

A segment of the universal history of art between both world wars – is undoubtedly the era of the triumph of cinema.

Other arts in this interval of time move feverishly along the path of disintegration and collapse.

Expressionism. Suprematism. Dadaism. Surrealism.

The collapse of form, image, thought.

An elemental flight back to the primitive.

Apparently the latter achievements lock themselves in a mortal ring together with the first steps of culture and art.

The snake of the well-known emblem forever swallowing its own tail.

Frozen into immobility...

No period in the history of the arts had such an impasse of art as that beginning this epoch of wars.

Reaching the highest point of development, art suddenly was dissipated into nothing.

Cinema alone, in its best examples, stood its ground before this whirlwind of collapse.

And because it was the youngest – it began from the point all the other arts reached in their collapse.

* * *

Art – is the most sensitive seismograph.

And the tragic impasse of it in the last years reflected only the degree of tension into which the world has been plunged by its lacerating contradictions.

These contradictions exploded into world slaughter on an unprecedented scale.

Neither the paradoxicality of what is happening, neither the scale of what has already happened, nor the perspective of what awaits the world to experience – can be grasped by a single consciousness.

We know firmly – ahead there will be victory over darkness.

Ahead – there is light.

But we are still not able to assimilate its rays, to examine the new life in these new rays, to move along the new paths illuminated by them.

We foresee, have a presentiment, and have a foreboding of it.

But this light is only now being born in the truly apocalyptic madness in which the universe is now enveloped.

Humanity is stretching out to it, toward this new unknown light of the future.

On the way to it, smashing the forces of fascist darkness, heroic humanity is laying down its bones, clearing the path for future generations.

And there are no words to describe the sacrificial heroism with which it is doing this.

We will not debase the figure of this future by quick guesses, we will not belittle the greatness of it, born out of the blood of millions of human lives, we will not give ourselves airs in an attempt to reconstruct the features of its future face.

We will only recall one thing: the hymns of the new unprecedented art, the art of the postwar epoch of World War II, will be a reflection of this unprecedented new face of humanity that, triumphantly, will rise up to life, having conquered the monster of fascism.

And as the actual image of the future is inaccessible to our conjectures, so the future form of the renewed arts must still inevitably escape any assumptions and deductions, whatever we might imagine it to be.

Three things are in store for us:

to wait,

to hurry,

to be prepared.

To await this new era.

To hasten its approach, giving one's full strength, whole life, any sacrifices for hastening its arrival.

And to be ready, fully armed with the experience of the past, to prove to be worthy of perceiving and moving ahead that which this unprecedented future will bring us.

There is something exciting in this expectation of the future fertilization of the art of the new zones and pages of life.

In the consciousness of one's torpor until the moment of its arrival.

Thus in torpor young brides await the moment of yielding themselves to the love of an unknown groom, and thus in torpor the earth, sprawling, lies in trembling expectation of the fertilization of spring shoots.

There is something intoxicating, not only in the consciousness of the freedom of the spirit but also in the sensation of historical limits put on the stage of life just passed, before receiving from its takeoff ordination to a new stage in the development of art. At such moments you feel the vital action of the historical movement of the universe.

Let the lamps in our hands waiting to be lit be pure and ready for that moment when it is necessary for our art to express the new word of life.

In the service of this task, apart from our work for the front, is our stern duty to the culture of our time.

To sum up what has passed in the interests of what will come – this is one of the duties on the front of the theory of our film art.

"Don't touch my circles!" – we must cry out together with Archimedes[83] in the face of a barbaric enemy, trampling on the fruits of the thought and work of a whole army of people, working in cinematography.

Therefore I am not embarrassed to print, in the full height of wartime activity, the present collection of summary articles and forecasts in such a special branch of film culture as montage, which in many ways has been the backbone of Soviet film stylistics.

For the last few years this line has subsided and gone out of use in Soviet films. Historically, this is probably not accidental.

In this collection of articles, I wanted to introduce the idea that montage – is an organic feature of any art.

And, in tracing the history of the rises and falls of the intensification of the montage method during the history of art, one concludes that, in the epoch of social stabilization, when art has the task of reflecting reality, the prominence of the montage method and composition will invariably diminish.

And, on the contrary, in periods of active intervention in the breaking, constructing, and recutting of reality, in periods of the active reconstruction of life, montage as a method of art grows with ever-increasing intensity [...].

This was written in distant Alma-Ata in October 1942.

Today, when I cite this, in the rays of final victory, the great May of 1945 rejoices outside my windows.

The premonition of new forms of montage, new stages in the development of its principles, have already become a concrete reality.

And we can see how a new stage of organic audiovisual montage has arisen and is now approaching us.

We hear the step of the pulsation of a new montage form.

We feel it with our hands from those examples that arose during the war years.

We perceive new features in it.

This is something new, no longer the prewar impasse of a subsiding montage form.

And this is no longer the palliative of outlived traditions of the "naked" and "obvious" montage of silent film, artificially stuck into sound film.

From the two or three attempts at such a restoration already made during the war exudes something terribly outmoded and decayed.

One persistently feels that the stage of "naked" montage passed over into history.

But this does not mean a denial of method, not carelessness, not a lapidary primitivism of the cinema of the premontage era.

Now the Soviet country is stronger than it has ever been before, both in military power, world prestige, unfading glory, and the results of the actions of its all-shattering Red Army.

Art – is the most sensitive seismograph.

And stylistic changes under the conditions of these most powerful social events is inevitable.

In terms of our country, this is not a "change," presupposing basically qualitative modification – as was the social "change" in the epoch of the Civil War.

Today's power of the Soviet land – is only the natural growth and consolidation, at the level of greatest luster, of all those social forces that Soviet power cherished and nourished in the years of the Five Year Plan.

Now, passing through the fires of war, the Soviet land has achieved that degree of monolithic fusion that had been tirelessly forged through all the years of Soviet rule. Is this at the expense of the oppression of one part of the country by the other? Is this at the expense of the interest of certain individuals in the name of the interest of others? Was something independent forfeited in this fusion?

No, no, and a thousand times no.

The striking quality of the structure of Soviet power – in terms of the problem of personality – has also been preserved in this surprising harmony of the single and the general, the collective and the individual, the distinctively national and the socialist.

I think that to presuppose the reflection of such features within the stylistics of the cinema of the war years is quite natural.

And if one looks at the most characteristic stylistic sign of cinema – at its defining nerve – *at montage*, then, at least in one picture, made by us during the war, one can clearly discover within its montage counterpoint this tendency toward knitting together into a more compact fabric.

I repeat, only to a shortsighted observer may it appear as a rejection of the culture achieved by "obvious montage" and "perceptible counter-point," and to whom the actual method might seem to be a return to the bosom of premontage cinematography.

This is a distinct step forward along the line of development of montage aesthetics, and, if someone cannot distinguish ordinary regression from this notorious "apparent reversion," in whose forms, developing in the usual way, phenomena move to new stages of development, then, God knows, the fault here lies in the misfortune of the "observers" and certainly not in the "pictures" themselves.

The film I have in mind is, of course, *Ivan the Terrible. Ivan the Terrible*, which, by the method of its contrapuntal montage composition continuing the original traditions of *Potemkin*, is not only distinguished from them but, in its audiovisual structure, is already the next step of development in relation to *Alexander Nevsky* as well (whose audiovisual montage is analyzed in detail in my articles on vertical montage in the journal *The Art of Film*).*

However, why has the analysis of how *Ivan the Terrible* functions been put into a collection devoted to *Potemkin*,[84] and not into an article or monograph concerning the film about the first Russian tsar?

And it is just because, in the consecutive triad of films, it is natural to assume a stylistic and methodological similarity between the *first* and *third* member, for in their development montage forms also move along the paths of the negation of the negation.

And, if the hoofbeats of the knights' attack in *Nevsky* grew directly out of the drumming of the soldiers' feet on the Odessa steps, then much of what has been done by the "audiovisual" method in *The Terrible* does not so much continue what was done in *Nevsky* as seizes what had been projected in its own time in *The Battleship* and, using sound, brings it to its essential culmination.

And this is just that part of *Potemkin*, which until the arrival of sound in film worked as "hidden sound" – as the *music of landscape*, that is just what we have been analyzing in this work.

And it is in the scene of the mist that we have an example, not of naked construction, but of the "fused" structure of contrapuntal currents in contrast to the "exposed nerve" of montage in other "accented" scenes of the film.

The montage structure of such "accenting" scenes is so obvious and clear, and it created first of all the fashion that until this very day is called "Russian cutting" or "Russischer Schnitt."

And if one believes what E. V. and M. M. Robson write in the book *The Film Answers Back* (London, 1939), that "*Battleship Potemkin* for its time, but only for its time, registered an immense advance in film technique and content" (p. 150), then this influence turned out to be the montage of just these "accented" scenes (for example, "The Odessa Steps"). And this is understandable: The structure of the montage of soldiers' feet above all bore the elements of the fertilization of montage *methods* of silent film.

The principles of the scenes "Mourning for Vakulinchuk" and "The Odessa Mist" did not have to so much determine the methodology of silent montage as to develop fully in *audiovisual montage*.

And therefore it is natural to finish the analysis of the problem of musical landscape and plastic counterpoint by a short description of how, twenty years later, those same principles, enriched by the possibility of sound and music, continue the traditions of the polyphonic

* [See *Film Form*, op. cit., pp. 150 and 178 – HM.]

Figure 19. The "Odessa Mist" sequence from Eisenstein's film *Battleship Potemkin* (1925).

montage of *The Battleship Potemkin* in a new quality in *Ivan the Terrible*.

In terms of this, the *montage composition* of *The Terrible* corresponds in a curious way to what occurred in the psychological drawing of characters in the plays...of Chekhov in the theater.

The cultivation of the refined and profound *musical nuances of the mood of the action* in Chekhov's plays created the impression of the disappearance of the *theatrical principle* in what was presented on stage.

The lines of nuances were woven into such a finely interwoven fabric that it seemed *the perceptible theatrical effect* was lost because of it.

And naturally, in opposition to Chekhov's theater, as a form of a protest, there came the theater of very strongly emphasized "theatricality."

The turn to the technique and traditions of the comedy of masks[85] was like a jolt back to the side of perceptible and "naked" counterpoint, perceptible in the "crude" mutual play of the dramatic lines and threads of the action of separate characters, in contrast to the *blending polyphony* of the nuances of the Chekhovian heroes.

In terms of the history of theater in general, it is interesting to note that the process of the submersion of bared "foundations" and "abutments" of the very material into complex patterns and drawings on the surface of the fabric occurs here, in theater, in exactly the same way as it occurred on the paths of the development of Chinese painting.

An increasing number of voices, an increasing number of nuances enter into the primitive polyphonic scheme, and planal interrelationships are replaced by interrelationships of chiaroscuro.

And the comedy of masks has developed in exactly the same way in the theater of Molière or Marivaux,[86] Beaumarchais[87] and...Griboyedov.

For if one "scrapes" Skalozub, Famusov, or Liza,* then, under all the richness of the everyday domestic and social features of the epoch, the basic outlines of the stage figures come through distinctly – the Captain, Pantalone, and Esmeralda.

The Italian comedy of masks in this sense is very unique, and it is quite natural that "relapses" of theatricality had to take it up. Here the threads of behavior and the lines of the characters had all been given earlier, and the whole attraction of the action is preserved only by newer and newer *contrapuntal combinations* – in stage business and *lazzi*[88] – between these masks of characters who had been established once and for all.

It is interesting how this limitation on the *very choice itself* forces us to recall China with its quantitative limitations on motifs – no matter whether they be representational elements in painting or the 106 groups of permissible rhymes in poetry!

Just as tangible is perceived the "eternalized" choice of traditional

---

* [In Griboyedov's *Wit Works Woe* – HM.]

theater masks (they are "eternal" because in them the images of reality most pregnant with stage possibilities were consolidated in most complete perfection), and even among the heroes of such an "everyday life" dramatist as A. N. Ostrovsky! Glumov is Harlequin, Mamaev and Krutitsky – the typical Old Man, Gorodulin – a new aspect of the Captain (they speak of the "captains of industry"!),* etc., etc.

However, the traits of tangibility become more and more refined, and the nuances of Chekhovian characters and moods leap into other stages of development of stage counterpoint, where it is now more difficult to feel the skeleton of conventional theatrical tradition.

It is very amusing that something similar is occurring now around the unexpected stylistics of the montage composition of *Ivan the Terrible.*

Here montage, after the stage of "jumping montage" of the *naked* montage form, passes into forms of blended polyphonic means of expression.

And it is surprising that just as in its time they shouted that the theater of Chekhov was not theater, now there are voices that shout that the montage of *Ivan* is actually not montage (!), and the film itself is not – cinema.

We know well enough that Chekovian theater in the end "turned out to be" and nevertheless remained theater.

And we will also certainly continue to assume that the montage of *Ivan* is nevertheless *montage* – true, in a new phase of development, and therefore an analysis is necessary of what was done in *The Terrible,* particularly in the light of what was done in its time in *The Battleship.*

Of course, for me, having just come from the ultratheatrical "left" theater – from its circus wing – it is particularly amusing now to hear in respect to the montage of *Ivan* the same accusations, which had been expressed because of the absence of "theatricality" in Chekhovian theater! I even had to hear one opinion on how the montage of *Ivan* wiped out all I had done to confirm the montage method in general (!), when what was done in *Ivan* grows completely out of and develops from what was done in *Potemkin.*

Thus, an explanation is evidently called for here! And that is what we will concern ourselves with!

In order to do this, for purely academic reasons, we must first recall what is the basis or, more precisely, on what psychological phenomenon is based the possibility of an equal combination of audiovisual elements – elements of audiovisual polyphony?

---

* "In all European countries, especially in England, a class of commanders and captains has to a certain degree already formed over people that may be recognized as the germ of a new real, and not imagined, aristocracy: they are captains of industry." [Thomas Carlyle, 1841.[89] Eisenstein quotes from the Russian anthology *Marx & Engels on Art,* Moscow, *Iskusstvo,* 1937, p. 288 – HM.]

Of course, everything is based on that same *synaesthetics* – that is, on the ability to gather *into one all the variety of feeling brought from different areas by different organs of sensation.* I have already more than bored the reader with the description of this phenomenon in my articles on vertical montage and in the description of the elements of the "chiming" Chinese landscape.

If I did not now have at hand one more amusing and fascinating example from this area, I would have limited myself, of course, only to designating this phenomenon and to references, and I would not have given examples and descriptions of it once more.

But unfortunately into my hands fell the second volume of *La Mouche causeuse* [*The Talkative Fly*] of Eugène Sue[90] (it is a continuation of his two-volume *The Cockroach*), where, in the story *Physiologie d'un appartement* [*Physiology of an Apartment*], excerpts are brought in from an imaginary book *Sur la musique appliquée à gastronomie* [*On Music Applied to Gastronomy*]:

...If I had thought of deepening the great increase in the influence of intoxication or, more precisely, the poetry of port – poetry that is pensive, serious and sad – I would have dined alone, and there would not be anything except meat, black and *meagre* – a filet of boar or middle-age deer, in this way achieving the harmony of the *juices* of solid food with the *spirit* of wine, for if the *dish* – is *the body of intoxication, then the wine – is its spirit, and one must observe the most perfect correspondence between these two principles*...[can it be that 1,000 years later the Chinese of the eighth century are not recalled here?! – SE]...And the light that would illuminate me would have to be pale and (*douteuse*) vague; and the music that would be played to me (*I will not think of dinner without music, without excellent music*), would have had a character both gloomy and imposing: it would have consisted of several pages of *Don Juan* – this powerful and terrible epic of Mozart's – or from the grandiose oratorio *Moses*.

And then through the body, soul and spirit of mine, intoxicated by the triple intoxicants – dishes, wines and music – I would achieve the highest spheres of pleasure, both intellectual and material...

But then I would think of surrendering to the lulling carefreeness and mad poetry of cool champagne, I would suck atoms out of any roasted delicate and brilliant birds, for example, from the little wing of a gilded pheasant with purple claws...And then – the gleam of thousands of candles, colors, silver, a woman and the cry of love and joy...And, crowning in my ecstasy, let there ring out sparkling tarantellas from *The Mute* or divine music of *The Barber*, the intoxicating music that laughs, sparkles and overflows like trembling gauze over silvery tulle!...

If one compares this healthy and carnivorous synaesthetic polyphony of the beginning of the age with an example of what it degenerated into in the epoch at the end of the century, decadence, then – next to this cheerful organic whole on the pages of Sue – the famous stylized "black dinners" from a selection of certain black plates (caviar, truffles, etc.), black in themselves, for their sake and for the sake of a "general picture," down to the candles of black wax and the Negro woman servant – then these "black dinners" of Des Esseintes – the hero of Huysman's novel[91] – seems justifiably typical. . . . "formalism," that is, an artificially conceived and totally inorganic combination, imposed only as a purely external formal sign!

Thus, the audiovisual polyphony of the increasingly profound blended composition is possible only under the strictest "synesthetization" of separate areas of visual and audial expressive effects.

The paradoxical conception of the "montage of attractions," which twenty-odd years ago seemed merely eccentric tricks – a *boutade* in the theater – now turns out to be not only not a "shocking" device but, under the conditions of the unlimited possibilities of audiovisual polyphony, an absolutely basic and necessary prerequisite[92] for the construction of even the smallest seriously conceived and compositionally planned audiovisual scene.

I have in mind the introductory part of the "Declaration" of 1923 concerning "The Montage of Attractions" (*LEF*, no. 3, 1923). As an attempt to make all various areas of the theater commensurable, proceeding from their basic principle – the effect on the viewer – this declaration of the synaesthetic principle has preserved its significance even today.

The spectator himself constitutes the basic material of the theatre; the objective of every utilitarian theatre (agit, poster, health education, etc.) is to guide the spectator in the desired direction (frame of mind). The means of achieving this are all the component parts of the theatrical apparatus: Ostyzhev's* "chatter" no more than the color of the prima donna's tights, a stroke on the kettledrum as much as a soliloquy of Romeo, the cricket on the hearth[†] no less than a salvo under the seats of the spectators. In all their heterogeneity, all the component parts of the theatrical apparatus are reduced to a single unit – thereby justifying their presence – by being attractions.[‡]

This systematic unity – observed independently of the *area* of the effect, only from the point of view of its possibility – was called an "attraction."

Of course there never was nor is any real basis for disputing such a thesis. My montage of attractions underwent "persecution" in its time because, in broadening this principle, I said that effective compositions are possible also *outside* of a unified plot, and the plot itself I considered

---

* Alexander Ostyzhev was a well-known actor of the period who appeared as Romeo, Othello, and in many other classic roles.
† A reference to the dramatization of Dickens's *The Cricket on the Hearth*, presented by the First Studio of the MAT in 1915.
‡ [Translated by Prof. D. Gerould in *The Drama Review*, March 1974, p. 78 – HM.]

to be *one of the varieties of the unity* of effect that is *by no means obligatory in all cases.*

This assertion was really more a *guide*, that is, transient, personally stylistic and not obligatory for anyone.

In terms of the *principle of synaesthetics* at the basis of the structure of things, this question is one of general method and, of course, preserves its essential meaning even now.

The approach to or departure from the principle of synaesthetics in different periods of the development of art is different, and depends on the specific social form of the epoch, dictating the style and form of its time.

Besides, the nature of *how this principle is understood* and applied is different, in different epochs.

Thus, the emphasis of the principles of synaesthetics has equal place in the epoch of romanticism and in the period of the domination of impressionism. But the major difference in understanding and applying these principles in these different historical epochs is quite obvious.

What cinema does is just as distinct from both of them, given its possibilities concerning it and its *realistic orientation* in using it.

This is one more reason why we are not only interested in analyzing what has been done in *Ivan the Terrible* but also in tracing retrospectively how what was done in this direction in *Ivan is derived in method from what had been done in Potemkin.*

Therefore, it is natural, in the interests of this examination, to choose scenes that are inwardly similar *in both* films.

In both there is a scene over a dead body.

In both they are grieving over a victim who perished in the battle for an idea.

In both there is mourning.

And further...almost according to the principle of yin and yang.

There – someone murdered:

A sailor.

Here someone poisoned:

A tsaritsa.

There the collective is grieving for a fighter for the common good.

Here an individual is tormented over the body of the one who supported him in battle.

In the first case the theme of mourning is unfolded *into differentiated acts of separate people* from the crowd, from the masses.

In the polyphony of common grief there participate

the singing blind men, the grieving women, and groups of two, three, four, and five faces: sad, angry, or indifferent (in order to give nuance to all shades of grief of the other faces) – faces of the young and old, workers and intellectuals, women and men, children and grown-ups.

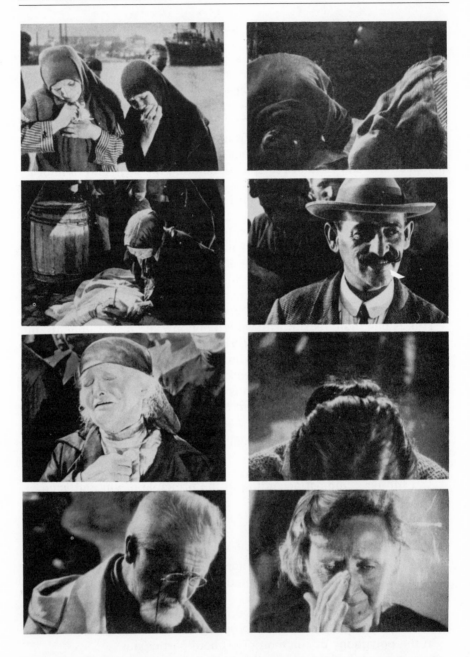

Figure 20. The "Mourning for Vakulinchuk" sequence from *Battleship Potemkin*.

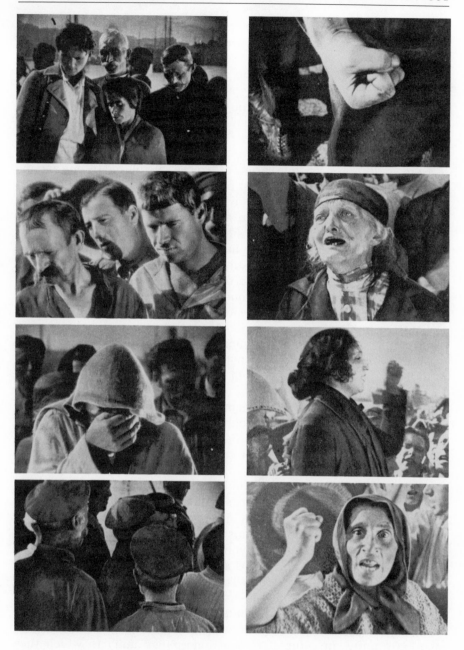

Caption to Figure 20 (*cont.*)

In the second place, in *Ivan*, the theme of mourning is gathered in one person (this person justifiably incarnates the government of a huge and multitudinous country):

But the polyphony of despair and grief is played here "by voices": now by the moan of the tsar, now a whisper, now the thump of a crucifix and a candlestick falling to the foot of the pedestal; now the white spot of his face half-devoured by shadow; now the head thrown back and forth; now a face with panic-stricken eyes rising from behind the chiseled tomb and a barely audible whisper: "Am I right?!"

Here, in this case, a whole variety of "voices" are played by *one and the same figure* of the same character-protagonist:

now down on his knees, now lying prostrate, now slowly walking around the catafalque, now in an attack of rage, toppling over heavy candles and breaking the solemn silence of the cathedral with a furious cry: "You lie! The Muscovite tsar has not yet been overthrown!"

In this respect, it is characteristic that different positions of one and the same tsar are presented from different points of view around the coffin *outside the transition from one position to another*, that is, almost as if a series of separate, independent characters had been depicted, chosen by the camera not as a sign of physical and spatial coexistence, but *to the degree of a single current of growing emotion.*

Thus the increasing grief is constructed through changing close-ups of different people over the body of Vakulinchuk.

And thus different shots of Ivan replace each other in the increasing *pathos* of position and camera angle.

The figure of Ivan passes through a strict sequential composition of positions: beginning with the knee-bending position at the foot of the catafalque (when he appears at the beginning of the episode at the end of the initial pan from above down) – through a position sprawling flat on the floor after the words "Is this not Divine punishment?" – to the figure stretched upward, with his head tossed as far back as possible (after the news about Kurbsky's betrayal – in the words of Pimen: "Defamation ravaged my heart, and I am exhausted.").

As we can see, here the polyphony is built on the changes and interweaving of different positions of one and the same figure.

But not through this alone: There is also interwoven into this polyphony the separate play of separate elements of the same figure; these elements seem to be independent and to merge by their own whim into a new, higher unity through consecutive actions – into a new, higher emotional unity, in contrast to that amorphous unity to which they belong from a purely physical point of view.

This perception of the figure mainly as a *distinctive orchestra of parts independently composing it* by no means is foreign to our figurative representation in general; and if it may sound unexpected in the plastic

Figure 21. The "Ivan at the Coffin of Anastasia" sequence from Eisenstein's film *Ivan the Terrible, Part I* (released 1942).

Caption to Figure 21 (*cont.*)

and dramatic sense, then in the area of verbal imagery we have become used to such expressions as "the right hand does not know what the left hand is doing," that the legs of a drunkard have "split asunder," or that a "man ran so quickly that his shadow was barely able to keep up with him (as they say in the East)."

However, the possibility of a similar playful and plastic construction demands that a single compositional principle penetrate the structures of all separate elements entering into this type of complex polyphony.

So that the *action* and the shot, which catches it, "sing" harmoniously, it is necessary that those same elements be put in the spatial composition of the action constructed by the rectangular "framing" of the shot;

so that there be harmony of action and spoken word, it is necessary that the elements of the mise-en-scène bear the same signs of spatial "blank verse" as if the text had been written in blank verse;

so that the music (or chorus) and the environment resound in unison – it is necessary that the tonal picture of the mutual play of light and shade repeat the timbre, melody, and rhythm of the sound element that will penetrate the screen space.

And, mainly, it is necessary that everything, beginning from the actor's performance and ending with the play of the folds of his clothes, be equally immersed in the sound of that single, increasingly defined emotion that lies at the basis of the polyphony of a whole multifaceted composition.

It is interesting that even here we are again coming into conflict with the traditions of the Chinese Orient.

Scholars and connoisseurs of this area repeatedly note that the surprising harmony of Chinese landscape is also achieved by *cultivating* and nourishing the canonical principles of its structure, shifting into painting first of all through real *landscapes*, however artificially constructed by no less strict canons, and, in addition, *by those same canons* that later govern the principles of painting!

The first objects of painting were parks and the environs of palaces and temples where, by the skilful hand of masters, an apparently free landscape was *artificially* arranged; and skillful hands, catching with their eye the contour and silhouette of a distant mountain chain, knew where to fling piles of wild stones, where to dam up a stream and allow it to explode as a waterfall, where to leave the curving trunk of a pine, having freed it from the confused surroundings of haphazard bushes, and where to leave an intentional thicket of an overgrown bunch of reeds.

Here within the elements of real nature, sequentially composed in exactly the same way, alternate the same opposite elements of *the fluid and the solid, the material and the airy, what is close and what is revealed in the distance.*

Here, on the one hand, is an apparent similarity to romantic principles in the unexpected characteristics of English parks that, with its garden aesthetic, overturned the vigorous aesthetic of the tradition of Versailles and the parks of Le Notre.[93]

But, on the other hand, under this apparent freedom beats that same strictly pulsating organizing law of the same principles of yin and yang.

But who taught the elegance of artificially created gardens and park landscapes to these masters of antiquity?

Who in the final account is the everyday and immutably great teacher, even in areas of the most intricate compositional and stylized methods?

Of course, always and especially – nature herself.

Once in his *Journal* Delacroix[94] apparently compared nature to an ABC book, from where the painter draws words for expressing his ideas.

And these words of Delacroix somehow veiled the fact that not only the words but also the structure of pictorial phrases, plastic turns of speech, stylized devices, and compositional laws are invariably born from nature as well.

This documentary "naturalism," of what we consider to be the most refined *stylization*, first struck me in Holland.

Canary-yellow bridges, raised in the azure blue of the sky from the poison green shroud of the meadows, always seemed to me in their palette like the colored frenzy of van Gogh. Known to me only by his canvases, they seemed to be the fruit of a fantastic palette distillation of the colors of his imagination, colors that in themselves are probably just as normal and restrained in nature as in our bridges, streams, and meadows.

The shrillness of color of van Gogh's landscapes always seemed to me like purified spirits passing through the brain, eyes, and feelings of a man who, by the strength of his emotional perception, surpasses all the facets of reality available to nature.

And suddenly, wandering along the cobblestone roads of the Netherlands, which have been saved by God under the protection of the Kings Whilhelm, time after time you come upon a chain of invariable quotations from van Gogh: here point by point is that same yellow bridge, here a field, here the wall of the little house painted in such pure tones – light blue, orange, yellow, green, cherry – so they seem like the little bricks of watercolors, set between the walls of enamel boxes that we had as gifts in childhood, and involuntarily you search along the thresholds of these little houses...for a set of brushes.

The little houses painted in the purest colors burn like topazes, emeralds, or rubies. They burn like van Gogh's palette, burn like the rays of the sun shattered by the glass facets of a prism.

And suddenly, simultaneously with the worship of representation of untouched nature, you begin to worship even more the great artist whose greatness lies in humility: not in overcoming nature, but in worshipping it, and whose charm lies in the childlike naïveté of lips able to sing with such purity of soul and heart the genuine fullness of its virgin beauty.

But perhaps only the "madman" van Gogh was like this?

Then let us look at another example, and let us turn our glance from the West to the East.

What could perhaps be further from the photographic imprint of simple "living" nature than the fragile refinement of a finely stylized Eastern miniature?

Figures stand strangely, on ledges, without perspective and foreshortening. Geometrically outlined circular silhouettes of trees of an inklike color. Goats with hides sprinkled with severely drawn, repeated ornaments.

Billy goats cut in two by color: black in front, white in back.

One need not go all the way to India or Iran.

It is enough to go to Samarkand and Andizhen, to suddenly understand that almost all the elements of the charm of miniatures are literally scattered around us at every step.

Ink spots of trees stretch from the blackness of the *karagach* [Central Asian elm] amid a dusty, faded landscape and seem like a gigantic prune of dark indigo. The figures of three white Uzbeks on three ledges, covered with red carpets of the verandas of Central Asian tearooms, with a squint look down, also do not intersect each other compositionally, as in classic miniatures.

Pruned crowns of mulberry trees, running along irrigation ditches, with their deformed trunks under geometrically severe caps of leaves, seem to be running with ornamental decorations of Arabic manuscripts.

And on the day of the bazaar on all the surrounding roads dozens of shaggy horses are turned toward Bukhara, as if they were a routinely drawn black and white geometrical ornament, and out of a dozen herds rushing in the heat jumps a big, long-haired billy goat – divided exactly in two by black and white color...

Andrey Bely[95] (in *Wind from the Caucasus*) noticed the similarity of the cracked mountain fissures to the uniqueness of the broken-up violet-brown strokes with which Vrubel's *Demons** were painted.

A traveler in the area of Alma-Ata, in the morning hours, is invariably amazed at the picture of the slender trees drawn on the milky-blue background of the blue sky. But weren't there mountains on this side

---

* [Mikhail Vrubel was one of Russia's greatest artists who painted in the symbolist manner at the end of the nineteenth century. He created a series of pictures on the theme of the Demon from Lermontov's narrative poem, one of which shows the demon's body smashed on the cliffs of the Caucasus, his beautiful peacock wings covering his body – HM.]

yesterday evening? The question is barely formulated in your mind when, suddenly, way up high in the sky – at a height of inconceivable proportions overhanging the trees, your eyes catch sight of a mountain chain with those same "brush-stroked" foothills that we saw a hundred times in Chinese prints and paintings, where this purest "phenomenon of nature" captivates us as an artistically found pictorial device. The mountain chains and foothills around Alma-Ata lead us again to China. [...]

And the many seemingly "stylized" visions of the Chinese landscape are no more than the wonder of the Chinese landscape itself, multiplied by the no less wonderful ability of the Chinese eye to see and be intoxicated by what living nature offers.

Here is the obvious cradle of repeating motifs of mountain chains arranged in "planes," becoming dimmer as they recede into the distance; here are the sources, apparently, of single mountain peaks arbitrarily stylized into kinds of granite columns; here, in the flow – breaking and interruptions of the contour smoothness of separate knolls – is the undoubted key to the system of canonized types of graphic strokes, by which it is acceptable to paint mountain slopes in contrast to waterfalls and contours of ravines rather than silhouettes of old tree trunks.

The Chinese graphic artist has several types of brushstrokes that, in the strictest way possible, are connected with elements of landscape, allowing their application only in very precisely designated cases.

The unquestionable influence of this corner of real nature on the conventional painting canons of China has been preserved in a legend about a painter who, hundreds of years ago, climbed these mountains and recorded the landscapes that excited him. The success of these landscapes was so great that it began to be considered proper to paint in this style landscapes whose form did not even resemble this striking mountain symphony.

Thus, a vivid impression lies at the basis of a whole canonically developed aesthetic system.

Real landscape teaches the creation of an artificial landscape – a garden or park.

And both garden and park in their turn influence the painting canon, conquering the surface of silk and drawing paper.

Thus, the similarity of method is interesting, whereby an occurrence or action, object and space, event and landscape, before one's eyes, is organized and arranged by the drawing paper and brush of the Chinese artist, in exactly the same way as these same elements are constructed by the will of the director facing the complex system of the audiovisual camera!

An amusing example of a "correspondence" to this can be found in the branch of literature concerned with the complication of the plot.

In relation to Chesterton,[96] V. Shklovsky[97] noted this in his *Journals*[1] (1939, p. 141), where with good reason he writes:

"In his novels and novellas special offices create plots for the amusement of clients." Here we only have a case made concrete in pure form of what every writer does: He composes the "objective course of events" so that afterward he may catch it on pages of description.

And woe to that writer who, not having created this objectively existing world, tries to write without seeing and hearing before him the reality of what he expounds on paper! How many angry pages, lines, and whole articles of Lev Tolstoy or Gorky would seem to be written specially for him!

Of course, the case of Chesterton serves as a curiosity here – where this part of the invention and creative laboratory of the writer is included into the actual exposition of the subject.

We can find a more complex and paradoxical case in Huxley[98] on the pages (so near to us in name) of the novel *Point Counterpoint*; here the author interweaves the process of the creation of the book with the process of the unwinding of the events entering into it. In this case it also puts its imprint on the specific stylistics of the writing itself.

Of course, I cannot restrain myself here from putting alongside these examples (which concern the inner, often microscopic, mechanics of construction and composition of works), examples of the same type, but now on a tremendous scale, if one takes into account that in this case whole armies, battleships, and bloody conflicts were acting. And all this basically with the single goal of serving as material for future description: sensational material for newspapers so that by this device their circulation would swell and increase! Such adventures are due, of course, only to people of the ilk of the notorious Randolph Hearst.[99]

And we have such an example from an early period of his newspaper career: A career that later buried itself deeper and deeper in the gold, dirt, and blood of blackmail, jingoism,[100] forgery, and crime [...]

This was done to the loud cries of a "struggle for independence and liberation of the Cubans from under the Spanish yoke."

This was essentially raised to tremendous scale by calling to life events with one basic aim in mind – "to have something to write about."

This story, which begs to be applied to Chesterton's "The Club of Ingenious People," begins with two notorious telegrams.

A reporter of Hearst's – Remington – is sent to Cuba with other artful dodgers from the Hearst clique. The aim of their activity – to scatter about sensational data about possible political scandals and international conflicts.

Remington is bored. He wants to go home.

He telegraphs the "boss":

Everything is quiet. There is no trouble here. There will be no war. I wish to return.

Remington.

The "boss" answers briefly, imposingly, and decisively:

Remington. Havana.
Please remain. You furnish the pictures and I'll furnish the war.

W. R. Hearst.*

Supporters of Hearst try in every way to convince everyone that these telegrams are apocryphal, but in two lines they state so precisely the essence of his efforts and attempts that, like many apocrypha that are part of history, they are more truthful as "human" documents than numerous historical documents.

Later the earthshaking phantasmagoria of Hearst's role in the Cuban war follows, and the grandiose growth of the kingdom of this uncrowned king of the press.[†]

Thus, recalling everything that has been said above about polyphony and counterpoint, let us disclose the principles of the compositional canvas of the scene at the catafalque of the poisoned Tsaritsa Anastasia from the film *Ivan the Terrible*.

The basic theme is Ivan's despair.

In spite of the fact that Ivan is a progressive man of the sixteenth century, looking far ahead, he is still a man tied to his own time – to the beliefs and prejudices, to the superstitions accompanying the religious fanaticism of the epoch, to the concepts that are an integral part of the Russian Middle Ages, which is developing into the Russian Renaissance.

And therefore Ivan's despair creates doubt – and the *theme of despair* grows into the *theme of doubt*: "Am I right in what I am doing? Am I right? Is this not the chastisement of God?"

Interwoven into this basic theme is: the reading of the psalms of King David by the Metropolitan Pimen and the reading by Malyuta of the dispatches on the boyars' misuse of "the right of departure," their escape beyond the borders of the Muscovite state and crossing over to the side of the foreign enemies of the tsar.

These two readings proceed as a distinct antithesis – in two voices. By the tone and rhythm of the reading they are similar.

---

* [John Winkler, *William Randolph Hearst*, Jonathan Cape, London, 1928, p. 144 – HM.]
[†] I should also add that it was here, in this fuss made around the Cuban war, that screaming headlines in large script were applied in newspapers for the first time.
I cite John K. Winkler, *William Randolph Hearst*.

By the text, they seem to continue each other.

The words of the dispatch seem to reveal the concrete meaning of the words of the psalm.

The words of the psalm seem to comment emotionally on the meaning of the dispatch.

At first Ivan is deaf to both.

("Ivan's eyes are fixed on Anastasia.

He has no ears for either the dispatch or the prayer.")*

I do not know where I got the notion of applying this dual-voiced reading here. I think, however, that it occurred to me from an actual vivid impression – from the first time when I was to overhear in the distance a similar antiphonic dual-voiced reading.

True, this reading was in Latin.

Both voices had the same theme.

And it resounded under Gothic arches, almost exactly the same way it did later in my film, having become lost in the darkness of unreachable heights.

It was in Cambridge.

In 1930.

In Trinity College

In the huge Tudor dining hall.

And although I was sitting next to (actually, at the moment, I was standing next to) such a powerful supporter of the materialistic unmasking of the mystical secrets of nature as P. L. Kapitsa[101] – then working in Great Britain –

nevertheless this was...a Latin prayer before the meal.

And also it was read by the luminary of the exact physical sciences – rector of the university – laureate Nobel Prize winner, J. J. Thomson[102] [...]

On that memorable evening of the late dinner in Cambridge, the voice of the rector was repeated in response by the voice of the vice-rector.

Candles. Vaults. Two old men's voices resounding in the boundlessness of the dark hall.

The strange text of the prayer.

The gray heads of the two old men.

The black university gowns. Night all around...

I thought about all this least of all when I was writing the scene of Ivan over the coffin of Anastasia in the scenario of *Ivan*.

But now I think this episode of the film is definitely connected with the vivid impressions of that evening long ago in prewar England.

In our scene, however, in the external similarity of tone and tempo,

---

* [Quotes from the film script *Ivan the Terrible*, I. Montagu and H. Marshall, trans., Simon & Schuster, New York, 1962, p. 122 – HM.]

manner of reading and rhythm – the dramatic *direction* of both readings were also *diametrically opposed to each other.*

There is a reason why one of them is spoken by the deadliest enemy of Ivan, and the other is read by his most devoted friend and "faithful hound."

This inner struggle of the two readings – is like an inner struggle "for a soul."

As on the *lubok*s* or medieval miniatures, here two principles struggle – the positive and the negative – for the possession of a human soul.

But, despite tradition, they are fighting here not for the soul of someone dying but for the soul of someone crying over her – for the soul of someone living, for the soul of the tsar.

And one principle, one reading drags the tsar's soul to despair, darkness, and ruin.

And the other – to activity and life.

One reading is directed to finally breaking the will of the tsar, to crush and destroy the tsar, to make him an obedient and slavish tool in the hands of the boyar clique.

This is the reading of the pages of Psalms, full of despair:

I am weary of my crying:
my throat is dried:
mine eyes fail...

Another reading is directed toward arousing Ivan to activity, to compel him to abandon the paths of doubt and the anger of despair, to compel the tsar to grasp the matter with all his energy, to continue the battle with redoubled strength.

The reading grows louder.

The alarm of the message increases.

The emotional despair of the lament increases, trembling from the pages of the psalter...

And now the final destruction of will, the last blow is dealt by the one whose report was to evoke renewed strength!

Malyuta reports Kurbsky's betrayal.

With the moan of one beaten, Ivan responds.

His head is thrown back onto the coffin.

In the vaults resounds hysterically the concluding part of the *prokimen*[103] following "Peace be with the Saints."

The end. Period.

The culmination.

* [Woodblocks or engravings in Russia made for popular consumption which often contained satiric or folklore material – HM.]

But at the culmination (and it often happens) – in this ecstatic moment of dramatic construction – a sudden switch to the very opposite occurs.*

And if Malyuta's information deals a final blow to the tsar,

then as a reverse shock what returns the tsar back to battle is

the voice of the one whose entire efforts have been directed to destroying the tsar.

Raising his voice, Pimen's words are shattering with the accusation:

Reproach hath broken my heart;
and I am full of heaviness...
And I looked for some to take pity,
but there was none;
and for comforters,
but I found none...

But this is now like a drop overfilling the cup of long-suffering and misery.

Like a wounded animal, Ivan roars in response:

"Thou liest!" – etc., etc.

I only wanted to *mention* briefly the emotional current of the scene.

I must also add that the white figure of Anastasia in the coffin enters rhythmically into certain intervals of this sequence;

that a distant choir is singing "Eternal memory," passing into "Peace be unto you";

and that the scene begins with a long panoramic shot from the top of the coffin with the face of the dead tsaritsa down to the foot of the heavy candlesticks, to which Tsar Ivan is pressing himself in despair...

For a complete picture one must keep in mind that the separate lines within the general theme are also supported by including another series of faces participating in the general performance.

The line of *death and constraint of will* enters with the immobile face of the dead Anastasia, passes into the constrained, immobile shots of Ivan, develops in the theme of Pimen's reading ("*exhausted* from wailing," "my throat *dried out*," "my eyes grew weary"), and is crowned by shots of the vehicle of the theme of death and its actual culprit – the poisoner Staritskaya.

The line of affirmation – Malyuta's line – is taken up by the Basmanovs (father and son), the inflammatory nature of the old man's speech passes into the fiery "Two Romes fell, and a Third stands" of the tsar, and ends with the flight of servants in the real fires of the torches.

At this point the theme of death "is removed," and the apparent *smile* of approval at Ivan from the dead tsaritsa, "as if she revived" in the

* About this, see the detailed discussion in the article "On the Structure of Things."

coffin, had to be the culmination of this ("The face of Anastasia seems to light up with approval") at the moment when Ivan, having overcome his doubts, again sets out on the path of battle and life.

Unfortunately, rhythmic *miscalculation* over several frames (temporal) and the filming of the smile being made *too concrete* (the plastic element) disrupted the emotional effect to this detail (I cut it out later when the film was already showing on the screen.)

The miscalculation was that this smile, conceived of as "*appearing fleetingly,*" in practice turned out to have been *perceived as persisting,* and therefore evoked either bewilderment or laughter or irritation (depending on the temperament of the viewer!).

I myself once was forced to become convinced of how decisive a portion of one second turned out to be in a showing of *Potemkin.*

It was in London. In 1929 our composer – the now late Edmund Meisel – directed the orchestra, using his own music for the film. In addition, at his own risk – in the interests of the music – he made arrangements with the film projectionist to *slow down slightly the tempo of the projection.* For one part of the film this turned out to be fatal: for the jumping marble lions.

Usually this "sculptural metaphor" passed by so suddenly that the analyzing capability of the viewer was not able to be delayed at this point; the jumping lions entered into one's perception as a turn of speech – "the stones roared." Due to the attention drawn to it by "overexposure," the immediacy of the "shock" at one's perception passed into the *realization of a device* – into an "exposure of the trick," – and the auditorium responded instantly with the inevitable reaction – amiable laughter – unavoidable in all those cases when the "trick failed to come off."

In my memory this is the only time this piece evoked laughter, and the fault was due to the destruction of the duration of those parts of the seconds that decided whether it was a construction by *metaphor* or by *an anecdote told in its own words*!

At the indicated point of *Ivan* a well-conceived part, written correctly in terms of the scenario, "broke down" because of the compositional blunder in the picture's methods mentioned above!

We allowed ourselves the luxury of a somewhat emotionally decorated paraphrase of the scene of Ivan at the coffin.

Now let us try to arrange it into those effective means by which the polyphonic structure of this scene operates like voices or instruments.

The object of despair – the dead Anastasia in the coffin.

The vehicle of despair (the subject of despair) – Tsar Ivan.

The means of effect:

A. *The performance of Ivan*

It is realized in three planes:
1. He himself performs (experiences, behavior, and actions of Ivan).
2. They perform for him (the frame of the shot, the light, partners).
3. They perform on him (components of the scene as a whole).

B. *The screen image of Ivan*
    1. Visible
        Static (by camera angle)
        Pantomime movement
        Figure in detail (gesture, mimicry)
    2. Audible
        Voice off screen
        Voice with representation

C. *Music*
    The singing of the choir as the musical solution of the theme of despair and mourning of Ivan, as the permeating action of the theme of despair in *sound*.
    The singing goes on continuously through the whole episode (up to when Ivan turns to the Basmanovs and Malyuta: "There are few of you!").
    In addition, the singing now moves ahead, now yields to the antiphonic reading of the voice of Ivan.
    The chorus works doubly:
    1. Outside of the text (as musical construction)
    2. As text (as the meaning of the content of the text)

D. *Irradiation of the theme and supporting components*
    1. Reading of the psalm,
            and opposing it –
    2. Reading of the dispatch

Reading of the psalm:
    As the content of the text (the principle of meaning prevails)
    As music (the melodious intonational principle prevails)
    Both principles blending
    To speak with a voice off screen
    The representation of Pimen
    Both together

Reading of the dispatch:
    Malyuta: the text
        Malyuta as representation
        Voice and text of Malyuta off screen

E. *The purely representational elements*
    1. The interior of the cathedral (the people, the coffin, the candles – only as attributes of the cathedral, the cathedral as a whole "sings" the basic "score").

Figure 22. Eisenstein's sketch for "Ivan at the Coffin of Anastasia" with dialogue.
[The tsar]: "We are scum!" Fedor responds firmly: "We are!"

2.   The characters, as an ensemble:
     In combination *with the cathedral* ("to the accompaniment" of
     the cathedral).
     As separate groups *outside the sensation of the cathedral.*
3.   The characters as *groups among themselves* ("chords"):
     Pimen, Ivan, the coffin with Anastasia, Malyuta
     Pimen, Ivan, and Malyuta
     Pimen and Ivan
     Ivan and Malyuta
     Anastasia and Ivan
     Ivan and Anastasia
The order of arrangement of the names corresponds to the interrela-

tionship of the characters according to the depth of the shot: The one occupying first place dominates in the scene either from a plastic or dramatic aspect, that is, he attracts attention either by plastic means or by means of performance.

An example of the first may be the enlarged visual depiction of the actor that is strongly pushed forward — into the "foreground" (for example, the close-up of Pimen and the depressed figure of Ivan in the distance).

An example of the second may be Ivan's behavior when the attention is distinctly focused on the tsar while he and Malyuta are arranged in one plane and in one dimension.

4. Close-ups of separate characters *taken separately.*
    (Outside the "plastic accompaniment" of the background — is the cathedral, and not in the "spatial chord" of a combination actors).

Ivan	Malyuta
Anastasia	Basmanov
Pimen	Staritskaya

Instances when we have before us "Anastasia's face on the background of the cathedral," or "the group Ivan–Malyuta in the background while Pimen's face is strongly moved forward," correspond *plastically and spatially* exactly to what we mentioned when we analyzed the mist of *Potemkin*. There also, a buoy or mast protruded in the foreground and the mist receded into the depths, or the whole space of the shot was swallowed by the "close-up" of the water and the details of the port only bordered on the water-filled space, etc.

We noted that through the whole scene runs the *continuous singing of the choir* ("Eternal memory" and "Peace be unto you"). It now enters into the foreground, then yields to Ivan's words or to the two readers, now, finally, growing into a roar, merging with Ivan's voice: "You lie!"

The same role of the plastic chorus is played by the cathedral itself in the composition of its visual depiction.

Its vaults are like the peals of church singing that have become petrified into stone cupolas.

This plastic organ of the general pervasive background resounds not only with the cuts of the shot *but especially with tonal melodiousness* — with light, or rather, with darkness.

And in a few moments this organ dominates the scene as a whole (examples are the initial shots and the shots at the end, when the people are rushing into the cathedral with torches).

The permeating line of "filling with darkness" in the experienced hands of Andrey Moskvin leads the cathedral through the same kind of chain of tonal variations and light nuances that penetrate the sound of the funeral choir beneath its vaults.

Figure 23. Still from *Ivan the Terrible, Part I*: The *oprichniki* surround Vladimir.

This line of gradual tonal light "animation" of the cathedral – that is, the movement of the cathedral "in tune" with the whole scene – from the darkness of death to the fiery activity of life affirmation – passes through a series of distinctly outlined phases of illumination.

They are as distinct as those verbal terms that from episode to episode may characterize these consecutive "states" of illumination of the cathedral.

1. The *darkness* of the cathedral.
2. The *dark* cathedral.
3. *People in the dark* cathedral.
4. The cathedral *animated with torch flames.*

These almost identical verbal terms actually conceal within themselves great variations of light.

I think this is so clear and obvious that I am not sure whether it is necessary here to *chew the cud* and comment on the obvious principal difference as to whether it is a question of a "dark cathedral" or the "darkness of a cathedral."

In one case the *darkness* of the cathedral must "resound" above all, while in the other the *cathedral* itself must "resound" above all – in this case distinguished by its darkness from other "states" of the cathedral – from a bright cathedral, a cathedral plunged in twilight, or a cathedral drowned in the sun's rays.

If one does not catch the nuances of similar verbal terms, if one does not understand why, let us say, Selvinsky[104] writes in one line somewhere about a river that "shines, shimmers and sparkles...," each time having in mind a completely independent "nuance" of shining, and, what is most important, if one does not have the ability to *see before one, tangibly in sensuous images*, the real phenomena, corresponding to these *verbal nuances*,

then, ...there is no point in delving into the analysis and assimilation of audiovisual phenomena and structures! It is better to resemble, in one's ignorance, Monsieur Lepic, from the novel of Jules Renard,[105] *Carrots* [*Poil de Carotte*] and continue to stay bewildered and leave behind "empty solicitude" in audiovisual matters.

This is what Monsieur Lepic writes to the hero of the novel – his son Carrots:

My Dear Carrots,

Your letter, which arrived this morning, greatly astonishes me. I have reread it in vain. It's not in your usual style at all, and you speak of things which seem beyond my competence as well as yours.

As a rule you relate your little adventures, you tell us about your places in form, the merits and faults you discern in the various masters, the names of new boys, the state of your linen, whether you sleep and eat well.

That is the sort of thing that interests me. To-day I cannot make head or tail of you. What is the point, if you please, of this excursus on Spring, when we are in midwinter? What are you trying to say? Do you want a muffler? Your letter is undated and one can't make out if you are addressing me or the dog. Even the shape of your handwriting seems to me altered, and the arrangement of the lines and the use of capitals I find disconcerting. In short, you appear to be making fun of somebody. Of yourself, I can only suppose. I don't want to make a fuss but merely to point this out.

Carrots's answer:

My dear papa!

Two words in a hurry to explain my last letter to you. You didn't notice it was written *in verse*.

I allowed myself this digression because, unfortunately, among those who saw *Ivan the Terrible*, there were more than a few Monsieur Lepics

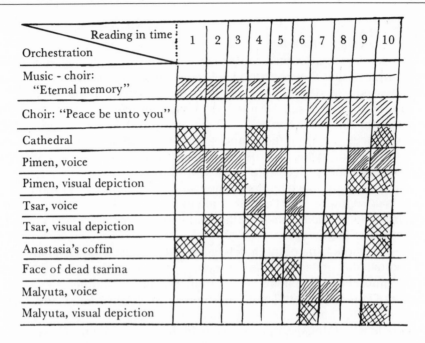

Figure 24. Polyphonic chart of the sequence "Ivan at the Coffin of Anastasia."

who, having noted that many of the usual things were lacking, totally missed the point that the film is constructed on totally different principles.

And many of their views sounded to me exactly like the bewilderment of the papa of Carrots, whose "arrangement of lines and the use of capitals I find disconcerting"!

They also did not notice that the film was shot and assembled...in verse!

True, perhaps in several parts of the film it is not only necessary to *look* and *listen*, but to *look closely* and *listen closely*.

But it is interesting to note that in the majority of cases, the Monsieurs Lepic turned out to be those who should have been the very first to look closely and listen closely to this film in the interests of developing the methodology of the composition of our films in general!

Let us try, however, to gather together into a conventional chart the interaction of a series of those components from which the general polyphony of a scene is formed.

We will discuss here only the main divisions – only the designation of what particular groups of instruments and what particular means are brought forward into the foreground, no matter which progressive passage of the movement of the whole scene is "performing."

From this point of view, one would have to introduce a supplementary chart for each horizontal line. The chart would be concerned with how, within each separate expressive "complex" ("the tsar," "Pimen," "Malyuta"), its own share is divided each time into the separate effective means available to it.

This would mean the clarification, for example, of which elements of a spoken phrase would predominate: the sense of the text, the rhythm of the text, the rhythm of pronunciation, the timbre of the voice, the emotional vibration of experience, the melodic principle, the combination of text and facial expression, etc., etc.

But this would obviously carry us too far from the subject.

Also we will not make this chart an exact copy of how, beat by beat, all these combinations actually twine through the whole scene.

This would result in an overabundance of material. We will limit ourselves to giving a *typical example* of how the audiovisual link occurs and is realized inside the polyphony of the scene of Ivan at Anastasia's coffin.

1. Here intentionally the sound elements are not divided from the visual, but are presented as totally interwoven, so that the impression is created that the contradiction between both areas can be considered "removed."

2. If several cells of sound are filled in in the vertical

column, this means that the *combined* sound of several audial lines is occurring (5, 6, 8, 9).

3. If several cells of the visual depictions are filled in in the

vertical column, it means that those actors are seen together in one shot (6, 10).

Such is the polyphonic composition, interwoven from various spheres of influence, as it unfolds before us in one separately chosen episode of the film.

But this episode has not been chosen arbitrarily, and in many respects it is a "key" episode.

Not only in the method of its construction, but especially because of its dramatic effect.

This episode is a turning point.

For in it Ivan's words resound for the second time: "Two Romes fell, and the third stands," and here they are no longer just a program of action, as they were during the coronation, but they now resound as a battle cry ("for deeds of greatness, relentless"); this slogan becomes a call to battle.

Between the two utterances of these words passes the whole first period of Ivan's reign, just as the second stage of the battle and life of Tsar Ivan passes between the concluding words of the first series "For the Sake of the Great Russian Kingdom" and these words at the end of the second series.

With the episode at the coffin begins the second part of the three series "triptych" of the first Russian tsar.

In terms of method, I have already repeatedly pointed out that it is in these main scenes, made naturally at the highest stage of creativity, that there is revealed most completely those *new formal characteristics* that the film contains ("The Odessa Steps" and "The Mist" – in *Potemkin*, "Where Should the Commander Be" in *Chapayev*, "The Vow over Anastasia's coffin" – here).

The compositional features of such scenes usually contain a set of elements characterizing stylistic features of the film as a whole.

And so it proves to be true here.

Polyphonic composition, the principles of the fugue and counterpoint, growing out of the principles of the composition of *Potemkin*, here, in this episode, achieve their greatest dramatic effect; but they are characteristic not only of the composition within separate scenes of this film, but they define the entire *basic stylistics* of *Ivan the Terrible* as a whole.

And here it is especially important to note that the *audiovisual solution of a film totally repeats the way in which the film as a whole is taken dramatically and thematically* ("how to take a film – this is the important thing" – we might paraphrase the words of Serov* at this point![106]).

We looked at one episode *taken* separately – in the scene at the coffin – how a separate emotional theme has been "taken" – despair, and how it has been "divided" into separate parties and voices.

We see how its movement within its main vehicle – Ivan – passes along the line from total depression due to despair to an explosion of rage and to overcoming this despair. We see how this theme is divided in the voice antiphone of Pimen and Malyuta, and how this antiphone reveals the battle of opposites *within the theme of despair*, developing the active and passive tendencies included within it ("Subdue yourself – or be subdued").

We see how the secondary characters – Staritskaya and the Basmanovs – are interwoven, extending the battle of these opposites.

---

* [V. Serov: important Russian portrait painter at the end of the nineteenth century – HM.]

And the interweaving of the functions that these separate characters bear, while adding color to the basic conflict within the theme of despair, seems to be an embodiment *externally* of everything that is raging in the internal battle of Ivan.

But the range grows broader, and into the general performance there enters light and darkness, the mise-en-scène, the shot, the effect resulting from the performance and the singing, and from the rhythm of the combination of separate effective elements.

The basic conflict in the tsar's soul – "right or wrong" – whether to continue the cause or reject it – seems to grow out of the interaction of all the elements of the scene, which act as separate phases of this inner struggle and blend into one at the culmination of overcoming his doubts and the tsar's transition to a new stage of battle.

As here, for each episode a single theme (despair) is refracted through all the elements and in each of them quivers in its own way, so for the film as a whole its basic theme – power – is "divided" in the same way into all possible nuances of the main attitude toward it.

Every "voice" inside the human ensemble of the film carries this basic theme in its own way, with its own position, and according to its own social and political point of view.

In the words and actions of Ivan the problem of the unity of state power is higher than isolated personal interests:

the interest of the state is higher than personal interest.

This position is opposed by the great diversity into which the opposite point of view disintegrates.

And the unselfish service to the idea of the state on the part of Ivan opposes all possible nuances of selfishness and egoism.

Here there is also the personal unselfishness of "the idealist of feudalism," Metropolitan Philip, acting, however, in the interests of the caste selfishness of the nobility; here there is also the Bonaparte vanity of the wounded egoism of Kurbsky, pushing him to open betrayal; here is the unrestrained thirst of power of Staritskaya who, in trying to achieve her goal, urges her own son to destruction – that son for whose sake she has tried so hard to obtain this power; there is the maniacal fanatic of church power, Pimen, ready for any crime if only it would destroy and bring the crushed tsar to his feet; here is the old man Basmanov, dreaming of a new tribal caste of landowners to replace the feudal lords being thrown out of the historical arena, and hoping through his descendants to "be measured" with the descendants of Ivan; here is Shtaden – simply a self-seeker, robber, and adventurer; and even weak-minded Vladimir, who "has no objection" to occupying the throne, if only it were not connected to a lot of troubles, blood, and a possibly bad conscience.

We can see that in the actual *dramatic effect of the scenario* about

Ivan, we are again concerned with a construction of the fugue type as in the *audiovisual* solution of the scene at the coffin.

Actually, it is enough to briefly enumerate the most general features of the fugue for it to be clearly understood.

I will quote the textbook of Professor E. Prout, *The Fugue* (Moscow, 1922):

2. At the basis of the composition of a fugue is a set theme, which is first stated by one voice and then subsequently imitated by all the others...

In the picture this is − *the theme of power.*

8. The subject or *theme* of the fugue, as it is called, appears at first in the beginning of the composition as single-voiced, without accompaniment, and on which the whole fugue is then constructed...

Even this condition is observed almost literally: The theme of the film − the theme of power − is developed from the very beginning as the subject − and single voiced at that − in the monologue on autocracy in the coronation scene in Uspensky Cathedral. In addition, the first condition − producing the theme designated for the fugue − is *tonal clarity and precision.*

Ivan has to complain of so many things, but not of the clarity and precision of the exposition of his outlaid program.

...From what has just been said, one should not think that the subject must be heard constantly in the rest of the composition, which would lead to tiresome monotony. Saying that the subject lies at the basis of the whole fugue, we wish to say that it appears repeatedly in the greater or lesser intervals of time in the course of the whole fugue...

The line of Ivan penetrates the course of the entire film, and inevitably carries the basic theme of the unity of the state in all its possible variations (declaratively − during the coronation; propagandistically − in the scene of the wedding; in military action − at Kazan; in a tragic aspect − on his knees before the boyars; in accusatory speeches − before the scene of sending off the envoy to Queen Elizabeth; in his battle with his doubts − at the coffin with Anastasia; in the program of ruthless battle − at the end of this scene, etc).

The subject is contrasted to the *answer* or *countersubject.* It is interesting that this companion is the subject transposed to another key:

9. The *answer* or *countersubject* is the subject transposed to the key lying a fourth or fifth higher or lower than the given key...

It is more interesting that often the answer is understood to be something opposing the subject:

...20. There are fugues in which the response is not the subject transposed, but the subject taken in reverse, multiplied or reduced...

Unintentionally it seems that both basic companion opponents of Ivan, of which one is Kurbsky, who, with the makeup and face of a blond man, seems even externally to be the "reverse" of Ivan, and the other – Efrosinya Staritskaya – in one scene of the second series she scares even Malyuta by her resemblance to the look and face of the tsar, "transposed" into the face of the tsar's aunt.*

As for the other characters, whose fate and actions are interwoven in counterpoint to the actions and fate of Ivan, it seems that the very nature of their opposition to his work finds its most precise definition in the fact that

...10. the counterpoint which persistently accompanies the subject or theme is called the *countersubject*. It is not obligatory that the countersubject remain unchanged in the course of the entire fugue: there are fugues with several countersubjects...

And finally, the most important condition that must be present no matter what liberties are allowed in the various parts and details:

...23. The only thing that is obligatory is that the fugue must represent an organic whole; this is achieved by the fact that the thematic material is taken exclusively from the subject or countersubject...

As we can see – they coincide completely.

And we should not be surprised, for, according to the definition of Bach, the "father of the fugue," the form of the fugue is apparently a "conversation [confirmed in the orchestra] of several participants. And when one of them has nothing to say, it is better for him to keep silent."

Constructed according to this principle, both as a whole and in its separate parts, the film in this way is perceived both polyphonically and "symphonically."

I am very glad that I can use someone else's words to characterize it this time, and not have to use my own.

S. Yutkevich in a review of *Ivan the Terrible* writes;

...Eisenstein's film brings us back again to an understanding of film as an art that has a powerful influence on the viewer. Here I would probably apply not a term from painting, but one from music – I would call *Ivan the Terrible* a symphonic film.

Eisenstein does not copy a picture gallery, he does not turn the film strip into a set of slides. He puts all his tremendous culture of cinematographic expression

---

* "...His aunt's eye, resembling Ivan's, looked at Ivan's eye
And from the eye of this acquaintance
To the broad bear-like shoulders
His red shaggy head
Malyuta hides.
And walks backwards to the door.
With a clumsy gait. F.O."

into the service of his theme and, as in no other film of his, he achieves a unity of the different expressive means available to the cinematic art.

This is not only a brilliant duel of remarks and glances, but a passionate battle of sound and silence, light and dark. Brightness and shadow, color and texture – all influence one's mind and feelings...

...The black silhouette of Princess Staritskaya, created with such talent by S. Berman, sprawls like a sinister bird over the silver cradle of Ivan's heir; contrasting with it is the whiteness and severe sculptured quality of the figure of the Tsaritsa Anastasia. This play of black and white, dark and light, as well as the contrasts of the folk choruses and brilliant music of S. Prokofiev, the shadow from the astrolabe and the silver cross, swinging on the tsar's chest; the twisted candlesticks and the semicircular vaults; the fiery parabolas of castiron balls scattered along the walls of the Kazan fortress, and the patterned fields of Tatar robes, and the white snow of the Moscow area – all this blends into one symphonic poem about the strength and beauty of the feat done in the name of the state power of our native land.*

In terms of the key episode "Ivan at the Coffin," which we analyzed above, if we wished to delve into a more delicate analysis we would have had to use many more diagrams.

However, it is very interesting to establish where, when, and how the effect, while alternating, proceeds from *action* (performance) and then from the *shot* (plastic formation): This is why their connection is as refined and vivid as the effect obtained in combining *words* and *music* in a musical drama, rather than in an audiovisual drama as here.

Here, in the interweaving of visual representation and sound, is achieved what was achieved in musical drama given the possibilities of the combination of *music* and *word*. In one of his articles, Saint-Saëns brings in "one of a thousand samples" of how similar combinations were achieved by Wagner.

Tristan asks "Where are we?" "At our goal" answers Isolde to the sound of the music, which before this had repeated the words: "Heads doomed to death" – words she uttered as a prophetic whisper, looking at Tristan, and immediately it is clear which goal, which limit, which end is meant here.[†]

However, we must now focus on one element of composition, in what way the "link" of large divisions that has been described is repeated by the "microscopic" link between *the flow of the music and the performance.*

In the analysis of *Alexander Nevsky* we have already discussed the fact that "as a rule the borders of the division of music (for example,

---

* From "Dalekoye i Blizkoye" in *Sov. Iskusstvo,* February 6, 1945.
† See C. Saint-Saens, *Portraits et Souvenirs,* Société des Editions Artistique, Paris, 1900, pp. 284–5.

measures) and the borders of the division of visual objects (the transition from shot to shot) do not coincide and need not coincide."

What has been described and recommended was "bricklaying," that is, the overflow of divisions into each other: a unique application to the combination of sound and visual depiction of what in poetry is known by the term "enjambment." *

The "bricklaying" is achieved by the stability of the *combination* of the basic elements of a sound track and running ribbon of visual representation.

But this principle takes root even more deeply: *inside the shot* and *inside the musical beat*, pursuing even here that same task of *organic fusion*. And so that the unity of method penetrates the work as a whole, the observance of these obligatory principles must diffuse also into the *inner divisions* of the "pieces" of music and the "pieces" of visual representation. The *accents of sound and movement* (stresses) inside these and other pieces serve as the perceptible skeleton of these "inner" divisions.

In its development, to a significant degree vertical montage *also changed much in the principles of "linear" montage*, that is, in the principles of montage of purely *visual pieces* within those *plastic components*, which each time participate in the general composition of the audiovisual montage structure.

This occurs at the basis of what, at the time, fell to the lot of silent montage – not only to carry on the course of the *visual representation*, but

---

* "Enjambment" occurs when the divisions and ends of *sentences* do not coincide with the divisions and ends of *lines* in a poem. Passing from line to line, the sentence thus appears to connect the lines. See, for example, in Pushkin at the end of *The Bronze Horseman*:

...A little island
Lies off the coast. There now and then
A stray belated fisherman
Will beach his net at dusk and, silent,
Cook his poor supper by the shore,
Or, on his Sunday recreation
A boating clerk might rest his oar
By that bleak isle. There no green thing
Will grow; and there the inundation
Had washed up in its frolicking
A frail old cottage. It lay stranded
Above the tide like weathered brush,
Until last spring a barge was landed
To haul it off. It was all crushed
And bare. Against the threshold carried,
Here lay asprawl my luckless knave,
And here in charity they buried
The chill corpse in a pauper's grave.

[Walter Arndt, trans., *Pushkin Threefold*, Dutton, New York, 1972, p. 144.]

also to realize the rhythmic outline and its physical beat, that is, what now in sound film is found almost totally in the sound track.

To achieve this montage, the silent film had to lay a strong emphasis on the greatest physiologically *effective* element within the system of shots.

An example of such an element, *without an illusory visual representation and having a direct physiological effect* (as the rhythmic pulsation does), was the *junction between pieces of visual representation*: the physiological sensation of the jolts of varying strengths from the shift of visual representations of varying size, varying direction, varying lighting, etc.

The system of such collisions of pieces and the sequence of jolts engendered, *through* the continuous flow of visual representations, an apparent second line, which in *another* dimension carried that same theme (of course, only in those cases where the development of the montage was adequate to the rhythmic beat of the theme!)

In the course of the silent visual representations this was achieved by the same *biunified course* we have in music, which in its most primitive construction carries on *two basic lines simultaneously*: melody and accompaniment.

And the course of *the beat of the montage junctions through the melody* of continuously flowing pieces of visual representation is very similar to what the "bass" part in the left-hand accompaniment usually resembles – under the melodic line of the right – in a piano score.

This creation of a *double series* (varied series) of *two dimensions* from the elements of *one* and the same dimension has been encountered by us in many cases in extremely varied areas.

Thus, for example, in folk poetry part of the verbal material works not in a *thematic-representational* way but as *musical* accompaniment, consisting of turns of speech and words. A. N. Veselovsky writes about this:[107]

"...The language of folk poetry is full of hieroglyphics, which can be understood not so much figuratively as musically; not so much as presenting as tuning up; one must remember this in order to analyze their meaning..."*

To a certain extent the same abstractly musical role is played by the notoriously complex Homeric epithets; you do not so much ponder over their significance as listen attentively to their rumble and peal.

This perception of them is very distinct in their repetitive use, where they figure as an individual musical leitmotif, accompanying each appearance of a character.

---

* *Collected Works*, Vol. 1, p. 168.

It is interesting that this example is used by Feuchtwanger[108] in written prose.

In his novels many characters are also inevitably accompanied by a similar ornamental, stereotyped, descriptive formula whenever and wherever they appear!

However, this feature mentioned by Veselovsky has a direct correspondence especially to what is known in Japanese poetry as "makura-kotoba" ("word-breathing").

In relation to the decoration of Japanese verse it must be remembered that archaic Japanese poetry had but scanty means of embellishment at its command. The language was the court-colloquial of the time, slightly poetized by such devices as the use of "empty" or enclitical words, *shi, no, ka, ya, yo, na,* and the like, or compounds of these, employed much as similar words are employed in Homeric verse – not, however, as mere chevilles, for they round out the sense as well as the metre.*

These words involuntarily bring to mind my conclusions about the performance of *Wit Works Woe.*

This comedy is surprisingly clumsy in the majority of its performances.

And, perhaps, most of all in the Moscow Art Theater of the USSR.

And this is because of deficiencies in it of certain features, almost analogical to what Veselovsky was talking about in connection with folk poetry.

I think the unusual heaviness of the performance of *Wit Works Woe* is based on the whole verse text of the comedy being considered "performable." Moreover, I think a large portion of it is above all music, which catches the basic themes of the action and discourse. Understood accordingly, this part of the text should not be performed in an everyday fashion, but as melodic accompaniment.

I think this consideration is based on comedy as a distinct genre, for, of course, it is completely within the tradition of vaudeville raised to a "monumental" scope.† Actually, the knot of the "comic" situation is built on a purely verbal pun – *on a play on words typical of vaudeville.* The cry that Chatsky is "mad" in the *figurative* and "*broad*" sense of the word is taken in the *literal sense* – as a real fact; why not permit the idea that music, which is just as compulsory for vaudeville, grew into the verbal fabric of the comedy?!

This point of view should not surprise us! Actually, what has *not* been written into the texts of plays in the course of the history of theater, to conform to the stage conventions in which they were created!

---

* F. V. Dickens, *Primitive and Medieval Japanese Texts,* Oxford, 1906, p. xxx.
† "...Vaudeville is the thing, and everything else is nonsense..."

Sometimes these were even...decoration (a phenomenon much farther from the text than music!): Actually so many *descriptive* monologues even in Shakespeare (beginning with the moonlit night in Romeo's monologue) serve to evoke before our eyes the imagined landscape, situation, and mood!

In other cases the text of a play must use very unusual means to convey the sensation of the duration of time.

I would like to discuss one such case here just because the text is used as a graphic modification of the visual representation, which it is forced to describe in words.

This is a famous scene in *Hamlet* before the king's prayer and the duologue of the Danish prince with his queen-mother:

POLONIUS: My lord, the Queen would speak with you and presently.

HAM.: Do you see yonder cloud that's almost in the shape of a camel?

POL.: By th' mass, and 'tis like a camel indeed.

HAM.: Methinks it is like a weasel.

POL.: It is back'd like a weasel.

HAM.: Or like a whale.

POL.: Very like a whale.

HAM.: Then will I come to my mother by-and-by. – They fool me to the top of my bent – I will come by-and-by.

POL.: I will say so.

HAM.: "By-and-by" is easily said. – Leave me, friends.*

This part of the tragedy has usually been given a great variety of interpretations, proceeding from the idea that the cloud keeps its outline, but the prince arbitrarily changes his interpretation of its contours.

Therefore the scene is usually treated as Hamlet's mockery of Polonius or the continuation by the Danish prince of the game of madness.[†]

I do not think this is quite true, and especially because no one really imagines those contours of the cloud we are discussing here.

And moreover the sequence of the contours of a camel, weasel, and whale – are very logically consecutive phases for a cloud *changing its shape*.

Actually, we will draw these three contours in diagrams.

And what do we see?

The first contour pours over into the second and later into the third as a normal sequence.

---

* [*Viking Portable Shakespeare*, Viking, New York, 1974, p. 73.]
† This is how Kuno Fisher interprets this passage (*Shakespeare's Hamlet*, Moscow, 1905, p. 118), who sees in this scene basically the prince's mockery of the toadying of the courtiers (in addition, Fisher alludes to the analogous scene with the hat of Osric).

 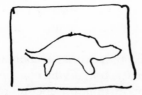 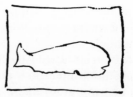

Therefore I think that the three consecutive comparisons define primarily *the course of time* – the time in which a cloud is able to change its shape twice.

One has to consider that the cloudy sky is not calm, for this double change of outline occurs in the course of six short remarks – one has to consider that the clouds are rushing by quickly, and are quickly changing shape.

Why is this double characterization necessary – the flow of time and the feverish flight of the clouds?

I think in order to emphasize two elements in the behavior of the Danish prince: Time rushes by because the prince is thinking, and the prince thinks – in a feverishly quick manner.

Let us not forget what a serious place this scene occupies in the general course of the increasing number of events threatening Hamlet.

In the conversation with Guildenstern, he just said: "'Sblood, do you think I am easier to be play'd on than a pipe? Call me what instrument you will, though you can fret me, you cannot play upon me." [p. 72]

This shows that the prince already knows that the ring of intrigue is closing in around him: His friends have already been recruited into it, and now unexpectedly comes his challenge of the queen.

In eight remarks there will be a short monologue on the forthcoming unpleasant scene of the encounter with the queen ["O heart, lose not thy nature...Let me be cruel, not unnatural." (p. 73)].

Between these scenes you see the prince, through whose consciousness rush feverish thoughts, changing shapes, and these thoughts echo the flight of changing shapes of clouds surging through the heavens.

In the short intervals of being deeply immersed in the flight of his own thoughts, the prince raises his eyes.

Before him rushes the changing forms of the cloudy sky.

Remarks on the changing comparisons, casually tossed off, distract Polonius's attention.

And in a feverish flight of his most anxious moments, they provide the prince the possibility of realizing everything that now pours out in his short monologue before the scene of the king's prayer.

But at the bases of its structure, poetry also has something similar to it. Not only the rhythmic beat, but even the system of rhyme is for verse exactly what a "support" like the montage junction is – for montage. Somewhere a quotation of Richeau, caught by me, is very convincing on this subject:

"If poets would be frank, they would recognize that rhyme not only does not hinder their creativity, but, on the contrary, evokes their poetry, appearing more like a support than an encumbrance..."

To those inclined to see formalism everywhere and to be frightened by it, this quotation does not give grist to their mill, for the "play" of those rhymes "evoking poetry to life" is by no means arbitrary – it is the same original basis of a conception, the same first "fling" of creative intention – necessarily thematic – as any element one uses to begin to embody a conception.

Let us recall here what Mayakovsky wrote about this:

["Most frequently the first thing is the main word – the main word characterizes the meaning of the poem or the word underlying the rhyme. The other words come and are inserted, depending on the main one (*How to Make Verse*)."]

In the same way *the first rhythmic beat of the course of future montage structure* is not arbitrary at all, but is *a thematic solution, expressed in its largest dynamic divisions* and *in the most generalized development of it*.

Moreover, one should add that, purely in terms of creation, finding this first general rhythmic design – is the most difficult thing. It is at this point that there occurs the transposition of a vague emotional "feeling" of a scene into a strict mold of a distinctive form, which should be adequate to the author's experience.

For this very first, initial rhythmic formula, for this rhythmic contour – simultaneously the bones and skeleton of the future structure of the scene – one must..."pay money."

Everything that follows demands not so much *inspiration* as simple talent and ability.

This is why S. S. Prokofiev and I always bargain so long for "who is first": to write the music to unedited pieces of visual representation, so that one could create montage by proceeding from it, or to look at a scene edited in its final form and write music to it.

And that is why the first has the *basic* creative difficulty: to determine the rhythmic *development of the scene*!

For the second – it is "now easy."

What "remains" for him is the erection of an adequate building using the means, possibilities, and elements of his sphere.

Of course, the "ease" here is quite relative, and I speak only in comparison with the difficulties of the first stage. I know the inner mechanics of this process quite well.

This is a very feverish, although very attractive, process.

And to accomplish it, you must above all "see" very distinctly in your mind all the plastic material available.

Then it is necessary to listen endlessly to the recorded phonogram, patiently waiting for the moment when certain elements of one series suddenly begin to "correspond" to certain elements of the other:

the texture of the object or landscape and timbre of a certain musical passage; the potential rhythmic possibility in which one may synchronize a series of close-ups with the rhythmic pattern of another musical passage; the rationally inexpressible "inner harmony" of a certain piece of music and a certain piece of visual representation, etc., etc.

The difficulty, of course, is that the pieces with visual representation are still "in chaos." And the "spirit of combination" that hovers over this "primeval chaos of representation," caught up by the laws of musical development, is forced to keep jumping from the end to the beginning, from piece to piece, in order to guess what combination of pieces will correspond to one or another musical passage.

You should not forget that at the basis of each piece of visual representation there are certain laws, and if they are not taken into account, these pieces cannot even be combined purely plastically.

Strictly speaking, here there is no basic difference from what we are doing now in the era of audiovisual montage.

The only difference is that then we did not "select" pieces to correspond to the incomparable music of S. S. Prokofiev but to the "score" of what was "being sung" within us.

For no montage can be constructed if there is no inner "melody" according to which it is composed!

This melody is often so strong that sometimes the whole rhythm of one's behavior is predetermined on days when one is editing scenes according to the sound.

For example, I remember very clearly the "wilting" rhythm in which I carried out all my everyday activities on the days when editing "Mist" and "Mourning for Vakulinchuk": – in contrast to the days when "The Odessa Steps" was being edited: Then everything flew head over heels, my gait was precise, relations with my domestics – stern, and conversation – sharp and abrupt.

Involuntarily, one recalls Chekhov – this time Michael[109] (and other temperamental actors) – who, when playing a distracted man in the evening, from morning on would stumble on chairs, turn over cups, and smash dishes at home!

How this occurs "in the soul" of a composer I am not able to say in great detail. But I noticed something like this in the work of S. S. Prokofiev.

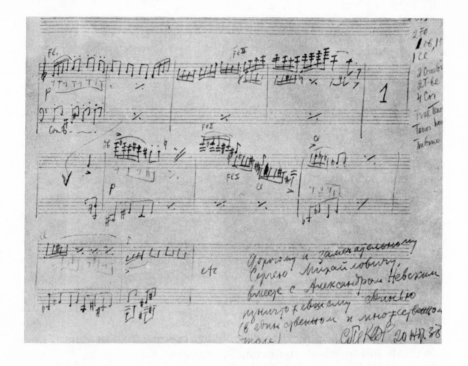

Figure 25. Page of original score by Sergei Prokofiev for *Ivan the Terrible*, inscribed: "To dear and wonderful Sergei Mikhailovich..."

And now I will allow myself time to discuss what I figured out about this in the form of a small "detective story."

THE TELEPHONE ACCUSER

In several hours it will be New Year's, 1945.

I will call S. S. Prokofiev on the phone to congratulate him.

Without looking at my little phone book, I dial the number:

K 5-10-20, extension 35.

And I stop...

I do not have a bad memory.

But probably it is because I am stubbornly trying not to bother it with memorizing telephone numbers.

I purposely cross them out of my memory and note them down in a little gray book of microscopic size.

Why was it so easy for me to remember the telephone number of Sergey Sergeyevich's new apartment, where he had just recently moved?

The numbers:

K 5-10-20 ext. 35.

Why did they settle in my memory?

"...Gordon Craig[110] was as handsome as a fair young god.

And he was very poor.

All the furniture of his garret consisted of one small rug.

When I went to see him, he looked at me and took off his clothes.

Naked he was even more dazzling.

The furnishings of his garret consisted of one rug.

On this rug we spent two days...."

This is a paraphrase in my own words of a page from the diary of Isadora Duncan.[111]

Next to me in the recording booth is Sergey Sergeyevich.

He just told me that he finally moved out of the hotel into an apartment.

On Mozhaisky Chausee.

That the gas is connected,

and the telephone.

But there is no furniture at all.

How could one not recall Duncan at this point and her meeting with Gordon Craig, described in the very shameless book of her memoirs.

Sergey Sergeyevich laughed for a long time, while the orchestra, exerting itself, achieves the clear purity of the musical number then identified as "Ivan Implores the Boyars."

On the screen, Cherkasov, in the character of Ivan, moves on his knees, begging the boyars to swear allegiance to the heir – Dmitry – so as not to subject Russ to the danger of new invasions by adding new conflicts, and to ward off the collapse of one government into warring feudal princedoms.

Incidentally, if you saw the film, then you probably remember this episode, even if only because of the very harmonious combination of action and music, resolved basically by the double basses, led by the incomparable performance of Joseph Frantsevich Gertovich.[112]

I have written extensively about the laws by which the harmonious combination of sound and visual representation was achieved.

I was given the solution to this by working with Prokofiev on *Alexander Nevsky*.

In *Ivan the Terrible* I was interested not in the *result* but in the *process* by which these harmonious combinations are achieved.

I am trying with persistent curiosity to find out how, in two to three reruns of the film, Sergey Sergeyevich was able to capture the emotional effect, rhythm, and structure of a scene so that *the next day* he could engrave *the musical equivalent of the visual representation* – into a musical score.

In the scene, which is being screened the tenth time for the orchestral rehearsal, the effect was particularly striking. The music was written to a completely edited episode.

The composer was only given a timing in seconds of the whole scene.

And nevertheless within the *sixty meters* not a single "cut-in" or "cut-out" of the edited pieces of visual representation was needed, for all the necessary accents of the combination of visual representation and music "found themselves" synchronized in an absolutely irreproachable manner.

Moreover – they were arranged not by a crudely metrical *synchronization* of accents but by a complex course of *interweaving* of accents of action and music, where *synchronization* is only a rare and exceptional phenomenon, strictly conditioned by the editing and by the phase of the unwinding action.

This method of "ligature" corresponds to the "bricklaying" of the brick layer or what is conventionally called "enjambment" in the work of the poets.

Again and again I keep thinking about the astonishing ability of S. S. Prokofiev *to achieve this result...*

However, the orchestra has finally mastered the score.

In a frenzy the conductor Stasevich[113] starts to rehearse it for the sound recording.

The sound engineer Volsky[114] has his earphones on.

The recording apparatus starts turning.

And like wild beasts we glued our eyes to the screen, watching the realization of the audiovisual "ligature" of visual representation and orchestra, whose precursor – the piano – had merged both series so monolithically.

They played once,
twice,
three times,
four times.

The fifth "take" was irreproachable.

The impetuous composer was already wrapped up in his checked scarf.

Already in hat and coat.

Quickly he shakes my hand.

And, running off, he tosses me his telephone number.

The new telephone number of the new apartment:

"K 5-10-20, extension 35!"

And...out of his head gives away
his method.

The sought-for secret.

For the telephone number he pronounces:

K 5! 10!! 20!!! extension 30!!! 5

I permit myself this inscription in the manner of the early Khleb-nikov[115] or Tristan Tzara, in order to note down precisely the course of the *intonational emphasis* with which Sergey Sergeyevich had yelled out the telephone number...

"So what?" you ask. "Where is the key here to the mystery of the creation of Prokofiev's music?"

We will tell you!

Meanwhile, I am not looking for a key to the creation of music and the inexhaustible wealth of images and sound combinations that Sergey Sergeyevich carries in his head and heart (yes – I will not allow anyone to deny this *warm heart* to the *wisest* of contemporary composers). I am now seeking a key only to the striking phenomenon of creating a musical equivalent to any piece of visual representation thrown on the screen.

Mnemonics is extremely varied.

Very often it is simply a matter of association.

Sometimes it is compositional (a series of words, which are to be memorized, are connected in action and subject matter, and thus form a *concrete picture* in your memory).

One well-known telephone subscriber is easily memorized by a double pun on the theme of the term "ochko (K 0-21-00)."*

The mnemonic manner of a man is, to a great extent, the key to the particular nature of his mental activity.

In Sergey Sergeyevich the mnemonic device is strikingly close to what one might guess to be the manner of his perception of visual representa-tion, which he so unerringly translates into a sound series.

Actually, what does Prokofiev do?

The accidental series of numbers – 5, 10, 20, 30 – he instantaneously interprets as following a certain regularity.

This series of numbers is really the sequence we know as the conventional formula for *increasing quantity*:

"5-10-20-30-"

A similar example is "100-200-300."

Or in another area: "Ivanov, Petrov, Sidorov."

However, this regularity is fixed in Prokofiev's memory, not by *speculation* but according to that same *emotional premise* that is then made graphic by the given formula.

This is not simply an increase in *loudness*, corresponding to an increasing quantity, not simply the rhythm of a phrase, meaning number, which is automatically imprinted in one's memory. However, for many

---

* [Points in a game – HM.]

orchestra players this is the mnemonic means of memorizing telephone numbers.* The difference between the composer and the orchestra player probably is that Prokofiev pronounced this series with an increasingly *excited* intonation, as 5!–10!!–20!!!–30!!!! thousands of rubles won or woodcocks bagged.

There is no real necessity for an intonation of *excitement*.

It could have been the intonation of *fright* just as well, in reaction to a group of advancing tanks or dive-bombing planes.

The nature of the emotional "subtext" under the discovered regularity is the work of the author and, in an example allowing for any interpretation, it can be dictated by any attendant motif.

The "joyful" interpretation of the given sound sequence in Prokofiev was probably determined...by the unspoken joy of finally, after wandering around hotels, finding his own quiet apartment on Mozhaika Boulevard...

Let us forget Mozhaika and the telephone.

And let us remember the basic point about Prokofiev's creative mnemonics.

He is able to interpret an "apparently" accidental accumulation of phenomena as corresponding to a definite regularity.

He gives an emotional interpretation to this found regularity.

The means by which a formula is mastered sensually – is unforgettable.

It is impossible to toss it out of one's memory.

The telephone numbers are memorized through intonation.

And *intonation* – is the *basis of melody*.

By the same method Prokofiev is able to interpret the intonation of the edited sequence of pieces projected on the screen.

For intonation, that is, the melody of the spoken "tune," lies at the basis of music as well...

With this the story essentially comes to an end. We should add only that for this type of musical composition, the "visual music" must be constructed according to this same principle, that is, the visual representation must be edited according to this principle.

And thus the experience of the montage construction of silent film has turned out to be very useful. Silent film demanded that the musical development be included into the combination of shots, equally and indissolubly synchronized with their narrative presentation of events.

And actually, it is only now – in the epoch of sound film – that you can see how the strict organization of such composition has become part of our flesh and blood after the period of silent montage.

---

* Among them I have known more than one who memorized melodies by tying knots to match them!

The indispensable repetition of expressive groups of sound combinations in music is also true of rhythmic and montage groups of visual representations moving in sequence.

And we can see numerous examples of how a completed element of music – the "piece of the phonogram" written "for" a certain part of a scene – also fits exactly its other parts.

What is remarkable is that not only is there a correspondence of large sections and a "general mood" as a whole, but there is also the same identity of audiovisual "mortise and tenon" joining of pieces of visual representation and music, as in that part of the scene for which the music was originally composed.

At another point I showed this to be true for minor elements in the musical articulation of "The Dawn Scene" in *Alexander Nevsky*. There I traced in detail how *the same compositional scheme* was *repeated in diverse areas of plastic possibilities.*

In the course of the development of the film, this can be observed in *Ivan the Terrible*, in the scene mentioned above, when Ivan begs the boyars to swear allegiance to Dmitry. In this case the phonogram composed for the *first half* of the scene – before Kurbsky's entrance – fits with inflexible inevitability the *entire second half* as well.

And not only in terms of "general length" but also in all the synchronization and preconceived nonsynchronization of the accents of action and music.

This is possible for two reasons: first, because of the persistence of the basic emotional mood passing through in the variations of individual phases of the scene, and second, because the structural regularity of separate parts strictly follows the same design.

Strictly speaking, there is, of course, only *one* reason here, and it is that for a given emotional solution that compositional structure is found in which it is expressed most completely. To interpret it from the editing and to transpose it into the system of sound combinations producing that same emotional effect is the problem of the composer.

As I said before, this is developed in a more detailed, scholarly way in my article "Vertical Montage."*

Here I would only like to briefly add a nuance to the development of the compositional counterpoint as it occurs in *Ivan*.

In the analysis of the "Dawn Scene" in *Alexander Nevsky*, we had a typical analogue to the Chinese picture scroll *unrolled horizontally.*

There this can be read as two horizontal, parallel lines of a score – the line of sound and the line of visual representation – just like the line of air, water, and earth in a Chinese landscape; here, then in *Ivan the*

---

* [See S. Eisenstein, *Film Sense*, Jay Leyda, trans. and ed., Faber & Faber, London, 1943, pp. 58–86 – HM.]

Terrible, we apparently have an instance of a roll of film "uncoiling" – so complicated is the interrelationship and interweaving, and so great are the number of elements constituting the general emotional effect.

Although our detective novel has ended, as we have said above, tradition nevertheless demands that not only the crime be revealed at the end but also a hint of the method by which it was discovered.

And therefore, in conclusion, we will briefly discuss the sleuth-detective and his methods.

But one must keep in mind that there are two basic types of detectives.

Just as in the case of graphologists, there is the private detective.

One of them is a type like Ludwig Klages,[116] who essentially operates in an analytic manner.

Thus, for example, among other features of Klages's analysis, a great role is played by the elucidation of the precise interrelationship in handwriting of *straight, angular*, and *sharp* elements in their combination with *rounded, smooth, flowing* elements.

In Klages's somewhat primitive system, the first are connected with conscious and willful elements, and the second with emotional, instinctual ones.

Of the huge multitude of possible "signs," which include the size of the letters, the slant, the closed-in and the open, the explosive and the indissoluble, etc., I have intentionally chosen only the following principle (based on Klages): In it is contained the whole system of yin and yang in the great blossoming of the twentieth century!

This more than confirms how strong original traditions are, as soon as you come into conflict with phenomena *where the exact* sciences have not yet penetrated, and the phenomena themselves relate to the division of the natural and the organic.

Let us not forget, however, that this tradition is strong not only in such scientifically suspicious areas as...graphology!

Actually, Wölfflin's famous classification of styles based on a system of opposites* and the observation of all of art history as a system of uninterrupted transitions from one opposite to the other, also bears the distinct imprint of the Chinese tradition.

In any case, the first type of graphologist (and detective) is the analytic type. In both cases, features and signs, or evidence, are grouped together;

* "The linear and the painterly," "surface and depth," "enclosed and revealed form," "multiplicity and unity," "distinct and indistinct (see H. Wölfflin, *Kunstgeschichte Grundbegriffe*, Bruckmann, Munich, 1929).

in this way the outline of the character or the image of the criminal and the picture of the crime are drawn up.

In graphology this method even tends to become "mechanical."

In America, a little book, Jerome S. Meyer's *How to Read Character from Handwriting*, 1927, has been published.

It is constructed so that the handwriting that interests you is laid consecutively under lined sheets of tracing paper.

On one you determine the degree of the slant of the letter; on the other, the slant of the actual stroke; on the third, the size of the letters; on the fourth, the character of the separate inscriptions, etc.

Each sign is numbered. The number and certain combination of numbers have a corresponding "interpretation" in the "keyed" part of the book.

To a certain extent this is also the classical model of the Sherlock Holmes type of detective.

The other type of detective and graphologist work in another "physiognomically" (in the broadest sense of the word) or, if you like, synthetically manner.

Among graphologists, one example is Raphael Sherman, who has become very famous since 1929, when he foretold the death of Stresemann[117] three days before the catastrophe (by a fragment of a letter one of his colleagues of the German Foreign Ministry brought to Sherman for analysis).

Here the affair is quite different.

Sherman does not analyze handwriting elements but tries to extract some general, synthetic, graphic image from the handwriting (essentially from the client's signature, which in many cases is like a person's graphic self-portrait).

This "ideogram" is usually concrete, and Sherman himself in his booklet describes those outlines of objects that he reads from the drawing of the signature and that serve as a key to him for discerning the basic psychic "complexes" of his patients.

But another "trick" with which Sherman literally amazes you at the first meeting is much more curious.

I personally became acquainted with him in Berlin in 1929 and experienced it myself.

When you enter his study, this hypersensitive man of small stature with a pale face and sharp, explosive movements convulsively grabs a pen and begins to write on a piece of paper... *with your handwriting*!

If there are certain mistakes in the details, still the basic nature and basic character of the handwriting are caught perfectly.

Another analogous routine of his is when he can just as easily use a painting of an artist to reproduce... his signature!

Is this a miracle? Or a mystical power?

It is neither.

And, although the effect is truly amazing, the basic premise has absolutely nothing to do with supernatural powers.

It is a matter here of *imitation* or, rather, in the *degree of imitation* with whose help Sherman, having "captured" you at first glance, instantaneously *reproduces you.*

And his graphic imitation does not differ in any major way from *plastic imitation* and "mimicry," so often accomplished with such perfection by professional impersonators, without even having recourse to makeup or props.

Let us recall, say, Andronikov[118] and his terrifyingly vivid imitations of Pasternak, Chukovsky, Kachalov, Alexey Tolstoy.

Here the good impersonator grasps the basic external characteristics "*en route,*" *as a whole*, and does not "concoct" an image of the imitated person from distinctive "attributes."

In this way he captures the basic "tonality" of a person, which is formed first of all from the *rhythmic characterization* of the whole complex of the person's functions.

But the *rhythmic characterization* is the external imprint of the *characterization of inner relationships and conflicts* in the "inner system" – in the person's psyche.

And, therefore, the once-captured, basic, tonally plastic characterization also provides a certain access to the inner psychological mechanism of the imitated person.

In Heracles Andronikov's imitations, for example, what is so striking is not so much the external reproduction of a man as the terribly simple way he penetrates into the inner image of the person depicted.

Thus, while imitating the melodious and particular manner of Pasternak's poetry reading, Andronikov improvises the text in the Pasternak style, not only in form but also in the details of the actual *process of formation*, by a system of accompanying digressions and commentaries to it by the "author" himself.

It is now easy to understand why Sherman, who has mastered the ability to "reembody himself" into another person perfectly at first glance (the first impression is usually the sharpest), easily captures the rhythmic nature of his *handwriting*. For it is in the rhythm of the handwriting that the dynamic characterization of a momentary emotional state or habitual emotional state appears so distinctly, that is, the material that provides the possibility of judging character!

It is not surprising that another curious phenomenon is also built on this same principle of imitation. This phenomenon again leads us to China.

Chinese banking houses and offices have perfectly assimilated European and American banking methods.

But in one point, and a very sensitive one at that, the Chinese have not grasped this methodology: on the question of how to recognize the solvency and respectability of the client.

And now in the Chinese banks, besides the usual set of guarantees demanded by the bank, they subject the client to one more test by...a fortuneteller.

And here, along with the calculating machines, safes, telegraphic equipment, and other "apparatus" of the bank, in a separate little window appears the mysterious figure of the fortuneteller, with his thin fingers sorting out small, thin sticks with mysterious markings.

The fortuneteller stares at the client and his fingers automatically sort out stick after stick with convulsive movements, from the many dozens his hands quickly run through.

By the signs on the sticks that have been sorted out, the fortuneteller finds the "answers" in a huge, mysterious book, and only if the combination of answers provides a generally favorable picture of the moral image of the client will the bank agree to give him credit. Without this verification, none of the other guarantees of solvency, no matter how impressive they be, have any force...!

In what does the secret lie?

I know about it, strange as it may seem, if not firsthand, then at least secondhand.

Once while I was in New York I was taken to look at the Sing Sing prison by a certain Dr. S., who was a friend of ours through his work with the International Workers Aid through the Red Cross.

On the way from New York to the small station where, in the center of a large prison, the notorious electric chair was set up, Dr. S. and I talked about themes that are close to what I am writing about.

I told him about Sherman, and he told me the secret of the Chinese fortuneteller. He learned this secret from his Chinese pupil, a medical student, the son of one of these fortunetellers in one of the banks of either Canton or Shanghai.

It turns out that this is built on precisely the same system of imitation.

The fortuneteller, having looked at the client carefully, reproduces his psychological *habitus* in exactly the same way as Raphael Sherman does, and thus catches his own personal impression of the degree of "moral trustworthiness" of the one being tested.

And the little sticks?

The experienced fortuneteller has mastered his sticks so well that their play almost by reflex repeats the nuances of the movements of his fingers, and certain sticks fly out under a certain movement of his fingers. And in the fortunetelling, the fortuneteller selects just those sticks with those signs that provide that characterization of the client,

which the experienced imitator and physiognomist-fortuneteller interpreted from his face, appearance, and behavior.*

I think that for us professionals there is something less miraculous here
than appears at first sight.

For does not each of us directors have to constantly "crawl into" and
"crawl out of" not only the individual characters his artists play but also
the actual individuality of the actors themselves, without which he
cannot help them in the complex process of the mutual "penetration" of
the character – performer, and the performer character, let alone the fact
that without this ability of the director, it would be impossible to transfer
the problems of drama into a chain of concrete acts of real, existing
characters.

However, no matter how strange, you will feel this most strongly in *the
work of typecasting*, rather, in the process of selecting types.

It is true that the construction of a suite of types, composed of separate
close-ups, appearing for only a moment before the viewer, demands
basically two conditions:

first of all, that the expressive "resonance" of such a face be absolutely
precise, like a chord or note, not allowing anything false in a given
combination;

second, that this precision be expressed with maximum clarity and
directness, so that a certain image of a completely defined human
characterization could be formed from a short, momentary appearance to
the viewer's perception.

The suite of faces grieving over Vakulinchuk's body was constructed
in this way.

Each face appearing for a moment bears not only a completely defined
chord or note of grief, but also a sign of social class, of accompanying
everyday associations, etc., etc.

Their correct selection also provides the sensation of the "universality" of the grief over Vakulinchuk – grief uniting the old and the young,
the intellectuals and the workers, the sailors and the women.

Therefore, the process of selection demands great exertion when, for
example, we have before us dozens of "gray-haired old men" summoned
by a private announcement.

And now you must, first of all, catch the nuance of emotional

---

* The degree to which a person's character provides an imprint of his whole appearance
and the degree to which the trained eye of the observer can interpret him from such an
appearance can be well illustrated by a line from Sainte-Beuve[119] (*Causeries du lundi*, III,
Garnier Frires, Paris, 1924/28 pp. 231): "They say of Abbot Morelle, pedant and fanatic of
great precision, that he even walked with sharply drawn-in shoulders in order to get closer
to himself..." (!) One recalls a similar characterization of the miser-father, Grandee, in
Balzac.

resonance stimulated by the tired eyes of one in contrast to the submissively compressed, toothless jaws of another, or the transparency of the pale skin on the temples in a third, in contrast to the scattered wrinkles on the shriveled face of a fourth.

And, second, to take into account what these separate faces with different nuances of emotional "resonance" provide in combination with the others.

And now you look, "immersing yourself" into such a face, and unintentionally you enter into the whole system of living drama engendered on the old man's face by these furrows of sorrow, these deep features of grief.

Of course, without guessing the physical details of such a life (and this is really not necessary), you enter emotionally into the tragic rhythms of the whole life that shines and flashes for a moment before you on the screen.

If this is the nature of the encounter with a senile face that, like a member of the Synodik,* has engraved traces of the history of a whole life on his parchment, then, no matter how strange it may seem, the process is even more sensitive in those cases when one must select children's faces.

This concerns young boys of eight–ten–twelve years of age.

If the face of an old man or old woman leads you back to the distant past by the imprints left on their faces, then the drawing of the features on a child's face forces you to look into the future. The features of a child's face seem to be the imprint of all inclinations within him, like a cluster of those possibilities that, once having developed, greatly define the image, character, and vital activity of the future person.

To immerse oneself into such faces is even more tormenting.

Here the inherited traumas and often horrible and depraved inclinations have not yet been overcome or smoothed away by the long toil of one's life path or worldly encounters that smooth and level their scandalous direction.

Here is a feature predisposed to vice, shining in all its glory.

Here a feature of a psychological flaw or inferiority cannot be hidden by the art of pretence.

Also purely physical badness is still not mollified or leveled down in the process of growth and development.

And now before your "spiritual gaze" this cluster of possibilities begins to unroll, inclinations without the unavoidable leveling correctives of practical life – grow "directly" to exhausting fullness...and you shudder at the picture of what a monster this child's face has grown into,

* [List of the dead to be read in church – HM.]

with the imprint of future sufferings and griefs in his childish features!

No, the process is even more terrible.

It is even more terrible because it occurs not before your "spiritual gaze" – indifferently and objectively – but you yourself, "in the skin" of this child who stands before you with wide-opened eyes looking at the "famous director," experience all the torment of his possible future development.

It is good that this lasts for only a moment, and by the sign of your eyes the diligent assistant leads the child away to the group of those considered suitable or unsuitable for the shooting.

But how horrible it is when you have to look over 50, 100, 200 children in one morning...

The detective technique – at least on the pages of a detective novel – is very good at this method.

The detective tries to "get inside" the train of thoughts and feelings of the criminal who is unknown to him, and in this way to possess his living image, so that he can guess the picture of the crime and the action of the criminal.

The classic example of such an approach is the famous Dupin,[120] conceived by the official founder of the genre, Edgar Allan Poe, who in his *The Purloined Letter* reproduced the complete thought processes of the person with whom he was conversing.

Of the newer ones, one should recall the detective from the novel *The Invisible Portrait* by Joseph Collomb (1928), where the person who is being sought is reproduced by this very method from the elements of usual surroundings – books, furniture, etc.

And, of course, to a great extent this is Chesterton's *Father Brown*; this little simple-hearted priest, preserving in his soul hundreds of monstrous crimes entrusted to him during confession by inveterate criminals; the image of the funny little priest, capable in necessary moments of "implanting himself" into these criminal natures, thereby deducting the various artful designs of their crimes.

Thus, to the second type of detectives belongs the detective who set out to find solutions to S. S. Prokofiev's work methods.

And the solution is made easier by the fact that the detective (and that's me) works exactly the same way.

I can illustrate this briefly in the material of this article.

The search for a certain regularity in the juxtaposition of apparently unrelated phenomena is the great passion of its author!

The embodiment of it or the case of the simplest "materialization" of this attempt was probably montage constructions like the "Jumping Lions," where three independent positions were synthesized into the normal phases of a single process of movement (in *October* the examples were even more "dashing" in this respect!).

But the majority of examples introduced in the course of this article arose in exactly the same way.

We have written in reference to Prokofiev:

"...The accidental series of numbers – 5, 10, 20, 30 – he instantaneously interprets as *following a certain regularity*..."

We could generalize these considerations by recalling the words of Rémy de Gourmont:[121]

"...To elevate one's own personal impressions into a law of regularity – this is what composes the great striving of man, if he is sincere..."

The same thing occurs here as well.

One must only add that the actual calling of attention to these separate elements is dictated, above all, by *emotional enthusiasm*.

And without enthusiasm such a process can hardly be realized!

But let us not tire the reader, and demonstrate all this in practice.

Earlier, in discussions on *pathos*, we illustrated an "ecstatic explosion" through the comparison of two of Piranesi's etchings from different series, from different periods of his life, and from different cyles of his activity.

The "montage effect" from the combination of the two engravings is undoubtedly no less than from the "Jumping Lions."

But basically they are all subject to that same set of laws, "detected" in several (here two) actually unrelated phenomena.

(And, perhaps, here it is even appropriate to speak not only about the "detecting" of sets of laws, but also about their "creation," for here, of course, the passive "detection" merges with the active "establishment" of laws; however, this has no decisive significance here.)

I am simply in love with Piranesi.

And I have been for a long time.

And especially the series *Dungeons*.

Now, when we analyzed the principle of the fugue that penetrates his etchings and compared them with the principles of how I construct my films, this earlier enthusiasm is very comprehensible as an index of a propensity that had not yet been formed in my own work.

I looked for etchings of *Dungeons* for a long time without success.

And then I accidentally found myself in one of the provincial cities of the Soviet Union.

In connection with looking for materials for a film about Frunze, which I had once thought of making.

I accidentally found myself in the city museum, organized on the basis of the collection of some merchant (in his private residence).

And totally unexpectedly I saw separate examples of Piranesi in several glass cases – and from the series *Dungeons*.

By a prolonged diplomatic operation (with the help of the local department of film distribution!) I was able to barter two sheets of

Piranesi for a whole package of other engravings that I proposed to the museum as an exchange. Both sheets have been framed and now hang in my yellow corner room.

Satisfied with the favorable outcome of the "transaction," for long hours I sit and admire the engravings.

But the "itch" for establishing interrelationships does not give me any peace.

Quiet "contemplation" without fail slips into "comparison."

And then suddenly and unexpectedly a "dynamic" tie is established between both engravings, as has been shown above, historically separated from each other by twenty years in the life of Piranesi himself.

And we obviously see that the predisposition of a detective is absolutely of the sort to puzzle out the secret of the one he is pursuing!

And that he tries to solve the puzzle of this other person "through himself."

And again we recall the Chinese, who even on this occasion, as always, have a charming story.

WHAT MAKES FISH HAPPY
Chuang Tse and Hue Tse stood on a bridge across the river Hao. Chuang Tse said:

"Look how the fish dart about. This is the way they express their joy."

"You're not a fish," said Hue Tse, "how do you know what makes fish happy?"

"You, not I," answered Chuang Tse, "how do you know that I don't know what makes them happy?"

"I, not you," asserted Hue Tse, "really don't know you. But I also know that you're not a fish, and therefore you can't know a fish."

Chuang Tse answered:

"Let's return to the first question. You're asking me how I know what makes fish happy? But you know that I know, and yet you're asking me this question. But never mind, *I know about this by the joy which the water gives me.*"*

However, let us return to the problems of montage.

We wrote above that in the montage of silent film the "rhythmicization" of separate passages, at least in the large section, is achieved mainly by editing.

Here editing established both the change of the precisely established *length* of changing impressions, as well as the systems of *rhythmic pulsations that are actually felt*, permeating the pictorial passages.

At the same time, editing also carried out the necessary *articulation* of this uninterrupted flow of the pictures.

Without such an articulation, any perception, be it emotional or

* From *Der alte Chinese Tschuang-Tse. Deutsche Auswahl von Martin Buber*, Insel-Verlag, Leipzig, 1910.

cognitive, would have been impossible, and so would the effects calculated earlier.*

Now, with the arrival of sound, the basic solution of such "secondary" problems, which formerly were based on *the change of visual depictions*, completely passed over *into the area of sound*.

From this position and point of view I welcomed the arrival of sound in film as early as my address at the Sorbonne (Paris, 1930).

The sphere of sound, of course, took upon itself the *rhythmicization of the screen event* more easily and naturally, for under these conditions it was possible to achieve this even when the visual depiction itself was invariable and *static*!

But this changing situation, as we said above, could not help but influence fundamentally the very principles by which "linear" montage is constructed – that is, the combination of visual depictions of passages *within the actual visual components of the audiovisual construction*.

The new position was expressed in the fact that under the new conditions the very *center of support* of visual montage had to be moved to a new area and to new elements.

This support, as we have shown above, was, although often excessively "aestheticized," the *juncture between pieces*, that is, the element lying *outside* of the depiction.

With the transition to audiovisual montage, the basic support of the montage of its visual components moves *into* the passage, *into the elements within the visual depiction itself*.

And the basic center of support is no longer the element between the shots, the juncture, but the element within the shot, the *accent within the piece*, that is, the constructive support of the actual structure of visual depiction.

(Here again the same process we pointed to earlier in a series of other examples seems to be repeated: in the Chinese picture scrolls, in the principles of literary writing, in Peruvian ceramics, etc.)

One must not view accent here in a vulgar way, that is, not only as a mechanical jolt; just as in the editing of silent film, the work is built

---

* In the theater such an articulation is achieved by the "predecessor of montage" – the atypical mise-en-scène. In opera especially. I once wrote about this in connection with a performance of "Die Walküre" in the Bolshoi Theater of the USSR (1940–1):

"...While the flow of music was articulated to the end by the system of plastic action, the mise-en-scène was also able, by a system of 'close-ups' (as we would say in cinema), to separate expressive phases of the general course of the sound flow."

In this visual presentation of separate consecutive links of music, *the music itself begins to acquire that visual tangibility*, which is also the production principle of "Die Walküre."

Here the first attempts had been made in this direction, but I think this must in general become part of the methodology of staging musical dramas, and not only those of Wagner (*Theater*, No. 10, 1940).

certainly not only on jolts between pieces, like the blows of buffers between train cars, and in music the stress is certainly not always on the first quarter note!

The accent within a shot can also be the changing light tonality and the change of characters, the movement in the emotional state of the actor, or an unexpected gesture, breaking the smooth flow of the piece, etc., etc. – in a word, everything that is suitable, with the condition, of course, that, while interrupting the inertia established in the preceding part of the piece with a new flight, turn, or step, it must attract the attention and perception of the viewer in a new way.

Such accents of action and behavior within a piece naturally conflict with the accented articulations through which pass the musical, intonational, spoken, or sound movement on the sound track.

And the combination or conflict of the system of these accents, these *junctures* "in a new quality" – *on the vertical* – cannot be composed accidentally or unskillfully.

In them there apparently must be similar, and perhaps even *the same*, *laws* of interweaving that govern the interweaving of the large articulations of the "bricks" of audiovisual "bricklaying."

At least we strictly held to this principle in *Ivan the Terrible* in those scenes where the audiovisual merging of the elements of music and action was achieved with maximum success (for example, in the scene when the sick Ivan entreats the boyars): The audiovisual articulation proceeded along the line to extend also this principle of "bricklaying" to the mutual play between accents of a piece of action and the music accompanying it.

The following graphs illustrate the basic possibilities of the combination of accents, and the notes to them characterize separate features of the effects as well as those from combinations that are especially characteristic of the manner of montage of the scenes in *Ivan the Terrible.*

In addition, it is quite conventional to take the four-beat measure with a strong accent on the first quarter note, and the second strongest – on the third, and for a passage of visual depiction the same accents are suggested – one main one, and a second somewhat weaker than the first.

At the same time, it is perfectly obvious that these performance accents may be not only of varying power or intensity but also can belong to different dimensions – to varying spheres of action (for example, the accent of maximum power can be *sharply transposed*, and the second in power – be the changing light tonality of the piece).

It is also quite obvious that in practice this also can be any syncopated distribution, both in the accents of music and in the innershot accents of visual depiction; an even articulation in the music can contrast with an unevenly accented articulation within the visual depiction; and, of course, as many as you like consecutive variations and dislocations of all this from piece to piece – right up to what might correspond to the phenomenon of two striking accents within one word: I myself, for example, recall how the late Mayakovsky at rehearsal of *Mystery-Bouffe*, demanded that the words:

...my avstraliĭtsy.
U nas vsë bylo...*

should definitely be pronounced with two accents:

...my avstralíĭ-tsý.
U nas vsë bý-ló...

With this reservation let us turn to the actual graphs of the combinations.

I will take only four of the most obvious cases and one example of complicated construction.

Schema 1

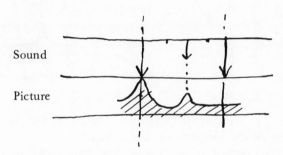

Sound

Picture

All articulations coincide in location as well as intensity.

1. The juncture of picture with the articulation into beats.
2. The main accent of picture and the main accent in the music.
3. The secondary accent of picture with the secondary accent in music.

This is an example of "nonbricklaying."

Schema 2

not: *but:*

---

* ...we are Australians. We had everything...

According to the main articulation, this is also not bricklaying; but the principle of *ligature* is set forth as the strong and weak accents of the music and picture already moving while interweaving.

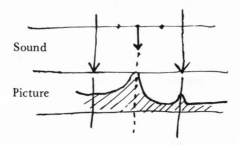

(The weak against the strong, the strong against the weak)

Schema 3 Bricklaying I

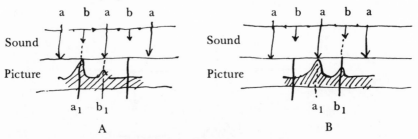

A   B

This is a case of "bricklaying" laid bare: The ends of the musical beats and the borders of the pictures do not coincide.

The secondary ligature in the case of A is maintained in the fact that the weak stand opposite the strong, and vice versa ($a-b_1$, $b-a_1$).

It is weakened by the fact that the juncture of montage coincides with the strong accent a_1, inside the picture itself.

In the case of B, the secondary ligature is established by the fact that the linear montage juncture appears on the weak accent b_1.

It is weakened by the fact that the vertical audiovisual juncture is constructed on the principle: the strong opposite the strong, the weak opposite the weak ($a-a_1$, $b-b_1$).

Schema 4 Bricklaying II

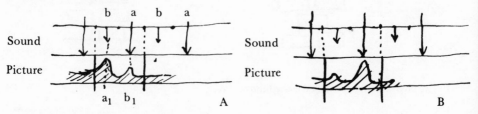

A   B

Classic "bricklaying."

Case A is distinguished from the preceding by the fact that the montage juncture does not coincide with the accent within the piece, and the inner ligature is maintained in the graph of weak accents opposite strong (a_1-b, b_1-a).

Case B is distinguished from A by the fact that the inner ligature in it is weakened: strong opposite strong and weak opposite weak (b_1-b, $a-a_1$).

The merit of graph 4 against graph 3 is that in the actual laying of large articulations there is an easy movement from *complete symmetry* (which always carries a certain element of conventionality) – this occurs because the *montage junctures* do not fall here in the *middle* of the beat (opposite the weak accent) as there.

Here the junctions fall opposite the *unaccented* quarters.

Schema 5 Bricklaying III

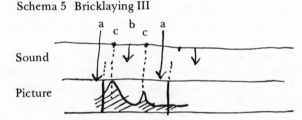

Distinguished from the preceding graph by the fact that here the accents of the picture now fall on the unaccented elements of the music (a_1-c, b_1-c).

The innershot ligature is even smaller. But there is now a danger that this ligature, if poorly understood, will generally be weakly felt or hardly perceived at all.

The same thing occurs with large articulations, which with great risk go from "bricklaying" to "the laying of pillars" (a montage juncture of the picture comes close to coinciding with the articulation of the music into beats).

The next step will be the case when the accents of the picture no longer fall between stressed accents, as here (a_1 opposite c, lying between a and b), but between stressed and unstressed (between a and c or c and b). This kind of "ligature" will almost not be understood and will be felt like the accidental co-occurrence of the music and picture.

In this case essentially nothing really corresponds to anything.

In conclusion, let us introduce an example of complex construction. In it one can observe constructive correspondences, despite the fact that both the time and the number of accents change from beat to beat.

In terms of practical application, basically the audiovisual ligature is maintained by "classical" bricklaying – varying, becoming remote, or approaching it, and passing into other forms.

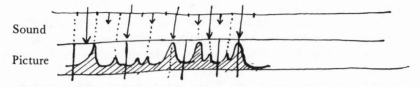

Graph 1 – is a complex, very strongly acting accent (the complete coincidence of all individual accents); it is recommended to be used in very strongly accented positions (in the scene "At the Coffin of Anastasia" it applies especially to the episode when Ivan hurls the candlestick; at the same time, the scene as a whole basically is maintained by variations of graphs 4 and 5).

One must not forget, however, that the strongest positions are sometimes more profitably built in a *contra-accent* (see above, in the analysis of the general question about "reverse decisions").

The coinciding of accents with the ends of pieces produces a scanning effect – also sometimes in special cases a real, desired, and necessary effect.

The too-frequent coincidence of inner accents of music and picture inevitably gives the feeling of a marching type of people's behavior, especially if the musical accent also coincides with their *movements*. This produces a rather comic effect, and therefore it often is used in comedies, in this case as if laughing at the very principle of the correspondence of music and picture. The baring of the actual principle translates it from the area of the *organic* into the area of the *mechanical*, and it inevitably seems funny in its application to the conduct of living beings. (The *bared* application of the principle of "repetition" is just as funny.)

If one looks at the graph of the basic principle according to which audiovisual combination occurs, then a curious thing is revealed:

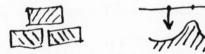

Just as in the actual "laying" of brick articulations, also in *the mutual play of accents* – where the accent of one row tries to lie between two accents of the second row – we essentially have the same rudiment of opposition of *odd/even*: *one* brick opposite *two*, or *one* accent *between two*!

Thus, having begun with the question about the music of landscape, about "nonindifferent nature" in the narrow sense of the word, we imperceptibly moved into whole performance complexes into which the landscape grows and toward which it develops.

On this new stage it is now a question of the "visual music" of whole fragments of the action complete in themselves.

As we will see, both the theme and the problem grew way beyond the frame of the *music of landscape* into problems of *the music of each plastic construction of the shot in general* – no longer only emotional and visual, but also in terms of performance!

We also traced how *hidden plastic music* grows out of the depths of the landscape into real music with the transition from silent film to audiovisual cinema.

And we traced how the music and picture merge in audiovisual counterpoint, and it seems that the music, while permeating the texture of the landscape, seems to pour back again into the plastic medium from which it was formerly overheard, emerged, and was born.

However, as we have seen, an emotional quality can be sensed from the plastic structure, and this is true not only when we are concerned with pure landscape and pure mood.

An "eventful" dramatic shot can engender its own music through the plastic nature of its composition in exactly the same way.

For landscape, as we have shown, is least of all a catalog of trees, lakes, and mountain tops.

Landscape is a complex bearer of the possibilities of a plastic interpretation of emotion.

And if a tragic scene in its narrowly plastic form is not at the same time a unique "tragic landscape" understood emotionally, then a major portion of the effect of the scene will disperse like smoke.

For not only is a pure – almost abstract – emotional effect of mood accessible to landscape.

A strong dramatic effect is just as accessible to a no less degree.

And there is even more to this.

Landscape can serve as a concrete image of the embodiment of whole cosmic conceptions, whole philosophic systems.

The numerous series of Chinese landscapes of the tenth, eleventh, twelfth centuries, and especially the compositions painted for the emperor (Sung dynasty, 960–1127) by Huang Ch'üan (919–65) show us a piece of craggy mountains, a broken tree, some other details, and, in the middle of them turned three-quarters from us, with his gaze directed into the depths of the picture, is the figure of a sage, standing, sitting, or resting, with his head leaning on his curved arm.

If one mentally traces the direction of the gaze of this figure of the sage, then, while passing over the vague outlines of vegetation, valleys, and mountain contours, this gaze inevitably turns out to be directed at "nothing" – at the actually *white background* of the picture, free of the slightest hint of objects or their depictions!

A certain special cosmic calm wafts from these pictures. Just as with the somnolent smile of Buddha in sculpture or in figurative painting, this type of *paysage*, in part of a landscape painting, probably is the greatest of all possible approaches to the experience of that immersion into "nothing," which the Indian East designates with the word "nirvana.". . .

And this is not by accident,

for the white space in the field of the picture, toward which the gaze of the sage is directed, is certainly not a part left for the text of a greeting, the program of a performance, or a menu; the combination of this spot with the gaze of the sage, directed toward it out of all the "bustling" variety of nature, is, according to the artist's conception, a symphony of the sage's immersion into himself, into self-contemplation and through this into the original Nothing, which has given birth to Everything. . .

The philosophically directed mind of the Chinese found this canon of representation for the embodiment of the bases of his worldview.

He consolidated it into the traditional type of landscape picture.

This immersion into self, into the "great Nothing," which at the same time "gives birth to Everything," is, of course, basically a poetic interpretation of that exalted state that seizes every person when he remains completely alone with nature. In such moments an unusual feeling seizes him like a dissolution in nature and a union with it, and in this feeling there seems to him to be a removal of the contradictions between the universal and the individual, usually opposing each other, just as man opposes the landscape.

The opposition of man and nature occurs very sharply in those cases when, besides everything else, man turns out to be alien to the given landscape – for example, when coming from another region.

D. H. Lawrence wrote very beautifully about this in application to America,[122] simultaneously noting both the yearning for union and the palliative form in which James Fenimore Cooper strove to realize this*:

...The American landscape has never been at one with the white man. Never. And white men have probably never felt so bitter anywhere, as here in America, where the very landscape in its very beauty, seems a bit devilish and grinning, opposed to us.

Cooper, however, glosses over this resistance, which in actuality can never quite be glossed over. He *wants* the landscape to be at one with him. So he goes away to Europe and sees it as such. It is a sort of vision.

And, nevertheless, that unity will surely take place – some day.

Dostoyevsky has separate moments of similar illumination in the unity of harmony, having described them with the words of Kirillov in *The Devils*:

"...There are moments, no more than five or six, and you suddenly feel the presence of eternal harmony, totally accessible...," etc.

* See D. H. Lawrence, *Studies in Classic American Literature*, New York, 1923 [reprinted by Penguin, 1977]; chapter entitled "Fenimore Cooper's Leatherstocking Novels."

George Sand writes something similar:

...There are moments when I crawl out of myself, when I live in vegetation, when I feel like the grass, the birds, the top of a tree, a cloud, running water, the horizon, a flower, form and feelings, changing, transforming, indistinct; moments when I run, fly, swim, drink the dew, spread out in the sun, sleep under the foliage, fly with the swallows, crawl with the lizards, twinkle with the stars and planets, when I, in short, live in what composes the milieu of evolution, seeming to appear as the extension of one's own being..., [etc.] (*Impressions et Souvenirs*).

The example of the same mutual dissolution into each other, but with the interpretation that nature enters into man and dissolves in him, is given us by Maupassant in the words of Paul Bretin (*Mont-Oriol*):

...I think, sir, that I am quite open, that everything enters into me, forces me to cry or gnash my teeth. Well now, when I look at that slope opposite us, at this large green fold, at these hordes of trees climbing up the mountain, the whole forest in my eyes; it penetrates all of me, seizes me, flows in my blood, and I even think that I am eating it, that it fills my insides; I myself have become the forest (Guy de Maupassant)...

In a more aggressive shade, we find that same motif in the words of Courbet,[123] addressing a journalist at the moment when he came out of St. Pelage prison.* He wanted to "seize the earth of the fields by the handful, smell it, kiss it, taste it, bang against the belly of the trees with his stomach, throw stones into the meadows, eat, devour nature."†

And to complete the examples, we could bring in Tolstoy's Pierre Bezukhov:

...High in the bright sky stood the full moon. The forests and fields outside the camp, invisible before, were revealed now in the distance. And even farther, beyond these forests and fields, the bright, wavering, endless distance was seen calling to you. Pierre glanced at the sky, into the depths of the playful, twinkling stars. "And all this is mine, and all of this is within me, and all of this is me!" thought Pierre. "And they caught all of this and put it into a shed boarded up with planks." He smiled and began to lie down to sleep with his comrades...‡

We will not study the nature of this extreme feeling and the psychological predispositions for it in any more detail. This is a separate topic I studied a long time ago in a separate work.

---

* Where Courbet was imprisoned in connection with the affair of the destruction of the Vendome Column.

†["Et, le jour qu'il fut libéré, comme un journaliste le visitait, il lui dit qu'il voudrait 'prendre la terre des champs à poignées, la flairer, la baiser, la mordre, donner des tapes sur le ventre des arbres, jeter des pierres dans des trous d'eau, barboter à même le ruisseau, *manger, dévorer la nature*'..."] Françoise Benoit and Henri Bouchot, *Histoire du paysage en France*, Laurens, Paris, 1908, p. 295].

† *War and Peace*, Vol. IV, pt. II (Russian), Kushnerev, Moscow, 1909.

Here the cited examples are enough if only because, *to a certain extent,* such a feeling is not strange to any of us. However, none of us has begun to make metaphysical calculations and conclusions from this. Moreover, we especially experience this feeling, not only in its early "pantheistic" form but in its highest and most perfect form – on the social stages of development.

This is what the feeling of merging with the collective and merging with class is like; the experience of indestructible unity with one's nation, with the best part of humanity as a whole.

We experience these great moments, and God knows how many times this has happened during the last years of the trials of our Homeland – in the moments of the greatest upheavals, when "human fates, national fates" are decided by history.

This feeling strengthens us in sorrow, it pours new strength into us in years of misfortune, it makes us indestructible in days of battle, it causes us to rejoice in moments of Victory.

And in these great moments, the narrow frame of personal life, of personal fate, of the personality itself seems to open up and to experience the greatest joy of ecstasy in merging with the collective:

whether we build, whether we go into attack, whether we rejoice, meeting the heroes of the world war.

From the heights of these feelings we can also fully understand and imagine this historical, evolutionary, precursory form of the ecstatic feeling of merging with nature.

On those stages this is the only conceivable form of achieving harmony.

On all such stages lies the same imprint of *pathos* – it is all the same whether it be in a rebellious representation of the active removal of oppositions or in the lyric feeling of the passive dissolution of opposites into each other.

And here at one "pole" stands the active *pathos* of the Spaniard, at the other – the East, immersed in the self-dissolution of nirvana.

But in both there is basically the same psychological phenomenon of the apparent removal of the contradiction between nature and the individual – from where the concept about the removal of contradictions from any pair of opposites in general was born.

However, the forms are different.

Unrepeatable.

Unique.

History forms the pervading tendency.

The forms are the stage of development of social formations.

And at every stage the artist prophesies about this with his own tongue.

We have already written above concerning Chinese painting that landscape is largely a portrait, and very often a self-portrait applying to oneself and dissolving the person in oneself.

And is this not the source of the perfection of this organic development of musical landscape into an image of the musical nature of a human portrait?

Is this not the source of the unexpected harmony of the plastic images of the portrait of man and the plastic art of the landscape in *Ivan the Terrible*, although location and the studio were shot by such remarkable but still so profoundly different masters as Moskvin and Tisse!

We traced this process in Eastern painting from the invisible coexistence of man and landscape in a plastic metaphor, from the visible – in the traditional landscape drawing of the philosopher immersed in a contemplation of nature, and from the material – in the landscape of the painted kimono that clothes a real person.

Everywhere this was the emotional landscape, dissolving into itself the human being, or more precisely:

Everywhere the emotional landscape turns out to be an image of the mutual absorption of man and nature one into the other.

And in this particular sense, the actual principle of emotional landscape bears the imprint of the inspiration of *pathos*.

And it is characteristic that even in the West one of the first "pure" landscapes, that is, one from where for the first time the real representation of human semblance has slipped away, and out of all the examples that have come down to us, is possibly the most ardent self-portrait of the "soul" of a human being – its creator.

This is El Greco's *Storm over Toledo*.

In addition, one must have in mind that this principle of "self-portraiture" in landscape certainly does not occur everywhere and is certainly not "obligatory."

Typical, for example, are the watercolor landscapes of Dürer belonging to a somewhat earlier epoch.

In the interests of "objectivity" I will provide a brief characterization from a very voluminous chapter about the landscape in Dürer from one of the best works on him by Wilhelm*:

...Dürer's landscape is reality seen and, as painters say, "understood"; next to them the landscapes of Altdorfer[124] seem dreamt up and full of emotion. Dürer does not have gigantic pines whose ancient crowns rock with the mountain winds – he sees the mountains geologically and illustrates them as the result of the movement of the earth's core. At a time when the mountains of Wolf Huber[125] seem petrified explosions of subterranean fountains...

Here the following idea is also interesting (in the light of further deliberation):

* Wilhelm Waetzoldt, *Dürer und seine Zeit*, Phaidon–Verlag, Vienna, 1935.

...The combination of portraits with pieces of landscape was viewed as Dürer's originality, which deserved special praise.

However, Dürer certainly does not reveal a new area of compositional concepts in this combination of large, closely arranged faces with a landscape background painted very small. Heads and landscapes are placed here without any connection between them. The landscape is put simply where there happens to be free space next to the head that has already been drawn...

This basically relates to Dürer's sketches during his journey to the Netherlands, from where, properly speaking, his reputation as a "landscape artist" begins.

The lack of any "subjectivity" in Dürer's landscapes strikes you particularly when comparing them with van Gogh's, especially since, purely in terms of subject matter, they are frequently somewhat similar – roofs, little houses, prows of ships: for example, the sheds and tree in Dürer's watercolor *Ansich von Kalchreut* and [...]* of van Gogh...

But Waetzoldt is entirely wrong when he consider's Dürer a predecessor of van Gogh on the basis of a similar subject matter in both painters! In his misguided consideration, he refers to the sharp-prowed ships in the drawing of the estuary of the Sheld near Antwerp.

In silhouette they are actually similar to the very famous picture of van Gogh's – but what is more striking is the contrast between the cool objectivity of Dürer's sketch and the flaming self-dissolution in van Gogh's landscape, where a stroke or trace of a dab coils like the tortured clump of snakes on Medusa's head.

That same ardent subjectivity, as if rearing up, twists the stone pillars of the crags resembling the contours of monks in the almost delirious landscapes of Goya,† which seem like a copy of another landscape miracle from under the brush of El Greco – his *Mountains of Sinai* (1571–6).

This is where one could truly overturn the old formula of naturalism that says that "art is nature seen through a temperament"‡ and say that art is a "temperament bursting through nature."

However, for an emotional landscape it makes no difference from which end one reads this formula, for in the miracle of a genuinely emotional landscape we have a total unity in the mutual interpenetration of nature and man with all the overflowing variety of his temperament.

A typical example of this is one of the first independent and thematically self-contained landscapes in art history – the famous *Storm over Toledo*, which has already been mentioned.

---

* Missing in manuscript.
† The so-called *Landscape with Two Trees* and *The Landscape with a Waterfall*.
‡ "L'art c'est la nature vue à travers un tempérament" (Zola).

At least this current of boiling lava acts in exactly this way, erupting from the bubbling volcano of the very soul of the great Toledoan.

I will not describe the effects of this picture, resembling a mountain avalanche crashing down on anyone who has the great fortune to approach it in the halls of the New York museum.

Let the confirmation of what has been said be the vivid impression of another viewer, another epoch, another country, other efforts, other ideals – out of various authors I will cite at random Hugo Kehrer from his monograph on El Greco (1914):

In 1614 when, in my opinion, death already was extending its bony hands toward him, El Greco painted Toledo in a storm. He wanted to reproduce once again before us those tragic theatrical stages on which he experienced his moments of illumination, and where he shuddered before the horrors of Hell and the Day of Judgment. Darkness envelops the landscape around Toledo, flashes of lightning blind us, clouds tormented by storms rush past us. We are penetrated by the fear of the mysterious unknown and of the forces of nature full of demonic dread. We feel the inner laceration of El Greco, his soul deprived of peace, totally in the power of tireless rebellious unrest, pressure, bursts of passion.

With the strength of primeval power, he forces us to experience with him this grandiose spectacle, and like a tornado, he attracts us into the inner storm of his soul. For this is simultaneously a dream conceived by his scorched fantasy and embodied in the powerful duel of light and dark through this landscape image of the destruction of worlds...

With the infallible precision of a sleepwalker's movements, El Greco paints the lightning, how it creeps along, burning homes, churches, and bridges. Everything is lost in this dizzy summer lightning: forms spread, running into ephemeralness. The spirit obeys the material completely and turns nature into the image of its own experience. In the foreground, the painter's brush bursts into flames, burning up what is concrete; the crags lose their sharp outline and strict form, no longer crumbling into stone, but they acquire a velvety fluidity and seem to be lit by a light from within.

Thus everything concrete dissolves, becoming the grandiose embodiment of the inner states of El Greco. While raising this piece of nature to an expression of the metaphysical idea of the essence of the universe, he at the same time testifies to his complete rupture with reality...*

We know that in the last years of his life, El Greco was seized by madness.

[...] Some three centuries later that same cruel and, it would seem, barren, ascetic Spanish earth once more gives birth to a frenzied artist, with no less fury smashing the visible world and once more fusing it together in the image and likeness of his imagination, according to the laws guiding his own inner worldview.

Picasso!

* Dr. Hugo Kehrer, *Die Kunst des Greco*, Schmidt, Munich, 1914, pp. 83–4.

Figure 26. *The Bull* by Pablo Picasso, 1934.

We can see why the bullfight is still alive today in Spain.

For the image of the matador, who in the simultaneous attempt of the bull and man to rush at each other, pierces with his sword like a flash of lightning into the blackness splashed with foam, the blackness of the fiery element of the horned monster that, according to tradition, once kidnapped Europa – and damn it, I understand Europa's yielding to this black devil who tramples everything with his hoofs – this is simultaneously the image of both great Spaniards, El Greco and Pablo Picasso.

They also both seem to be, not for life, but for death (the sword – for the bull or the horn – for the matador!), grappling with nature itself; also, in the same way the horn or sword penetrate each other; they penetrated each other in a similar great moment of the mutual merging of life and death, bull and man, instinct and craft: animal nature and the art of man!

The merging in the unity of Man and Beast!

Through death.

Hegel calls love the feeling in which "isolation undergoes negation," and as a result "the single image perishes, not having the strength to be preserved..."*

To perish there – to perish here.

* Hegel, *The Philosophy of Nature*, Sotzekgiz, Moscow – Leningrad, 1934, p. 513.

Here – in death, just as there in love – in the twinkling of one radiant moment – solitude and isolation perish.

But in this case the payment for this merging into one is not the destruction of a self-seeking "solitary image" completely dissolving; in this case life is the payment.

The horn pierces man.

Or: Shining steel pierces the animal.

There is no other way out.

The price – is to perish.

The reckoning – is blood.

For a moment of freedom, rumbling in the roar of the many thousands in the excited crowd, in the bloody moment of this sacrifice, that experiences a moment of liberation from the age-old stress of contraries.

Even if the price be blood, man merges with beast.

Even if the price be life, the barriers separating them into distinct categories are torn down.

And this is what composes the great magic of this bloody spectacle.

Otherwise, what composed the magnetic strength of this spectacle, except the single roar uniting thousands of the multitude amid the quivering walls of the circus on the sunny days of the bullfight.

But this liberation is momentary, fleeting.

And what is worse, it is imaginary.

For true freedom grows out of another's sacrificial blood.

And only through a real abolishing of class contradictions – in the real miracle of a classless society – is spiritual freedom from the oppression of contradictions possible, just as a freedom from oppression, force, and social enslavement is both morally and physically possible only in this situation.

For ages humanity has been striving toward this, but, not yet having matured socially, not yet having matured to the heights of a socialist re-creation of the universe, it seeks an escape, through its striving, in palliative forms of another type of *pathos*.

And along the path of an imaginary abolishing of contradictions in an ecstatic experience of *pathos*, man achieves what is a presentiment of the final aim of his efforts – the destruction of the social contradictions that has been approaching since the fall of tribal structure.

This unquenchable desire finds a temporary satisfaction in the *pathos* of artworks and art forms.

However, the embodiment of the ideal is smashed on the rocks of historical prematurity.

And thus is born the tragedy of new contradictions between striving and possibility.

The materialistic wing of Hegel's followers has given its energy to the creation of the actual possibilities of realizing this dream.

The idealistic wing has given its energy to the glorification of its strivings.

And the followers of the idealistic line of Hegel's teachings cannot interpret the basic essence of these strivings other than through images of metaphysics and...mysticism.

And they write about Picasso in the same way.

Thus, for example, Fritz Burger* says:

...Here in Picasso we encounter forms of mysticism very directly, which the arts had dared not attempt until now. For mysticism...is not only opposite to, but is simply in its very essence alien to the system of logical division. It immerses the understanding into night and nonbeing. In the place of a divided unity, it raises the chaos of night, in which the beauty of form perishes...In its impatience with everything that is realized according to categories, here the general tries to swallow all possible distinctions. And where a logical attempt is directed toward differentiating everything so that each separate item acquires its own independent form, here the mystical striving achieves an absolute merging and devouring of oppositions. Mysticism is essentially alien to the principle of opposition, contrast, negation...If you consider the most profound essence of mysticism, then its position leads to quiet silence in the boundless fullness of religious experience...

For mysticism, the unity of opposites, which is the soul of the dialectic, is not in the active process of battle and mutual penetration, as *the basis of eternal movement*, but in their mutual devouring of each other, that is, in the metaphysical ideal of the static immersement in eternal peace.

...Picasso's images are, therefore, essentially not capable of being pretty or even connected with features of individual concreteness or with the expression of any inner spiritual potential. For the nature of mysticism consists of this indifference to the individual. The intellectual opposition of figure and space, the organic and inorganic, are subjected here to the attempt for complete estrangement, and before us we have the numbing chaos of crystals piled up one upon the other... (pp. 124–5)

There is no need for us to polemicize with Burger. What we have already said speaks for itself.

And to what has been said above one should only add one consideration of the unavoidable social tragedy of Picasso's position, as Max Raphael does[†]:

"...The inner division of Picasso was revealed as early as his 'blue' period; here it is partially revealed through the strong opposition of spatially limited figures (or groups) and an unlimited background..."

Picasso's passion for achieving unity forces him to fling himself from

---

* *Cezanne und Holder*, Delphin-Verlag, Munich, 1923.
[†] In his book *Proudon, Marx, Picasso – Trois etudes sur la sociologie de l'art*, Editions Excelsior, Paris, 1933.

extreme to extreme; from the "mystical" dissolution of one thing in another to a dominating concreteness and objectivity:

"...Now corporality merges with the background and is lost in it, and this is a symbol of the metaphysical absolute, and then, on the contrary, three-dimensional space dominates, and three-dimensional bodies symbolizing the material and earthly move into the foreground..." (p. 216)

In the most recent stage of his path of development these tendencies are defined more sharply.

The method of mutual penetration of bodies and space by a mutual effect on each other through different dimensions or opposite directions (upward–downward, foreground–background, right–left) is not sufficient to reproduce the actual concreteness of true reality. And Picasso finally solves this problem for himself by a unique squaring of a circle.

"In addition to the most abstract (illusory) spatial interrelationships, he applies real materials outside of art (wallpaper, pearls, wood, letters, etc.). Here Picasso encounters the most decisive problem within any ideology: the problem of idealism and materialism. However, the paradox forcing idealism to sound so abstract and materialism to sound so literal cannot be looked on as a solution to the problem, but just the opposite, it testifies to the complete impotence in finding such a solution..."

Picasso's method does not achieve a unity of both areas – the abstract and the concrete – but emphasizes just the reverse – a factual division, even more emphasized by a paradoxically forced approach of refined "opposition."

"...The increased emphasis of separate poles distinctly points to Picasso's inner turmoil without elements of dialectical possibilities and, on the other hand, the limitations of the boundaries of his idealism clearly seen from the material point of view. Both these facts are very closely connected and have a huge social significance..." (pp. 215–16)

It is interesting to note how this sign of bifurcation hovers over all of Picasso's activity right up to the present.

We know of his magnificent behavior during the revolution in Spain, his noble position during the occupation of France.

Finally, we see him decisively joining Communism as a member of the Party.

And yet the imprint of division is still apparent in him. We cited Burger's words referring to 1923. Raphael wrote in 1933. And here is testimony concerning the same thing relating to our own day.

In the April (1945) edition of the London journal *Cornhill Magazine*, there is a conversation between Picasso and the director of the Tate Gallery, John Rothenstein, after Picasso visited him in Paris*:

---

* I am citing the American magazine *Time* of May 7, 1945 (No. 19). The article: "Picasso at Home." Report of John Kewstub Rothenstein, director of the Tate Gallery, London.

...I asked him whether he did not find that there was something anomalous in the position of an artist, however illustrious, whose work was, after all, understood by relatively few, being publicly identified with a popular party, and whether revolutionary art, such as his, was not at bottom even resented by the revolutionary masses.

"There is just such a want of accord between the two revolutionary forces," he conceded. "But life isn't a very logical business, is it? As for me, I have to act as I feel, both as an artist and as a man..."

This profound dissociation of the revolutionary artist and the revolutionary man is very significant here, although his revolutionary decisiveness in both spheres evokes our admiration.

And we see that together with the achievement of inner harmony and unity, here we have before us just such an example of *tragic pathos.* Inner bifurcation, which in varying periods of history permeates the temperaments of great creators, doomed to live in such social conditions and epochs does not permit unity and harmony. Perhaps it is surprising to place in the same rank with the wonderful life-confirming temperament of Picasso...the figures in Michelangelo, Wagner, Victor Hugo. But basically the same inner contradiction is found.

In another place, in connection with the production of *Die Walküre,* I wrote about this bifurcation in Wagner, embodied in the tragic divided figure of Wotan...

The particular forms of the expression of Michelangelo's inner division within the plastic features of his sculpture has been noted by Ekhardt von Zydow[*]:

...If you look at his whole life, then you will be struck by the richness of ideas, projects, passionate beginnings, all full of an inflamed desire for glory. Nothing was too great for him – by the sculptor's chisel he wanted to turn mountains into images of human beauty. Nothing was foreign to him – being a sculptor, at the same time he created Rome's greatest paintings. Nothing was too insignificant for him: He followed the work of the stone cutters and the transport of stone blocks, but if one looks at his creations, then we will see fragments, unfinished beginnings, unrealized conceptions everywhere. Of course, the period itself did not provide much help to him: the change of popes, the chaos of wars, the caprice of clients. However, the basic guilt for the fragmentary incompleteness of his works must be borne by Michelangelo himself.[†] Eternally disturbed, eternally dissatisfied with himself and others, his temperament pursued him from one unfinished work to another. He worked not because it gave him joy – like Goethe, moving through his creativity beyond the frame of his own being – but as if driven, incited and torn by his own genius, as if by an alien force..."

[*] In the book *Die Kultur der Dekadenz,* Sibylen-Verlag, Berlin, 1922.
[†] See Romain Rolland, *Vie de Michel-Ange,* Hachetter, Paris, 1914.

A similar inner torment passes through the images of his sculpture. "...They are full of an inner conflict bursting out of them like an irreconciled opposition."

A. Riegl[*] captures fairly well this complexity. He reveals in an analysis of the structure of the figures *Night* and *Day* that a certain rotational movement lies at their bases,[†] a movement "that possesses that uniqueness in which all elements participating in it are found in movement without the whole moving; absolute peace – the absolute immobility of the parts...Figures as a whole are sitting, sleeping, but all the separate members are totally put out of balance..."

The author sees this as the reason for the indistinct behavior of Michelangelo's sculptural figures, an indistinctness that at times allows directly opposite interpretations, beginning with Moses; the moment in which he has been caught, in spite of the mountains of interpretation, has remained insoluble even today: It is unknown at what moment he appears before you – ready to jump in rage, simply staring excitedly, by sheer force of will forcing himself to remain seated. And this is true right up to the Madonna of the Medici Chapel, with such a strong opposition between the aesthetic assertiveness of the infant, who has grabbed his mother's breast, and the tragic despondency of the Madonna, a despondency worthy "rather of the goddess of Death."

Besides this inner antithesis of both figures (here it is probably appropriate, even thematically), here there is that same dynamically rotary arrangement of basic planes of one section of the whole group that again recalls Riegl's observation about the uniqueness of the movement of Michelangelo's sculptural figures.

We find the latter particularly interesting, and this is why our V. Serov borrowed the scheme of this mutual dynamic play of planes from this very sculptural group in 1904 for the compositional solution of the problem of Maxim Gorky's portrait.

This has been cleverly proved by L. Dintses in the article "V. Serov's Portrait of M. Gorky."[‡]

He notes how, thanks to this, M. Gorky's figure, originally conceived in two planes, "energetically developed in a spiral movement, destroying the boundaries of the canvas and attracting the viewer to itself..."

Perhaps even here, in these planes of a section seen from extremely different angles, one can catch cinematic features – a certain resemblance to the piling on of shots, this time taken not from above

---

[*] A. Riegl, *Die Entstehung der Barock-Kunst in Rom*, Schroll, Wien, 1908, pp. 35–6.
[†] Circular movement, characteristic of the so-called pairs of forces, is formed as a result of the fact that two equal forces pulling in two different directions are placed toward the ends of a balanced lever.
[‡] See the preface to the second volume of the publication of the Academy of Sciences, *M. Gorky. Materials and Research*, Academy of Sciences, Moscow, 1936.

downward, but in a strong conflict of setups, as if shooting running figures from all sides.

However, returning to Michelangelo, it is interesting to note that a similar "bifurcation" is embodied in literature in almost exactly the same way. The living witness of this is the endless list of antitheses into which any page of Victor Hugo's prose breaks up.

Take any convenient place from *The Ninety-third Year*. From any page of it, beginning with the antithesis of Goven and Simerden,[126] an unrestrained stream of an unreconciled series of oppositions rushes at you, hoping for an unattainable fusion in the *pathos* of the author, who was not given the opportunity socially and historically to fuse them into a unity.

But the phenomenon of bifurcation is so powerful that the aging Hugo was, in general, incapable of expressing himself outside the structure of antithesis.

Paul Gsell, in a book of his conversations with Anatole France, introduced an interesting recollection of France's about Hugo:

This was at the time when we founded *Parnasse*. We often met at the publisher Lemaitre – Coppée,[127] Leconte de Lisle,[128] Catulle Mendes,[129] and I – and the first number of our journal had to appear as soon as possible. We were looking for what might attract the attention of the universe to our newly born infant.

One of us, I no longer remember who, suggested asking Victor Hugo for a letter-preface. He was then in exile in Guernsey.

We grabbed the idea with great enthusiasm. And we immediately addressed a letter to the famous exile.

Several days later we received an unusual epistle:

"Young people, I am – the past, you – the future. I – only a leaf, you – the forest. I – nothing more than a candle, but you are the Magi. I – no more than a stream, you – an ocean. I – no more than a molehill, you – the Alps. I am only..."etc., etc.

It continued in this manner for all of four pages and was signed with the name V. Hugo.

The young writers doubted the authenticity of the letter.

They suspected a trick or a joke by the police censor, and made an inquiry of Hugo's closest friend, Juliette Drouet, who was living at the time "at the feet of her divinity." In her answer, the "poor woman" affirmed the authenticity of the letter. ...She was even surprised by our doubts since finally, she wrote, his genius simply stands out from all four pages of his letter!*

A more felicitous epoch, a more fortunate talent for the same talent in more felicitous moments of their creation – when they rise higher than just a reflection of their age to stages of prophetic foresight – are able to achieve an inner harmony through the organic wholeness of their works.

The social usefulness of such creations is that, while appearing as

---

* *Les matinées de la Villa Saïd: Propos d'Anatole France recueillis par Paul Gsell*, Grasset, Paris, 1921.

forms of harmony, they incandesce the striving inherent in the people to create a similar harmony in the actual reality of their social existence and environment.

However, their final social value is determined by whether they summon such creations to an immersion in the contemplation of possible harmony and inactive dreaming about it, or they summon them to "establishing," really and actively, a harmony of social justice where there is a chaos of social contradictions.

The objective value of the first, of course, strongly yields to the second or, in any case, lies like a shadow on the artistic perfection that the first can achieve.

This forces one to assign them rather to creations of a religious type, where there apparently is that same attempt to remove contradictions, but even in the best cases they are understood only as a compromise, and more in the area of "spirit" than in the area of concrete reality, connected with our sinful flesh.

The small human value of all this apparently occurs because such an imagined abstract spiritual feeling of harmony neither demands a system of complex psychological exercises for self-immersion into ecstasy nor complex attributes for achieving the effect of the "opium of the people" – not even opium is necessary for this – nitrous oxide is sufficient.

Actually, the fictional and imaginary liberation from contradictions can be achieved by a very simple means. This has been tested and described most recently by William James[130] in his work:

...It is impossible to convey an idea of the torrential character of the identification of opposites as it streams through the mind in this experience. I have sheet after sheet of phrases dictated or written during the intoxication, which to the sober reader seem meaningless drivel, but which at the moment of transcribing were fused in the fire of infinite rationality. God and devil, good and evil, life and death, I and thou, sober and drunk, matter and form, black and white, quantity and quality, shiver of ecstasy and shudder of horror, vomiting and swallowing, inspiration and expiration, fate and reason, great and small, extent and intent, joke and earnest, tragic and comic, and fifty other contrasts figure in these pages in the same monotonous way.*

In *The Varieties of Religious Experience*,† James returns to the same topic in great detail:

...The keynote of it is invariably a reconciliation. It is as if the opposites of the world, whose contradictoriness and conflict make all our difficulties and troubles, were melted into unity. Not only do they, as contrasted species, belong

* From William James, *The Will to Believe and Other Essays in Popular Philosophy*, Longmans Green, New York, 1917, pp. 295–6.
† [Modern Library, New York, 1936 – HM.]

to one and the same genus, but *one of the species*, the nobler and better one, *is itself the genus, and so soaks up and absorbs its opposite into itself.* This is a dark saying, I know, when thus expressed in terms of common logic, but I cannot wholly escape from its authority. I feel as if it must mean something, something like what the Hegelian philosophy means, if one could only lay hold of it more clearly...[!]

Thus art is divided in two by the difference in the aim that it sets for itself.

One branch of it is the branch of abstract dream, which merges with religious dream and through this "opium for the people" borders on hashish, vodka, and nitrous oxide.

The other, through powerful images of an active dream about the re-creation of the world, merges with the sparkling pleiad of social thinkers – from the Utopians to the pillars of scientific Marxism.

However, unusual phenomena can appear in art that are similar to the dual mythological beings of antiquity, which in Greece combined horse and man into the Centaur, bull and man into the Minotaur, and in India or Egypt, man and elephant, hippopotamus, crocodile, hawk,...

However, they most of all resemble the two-faced Janus of antiquity.

For one face of theirs – the creator-artist – looks powerfully into the future, and the other face – the preacher and teacher – is turned to the past, to what has been overcome, experienced, to what has hopelessly vanished – and to see the features of the imagined golden age of the future.

Balzac was like this in many ways.

Tolstoy also to an even greater extent.

And in this sense, the great reproach of history is again Tolstoy.

We will not cite the very famous words of Engels on Balzac.

We will not introduce excerpts from the classical works of V. I. Lenin on Tolstoy.

But let us introduce on this occasion the fairly detailed excerpt from Korolenko's article, "Lev Nikolaevich Tolstoy" (the first article, 1908).

On the background of other works on Tolstoy it is less quoted than others, but the nature of it comes very close to what we are concerned with here:

...Tolstoy says (if I am not mistaken, in *Confessions*) that at this time he was close to suicide. But here on a cheerless cross-roads, Tolstoy the artist extends his helping hand to the tormented Tolstoy the thinker, and rich fantasy raises before him the picture of a new spiritual spontaneity and harmony. He sleeps and sees a dream. The burning sandy desert. A cluster of unknown people in the simple clothes of antiquity stand under the sun's rays and wait. He stands with them, with his present feeling of spiritual thirst, but he is dressed as they are. He also is a simple Israelite of the first century, waiting in the sultry desert for the words of the great teacher of life...

And now *he*, this teacher, goes up the sandy hill and begins to speak. He speaks the simple words of the evangelical teachings, and they immediately instill his peace into the confused and thirsting souls.

This had taken place. This means above all it could be imagined. And the moving and clear imagination of the great artist was at his service. He *himself* stood at the hill, *himself* saw the teacher, and with other Israelites of the first century, he experienced the charm of this divine preaching...Now he preserves this spiritual system, into whose sphere his prophetic artistic dream had flung him, and unfolds it before the people. And this will be the benevolent new era of Tolstoy, essentially the old Christian faith which it is necessary to extract in the Gospel from under the most recent layer, as gold from under slag. Tolstoy reads the Gospel, ponders the original texts of the Vulgate,[131] studies the ancient Hebrew language...But this study is not the research of an objective scholar, ready to recognize the conclusions from the facts, whatever they may turn out to be. This is the passionate attempt of an artist to begin, no matter how, to restore the spiritual structure of the first Christians and the harmony of the simple, uncomplicated Christian faith which he experienced in his imagination. At the time, as the feeling of welfare and peace descended on him in a prophetic dream, he was an Israelite of the first century. But then – he remains one until the end. This is not difficult for him: a rich imagination at his service giving him the power of reality. That is first. And secondly, a deficiency which was also of service to his artistic mental outlook, which we spoke of above.

Tolstoy the artist knows, feels, and sees only two poles of agricultural Russia. His artistic world is the world of a rich agricultural system and its poor Lazaruses.[132] Here there are also virtuous Boazes and poor Ruths,[133] and unjust tsars taking away the little vineyard from the peasant. But there is neither independent city life, factories, plants, nor capital squeezed from labor, nor labor deprived not only of a vineyard, but of his own home, nor trusts, nor trade unions, nor political demands, nor class wars, nor strikes...

This means that nothing of this is necessary for the only blessing on earth – spiritual harmony. Love is necessary. The good, rich Boaz allowed poor Ruth to collect ears of corn in his cornfield. The widow humbly collects the ears...And God arranged everything for the blessing of both...Love is necessary, and not trade unions and strikes...Let everyone love each other...Is it not clear that then heaven will settle on this perturbed earth...

Tolstoy is a great artist, and Tolstoy also is a thinker, showing humanity the path to a new life. It is not strange that he never tried to write his *Utopia*, that is, to portray in concrete, visible forms the future society built on the principles he preached. I think this apparent peculiarity is explained quite simply. Tolstoy does not require any new social forms for his future society. *His utopia* – is partly *in retrospect*...the simple village life, which remains only to be penetrated by the principles of the *original* Christianity. All complications and superimposed structures of the most recent centuries must disappear of themselves. Tolstoy's city in its organization would in no way be distinguished from what we see now.

This would be a simple Russian village, those same cottages, those same log walls, the roofs would be thatched with that same straw and the same way of life would reign inside the village world. Only everybody would love each other. Therefore, there would be no poor widows, no one would offend orphans, the authorities would not rob. Cottages would be spacious and clean, the corn bins wide and full, the cattle strong and well-fed, fathers wise and benevolent, children good and obedient. There would be no factories or plants, universities or high schools at all. There would be no "trade unions," there would be no politics, there would be no sickness, there would be no doctors and, óf course, there would be no governors, police chiefs, policemen, or "authority" in general.

It might be this way in the world if people wanted to obey the Israelite of the first century of our era who himself heard the words of the great teacher from the hill in the midst of the sandy desert...He heard him so clearly, even if it was only in a prophetic dream!

I think I am not mistaken: in this *image*, which Tolstoy the artist presented to Tolstoy the thinker, and in the attempt of the thinker to develop in concrete form the feeling of benevolent spiritual harmony wafted to him in a dream, after the harmony attracted all the people to this dream – this is what composes both the law and the vice of Tolstoy the thinker and moralist. Here is the astonishing strength, and here is his no less astonishing weakness.

The strength is in the criticism of our system from the point of view of Christian principles recognized by this system. The weakness is in the inability to find his bearings in the confusion of this system, from which he wishes to show us the way out...*

Another branch of the thinking intellectuals of the nineteenth century looked at these questions in another way.

For them the golden age was pictured not as a return to a past that has vanished but as the energetic laying down of a road leading to its realization in the future.

Shchedrin writes:

...In the forties Russian literature was divided into two camps: the Westerners and the Slavophiles. At that time I had just left the school bench and, raised on Belinsky's articles, naturally joined the Westerners. But not the majority, who were busy popularizing German philosophy, but that unknown circle which instinctively stuck to France, not to the France of Louis Philippe,[134] and Guizot,[135] but to the France of Saint-Simon,[136] Cabet,[137] Fourier,[138] Louis Blanc,[139] and especially George Sand. A belief in humanity flowed to us from here, from here shone the confidence that the golden age can be found not *behind us*, but *ahead of us*.†

However, it was not for his outmoded criticism that we disturbed the great shadow of Tolstoy the preacher.

But in order to observe, long before his "departure" from Yasnaya Polyana,‡ how in an artistic image, through the magnificence of his

---

* See V. G. Korolenko, *Collected Works in 10 Volumes*, Vol. 8, Goslitizdat, Moscow, 1955, pp. 105–07.
† Shchedrin, *Abroad*, IV, in *Collected Works* (Russian) Gos. Tzd. Khud. Lit. Moscow, 1950.
‡ [His country estate – HM.]

immortal genius, appears the same tendency of a predestined departure from reality for the Elysian Fields of ancient harmony, with its ideals of the eternal rotation of nature and the unities of the living and existing dissolving in it.

We will linger here only on the fact of how this idea of dissolving in nature is interpreted in artistic images by Tolstoy in his own way, an idea so close to Taoism and Confucianism to which, along with early Christianity, Tolstoy himself was fairly close.

Gorky writes to Korolenko in his letter already cited* concerning Tolstoy's death:

...He spoke about Dostoyevksy unwillingly, with great strain, somehow avoiding the issue or somehow getting the better of it.

He should have become acquainted with the teachings of Confucius or the Buddhists; this would have brought him peace. This is the most important thing everyone must know...

...His foggy preaching of "not doing anything," "non-opposition to evil" – the preaching of pacifism, this is all the unhealthy ferment of old Russian blood, poisoned by Mongolian fatalism...

Such is the nature of the ideal inspiring Tolstoy's preaching, an ideal remaining so far behind.

But my God! How terrible and far from the quiet and humane image of self-dissolution in nature (as India and China of antiquity knew it) is that image through which Tolstoy revives it!

The time is different.

And the embodiment of Confucius' ideals or the Buddhist nirvana have acquired completely different forms in the setting of the police state of the Russia of Pobedonostsev and Nicholas the Bloody. One life and many lives are not enough to establish the foundation for the actual realization of the kingdom of harmony in the land of the Russian nation languishing in chains.

And meanwhile – this fictitious and imagined harmony is possible only in forms of self-annihilation.

Only through self-annihilation is self-dissolution in nature and a return to a single, continuous unity with it possible.

Through self-annihilation.

Through death.

And now almost ten centuries later, the exact same concept of the harmonious merging with nature no longer draws heavenly lyrical images of the Chinese landscape, but "Three Deaths," and to a far greater degree the exciting, tragic end of "Kholstomer." †

* [This is lacking in the final version of Eisenstein's text – Ed.]
† L. Tolstoy, "Kholstomer," in *The Invaders and Other Stories* [N. H. Dale, trans., Crowell, New York, 1887 – HM].

This is how a solitary being, once having left the universe, is included back into it:

That evening the herd passed by the hill; and those who were on the left wing saw a red object below them, and around it some dogs busily romping, and crows and hawks flying over it. One dog, with his paws on the carcass, and shaking his head, was growling over what he was tearing with his teeth. The brown filly stopped, lifted her head and neck, and long sniffed the air. It took force to drive her away.

At sunrise, in a ravine of the ancient forest, in the bottom of an overgrown glade, some wolf-whelps were beside themselves with joy. There were five of them, – four about of a size, and one little one with a head bigger than his body. A lean, hairless shewolf, her belly with hanging dugs almost touching the ground, crept out of the bushes, and sat down in front of the wolves. The wolves sat in a semicircle in front of her. She went to the smallest, and lowering her stumpy tail, and bending her nose to the ground, made a few convulsive motions, and opening her jaws filled with teeth she struggled, and disgorged a great piece of horse flesh.

The larger whelps made a movement to seize it; but she restrained them with a threatening growl, and let the little one have it all. The little one, as though in anger, seized the morsel, hiding it under him, and began to devour it. Then the shewolf disgorged for the second, and the third, and in the same way for all five, and finally lay down in front of them to rest.

At the end of a week there lay behind the brick barn only the great skull, and two shoulder blades; all the rest had disappeared. In the summer a muzhik who gathered up the bones carried off also the skull and shoulder blades, and put them to use.

The dead body of Sierpukhovskoi, who had been about in the world, and had eaten and drunk, was buried long after. Neither his skin nor his flesh nor his bones were of any use.

There is an even more penetrating example. This same idea sounds even more tragic in another ending. By another writer. In the reconciliatory epilogue to the tragic end of another being: the English old maid, whose whole life, its tenor and cast, morals and character, fate and biography were destined to be inaccessibly far from the all-embracing harmony of exultant nature. Thus Maupassant ends his short story "Miss Harriet." Having described the suicide of the poor English old maid, who threw herself into a well because of misunderstood and unrequited love, he writes:

For her everything was over now, and very probably never in her life did she experience the exalted bliss of being loved, nor even a hope of it.

Why else did she hide herself and run away from people? Why did she love nature and animals so tenderly and passionately, in a word, why did she love everything except man? And I understood why she loved God so much and hoped for a reward in the other world. Now she would soon turn into earth and would be reborn in vegetation. She would blossom in the sun, would be eaten by cows and nibbled by birds, and would turn into the flesh of animals and would again pass over into human substance, but what we call the soul would remain at the bottom of the black well. She no longer suffered. She exchanged her life for a whole series of lives into which she would be reborn...*

You will inevitably recall Laertes's tragically sick, lyrical cry of pain over Ophelia's body:

...And from her fair and unpolluted flesh
May violets spring!... (V, 1)

However, perhaps another excerpt from *Hamlet* is more appropriate here that shows how the extremely cruel form of the outcome of the "Human Renaissance" on the same theme contrasts with what the Chinaman of early centuries drew in soft forms of lyric harmony.

KING: Now, Hamlet, where's Polonius?
HAM.: At supper.
KING: At supper? Where?
HAM.: Not where he eats, but where he is eaten. A certain convocation of politic worms are e'en at him. Your worm is your only emperor for diet. We fat all our creatures else to fat us, and we fat ourselves for maggots. Your fat king and your lean beggar is but variable service – two dishes, but to one table. That's the end.
KING: Alas, alas!
HAM.: A man may fish with the worm that hath eat of a king, and eat of the fish that hath fed of that worm.
KING: What doest thou mean by this?
HAM.: Nothing but to show you how a king may go a progress through the guts of a beggar.

(IV, 3)

Thus we see how each stage of history, through the creations of its great representatives, was able to find its own unrepeatable image of expressing one and the same idea of the unity of nature and man! This is the transitional image of an embodiment in art of the idea of what can be actually realized once and for all only in the social re-creation of reality.

What a range of variety: Tolstoy, Picasso, Maupassant, Shakespeare, Hugo, and Hui Tsun.

Each has *his own* image.

And in each image is his epoch's rectification of the basic idea, *his* nuance of the form of embodiment ensuing from *his* understanding and feeling of the decisive theme and idea.

But they were all equally able, although each in his own way, to bring and express through an artistic image the leading philosophical

---

* Guy de Maupassant, "Miss Harriet," in *Short Stories of Guy De Maupassant*, Book League of America, New York, 1941.

conception of their ideas on paths toward the actual realization of these basic universal aspirations for unity and harmony in the future.

The solution in the form of completed productions and in an orderly system of aesthetic teachings of the reality of this principle of unity and harmony must lie on the shoulders of our still young art of cinema.

For the first time in the course of history and the existence of humanity, a social system began to be *ahead* of the creators of artistic works in the solution of these problems.

Here in our country the builders of real life outstripped the creators of artistic values, and before the artists of our country and epoch stands an unprecedented task – not to be above their time, not ahead of it, for neither is impossible here – but to be on a level with and worthy of their time, their epoch, their people.

Our cinema, as the most progressive of the arts, has this great task before it: to reveal in its works that profound unity and harmony, and that profound worldview that our socialist era has brought to humanity.

We have seen how artists of different periods and nations tried through the artistic images of their creations to embody the philosophical conceptions of their time, fashioning out of the elements of a real landscape the artistic image of a basic world outlook.

And involuntarily we recall the poet Novalis,[140] who had written earlier: "Any landscape is the ideal body for the expression of a definite system of thought."*

The philosophical mind accomplishes the reverse, penetrating the real landscape with its outlook.

It interprets images from it, which embody whole systems of philosophical conceptions of the world.

If he is a painter or photographer, he brings them to the canvas or the film, having liberated them from anything obtrusive or incidental.

If he is a philosopher, then he leaves us those same exciting "philosophical landscapes," as the young F. Engels does in his descriptions.

I quote:

On a stormy night, when clouds stream ghostlike past the moon, when dogs bay to one another at a distance, gallop on snorting horses over the endless heath and leap with loose reins over the weathered granite blocks and the burial mounds of the Huns; in the distance the water of the moor glitters in the reflected moonlight, will-o'-the-wisps flit over it, and the howling of the storm sounds eerily over the wide expanse; the ground beneath you is unsafe, and you feel that you have entered the realm of German folklore. Only after I became acquainted with the

* "Chaque paysage est un corps idéal pour un genre particulier de l'esprit" (*Novalis Fragments*).

North-German heathland did I properly understand the Grimm brothers'[141] *Kinder- und Haus-Marchen*. It is evident from almost all these tales that they had their origin here, where at nightfall the human element vanishes and the terrifying, shapeless creations of popular fantasy glide over a desolate land, which is eerie even in the brightness of midday. They are a tangible embodiment of the feelings aroused in the solitary heath dweller when he wends his way in his native land on such a wild night, or when he looks out over the desolate expanse from some high tower. Then the impressions which he has retained from childhood of stormy nights on the heath come back to his mind and take shape in those fairy tales. You will not overhear the secret of the origin of the popular fairy tales on the Rhine or in Swabia, whereas here every lightning night – *bright lightning night*, says Laube[142] – speaks of it with tongues of thunder.

Hellas had the good fortune of seeing the nature of her landscape brought to consciousness in the religion of her inhabitants. Hellas is a land of pantheism; all her landscapes are – or, at least, were – embraced in a harmonious framework. And yet every tree, every fountain, every mountain thrusts itself too much in the foreground, and her sky is far too blue, her sun far too radiant, her sea far too magnificent, for them to be content with the laconic spiritualisation of Shelley's[143] spirit of nature,* of an all-embracing Pan.[144] Each beautifully shaped individual feature lays claim to a particular god, each river will have its nymphs, each grove its dryads – and so arose the religion of the Hellenes. Other regions were not so fortunate; they did not serve any people as the basis of its faith and had to await a poetic mind to conjure into existence the religious genius that slumbered in them. If you stand on the Drachenfels or on the Rochusberg at Bingen, and gaze over the vine-fragrant valley of the Rhine, the distant blue mountains merging with the horizon, the green fields and vineyards flooded with golden sunlight, the blue sky reflected in the river – heaven with its brightness descends on to the earth and is mirrored in it, the spirit descends into matter, the word becomes flesh and dwells among us – that is the embodiment of Christianity. The direct opposite of this is the North-German heath, here there is nothing but dry stalks and modest heather, which, conscious of its weakness, dare not raise itself above the ground; here and there is a once defiant tree now shattered by lightning; and the brighter the sky, the more sharply does its self-sufficient magnificence demarcate it from the poor, cursed earth lying below it in sackcloth and ashes, and the more does its eye, the sun, look down with burning anger on the bare barren sand – there you have a representation of the Jewish world outlook.†

To continue with the religious character of various regions, the *Dutch* landscapes are essentially Calvinist.[145] The absolute prose of a distant view in Holland, the impossibility of its spiritualization, the gray sky that is indeed the only one suited to it, all this produces the same impression on us as the infallible decisions of the Dordrecht Synod.[146] The windmills, the sole moving things in the landscape, remind one of the predestined elect, who allow themselves to be moved only by the breath of divine dispensation; everything else lies in "spiritual

---

* [The words "spirit of nature" are in English in the original. In Shelley's works, in particular in *Queen Mab*, the pantheistic figurative symbol of Pan appears – HM.]
† *Telegraph fur Deutschland* No. 122, July 1840.

death." And in this barren orthodoxy, the Rhine, like the flowing, living spirit of Christianity, loses its fructifying power and becomes completely choked up with sand. Such, seen from the Rhine, is the appearance of its Dutch banks; other parts of the country may be more beautiful, I do not know them.*

I understand these pages of Engels very well. And it is probably because at one time I experienced something similar just as poignantly.

Fate found it convenient that I immerse myself very deeply – "with my whole head" – in the study of the dialectic in the surroundings of...Central Mexico (1931).

I was astonished, why from books (part brought with me, part sent me from my distant homeland) it was precisely here, in these circumstances, that I not only felt so clearly as something living but I would say *experienced* the basic dynamics of its (dialectical) principle – *becoming.*

I had long searched for an answer, and when I found it, I understood the secret of the completely inimitable charm of Mexico at the same time as the answer to this question.

There are three countries in the world – at least in those parts of it in which I have traveled – where you will experience this special feeling.

This is the Soviet Union, the United States, and Mexico.

If the prim immobility of the well-established wafts from England...a top hat on the head of an Eton boy[147]...the medieval guard of "Beefeaters"[148] and present-day "Bobbies"[149] at the foot of the Tower of London, the wig on the judge's head and a sack of wool under the seat of the Speaker in Parliament.

– then on the contrary, from France wafts the ephemeralness of the continually changing, the inconstant, and the transitional: the unbelievable contours of the boulevards of Paris floating in twilight, the coquettish curves of the Louvre, as if waltzing among the castles on her shores, the rococco volutes, like curls from under whose gold peeps gray hair of threadbare curves, the balls and musettes, the dances, where at the peak of a working day a young loafer runs to dance with his frivolous girlfriend for three rounds of a waltz – just as we all push into the whirlpool of quick-flowing life so that our biography would flash by even more fleetingly...

The static is there.

Excessive immobility is here.

And only the Soviet Union, the United States, and Mexico – each in their own way make you feel as if in three different phases and experience the *great principles of the dynamics of completion – of formation and becoming.*

* K. Marx and F. Engels, *Collected Works*, Vol. II [International Publishers, New York, 1975, pp. 95–7. SME quotes are out of sequence – HM].

The Soviet Union is the crown of this triad.

It resounds in all its fibers with the highest form of becoming – *social becoming.*

Here the eternal nomad has slipped down from his horse and camel and has settled into the collective way of life on earth.

Here millions of individual farms have merged into thousands of collective farms.

Here the barriers dividing people by the mark of race, class, or nationality...have been broken forever.

America...It buzzes and rings with *technical and material becoming.* In the whirlpool of people pouring down its streets, as well as in the millions of whirling wheels of its superindustry, you feel that the earth itself is whirling!

On approaching its New York shores, you feel just as strongly that the earth is a sphere.

For long hours and many miles before the steamboat passes under the protective canopy of the Statue of Liberty – there arises over the smooth greenish surface of the Atlantic Ocean rosy four-faceted columns. Their tops are in the morning sky, but they have no pedestal. The pedestal does not grow out of the surface of the water, and this is why the pedestal rests on that part of the earthly sphere that lies on the side of its linear contour, which we interpret as the juncture of sky and earth and call the horizon.

The pedestal of rosy-orange columns lies still further...behind the horizon, and the columns themselves – are the skyscrapers of Manhattan.

And as we approach, sliding by ship across the surface of the earthly sphere, the columns reach upward, growing into the sky. And their pedestal rises from the ocean's waters, the pedestal called Brooklyn and the Bowery.

But they no longer penetrate the sky like cheerful enema clysters of church spires directed, according to Anatole France, toward the behinds of small angels, but more like rocket missile explosions frozen in flight.

The tapering column of the second thirty stories explodes out of the broader shoulders of the first thirty, and the third thirty rushes like an even slenderer pillar to soar upward from the embrace of the second and stand still in the inaccessible heavenly heights, where upsurging elevators and staggering, twisting fire escapes strive to overtake them.

And from this point, as skyscrapers can grow no higher (Babylonian towers piercing into the very firmament) the steel city, in its insatiable thirst, takes airplanes and hurls them into the sky to conquer the stratosphere; and the age-old blueness of heaven's dome trembles before them and behind its sky-blue curtain quivers the Demiurge himself,[150] in expectation of meeting the man of the age of *victorious industrial becoming*...

And next to it is Mexico, into whose patriarchal depths the iron stain of industry has not yet penetrated.

Mexico – still unawakened and drowsing with the childish dream of its century plants and palms, sand, plains, bird sanctuaries, thickets, bays, and mountain peaks, like the matriarch of the tropics and the stern masculine force of the central plateau.

Mexico, where its favorite word is a lazy "mañana" ("tomorrow"), while its grandeur is recalled in the thousands of years behind or is foreseen in the vague contours of the centuries ahead...

Mexico, where everything breathes of primary and elementary becoming and at the same time – eternal.

It is as if the organic world looked just like this in the first days of creation.

Is this because today's Indian sits cross-legged on the stone, exactly as his stone image sits, carved out by his ancestor thousands of years ago? Or because one's feet cannot help stepping on the sculptured stone ruins of ancient cities and cultures along the thousands of kilometers of shrubbery in Yucatan?

Perhaps it is because the primitive's hut is built today from the same oval poles stuck into the ground with a light covering of straw, as depicted in the codex of the pious Father Sahagun of the sixteenth century or in the undated antediluvian frescoes discovered by excavations.

Or perhaps it is because of the interweaving of birth and death, which you see at every step, because of a constant feeling of the cradle in each sarcophagus, because of the view of a rose bush at the top of a crumbling pyramid, or because of the half-effaced prophetic words above a sculptured skull: "I was like you – and you will become like me."

Or perhaps this feeling is derived from "Day of the Dead" with its decorous principle that a family, amid candles at the grave of the deceased, participates in its sorrowful feast so that the young people, having become intoxicated, look after the continuity of the family and tribe by the grave of their ancestors.

This is the constant mixture of life and death, appearance and disappearance, dying and being born – at every step.

And little children on "Day of the Dead" stuff themselves with skulls made of sugar, and chocolates in the form of little coffins, and they amuse themselves with toys in the form of skeletons.

And the most naïve childishness also gazes enthusiastically out of the eyes of the full-grown bronzed Indian who even today, as once did Guatamokh on the brazier of the Spanish aggressors, could bear without flinching the torture and torments, saying: "And I am not lying on a bed of roses" – in answer to the moan of the weaker. That same childishness also shines in the landscape – in those moments at dawn or sunset, when

Figure 27. The General from Eisenstein's *Que Viva Mexico!*

the air is so transparent that it seems as if someone had stolen it, and distant slopes reddish mountains hang with blinding distinctness in the airless space between the ultramarine sky and the violet shadow of its own foothills – and suddenly you feel clearly that our eye cannot see, but feels and senses objects just as a blind man does with his hands.

And, perhaps, the sensation of this life-asserting growth and becoming comes from the thirst with which the violent greenery in the tropics swallows everything that falls in its path in its unrestrained thirst for life – just a few days of inattention by the railroad guard is needed for the liana to intertwine among the rails and viaducts, pumphouses, and semaphores, and, like snakes, it seems to entice into its coils a confused steam engine that fell into its deadly loops.

Or the sensation comes from the creeks, teeming with alligators, creeks full of floating brushwood from the Pacific Ocean coastline, where roots droop from the tops of trees and descend thirstily in their insatiable greed down toward the small lagoons; and pelicans, with heads turned characteristically to the side, dive into the depths of the golden waters of the small bay for silver fish; while the rose-colored flamingos fly like arrows over the blue surface of the ocean between our airplane and the bronze-green Atlantic coast that lies at our feet.

And is it not that same childishness in the measured communal breathing, in which the naked bodies of soldiers intertwine with "soldaderas" (women camp followers) who march unswervingly with them in their campaigns – and sleep on the white flagstones that pave the small courtyard of Acapulco's toylike fort; the moonlight silvers their bronzed skin, and then, in the darkness of the night, turns them to cherry-black?

The sentry walks with measured steps above them, along the narrow passages of the wall. And, bending down, you can see through the barrier dissolving in the dawn the contour of a seemingly single body of a people, a nation, a race – the "bronze race," as the half-breeds, with this name, love to flatter the bulk of the population of the country they captured...

It seems that not only does the small fort breathe with a single spirit, not only the tiny bay with the amber-colored water, but also the receding blue of the ocean, and the well-proportioned trunks of palm forests, rushing off in crowds into the depths of the country, the giant tortoises drowsing in the water, the flying fish rushing over them, and even the sand boiling in the blazing sun, the sand that collects the vital juices of the desert into the unexpected miracle of the fruits of the palmate cactus: A knife cuts across these pulpy clusters, which serve as pedestal for the dazzling rose flowers of the cactus, and teeth greedily bite into the violet piece of sweet ice – so cold is this fruit, growing in the very heart of a sandy hell – and the desert scorched by the sun.

Everywhere life forces its way out from under death; death takes away the obsolete; centuries lie behind, but also the feeling that *nothing has yet begun*, that much is not yet finished, and that from what has just arisen – there is the possibility of everything developing...

Emotional landscapes, as we have seen, are not only charming on the shining silk of the Chinese painting of the eighth century.

Images of a worldview do not only occur in the flickering graphics of the brush of Huang Ch'üan.

They are around us everywhere.

"...Be artists," writes Jules Renard. "It is so simple – you only have to know how to see..."

And eyes sufficiently open and a burning heart, so that the nature around us sings, speaks, prophesies...

But "where nature displays all its magnificence, where the idea that is slumbering within it seems, if not to awaken, then to be dreaming a golden dream, the man who can feel and say nothing except 'Nature, how beautiful you are!' has no right to think himself superior to the ordinary shallow, confused mass."*

Apparently it is here where the concept of "nonindifferent nature" celebrates the highest point of its joy and triumph.

Epilogue

A tall white house rises amid the sands of the desert.

It is trimmed with blue slabs and surrounded by luxuriant greenery.

This luxuriant greenery consists of several palms, but mainly – cactuses.

High cactuses and low cactuses, pigmy cactuses and giant cactuses, round cactuses and cactuses reaching upward like candelabra.

This is apparently the best collection of cactuses in the world – these porcupines that seem to have run by mistake from the animal kingdom into the plant kingdom!

I have never in my life seen such a variety of needles.

It is as if all the arsenals of the European Middle Ages shared the tips of their pikes with them.

Single, double, triple, quintuple; like a star, the letter "V," a lancet, spire, awl, or thick mass of yellow-green eyelashes, they protrude into the world from the fat bodies of the plants, resembling eunuchs warming their fat beinds in the hot sand.

Whose perverted fantasy planted these freaks in clumps of soil won back from the desert?!

Who is that sadist who hourly feasts his eyes on this crowd of Nürnberg iron maidens twisted inside out?

This maiden, as we know, was a hollow lead cupboard crowned with a woman's head, and furnished with needles inside.

The doors of the cupboard closed slowly – by a clock mechanism – and millimeter after millimeter the sharp thorns penetrated into the body of whomever the terrible maiden locked into her leaden embrace.

But this desert is not the Sahara.

It lies in California.

And it is densely populated.

And it is certainly no sadist who lives there.

---

* F. Engels, "Wanderings Through Lombardy," *Collected Works*, Vol. II [International Publishers, New York, 1975, p. 173 – HM.]

And the bloodthirsty songs of Lautréamont[151] or the pages of that very deceased Marquis[152] do not tickle his morbid ear.

And this is not only because the howl of Maldoror or the cold cynicism of the heroes of the "philosophy in a bedroom" do not reach him, because he is simply deaf: But, if desired, they could be shouted to this stately old man through a huge microphone dangling on his stomach.

But mainly because the needles of the cactuses here are not really connected with sadism.

Above all, they serve an inner aim – compensation.

In fact, the same person who planted a bristling forest of needles for himself and his home turns out to be the same person who inflicted the most horrible blow in the history of humanity on the bristles growing on the cheeks and chins of his fellow man!

Both the house and the cactuses actually belong to this man – King S. Gillette – inventor of the safety blade, the "Gillette" razor.

Of course, it is difficult to imagine that it is possible to suddenly meet the man who bears the name that has become so common for this small machine, which daily scrapes the chins of millions of men.

This person seems to be an abstraction or abstract concept, somewhat like Icarus among contemporary pilots, Hephaestus among colleagues of a crematorium, or Neptune jabbing his trident into the belly of a submarine.

Gillette has had a place for a long time on Olympus – next to Aristotle, Copernicus, Madame Curie, or Luigi Pirandello.[153]

And yet – he does not.

In 1930, the now-deceased legendary old man was just as alive as another California rarity: the first child born of the pioneers in that same land of California.

We saw that perky old man in a red flannel shirt and with a long beard, riding in a car to San Francisco, when he was going to look at antiques associated with the "Gold Rush" of 1848.

The old man allowed himself to be photographed, to be sold souvenirs, and to be shown tiny gold nuggets, hanging on a watch chain, which had come from former mines on the land of the famous Captain Sutter.[154]

The old man Gillette – himself an inventor – gold nugget, and even the chains in his home are gold, for, owning all his patents himself (which is a great rarity), at that moment he was valued roughly at 60 million – had been fined for not paying taxes, apparently up to one million dollars; and in the end was an ardent enthusiast of the "noble experiment," as the foremost Americans referred to our Soviet Union in those days.

But the old man King Gillette finds himself on the pages of this article, not because of the cactuses and the black marble of the bathroom with gold faucets and handles and the gold chain on which dangles an oblong pear with the inevitable inscription: "Pull!" – he appears here not for his project of creating a government based on collective and cooperative principles whose plan he published in 1897 (I have kept his autograph in a copy of this bibliographic rarity) nor because he wrote an even more radical book in 1930, so radical that his friend Upton Sinclair[155] refused to edit it – for being too "leftist"(!) – King Gillette appears here mainly because of his safety razor.

Rather, for the important instructions that guarantee the efficiency of its working,

for that easy half-turn, which has to be made in the opposite direction, right after it is wound as far as it will go.

And it is probably already quite clear to you why the "Gillette" razor appears on these pages of our discussion.

Ancient writings contained a whole series of books under the general title "didactic."

I also look on my films as being "didactic" to a certain extent; that is, those that besides their immediate aims, always contain researches and experiments in form.

These researches and experiments are made so that – in another interpretation and from another individual point of view – they could be used later collectively by all of us working on the creation of films in general.

Therefore, I am not constrained to speak of tasks that may have been mentioned a hundred times. Especially since "researches" or "experiments" had never been in conflict with a film's theme until now, or even simply separate from the content of the pictures. On the contrary, even certain "excesses" arose mainly as a very intense desire to express most fully one or another side of the theme.

Because of these motives and in the interest of those "didactic" aims, one should point out in an afterword to possible dangers resulting from too much consistency in paths once marked and chosen...

In the practical application of the principles of polyphonic montage, one must stick to that same "golden rule" of King S. Gillette – to maintain *a half-turn from the maximum point.*

For too consistent an application of these principles of montage can also be...dangerous!

It is apropos here to mention first what Saint-Saëns wrote in relation to Wagner – one of the undoubted predecessors and ancestors of the audiovisual polyphony of contemporary montage (true, under conditions so imperfect an apparatus as the theater was, even in Bayreuth).[156] Saint-Saëns wrote:

...There was a time when they gladly forgot about drama in order to listen to the voice and, if the orchestra was too interesting, they complained about it and blamed it for distracting attention.

Now the public listens to the orchestra, tries to follow the thousands of interweaving designs, the nuances of the play of sounds; it forgets to listen carefully to what the actors are saying, and loses from view the action.

The new system almost completely reduces to nought the art of singing and boasts about it. But, in this way, the main instrument, the single *living* instrument, departs from the role of carrying the melody; and instead this role falls to the instruments manufactured by our hands as pale and clumsy imitations of the human voice.

Isn't there something wrong here?

Let us continue. The new art, because of its extreme complexity, demands extremely hard labor, sometimes superhuman strength from the performer and even from the spectator. Extreme sensitivity, which is the result of the application of harmony and orchestration unheard of until now, makes the nervous system extremely tense and provokes an extravagant exaltation, going beyond the bounds of the aims that art must set for itself.

This music so excites the brain that it is capable of moving it off-balance. I am not criticizing: I am simply stating the facts. The ocean drowns, thunder kills: But the sea and a hurricane do not lose their grandeur because of it.

But let us continue. Of course, it is contrary to reason to transfer the drama to the orchestra when its place is on the stage. But one must realize that, in this case, it does not matter to me at all. Genius has its own common sense, which is by no means compulsory for common sense.

But I think that what has been said is enough to prove that even this art has its flaws, as does everything in the world, and that this art is still not perfect and polished...[...]*

But besides these considerations, there is one more great danger in this method – this is the danger of *the solipsism of audiovisual drama.*

The proclivity to egocentrism and solipsism in those who work in synaesthetics is quite well known.

The egocentrism of Wagner is well known.

And Plekhanov made fun of this proclivity for solipsism in Scriabin.

Solipsism, as we know, puts your "I" in the center of the universe. And, therefore, on meeting Scriabin in Geneva, on sunny days Plekhanov had the habit of ironically asking him: "Well, are we obligated to you, Alexander Nikolayevich, for this good weather?"[157]

Here before us we have the danger of similar features slipping into the very fabric of the work.

The perfection of the fusion of parts among themselves can easily slip into a distinctive self-enclosing of things into themselves.

They can shut off the canals through which creation draws the spectator to itself;

with knots they can plait antenna between themselves, which the production directs into the thoughts and feelings of the viewer.

Like a squirrel in a wheel, one can spin a work "within oneself," losing

---

* Camille Saint-Saëns, *Portraits et Souvenirs*, Societé des Editions Artistiques, Paris, 1900, pp. 295–6.

one's basic task of drawing in the viewer, and going off completely into a self-contemplation of the harmonic perfection of the composition of one's own parts.

This is particularly dangerous under the conditions of contemporary man's perceptions.

We are not able to be enthusiastic about the harmonic perfection of the forms of ancient sculpture, as Winkelmann[158] and his contemporaries were.

We cannot even be intoxicated with the extremely smooth surface of the nephrite bodies of Egyptian plastic arts, as Gaston Maspero[159] or Jean François Champollion[160] were.

We are more excited by the scribbled understatement of Mexican terra cotta or the chaotic piling up of separate details of its decoration.

And the audiovisual polyphony must diligently avoid degrees of fusion where all outlines composing its features disappear completely, totally, and forevermore.

Moreover, what is even more dangerous is: *the commensurate merging of sound and visual depiction*; that is, the phenomenon that we call "SYNAESTHETICS" is a typical feature of so-called *sensuous primitive thinking*.

With the evolution of a differentiating mind, we are capable only with an inner effort, or in bursts of inspiration, or under the influence of being seized by a work of art, of reverting to the vitality of those original sources of thought and feeling, where the most surprising thing is this: that there is still no division yet into thought and feeling.

Under "normal" conditions we experience this "original bliss" of *the undivided and the non-disunited* either in a state of intoxication (active) or in a state of dream (passive).

In any case, in states of "withdrawal" and "immersion."

And we know what it costs us just to enter into a condition that is the result of a certain psychic set of circumstances, which inevitably produces in us a psychological sensation of this set of circumstances.

And the result may be, in addition to "self-enclosure," a certain "drowsiness" of the general effect.

(The latter can to a great degree be promoted also by an insufficient rhythmic variation that produces a certain lulling effect on the whole.)

I speak about this from personal experience.

Several parts of the first series of *Ivan the Terrible* are barely kept from slipping into a series of slowly flowing, dreamlike visions, slipping by the viewer's perception – according to their own laws, following their own moods, almost for themselves – a kind of "plastic solipsism."

Fortunately, there are not many of them.

Fortunately, a strained nerve forces its way through whenever necessary.

And fortunately, the auditorium does not fall asleep.

However, discretion and honesty force me not to ignore this danger, and this is especially in the interests of the method itself – in the interests of the fact that partial breakdowns in the practical application of the method should not be in a state that would discredit the method and the forms of a new type of polyphonic montage, which, engendered as early as *Potemkin*, achieves its final culmination in the audiovisual construction of *Ivan the Terrible*.

And one more thing.

The stylistic tendencies in my work, as in any of our work, are certainly not maliciously far fetched or intentionally fantastic.

Our people and our time dictate to us what we should film.

The nation and the time define how we look at life.

And both how we look at things and our relationship to phenomena dictate the appearance and form in which we embody them.

The structure of a work, the principles of solution, and the development of methods are born totally out of the nature of the theme and the treatment of it.

This determines the vitality of the theme.

This engenders the progressive changes in method.

And this inevitably nourishes the inspiration for creativity and the inevitable search for something new.

Postscript

When you delve very deeply into analysis, sometimes you begin to be doubtful: Does anyone need this except me, and is all of this not "analysis for the sake of analysis," like the notorious *l'art pour l'art*?

Is so much space necessary to explain landscape and music, the musical construction of emotional landscape, the special features of the musical composition of landscape, etc.?

Does this not have merely a purely academic and historical interest?

And does this have any relationship to what is now being done in film and will be done in the very near future?

Well! This is far from being analysis for the sake of analysis, and is certainly not merely curiosity about what took place long ago; these are very essential themes of the most recent cinematography!

The technical mastery of color has barely begun, has yet to be realized and the aesthetics of it have yet to be mastered, even to a modest degree.

And in the light of the "color catastrophes," as almost all color films appear to be today, the theoretical work on the problem of the subject matter of a film, its color and combination with music is very significant.

The definition of a "color catastrophe," as the definition of aesthetic lack of mastery in the application of color in film, unfortunately does not only refer to those films where the color functions only as a recurrent

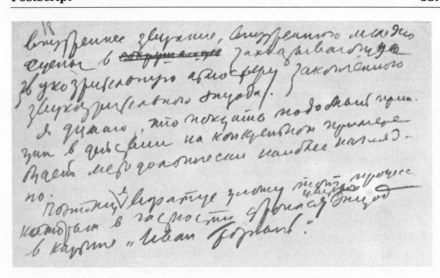

Figure 28. Last page of the manuscript "Color Cinema": lines written by Eisenstein the day before his death.

sensation – such as *The Thief of Baghdad*[161] and *Mowgli*[162] as well as *The Bathing Beauty* of MGM.[163]

Other such examples, alas, were two pictures of apparently quite different intentions, which I saw by accident, right in the midst of my work on the Chinese landscape for this article: These are *Bambi*[164] by my friend Disney[165] (which I encountered quite late) and *Chopin*[166] by Columbia Pictures (1944). I was particularly disappointed with the first film – it was so bad in the unmusicality of its *landscape* and *color*.

Disney – is the brilliant master and unsurpassed genius in the creation of audiovisual equivalents in music of *the independent movement of lines* and a graphic interpretation of the inner flow of the music (more often of the melody than of the rhythm!). He is surprising when it is a question of the structure of the comically exaggerated movement of the human characters, the masklike figures of the comic animals, but this same Disney is amazingly blind when it comes to *landscape* – to *the musicality of landscape* and at the same time, to *the musicality of color and tone.*

Already in the early works of Disney, in what I think is the best of his series, *Silly Symphonies*,[167] I was disturbed by the total *stylistic rupture* between the background, painted in such a weak, childish manner, and the brilliant perfection of the movement and drawing of the moving figures in the – foreground...

This is particularly striking in a masterpiece of the moving equivalent of music as the dance of the skeletons in *Danse Macabre* of Saint-Saëns

(1929), where the naturalistically shaded dead background is extremely ugly.

In the Mickey Mouse series[168] – especially the black and white ones – it is somewhat better, for there the landscape is mostly sustained in the linear-graphic manner with a concise black wash of parts of the landscape and background, as was applied in the drawing of Mickey and Minnie.

In addition, one should bear in mind that Disney bears the full responsibility for the failure of the landscape – (we* are forced to chase after effects of real nature and on our knees beg it for symphonic elements of sunsets and sunrises, misty dawns, or the threatening racing of clouds) – whereas he is really the complete master of the atmosphere and the elements of his landscape!

Moreover, the possibilities within the art with which he works provide totally unlimited possibilities for landscape elements (which are actually deformed) to live and pulsate in the tone and emotions of corresponding action.

Here the real *flow* and *true* formation of landscape are possible, transitions from one element of landscape into another, not only as a meaningless panoramic shot or as a tracking of the camera back from the crude, naturalistic dabs of background, as, let us say, in *Bambi*, where this is very objectionable.

It is much more than this. It is accompanied by a complete rupture of the stylistic manner between the flat drawing of *conventional volume* in the figures and *the false three dimensionality* of the *setting*, painted with all the painstaking care of a bad oleographic print.

The culture of the Chinese landscape could add a great deal here, for, in spite of everything, besides the effects of "seasons" (winter, spring) in the landscapes, somewhere there is the pretense of conveying an emotionally charged "atmosphere." However, in addition, we forget that only a definite "dematerialization" of the elements of this landscape could achieve this. Instead of this, what is presented is an oleographic painting of an *emphatically concrete* environment that, in contrast to the Chinese landscape where everything is done by nuance, *it does not subject itself at all to conveying mood.*

Here in *Bambi*, where it was no longer a question of the parody of the parodoxical, but of *genuine lyricism*, one should have confined oneself to the soft dissolution of forms in the setting and background, able to pass one into the other and repeat the change of moods, and by this flow, create genuinely plastic music.

In *Bambi* I think the retention of the former mode of Disney's drawing

---

* [Refers to those filmmakers *not* producing animated cartoons – HM].

was wrong, with its sharply confined linear contour and the continuous *outlining* of colored areas.

In Disney's earlier works this type of drawing corresponded completely to Mickey's paradoxical charm, which consisted in the very fact that Disney, within the self-contained, concrete representational form subjected it to an immaterial free play of free lines and surfaces. This is one of the basic springs of the comic effect of his works. In *Bambi* it is just the reverse.

Here the most important thing is lyricism.

With a proper resolution of the landscape, figures would genuinely merge with it, a resolution of unrestricted strokes such as we know from Chinese *graphics* – and soft spots of color with indistinct edges. This is also typical of Chinese *painting* in its treatment of fluffy beings – monkeys or fledglings.

What is even more sad and tedious is that this had apparently all been kept in mind in the sketches for the film *Bambi*.

In these sketches a complete harmony between the drawing of a character and the background was projected, but the very way both have been drawn, as well as the color resolutions, follow very closely to what so upset me here.*

A completely animated cartoon film, not able to find a *graphic and painterly method* for the complete expression of its aims or a *stylistic unity of setting and figures* – is a very melancholy spectacle.

Especially if one recalls that this had often been successful even in the theater, where the actual three-dimensional actor and the flat elements of the setting merged into one whole by means of color and light!

Another film presents a no less melancholy picture.

Strictly speaking, from the purely plastic aspect of a film, any *general surface of each shot* is a distinct tonal or color "landscape" – not because of what it represents but because of the *emotional feeling* the shot must bear, which itself is perceived as *a whole* within the consecutive course of the montage pieces.

If such shots, as a plastic equivalent, are intended to repeat the course of such profoundly poetic music as Chopin's, then it would seem that it is difficult to find a more charming and delightful problem to solve.

To create a picturesque symphony of tender fading tones (repeating Chopin's nocturnes and preludes) is a charming problem indeed.

Yet what do we see instead in the film *Chopin*?

A jumble of colored fragments with no combination within themselves or with each other, without a logic of the feelings or mood or atmosphere

---

* I know several of these sketches from the reproductions in a good book: Durant Field, *The Art of Walt Disney*, Macmillan, New York, 1942, pp. 112–15, and especially p. 119.

of the scene or, above all, most important of all, most necessary of all, without a unified course of the composer's musical thought!

And again we have before us the stubborn *colored painting* of separate objects instead of a general restrained colored space of the suite composed of them.

Again a play of *colored objects*, and not of *the color of the objects*.

This is particularly scandalous and insulting in the last part of the film, which had been conceived correctly – in Chopin's concert tour to collect money for the Polish uprising (I will not go into an evaluation of the historical justification of the subject itself). Here the basic musical theme of the film, a polonaise (which is understood as expressing the national feelings of the Polish people), is played continuously in the music, and at the same time the visual aspect of the episode is being continuously modified through change of European concert halls, where Chopin himself is playing the polonaise on the piano. Dissolving into each other, posters from various cities flash by, the varied forms of the halls, the changing forms of the pianos, the changing costumes of Chopin, who turns dark in unison with his increasing sickness – and mainly the colored velvet backdrop of the background.

This is well conceived, but its realization is terrible. For again the basic concept is forgotten, that *red velvet* cannot turn into *blue velvet*, and *green velvet* into *violet velvet*, *crimson* or *orange velvet*; and that this transition is accessible only to *color* – easily flowing from *red* into *blue*, from *green* into *violet*, into *crimson*, into *orange*.

The color, but not the velvet.

After this flow of color into color, each color can then freely "materialize" in reverse into surface, texture, folds, the general concreteness of velvet; but musical transitions are accessible only to tonally colored or textured values and not to pieces of varicolored plush stuffed with nails!

This failure is particularly disgraceful for film because even theater, and especially in the case of Chopin's music, was able to convey with great refinement *the colored sound of music* through *plastically colored stage action*.

I remember the ballet *Chopiniana*[169] in Fokine's production on the stage of the former Marinsky Theater, and, although this was about thirty years ago, I still remember this feeling of the complete merging of the modulations of music with the modulations of color from silver into violet, and from white into blue, and how the light and color repeated the dreamy, poetic movement of the ballerinas, gliding along the whiteness of their tutus...

I continue to believe firmly that the problems of color will have to be solved by our cinematography in particular, which, beginning with the period of silent film, has tirelessly striven to be audiovisual color.

I wrote about this in the newspaper *Kinogazeta* – in 1940*:

. . . The best works of our cameramen had long ago been potentially in color. Even if it was still a "minor palette" of the grayish-white range, in this best examples they never seem to be in "tri-color" because of a poverty of expressive means.

They are so powerful in terms of composition and color that they seem to be the intentional self-limitation of masters such as Tisse, Moskvin, and Kosmatov, literally wishing on purpose to speak with only three colors: white, gray, and black, and not with all the possibilities of the palette.

Thus, in limiting himself in a part of the *Iolanthe* overture, Tchaikovsky speaks only with brass.

Similarly, in Tchaikovsky's *Romeo and Juliet*, in Act II of the ballet,[170] suddenly, instead of the whole orchestra, only a few mandolins speak.

In the works of our greatest cameramen, black, gray, and white were not perceived as the absence of color, but always as a definite color gamma, in which (or in variations of which) not only the plastic wholeness of the picture's form was sustained but also the thematic unity and movement of the film as a whole.

A gray tone was the predominant range in *Potemkin*. It was composed of three elements: of the cruel gray gleam of the sides of the battleship, of the soft tonality of the washed-gray mists, reminiscent of Whistler, and from a third factor, which seemed to combine the first two – taking the gleam from the first and the softness from the second: This element was the variation of the sea's surface shot totally in this gray gamma.

The gray tone in the picture separated into extremes.

Into the color of black. Into the double-breasted black jackets of the commanders and into the black shots of the anxious night.

And into the color of white. Into the white tarpaulin in the execution scene. Into the white sails of the yawls rushing toward the battleship. Into the flight of the white sailor caps at the end, a flight that appeared like an explosion of the tarpaulin death shroud, blown to pieces by the high intensity of revolutionary 1905.

October is totally sustained in a velvety-black tonality. With a black gleam with which monuments, railings, and roads, wet with rain, shine in nature, and with which gold, gilding, and bronze shine in a photograph.

The Old and the New had a white tone as the leading color. The white state farm. Clouds. The streams of milk. Flowers. Through the gray motives of the beginning – destitution. Through the black motives – crime and evil. Again and again everything connected with the theme of joy and the new forms of the economy show through as white. The white color was born in the most tense scene in the picture: the scene of waiting for the first drop from the separator. And, appearing on the screen with it, the white color carried the theme of joy to the screen as shots of the state farm, as rivers of milk, as herds of animals and birds.

* "Not colored, but colorful," *Kinogazeta*, No. 29, Vol. 20, 1940.

In *Battleship Potemkin*, the red color of the flag exploded like fanfare, but it was effective because, above all, it was not just a color, but a concept.

And, in approaching the problems of color in film, one must think especially about the significance of color.

The same play occurs in Golovin's *Mother*,* although less clearly and less consistently than in Tisse: from the oily black beginning – blackened boots, the night search, and Rembrandt illumination – through the grayness of prison, to the whiteness of the floating ice, shaded by the dark human masses with their lit-up faces.

While preserving all the merits of the silent film in this area, *Nevsky* goes even further in this respect. The foreign press has been struck by the fact that in *Nevsky* it is not the traditional black that denotes the villain, but the blinding white color.

Goodness knows by what technological devices Tisse achieves a real illusion of color, but undoubtedly, in places, it is palpable.

I myself think that the sky in the Battle of the Ice sometimes seems blue, and the grass is at first gray-green. Similarly I remember shots of the funeral of the old man Bozhenka, golden shading into indigo, and the shots at the beginning of *Ivan* as blue-green.

With the arrival of sound, these moments of so-called uncolored photography begin to take on quite a different significance. For it is just through these qualities of photography that the most refined blending of sound and visual depiction occur, a melodic blending.

If, as we wrote long ago about film in our *Manifesto*,† "the image has remained decisive in an audiovisual combination...If the movement is rhythmic and the texture of the material shot is a way of using timbre to achieve the merging of visual and audial elements...Then the melodic blending with sound is probably achieved most distinctly through nuances of light which are inseparable from nuances of color..."

I cannot but recall here, at the conclusion, one remarkable literary example of an audiovisual symphony, which in addition is also *monotone color but with a blinding variety of textures and nuances of different material.*

This is one of the most charming examples of Zola's "symphonic" constructions taken from the scene "The White Sale" in his novel *Women's Happiness*:

"Oh! How unusual!" the women exclaimed. "Unheard of!"

They did not grow tired of this song of white which was sung by the fabrics of the whole store. Mureau had never yet created anything greater: This was the exhibition of the genius of his talent for arranging displays. In this white cascade, in the apparent chaos of fabrics falling literally at random from disemboweled shelves, there was a harmonic phrase: Nuances of white followed and unrolled one after the other; they were born, grew, and performed a whole

---

* [Cameraman of Pudovkin, director of the classic film, *Mother* – HM.]
† [See *Film Firm*, op. cit., p. 257 – HM.]

complicated orchestral fugue of a great musician, whose gradual development carried souls off into increasingly extensive flights. Everywhere there was only whiteness, but it was never the same; all these white nuances rose one over the other, contrasted, supplemented each other, finally achieving the shining of real light. The white symphony was begun by the dull whiteness of linen and. . . muted white tones of flannel and cotton, then came velvet, silk, satin, the rising gamut little by little becoming ignited by little flames on the edges of the folds; the whiteness flew upward in the transparency of the curtains, was penetrated by light in the muslin, guipure, lace, and especially in the tulle which was so light that it seemed the highest note lost in the air, and next in the depths of a gigantic alcove, even more loudly sang the silver of Oriental silk. . .

This example is particularly apropos here at the end of our work.

And not only because it gives a sparkling and blinding example of how one should work out color solutions, even in those cases when it is in the hands of an artist with a palette of every kind of color richness (and from this point of view it would be a good idea to recall and reread endlessly the novels of this astonishing master of color – Emile Zola).

And not only because we have an obvious example here of how the traditions and methods of the painting of China and the Orient flourish in the creativity and methods of the great French novelist, together with his like-minded impressionists, who so nobly enriched their own efforts and tendencies with the age-old experience of the East. And in this respect, this additional excursion is interwoven organically into our theme of the methods of Chinese landscape.

But above all, perhaps, because the musical visions of real phenomena, characteristic of Emile Zola's perception and exposition, greatly influenced the development of the methods of producing visual music in our silent film.

In terms of my own share in this general work, I will never personally be ashamed "to raise my glass" along with my other teachers to the great teacher of visual music – Emile Zola.

It is interesting that the literary tradition of "nonindifferent nature," generally proceeding from Zola, especially seems to have been captured by the cinematographic tradition of our silent film.

How characteristic it is that even Zola's film scenario – even *Thérèse Raquin*[171] and the film versions of *Money*[172] and *Nana*,[173] which had been modernized by Renoir – totally ignored this astonishing and profoundly musical-cinematographic feature of the great Frenchman.

The absence of this is particularly annoying, considering the generally high level of performance in such a very gratifying work as *The Human-Beast*.[174] In this film we did not see anything of the astonishing symphony of railroads, steamships, rails, machine oil, coal, steam, and semaphores that are so attractive in the rhythm, tempo, color, texture, and sound in the novel itself.

Several gray newsreel shots of arrivals and departures...several inexpressive corners of train stations...two or three empty railway platforms...perhaps they do answer the exhausted "slogan" of the school of naturalism, as it is understood scholastically. But in these films there is none of the range of fervor and trembling, passion and lyricism from the pages of the great magician, sorcerer, and, above all, poet – Zola.

And here, probably, is the key to the secret of why it was among us, in the period of our most temperamental cinema, that the predecessor of sound film has flourished so richly – the cinema of "nonindifferent nature."

For – damn it! – "nonindifferent nature" is above all within ourselves: It is not the nature around us that is particularly nonindifferent, but our own nature – the nature of man who approaches the world that he re-creates, not with indifference, but with passion, actively and creatively.

And the temperamental re-creation of nature in a work is, as it were, an image of that mighty re-creation of the world in which our great generation participates.

For around us is not a world "seen through a temperament," but a world created and re-created according to the commands of that creative revolutionary temperament of our inimitable country and epoch.

And the nonindifference of our own human nature, participating in the great historical act of the best part of humanity – is the invincible guarantee of the undying essence of the great arts, glorifying with every means available to it the greatness of Man – the maker and the creator.

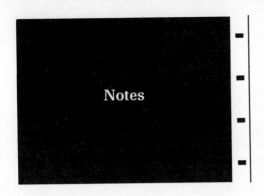

Notes

Poor Salieri

1 *...I fling the crutches of conformity to the Devil, a term used by Lessing.* Eisenstein must have in mind the following words of Lessing: "...It was always offensive and vexing to me, if I read or heard anything that tended to blame the critics...But, of course, as crutches help a cripple to move from one place to another, but cannot make him fleetfooted, so it is with critics" [G. E. Lessing, *Izbran, Proizvidenie* (*Selected Works*), Moscow, Goslitizdat, 1953, p. 606].

2 Quoted by Eisenstein in the original German. From Goethe's *Faust*.

I. On the structure of things

1 *Diderot deduces the compositional principles...in surrounding nature*, SME has in mind the views of Diderot on the nature of music, set out by Diderot in his book *The Nephew of Rameau* (*Le Neveu de Rameau*). SME deals with this in some depth in *Montage*, Herbert Marshall, trans., in publication (*Selected Works*, Vol. II).

2 *M. Sukhotin in a letter to Veresayev*, Sukhotin Mikhail Sergeyevich (1850–1914), husband of the daughter of L. N. Tolstoy Tatiana; Veresayev (Smidovich) Vinkenti Vikentyevich (1867–1945), Soviet Russian writer.

3 See V. V. Veresayev, *Memoirs*, in *Sobranye sochinenii, Collected Works*, Vol. 4, Izd. Pravda, Moscow, p. 433.

4 Drama on the Quarterdeck (literally "Drama at Tendre"). The mutiny on the Battleship *Potemkin* began on 14 June 1905 while it was docked in Tendrovsky Bay (near Ochakova).

5 *Plato*, (427–347 B.C.).

6 G. E. *Timerding*, Professor at the Higher Technical School in Brunswick, Germany, author of *The Golden Section*.

7 See V. V. Stasov, *The Exhibition of the Itinerants, Selected Works*, Vol. 3, Iskusstvo, Moscow, 1952, p. 59.

8 Citation from V. Nikolski, *The Creative Processes of V. I. Surikov*, Vsekokhudozhnik, Moscow, 1934, p. 68.

9 *Avvakum* Petrovich (1621–82), an archpriest, orator, and writer, author of the classic work of ancient Russian literature *Zhitie* [*A Life*], founder of the Old Believers, a clerical movement that arose as a religious protest against the innovations of Patriarch Nikon and grew into a protest against social oppression. The subject of the painting of V. I. Surikov was the tragic fate of F. P. Morozova (?–1672), a famous noblewoman supporting the schism and incarcerated in jail by the tsar.

10 *Frédérick Lemaître*, pseudonym for Antoine Louis Prospero Lemaître (1800–76), French actor, representative of the romantic theater, initiator of critical realism on the French stage. Eisenstein dedicated to Lemaître much of the section entitled "The Lion in Old Age" (see Chapter II).

11 See *Battleship Potemkin*, Herbert Marshall, ed., Avon Books, New York, 1978, pp. 301–7.

12 *Edmund Meisel*, German composer who composed music specially for *Potemkin* and *October* under Eisenstein's supervision.

13 *Ein Waltzertraum*, a German film-operetta (1925) produced by UFA Film Studios, directed by Ludwig Berger. It was filmed to the accompaniment of the previously composed music of Oscar Strauss.

14 Eisenstein has in mind the declaration of *The Future of Sound Film*, signed by himself, V. I. Pudovkin, and G. V. Alexandrov (see *Film Form*, Ed. J. Leyda, p. 25).

15 Kasimir Severinovich, *Malevich* (1878–1935), Russian artist, founder of the suprematist movement in modern painting.

16 *A curtain wastorn open. . . on Officer Street*. Eisenstein has in mind the opera-spectacle *Victory over the Sun* performed in Petersburg in 1913 by a group of futurists (text by A. Kruchenykh, music by M. Matyushin, decor and costumes by M. Malevich).

17 *A slap in the face of public taste*, the title of an anthology and declaration of Russian futurists (1912) that declared that with their art they threw a challenge to the generally accepted and, according to them, petty bourgeois taste.

18 *Comédie Française*, the oldest theater in France, "The House of Moliere," founded in Paris in 1650.

19 Matthew 27: 51.

II. *Pathos*

1 *The Holy Grail*, according to medieval legend the very cup Jesus Christ used for the Last Supper and in which eventually the blood of Christ was preserved. This legend served as the subject for many poetic works including the operas of Richard Wagner, *Lohengrin* and *Parsifal*.

2 Eisenstein has in mind an interview he gave in 1926 to the Soviet periodical *Kino*, 32, p. 152, August 10, 1926, in which he said (inter alia): "Why does the heart of the audience tremble when, under the thunderous rolls of Wagner's brass, the goblet of the Holy Grail of the Eucharist blazes like diamonds?

"What the hell do we need that Spanish vessel for?

"Better let the eyes of our Young Communists blaze before the shimmering of the metal Collective milk separator!"

3 Maurice *Bardeche* (1908–), French writer and critic. He wrote *The History of Motion Pictures*, together with S. Brasillach (1935; published in English in 1938, Ayar, New York).

4 *Hesiod* (c. 700 B.C.), ancient Greek poet. Author of *Toil and Days*.

5 *Virgil* (70–19 B.C.), ancient Latin poet. Author of the *Aeneid* and the poem *The Georgics* in which he sang of nature, village life, and agricultural labor.

6 *Dionysian lyricism*, in ancient Greece the festival held in honor of the god Dionysus, from which Greek drama developed.

7 *I have already written much on the subject matter...*, Eisenstein wrote about the theme of his film *The Old and the New* (or *The General Line*) in his essays *Triumphant Workdays* and *Experiments Understood by Millions* (see *Selected Works*, Vol. I).

8 Andrea *Mantegna* (1431–1506), Italian painter and engraver. In this case Eisenstein has in mind his painting *The Dead Christ* (1467, Gallery Brera, Milan), also known as *The Foreshortened Christ*.

9 *Jupiter, once kidnapping Europa...*, the Greek myth.

10 *Moses...*, Exodus.

11 *Golden calf*, Exodus 32.

12 *Shakhsi-Vakhsi*, refers to a procession during a Muslim religious ceremony in memory of the son of the Caliph Ali-Hosain, killed in a battle at Kerbela (A.D. 680) – a procession simulating the funeral of Hosain, accompanied by self-torture.

13 The "Flagellants," one of the very oldest Russian sects, originated at the end of the seventeenth century and was a branch of the larger religious movement called the "Old Believers" ("The Ritualists"). The "Flagellants" were mystics who believed in the possibility of the permanent incarnations of God in the individual...They organized secret meetings in which they attempted to call forth the presence of the Holy Spirit by means of ecstatic dances. These meetings at times terminated in orgies. This sect was in general associated with sexual license. Gregory Rasputin, who played such a tragic role in the fall of the imperial regime in Russia, was associated with the "Flagellants." G. Vernadsky, *A History of Russia*, Yale University Press, New Haven, 1961, p. 117).

14 *Hardly perceptible...the tonality of the shot*, a reference to Eisenstein's theory of "tonic and overtonic montage." [See his *Montage*, H. Marshall, trans., in publication (from Vol. II of the Russian edition)].

15 *Suprematism*, the Russian abstract school of painting pioneered by Malevich.

16 *I had reason to quote a perfect example of this...*, see *Montage*, 1938.

17 *Amplification*, one of the favorite terms of Eisenstein signifying the enlargement of the compass of an artistic image as a result of a deepened dramatic and directorial treatment. Thus evolved the film *Battleship Potemkin* from a sketchily outlined episode in N. F. Agadzhanova's 1905 script.

18 Claude *Monet* (1840–1926), French artist, impressionist.

19 *Ormazd and Ahriman*, the Hellenized names of the god-brothers Ahura Mazda and Angra Mainya [negative thought]. According to the beliefs of the Zoroastrian (ancient Persian) religion, they embody correspondingly good and evil, light and dark, the creative and destructive principle and are eternally fighting among themselves.

20 *Litany*, a form of prayer in which the clergy and the congregation take part alternately with recitation of supplications and fixed responses.

21 *Ratapoile*, a representative image of a French militarist of the period of the

Second Empire. He was the main character of a whole cycle of graphic and sculptural caricatures by Honoré Daumier.

22 *Rigalbouch*, a French singer and dancer of the period of the Second Empire and author of *The Memoirs of Rigalbouch*, 1860.

23 *The brothers Vasil'ev*, pseudonym of the Soviet film directors G. N. Vasilev (1899–1946) and S. D. Vasil'ev (1900–59) who, besides the classic *Chapayev*, created the films *The Volochayev Days*, *The Front*, *The Defense of Tsaritsyn*, etc.

24 Alexey Dmitrievich, *Popov* (1892–1961), Soviet theater director, people's artist of the USSR from 1935 – artistic director, then main director of the Central Theater of the Soviet Army. In the history of Soviet theater are his productions of the play by L. Seifullian, *Virineia*, 1925; N. Pogodin's plays *The Poem about an Axe*, 1931; *My Friend*, 1932; and *After the Ball*, 1934; Shakespearian productions of *Romeo and Juliet* and *The Taming of the Shrew*, etc.

25 Grigory Vasilyevich *Alexandrov (Mormonenko)* (1903–   ), Soviet film director, People's Artist of the USSR. He began his activity under the direction of S. M. Eisenstein in the Proletcult theater. From 1925 to 1931 he participated in the production of Eisenstein's films. He is the producer of the musical comedies *Cheerful Fellows*, *Circus*, *Volga-Volga*, *Spring*, *A Russian Souvenir*, and also the film *The Composer Glinka*, etc.

26 Maxim Maximovich *Shtraukh* (1900–   ), Soviet actor and theater director, People's Artist of the USSR. A friend since childhood of S. M. Eisenstein's, Shtraukh began his creative path with him in the First Workers' Theater of the Proletcult. In 1925–8 he became part of the "Iron Five" assistants of Eisenstein. (See Herbert Marshall's *Battleship Potemkin*, Avon Books, New York, 1978, p. 13.) The image of V. I. Lenin was created by the actor on the stage of the Moscow Theater of the Revolution (the production of *Truth*, 1937) and in film (*Man with a Gun*, 1938; *Yakov Srerdlov*, 1940; *They Call Him Suche-Bator*, 1942; *Tales about Lenin*, 1957).

27 Eduard *Manet* (1832–83), French painter, one of the founders of impressionism. Eisenstein has in mind here his picture *The Bar of the Follies-Berger* (1881) and *The Beerseller* (1878).

28 *Ragtime*, rhythm characterized by strong syncopation in the melody with a regularly accented accompaniment.

29 *Sequence* (music), the sequential alternation of homophonic and polyphonic musical structures in an ascending or descending direction. Eisenstein uses this term figuratively for signifying a certain method used by the director to develop an episode or scene in a film. Besides the scene from "Meeting the Squadron" discussed above, one may take as an example the well-known "Suite of the Mist" in *Potemkin* analyzed by Eisenstein later, in the chapter "Nonindifferent Nature."

30 *Tabernacle*, a portable sanctuary of the ancient Hebrews that accompanied them, according to Biblical legend, during their wandering after the "exodus" from Egypt.

31 François *Rabelais* (1494–1553), French writer and humanist. In the novel *Gargantua and Pantagruel* (1532–4), directed against the old feudal world and the scholastics of the medieval church, Rabelais with brilliant hyperbolization praised the joy of earthly life and human flesh.

32 Peter *Breughel*, the Elder, nicknamed the Peasant (born between 1525 and

1530, died 1569), painter, draughtsman, and engraver, representative of the Dutch Renaissance. With great strength, richness, and mischievous humor Breughel painted scenes from popular life (*The Battle of Carnival with Lent, Proverbs, A Peasant Dance,* etc.).

33 Peter Paul *Rubens* (1577–1640), Flemish painter whose works are permeated by an attempt for sensual, full-blooded perception of the world.

34 Percy Bysshe *Shelley* (1792–1822), English poet.

35 *Francis Bacon* (1561–1626), English philosopher.

36 *Die Gotterdammerung* (The Twilight of the Gods), the last opera of Richard Wagner's *Tetrology.*

37 Leonid Leonidovich *Sabaneyev,* musicologist, author of the books *Scriabin* (1923), *Recollections of Scriabin* (1925), and a series of articles.

38 Yuri Fedorovich *Fayer* (1890–   ), people's artist of the USSR, main director of Ballet of the Bolshoi Theater of the USSR.

39 Apocalypse: The Revelation of St. John.

40 *Sodom and Gomorrah,* according to Biblical legend the ancient Palestinian cities destroyed by earthquake and fire because of sins.

41 Walt *Whitman* (1819–92), classic American poet.

42 *Yggsdrasil* in the tales of the ancient German epic the Edda – The Tree of Life, Ash of the World [*Welt-Esche*], whose name means "Bearer of Sacred Terror." In his article "The Embodiment of a Myth" (the journal *Teatr,* 1940, no. 10) Eisenstein discusses the following characteristics of it given by the German scholar Carl Zimrok: "This tree is the grandest and most powerful of all trees: Its branches spread over the entire earth and tower far above the heavens. As a whole this ash tree represents an image of the whole world..."

43 In his *Sketches Abroad* (1880–1), M. E. Saltykov-Shchedrin refers very negatively to E. Zola's novel *Nana,* but makes the following remark: "In general I recognize this activity (besides of course, his critical essays) to be very remarkable and am speaking exclusively about *Nana,* since this novel provides the standard for determining the tastes and trends of the contemporary bourgeoisie" (M. E. Saltykov-Shchedrin, *About Literature and Art,* Iskusstvo, Moscow, 1953, p. 398). The French writer Henri Barbusse (1873–1935), whose novel *Hell* (1908) was written under the clear influence of Zola's work, devoted an entire book to him, *Zola.*

44 Walter *Pitkin* (1878–1953), American psychologist and journalist, author of works popularizing applied psychology.

45 Edgar Lee *Masters* (1869–1950), American poet known for his collection of epitaphs *Spoon River Anthology* (1915). The book *Walt Whitman* (1937), to which Eisenstein refers, also belongs to the pen of Masters.

46 *Bacchus,* the god of wine in classical mythology.

47 *Osiris,* one of the major gods of ancient Egypt, the god of water, vegetation, and the incarnation of Nature's cycles. *Phoenix,* a mythological bird that resurrects from its own ashes, a symbol of eternal renewing and resurrection of Nature.

48 *Osiris, Phoenix, etc.* At this point in the margins of the manuscript, the author made the following note by hand: "Shouldn't we here talk about montage as '*unity in variety,*' a method that, incidentally, was born in films of purely poetic themes, forms and structures."

49 Stefan *Zweig* (1881–1942), Austrian writer, author of the collection *Novellas* (1911), *Amos* (1922), and other works, especially several cycles of literary-critical biographies. Eisenstein devoted a chapter to Zweig in his autobiography (see *Immoral Memories: Autobiography of Sergei M. Eisenstein*, Herbert Marshall, trans., Houghton-Mifflin, Boston, 1985).

50 Gustav *Mahler* (1860–1911), Austrian composer and conductor.

51 *Franz Joseph I* (1830–1916), Emperor of Austro-Hungary.

52 Nicholas Semenovich *Leskov* (1831–95), Russian writer. Eisenstein devoted a chapter "Sue and Leskov" to the "Ironic Reinterpretation...of Forms of Pathos" by Leskov but left it unfinished.

53 Yuri Nikolayevich *Tynyanov* (1894–1943), Soviet writer, literary critic, and translator, author of historical-literary research and novels about A. S. Pushkin, A. S. Griboyedov, V. K. Kukhelbeker, and others. The story *The Waxen Personage* was written by him in 1931.

54 Henry Wadsworth *Longfellow* (1807–82), American poet. Author of the widely known *A Song of Hiawatha* (1855).

55 Edgar Allan *Poe* (1809–49), American writer, creator of the so-called thriller genre.

56 *What scope for "regaining the city,"* a rephrasing of a citation from the Epistle of St. Paul "Regaining the City of the future" – those seeking the City of God.

57 *...the fragments of Claudius's speech given above* (see "On the structure of things").

58 David *Belasco* (1859–1931), American dramatist and director.

59 Victorien *Sardou* (1831–1908), French dramatist, author of many melodramas.

60 Ambrose Bierce (1842–1914), American writer continuing the tradition of Edgar Allan Poe, master of short story "thrillers." Famous for his book of aphorisms *The Devil's Dictionary*.

61 Alexandre *Dumas(-père)* (1802–70), French writer and dramatist, author of popular novels: *The Three Musketeers* (1844) and *The Count of Monte Cristo*.

62 Félix *Pyat* (1810–89), French dramatist and political activist. Wrote melodramas protesting against tyranny and sympathizing with the poor. His best play is *The Parisian Ragpicker*, achieving great success in the revolutionary days of 1848.

63 Guilbert de *Pixerécourt* (1773–1844), French dramatist. Writer of pseudoromantic melodramas. Known as the "Roscius of the Boulevards."

64 *Edmund Kean*, central character in the play by A. Dumas-père: *Kean, or Genius and Dissipation*; *Don Caesar de Bazan*, hero of the same-name play by F. Dumas and D'Henry; *Father Jean*, hero of the melodrama by F. Pyat *The Parisian Ragpicker*; *Buridan*, main character of the play by A. Dumas-père; *Toussaint-L'Ouverture*, main character in the same-name play by the French dramatist A. Lamartin (1790–1869), dedicated to the leader of the negro slave revolt in Haiti; *Robert Macaire*, leading role of Frédérick Lemaître as the escaped convict in a melodrama by Anthier, Saint Amant, and Poliant (1823). In 1834 Lemaître himself wrote a comedy around the same character in which the speculator and murderer becomes a leading financier. Honoré Daumier created a cycle of gravures dedicated to Robert Macaire (1836–8 and 1840–41).

5 *Virgil* (70–19 B.C.), ancient Latin poet. Author of the *Aeneid* and the poem *The Georgics* in which he sang of nature, village life, and agricultural labor.

6 *Dionysian lyricism*, in ancient Greece the festival held in honor of the god Dionysus, from which Greek drama developed.

7 *I have already written much on the subject matter...*, Eisenstein wrote about the theme of his film *The Old and the New* (or *The General Line*) in his essays *Triumphant Workdays* and *Experiments Understood by Millions* (see *Selected Works*, Vol. I).

8 Andrea *Mantegna* (1431–1506), Italian painter and engraver. In this case Eisenstein has in mind his painting *The Dead Christ* (1467, Gallery Brera, Milan), also known as *The Foreshortened Christ*.

9 *Jupiter, once kidnapping Europa...*, the Greek myth.

10 *Moses...*, Exodus.

11 *Golden calf*, Exodus 32.

12 *Shakhsi-Vakhsi*, refers to a procession during a Muslim religious ceremony in memory of the son of the Caliph Ali-Hosain, killed in a battle at Kerbela (A.D. 680) – a procession simulating the funeral of Hosain, accompanied by self-torture.

13 The "Flagellants," one of the very oldest Russian sects, originated at the end of the seventeenth century and was a branch of the larger religious movement called the "Old Believers" ("The Ritualists"). The "Flagellants" were mystics who believed in the possibility of the permanent incarnations of God in the individual...They organized secret meetings in which they attempted to call forth the presence of the Holy Spirit by means of ecstatic dances. These meetings at times terminated in orgies. This sect was in general associated with sexual license. Gregory Rasputin, who played such a tragic role in the fall of the imperial regime in Russia, was associated with the "Flagellants." G. Vernadsky, *A History of Russia*, Yale University Press, New Haven, 1961, p. 117).

14 *Hardly perceptible...the tonality of the shot*, a reference to Eisenstein's theory of "tonic and overtonic montage." [See his *Montage*, H. Marshall, trans., in publication (from Vol. II of the Russian edition)].

15 *Suprematism*, the Russian abstract school of painting pioneered by Malevich.

16 *I had reason to quote a perfect example of this...*, see *Montage*, 1938.

17 *Amplification*, one of the favorite terms of Eisenstein signifying the enlargement of the compass of an artistic image as a result of a deepened dramatic and directorial treatment. Thus evolved the film *Battleship Potemkin* from a sketchily outlined episode in N. F. Agadzhanova's 1905 script.

18 Claude *Monet* (1840–1926), French artist, impressionist.

19 *Ormazd and Ahriman*, the Hellenized names of the god-brothers Ahura Mazda and Angra Mainya [negative thought]. According to the beliefs of the Zoroastrian (ancient Persian) religion, they embody correspondingly good and evil, light and dark, the creative and destructive principle and are eternally fighting among themselves.

20 *Litany*, a form of prayer in which the clergy and the congregation take part alternately with recitation of supplications and fixed responses.

21 *Ratapoile*, a representative image of a French militarist of the period of the

Second Empire. He was the main character of a whole cycle of graphic and sculptural caricatures by Honoré Daumier.

22 *Rigalbouch*, a French singer and dancer of the period of the Second Empire and author of *The Memoirs of Rigalbouch*, 1860.

23 *The brothers Vasil'ev*, pseudonym of the Soviet film directors G. N. Vasilev (1899–1946) and S. D. Vasil'ev (1900–59) who, besides the classic *Chapayev*, created the films *The Volochayev Days*, *The Front*, *The Defense of Tsaritsyn*, etc.

24 Alexey Dmitrievich, *Popov* (1892–1961), Soviet theater director, people's artist of the USSR from 1935 – artistic director, then main director of the Central Theater of the Soviet Army. In the history of Soviet theater are his productions of the play by L. Seifullian, *Virineia*, 1925; N. Pogodin's plays *The Poem about an Axe*, 1931; *My Friend*, 1932; and *After the Ball*, 1934; Shakespearian productions of *Romeo and Juliet* and *The Taming of the Shrew*, etc.

25 Grigory Vasilyevich *Alexandrov (Mormonenko)* (1903–   ), Soviet film director, People's Artist of the USSR. He began his activity under the direction of S. M. Eisenstein in the Proletcult theater. From 1925 to 1931 he participated in the production of Eisenstein's films. He is the producer of the musical comedies *Cheerful Fellows*, *Circus*, *Volga-Volga*, *Spring*, *A Russian Souvenir*, and also the film *The Composer Gïinka*, etc.

26 Maxim Maximovich *Shtraukh* (1900–   ), Soviet actor and theater director, People's Artist of the USSR. A friend since childhood of S. M. Eisenstein's, Shtraukh began his creative path with him in the First Workers' Theater of the Proletcult. In 1925–8 he became part of the "Iron Five" assistants of Eisenstein. (See Herbert Marshall's *Battleship Potemkin*, Avon Books, New York, 1978, p. 13.) The image of V. I. Lenin was created by the actor on the stage of the Moscow Theater of the Revolution (the production of *Truth*, 1937) and in film (*Man with a Gun*, 1938; *Yakov Srerdlov*, 1940; *They Call Him Suche-Bator*, 1942; *Tales about Lenin*, 1957).

27 Eduard *Manet* (1832–83), French painter, one of the founders of impressionism. Eisenstein has in mind here his picture *The Bar of the Follies-Berger* (1881) and *The Beerseller* (1878).

28 *Ragtime*, rhythm characterized by strong syncopation in the melody with a regularly accented accompaniment.

29 *Sequence* (music), the sequential alternation of homophonic and polyphonic musical structures in an ascending or descending direction. Eisenstein uses this term figuratively for signifying a certain method used by the director to develop an episode or scene in a film. Besides the scene from "Meeting the Squadron" discussed above, one may take as an example the well-known "Suite of the Mist" in *Potemkin* analyzed by Eisenstein later, in the chapter "Nonindifferent Nature."

30 *Tabernacle*, a portable sanctuary of the ancient Hebrews that accompanied them, according to Biblical legend, during their wandering after the "exodus" from Egypt.

31 François *Rabelais* (1494–1553), French writer and humanist. In the novel *Gargantua and Pantagruel* (1532–4), directed against the old feudal world and the scholastics of the medieval church, Rabelais with brilliant hyperbolization praised the joy of earthly life and human flesh.

32 Peter *Breughel*, the Elder, nicknamed the Peasant (born between 1525 and

1530, died 1569), painter, draughtsman, and engraver, representative of the Dutch Renaissance. With great strength, richness, and mischievous humor Breughel painted scenes from popular life (*The Battle of Carnival with Lent*, *Proverbs*, *A Peasant Dance*, etc.).

33 Peter Paul *Rubens* (1577—1640), Flemish painter whose works are permeated by an attempt for sensual, full-blooded perception of the world.

34 Percy Bysshe *Shelley* (1792—1822), English poet.

35 *Francis Bacon* (1561—1626), English philosopher.

36 *Die Gotterdammerung* (The Twilight of the Gods), the last opera of Richard Wagner's *Tetrology*.

37 Leonid Leonidovich *Sabaneyev*, musicologist, author of the books *Scriabin* (1923), *Recollections of Scriabin* (1925), and a series of articles.

38 Yuri Fedorovich *Fayer* (1890—   ), people's artist of the USSR, main director of Ballet of the Bolshoi Theater of the USSR.

39 Apocalypse: The Revelation of St. John.

40 *Sodom and Gomorrah*, according to Biblical legend the ancient Palestinian cities destroyed by earthquake and fire because of sins.

41 Walt *Whitman* (1819—92), classic American poet.

42 *Yggsdrasil* in the tales of the ancient German epic the Edda — The Tree of Life, Ash of the World [*Welt-Esche*], whose name means "Bearer of Sacred Terror." In his article "The Embodiment of a Myth" (the journal *Teatr*, 1940, no. 10) Eisenstein discusses the following characteristics of it given by the German scholar Carl Zimrok: "This tree is the grandest and most powerful of all trees: Its branches spread over the entire earth and tower far above the heavens. As a whole this ash tree represents an image of the whole world..."

43 In his *Sketches Abroad* (1880—1), M. E. Saltykov-Shchedrin refers very negatively to E. Zola's novel *Nana*, but makes the following remark: "In general I recognize this activity (besides of course, his critical essays) to be very remarkable and am speaking exclusively about *Nana*, since this novel provides the standard for determining the tastes and trends of the contemporary bourgeoisie" (M. E. Saltykov-Shchedrin, *About Literature and Art*, Iskusstvo, Moscow, 1953, p. 398). The French writer Henri Barbusse (1873—1935), whose novel *Hell* (1908) was written under the clear influence of Zola's work, devoted an entire book to him, *Zola*.

44 Walter *Pitkin* (1878—1953), American psychologist and journalist, author of works popularizing applied psychology.

45 Edgar Lee *Masters* (1869—1950), American poet known for his collection of epitaphs *Spoon River Anthology* (1915). The book *Walt Whitman* (1937), to which Eisenstein refers, also belongs to the pen of Masters.

46 *Bacchus*, the god of wine in classical mythology.

47 *Osiris*, one of the major gods of ancient Egypt, the god of water, vegetation, and the incarnation of Nature's cycles. *Phoenix*, a mythological bird that resurrects from its own ashes, a symbol of eternal renewing and resurrection of Nature.

48 *Osiris, Phoenix*, etc. At this point in the margins of the manuscript, the author made the following note by hand: "Shouldn't we here talk about montage as '*unity in variety*,' a method that, incidentally, was born in films of purely poetic themes, forms and structures."

49 Stefan *Zweig* (1881–1942), Austrian writer, author of the collection *Novellas* (1911), *Amos* (1922), and other works, especially several cycles of literary-critical biographies. Eisenstein devoted a chapter to Zweig in his autobiography (see *Immoral Memories: Autobiography of Sergei M. Eisenstein*, Herbert Marshall, trans., Houghton-Mifflin, Boston, 1985).

50 Gustav *Mahler* (1860–1911), Austrian composer and conductor.

51 *Franz Joseph I* (1830–1916), Emperor of Austro-Hungary.

52 Nicholas Semenovich *Leskov* (1831–95), Russian writer. Eisenstein devoted a chapter "Sue and Leskov" to the "Ironic Reinterpretation. . . of Forms of Pathos" by Leskov but left it unfinished.

53 Yuri Nikolayevich *Tynyanov* (1894–1943), Soviet writer, literary critic, and translator, author of historical-literary research and novels about A. S. Pushkin, A. S. Griboyedov, V. K. Kukhelbeker, and others. The story *The Waxen Personage* was written by him in 1931.

54 Henry Wadsworth *Longfellow* (1807–82), American poet. Author of the widely known *A Song of Hiawatha* (1855).

55 Edgar Allan *Poe* (1809–49), American writer, creator of the so-called thriller genre.

56 *What scope for "regaining the city,"* a rephrasing of a citation from the Epistle of St. Paul "Regaining the City of the future" – those seeking the City of God.

57 *. . .the fragments of Claudius's speech given above* (see "On the structure of things").

58 David *Belasco* (1859–1931), American dramatist and director.

59 Victorien *Sardou* (1831–1908), French dramatist, author of many melodramas.

60 Ambrose Bierce (1842–1914), American writer continuing the tradition of Edgar Allan Poe, master of short story "thrillers." Famous for his book of aphorisms *The Devil's Dictionary*.

61 Alexandre *Dumas(-père)* (1802–70), French writer and dramatist, author of popular novels: *The Three Musketeers* (1844) and *The Count of Monte Cristo*.

62 Félix *Pyat* (1810–89), French dramatist and political activist. Wrote melodramas protesting against tyranny and sympathizing with the poor. His best play is *The Parisian Ragpicker*, achieving great success in the revolutionary days of 1848.

63 Guilbert de *Pixerécourt* (1773–1844), French dramatist. Writer of pseudoromantic melodramas. Known as the "Roscius of the Boulevards."

64 *Edmund Kean*, central character in the play by A. Dumas-père: *Kean, or Genius and Dissipation*; *Don Caesar de Bazan*, hero of the same-name play by F. Dumas and D'Henry; *Father Jean*, hero of the melodrama by F. Pyat *The Parisian Ragpicker*; *Buridan*, main character of the play by A. Dumas-père; *Toussaint-L'Ouverture*, main character in the same-name play by the French dramatist A. Lamartin (1790–1869), dedicated to the leader of the negro slave revolt in Haiti; *Robert Macaire*, leading role of Frédérick Lemaître as the escaped convict in a melodrama by Anthier, Saint Amant, and Poliant (1823). In 1834 Lemaître himself wrote a comedy around the same character in which the speculator and murderer becomes a leading financier. Honoré Daumier created a cycle of gravures dedicated to Robert Macaire (1836–8 and 1840–41).

65 Theophile *Gautier* (1811–72), French poet, novelist, and critic.

66 Jules Gabrielle *Janin* (1804–74), French writer, critic, and journalist.

67 Roscius *Quint* (130–62 B.C.), famous ancient Greek actor who was born a slave and eventually achieved the highest honors. Ira Aldridge was called the African Roscius and Eisenstein called Frédérick Lemaître the Roscius of the Boulevards.

68 *Zaza*, American film produced by Paramount, George Cukor director.

69 Joseph Isadore *Samson* (1793–1871), leading actor of the Comédie Française, creator of the famous role of Figaro in Beaumarchais's *Marriage of Figaro*.

70 *Rachel* (Elisa Felix) (1820–58), celebrated French tragedienne.

71 Alexandre *Dumas*(-fils) (1824–95), French writer and dramatist, author of many melodramas including the famous *The Lady of the Camelias*.

72 *Ruy Blas*, drama by Victor Hugo (1802–85).

73 *...the task of comic composition....* Over many years Eisenstein intended to write a thesis on the nature of comedy. In his textbook *Regisseur* (see Vol 4. of Russian edition of *Selected Works*) Eisenstein dedicates a special section to the comic structure of stage action and its theoretical base. In addition, in his Archives are notes for a book on "The Comic," which remained unfulfilled.

74 Firmen *Jamais* (1865–1933), French actor and director who played an important role in reforming the pseudoclassic French theater style along realistic lines.

75 *Pliny* (the Elder) (A.D. 23–79), ancient Roman teacher and writer.

76 *Zeuxis* (420–390 B.C.), ancient Greek painter.

77 *Medea*, heroine of ancient Greek mythology, subject of the tragedy by Euripides (405 B.C.).

78 *Phaedra*, a heroine of ancient Greek mythology, subject of the famous play by Racine (1677).

79 *Horatii*, of Patrician stock in Ancient Rome.

80 *...through the ascetic and saint who is capable of "stinking,"* Eisenstein has in mind the character of the elder Zosimi from the novel by F. Dostoyevsky.

81 Apollon Nikolayevich *Maikov* (1821–97), Russian poet, in correspondence with F. M. Dostoyevsky.

82 Lucius Annaeus *Seneca* (54 B.C.–A.D. 39), ancient Roman philosopher, politician, and dramatist, author of nine tragedies.

83 Christopher *Marlowe* (1564–93), English dramatist, precursor of Shakespeare. Author of *The Tragic History of Dr. Faustus*, *The Jew of Malta*, *Tamerlaine the Great*, and other tragedies.

84 Ben *Jonson* (1573–1637), English dramatist, author of the comedies *Bartholomew Fair* and *Volpone*.

85 John *Webster* (1580–1625), English dramatist, author of *The White Devil*.

86 *Everyman in His Humour*, Ben Jonson, *Complete Plays*, Dent, London, 1910.

87 In the manuscript a note is attached here: "Quote from *The Storm* – find." In all probability this is the quotation Eisenstein had in mind: from Ostrovsky's play *The Storm* (Act 1, Scene 1.): "...Do you know, on a sunny day such a bright pillar extends downwards from the cupola, and in that pillar hovers smoke, just like a cloud, and it seems to me as if in that very pillar angels fly and sing...".

88 *The Seventh Seal of the Apocalypse*, an erroneous allusion by Eisenstein; the painting concerned is El Greco's *The Lifting of the Fifth Seal*.

89 Maurice *Barres* (1862–1923), French writer, author of the book *El Greco ou le Secret de Tolèdes*, (1912).

90 *This picture exists in four variants.* Actually there are seven canvases of *The Expulsion of the Moneylenders from the Temple* attributed to El Greco and several copies from his studio. It may be that he had in mind the four with the greatest variations from each other.

91 *Laocoon*, the painting by El Greco, created in 1606–10 (preserved in the National Gallery, Washington); *The Lifting of the Fifth Seal*, see note 88; *The Concert of Angels in the Clouds*, detail (upper part) of the El Greco painting *The Annunciation* (1593, Bilbao Museum, Spain).

92 ...makes such an astonishing and exciting *Storm over Toledo*. In a section of *Nonindifferent Nature* Eisenstein analyzes in detail the principle of the "pathetication" of landscape in the painting *Storm over Toledo*.

93 Andrea *del Sarto* (1486–1531), Italian painter of the Renaissance, representative of the Florentine school.

94 ...*contrast the Renaissance and Baroque.* Eisenstein has in mind the book by the German art critic Henrich Wölflin (1864–1945) *The Renaissance and the Baroque*.

95 Donato *Bramante* (1444–1514), Italian architect of the Renaissance, designer of the Milan cathedral and others. In 1504 began to work on a project for St. Peter's Cathedral, Rome.

96 Giovanni Battista *Piranesi* (1720–1778), Italian engraver and architect. Author of an enormous quantity of engravings, the themes of which are ancient and modern (for Piranesi) Rome and grandiose architectural fantasies. See G. B. Piranesi *Carceri*, Origo Verlag, Zurich, Switzerland, 1958. In the next chapter Eisenstein analyzes two engravings of Piranesi from his cycle *Fantasy on the Theme of Dungeons* (1745–50 and 1761.)

97 Alexandre Nikolayevich *Benois* (1870–1960), Russian artist, theater designer, art historian, head of the World of Art Group (Mir Iskusstvo), Petersburg. Eisenstein quotes from his *History of Painting of all Times and Peoples*.

98 This chapter does not have a title. Here is a note about it dated July 4, 1947, in which Eisenstein writes: "Strictly speaking the second theme in every chapter is or should be stamped out. Along the lines of "Helen or the Rescue of the Virtuous": "Piranesi or the Flux of Form."

99 Daniel *Marot* (1663–1752), French engraver and theater artist.

100 Gérard *Edelinck* (1640–1707), French engraver, master of metal engraving.

101 William *Hogarth* (1697–1764), English painter, engraver, and art theoretician, author of the well-known treatise *The Analysis of Beauty*.

102 Robert *Nanteuil* (1623–78), French engraver and draughtsman.

103 Claude *Mellan* (1598–1678), French engraver and draughtsman.

104 Jacques *Callot* (1592–1635), French engraver and draughtsman, whose basic works are considered his *Balli* (1629), *Capriccio* (1617–23) *The Disasters of War* (1623–33). Callot's two engravings "The Temptation of St Anthony" relate to 1615 and 1635.

105 ...the stair case, hurled from one world to another...*the Biblical legend of Jacob's dream*, see *Genesis*.

106 *Next – the young Picasso, Gleizes, Metzinger.* The French artist Paul Cézanne (1839–1906) declared: "Everything in nature is designed in the form of a sphere, cone, cylinder; one must learn to draw these simple figures, and if you are able to master these forms, you can do anything, you want." (*Masters of Art on Art*, Vol. III, Iskusstvo, Moscow–Leningrad, 1939, p. 219). With this formula Cézanne expressed the task of one school of twentieth-century painting – cubism, the program of which was laid down by the French artists Albert Gleizes (1881–1953) and Jean Metzinger (1883–1956) in Gleizes and Metzinger, *On Cubism*, Unwin, London, 1913.

107 "*No – you!*" In his monumental painting *Guernica* Picasso reflected the barbarous destruction of the city of Guernica by the German and Italian fascists during the Spanish civil war (1936–9).

108 *At the basis of the composition of its ensemble... lies that same 'dance' that is also at the basis of the creation of music, painting, and cinematic montage.* (This statement refutes the accusations of certain critics that Eisenstein transfers mechanically the laws of one art into another. In fact... Eisenstein seeks for the general aesthetic laws governing each form of art's specific shaping of expression, but in principle universal for all systems of art. [Russian ed. note]

109 *Trianon*, a palace in Versailles decorated with frescoes and sculptures in the Rococco style.

110 *Gopurams*, the great gateways of Indian temples, richly ornamented with sculptures. Alongside of realistic representations of animals are also figures of fantastic monsters, several of which Eisenstein describes.

111 Phineas Taylor *Barnum* (1810–91), famous American circus entrepreneur, whose touring circus covered America and Europe.

112 *Uxmal*, one of the ancient cities of Yucatan, founded in 897–1007.

113 Thomas *De Quincy* (1785–1859), English writer, author of essays on Shakespeare, Milton, etc., and author of the famous *Confessions of an English Opium Eater* (1821).

114 William *Wordsworth* (1770–1850), English poet.

115 Samuel Taylor *Coleridge* (1772–1824), English poet. Like De Quincy, Coleridge was a dope addict and his famous poem *Kubla Khan* was written under the influence of opium.

116 *Quietism*, a complicated religious movement that swept through France, Italy, and Spain during the seventeenth century. Quietism was essentially a reaction against the bureaucratic ecclesiasticism of the Roman Catholic Church. Its chief apostle was Miguel de Molinos who was eventually condemned as a heretic by the Inquisition and imprisoned for life. Eisenstein deals with the aesthetic expression of Eastern "quietism" – the contemplative philosophy of ancient India and China – in *Nonindifferent Nature* (see present volume, p. 216)

117 *Yosa Buson* (1716–83), Japanese artist and poet.

118 *St. John of the Holy Cross*, Eisenstein means Juan de la Cruse (1542–91), a Spanish poet-mystic, known as the Doctor Ecstatic and posthumously relegated to sainthood.

119 *Fra Beato Angelico* (Guido di Pietro) (1387–1455), Italian artist of the Florentine epoch of the Renaissance.

120 *Bodhisattva*, one of the incarnations of Buddha.

121 *The General Line*, the title of the first version of Eisenstein's film *The Old and the New* that was intended to show the general line of the Communist Party in agriculture. [See my other two books *Masters of Soviet Cinema*, Routledge

Kegan Paul, Boston, 1983; and *Immoral Memories*, Houghton−Mifflin, Boston, 1983.

122 Peter Andreyevich *Pavlenko* (1899−1951), Russian Soviet writer and script-writer. Together with Eisenstein wrote the script of *Alexander Nevsky* (1938). [See *Masters of Soviet Cinema*, op. cit. p. 40, 216−17 − HM.]

123 Eisenstein is working here with data from the American press that he had at hand. The principle of the multistage rocket predicted by K. E. Tsiolkovsky was realized in practice in the following years of Soviet and Western astronautics.

124 Gertrude *Stein* (1874−1946), American author, representative of modernism, author of the books *Three Lives, The Autobiography of Alice Toklas*, and others. She had a significant influence on the formation of the style of the young Hemingway.

125 Later in the manuscript, Eisenstein says: "At another point we will briefly touch on the technique of *pathos* in which the famous passage of the 'bird-troika' of *Dead Souls* was constructed in terms of composition. In a third passage the governor thumbs his nose at himself in *Dead Souls*." However, in the manuscript *pathos* does not turn out to be among the examples enumerated here. In Tsgali (The Central State Archives of Literature and Art of the USSR), the sketched plan has been preserved, precisely pointing out the content and passage, in the research on *pathos*, of two unfinished fragments on *Dead Souls* by Gogol:

10 June, 1947. "Gogol and Pathos." "Bird-Troika."

A *Gogol "Bird-troika."*
   i   Chichikov in the troika.
   ii The troika in general.
   iii Only a smart people could invent it.
   iv "Aren't you, too, Rus, a smart unsurpassable troika..." (formula of the atomic bomb)

10 June, 1947. Kislovodsk.

B *Gogol*. The formula of Whitman-Chichikov and the register of dead peasants (Vol. I, chap. VII). Right after and as a consequence of *The Covetous Knight* (Tsgali, f. 1923, op. 1, #1044).

126 *Inferno and Purgatorio*, the names, respectively, of the first and second parts of Dante's *Divine Comedy*. Eisenstein hints here at Gogol's conception of *Dead Souls*. The Russian literary scholar D. N. Ovsianiko-Kulikovsky, in characterizing this conception, wrote that the great poem of Gogol "had to first portray everything that was bad and dark" in the nature of Russian man, and then reveal the good inclinations hidden in it, and finally, to show Rus the way to rebirth, to a better future...The story about the adventures of Pavel Ivanovich Chichikov turned into a poetic contemplation of Rus "from a nice distance" into a mournful narration about northern Russian "darkness and the frightening lack of light," finally, into a moral-religious poem − about Russian "hell" (Part 1), "purgatory" (Part 2), and "heaven" (Part 3). Such was the conception inspiring *The Divine Comedy* of Dante, which Gogol never stopped rereading in Italy, where he also worked on *Dead Souls* (D. N. Ovsianiko-Kulikovsky, *Collected Works*, Vol. 1. *Gogol*, GIZ, Moscow−Petrograd, 1923, pp. 32−3).

127 Fëdor Nikiforovich *Plevako* (1843−1908), Russian lawyer and judicial orator. At the scandalous trial of the Mother Superior Mitrofanya, formerly the Baroness Rozen, who was connected by dark machinations to great speculators and con men, Plevako shouted: "Higher, build higher the walls of the society that believes in you, so that the world won't see the deeds created by you under the cover of a cassock and cloister!"

128 Jean *Cocteau* (1889−1963), French writer, artist, theater director and film director, member of the French Academy. Cocteau's ironic passage on fashion is cited by Eisenstein in his study *Montage* (see Vol. II. *Selected Works*, pp. 398−9).

129 At this point in the manuscript Eisenstein made the mark of a footnote; however, he did not bring in the quote. At Tsgali the following excerpt from A. Bely's book *The Mastery of Gogol* has been preserved, marked "On... 'Gogol−Piranesi'."

"his (Gogol's S. E.) description of the city is the most urban of the urban: Paris: struck...by the gleam of streets, by the disarray of roofs, thick chimneys, unarchitectural, solid masses of houses, plastered with the dense raggedness of stores, the ugliness of bare...side walls, on the roofs...on chimneys, by the light transparency of the lower stories...from mirrors... Paris...craters, fountains, flashing sparks of news...under the fashion of petty...laws...A magic heap blazed...houses became transparent, etc. Rome." [It is interesting to note that S. M. Eisenstein worked in Hollywood on a filmscript called *The Transparent House*; see *Iskusstvo Kino* (*The Art of the Cinema*) − HM.]

"Gogol in a unique way sees the playing crowd of walls, as we see it from a streetcar: with a jump in the houses that open and close the perspective: 'Sidewalks bearing...carriages with galloping horses that seemed not to move, a bridge stretched out and broke...into an arch, a house stood with its roof below, a sentry-box came reeling towards him'" (*Nevsky Prospect*), A. Bely, *Mastery of Gogol*, Gos Izdkhudlit. Moscow−Leningrad, 1934. p. 309 (Tsgali, f. 1923. op.

130 In his well-known "Five Theses" the French architect Le Corbusier wrote: "In a structure one can separate the unessential from the essential. Instead of the former foundations on which a structure rested without a controlled calculation there appear calculated foundations, in the place of former walls − separate columns...They rise directly out of the earth to 3, 4, 6, etc. meters and bear the first story on this height. Thus, the building is saved from moisture, they have enough light and air, the building turns into a garden that passes under the house." (*Architecture of the Contemporary West*, M. Izogiz, ed., State Publishing House of Fine Arts, 1932, p. 40).

131 Frank Lloyd *Wright* (1869−1961), American architect who had a great influence on the architecture of the twentieth century. The basic principles of Wright's work are a rejection of decorative stylization, the substitution of a flat facade for "three-dimensional" architecture, the attempt to connect the house with the surrounding landscape. Proceeding from these principles, Wright applies glass extensively, alternates closed spaces with open terraces and squares, achieving the "transparency" of a building and its "synthesis" with nature.

132 Valdimir Evgrafovich *Tatlin* (1885−1952), Russian artist. In 1922 he created the project of the monument to the Third International in the form of a colossal tower created in the spirit of constructivism.

133 *Galley*, an ancient ship propelled by both oars and sails.

134 *Helicopter*, a plane that can fly vertically.

135 *Gregorian chants sung in unison*, the performance by a male choir singing in unison Catholic religious works created during the late sixth and early seventh centuries with the participation of Pope Gregory I.

136 George *Gershwin* (1898–1937), American composer, setting the principle of so-called symphonic jazz. He used the melodies and rhythms of Negro folk music in his work.

137 Arthur *Schopenhauer* (1788–1860), German idealist philosopher.

138 Albert *Einstein* (1879–1955), one of the most important physicists and theoreticians of the twentieth century, discovered one of the fundamental laws of nature – the relationship between mass and energy. The formula of this law ($E = mc^2$) played a huge role in the development of nuclear physics.

139 *Introspection*, self-observation, direct observation of states of consciousness of those experiencing them.

140 *Theurgic*, one of the varieties of so-called mystical knowledge presupposing an entrance into a union with gods and spirits. The concept of theurgy was widespread in symbolist literature at the beginning of the twentieth century.

141 *Manresa*, a city in Northeastern Spain. The Dominican monastery where in the 1620s Ignatius Loyola gave himself up to self-flagellation is located in Manresa.

142 *Saint Ignatius Loyola* (1491–1556), founder of the Order of Jesuits (The Society of Jesus). Canonized in 1622. Author of *The Book of the Spiritual Exercises*, a carefully worked out system for Jesuit education.

143 *Gnostic*, here in the sense of one who knows.

144 *George Sand* (pseudonym for Aurora Dupin, 1804–76), French writer, author of the novels *Oras* (1841), *Consuelo* (1842–3), and others.

145 Alexander *Borgia*, Alexander VI, Roman Pope (1442–1503), representative of the aristocratic Florentine family, the Borgias.

146 Alexander Christoforovich *Benckendorff* (1783–1844), reactionary political figure of the epoch of Nicholas I, from 1826 chief of police and head of the Third Section, one of the ardent enemies of Pushkin.

147 Shams ud-din Mohammed *Hafiz* (1325–89), classic poet of Persian and Tadzhik literature, praising exalted love, joy of life, and nature to his gazelles.

148 Constantin Mikhailovich *Simonov* (1915–79), Russian Soviet writer. The lyric poem "Wait for me," mentioned by Eisenstein below, was written by him in 1941.

149 Eisenstein wrote about the connection between the principle of the hieroglyphics of the East and the laws of cinema montage in the article "Behind the Frame," *Film Form*, pp. 28–44.

150 Since the beginning of *The Kangaroo* in the 1930s, Eisenstein begins to become profoundly interested in problems of the creative process, trying to establish a link between the most general aesthetic laws and the laws of developing human consciousness. As a result of many years of research and observation, he came to the conclusion that in the process of the creation of a work of art, not only do those layers of the human psyche that correspond to the level of logical knowledge of reality take part but in them is included the deep spheres formed historically in the prelogical epoch, man's sensual knowledge of the world. Eisenstein conceived several works on prelogic and its influence on the construction of an artistic work, however, he was not able to finish any of them. In its general features, he discussed this concept in his address at the creative conference of workers of Soviet cinematography in 1935. Here Eisenstein jokingly compares human thought to Pandora's box, having in mind the ancient Greek myths about how the curious Pandora opened a box given to her as a present by Zeus, full of calamities that flew out and spread around the world and from which Pandora was able to keep back in her hands only deceptive hope.

151 Eisenstein made a note in the manuscript, intending to bring in "several examples of her writing and a fragment of a parody on them," "a rose is a rose is a rose," etc.

152 Here the well-known statement of Karl Marx is paraphrased: "Humanity cheerfully parts with past."

153 Emanuel *Swedenborg* (1688–1722), Swedish scholar, theologian, and author of the book *Heaven's Secrets*, an allegorical commentary to the Bible.

154 The representation of a person established by the theosophists, who invested the mystical content of his teachings into forms of speculative logical constructions.

155 English film shot in 1946 by the director Compton Bennett, a work of Sidney Box Productions.

156 Pierre *Curie* (1859–1906) and Marie Sklodovskaya *Curie* (1867–1934), physicists whose discoveries in the field of radioactive uranium set the basis for contemporary nuclear physics; Louis *Pasteur* (1822–95), French biologist, founder of the science of immunization.

157 *Joseph John Thomson (1856–1940), English physicist, winner of the Nobel Prize, one of the founders of the contemporary science on the structure of the atom.*

158 *Eisenstein brings in the name here and describes below the subject of the preparatory sketch for the picture St. Anne and Madonna with Child* in which St. John is substituted by a lamb. However, the principles of composition of the sketch are preserved and developed in the final version of the picture.

159 After this phrase Eisenstein made a note in the manuscript, intending to bring in an excerpt from Sigmund Freud's book *A Childhood Memory of Leonardo da Vinci*. Referring to an actual fact from the biography of the artist (Leonardo was raised in the home of his mother, and then in the home of a stepmother – the legal wife of his father), Freud interprets the subject of *St. Anne* psychoanalytically – as a cryptogram of the situation of "child with two mothers." In contrast to Freud, Eisenstein sees in the picture an image of the pathos of unity of generations, whose brilliant solution determined the unsurpassable significance of this masterpiece.

III. Once again on the structure of things

1 Eisenstein is referring here to the book *The Director*, which he was working on since 1934. The first volume of this fundamental work, which had almost been completed, has been published in Vol. IV of the *Selected Works* [*Izbrannye Proizvedeniye*].

2 "Home Sweet Home," a popular American song with the words of the poet John Howard Payne (1791–1852).

3 Bing *Crosby* (1904–77), American film and television actor.

4 *Mars* (the pseudonym of Anne Boutet) (1779−1847), a French actress who played major roles in the *Comédie Française* for a long time.

5 Marie *Dorval* (1798−1849), French actress and romantic.

6 Pierre *Bocage* (1799−1862), French romantic actor, partner of F. Lemaître and M. Dorval in the Theatre Porte St. Martin.

7 *Robin Hood* (1923, A. Duen, dir.) and *The Thief of Baghdad* (1924, R. Walsh, dir.), American "hits" with the popular actor of the 1920s, Douglas Fairbanks. *The Gray Shadow* (original title *The Mystery of the Gray Ghost*, 1917, E. Johnson, dir.) and *The House of Hate* (1918, D. Seitz, dir.), American serials of adventure.

8 Alexander Pavlovich *Lensky* (1847−1908), Russian theater personality and actor from 1876 and from 1907 artistic director of the Moscow Maly Theatre.

9 Maria Gavrilovna *Savina* (1854−1915), Russian actress, from 1874 leading actress of the Petersburg Alexandrinsky Theatre.

10 Marlene *Dietrich* (1902−   ), German film actress. Her acting activity began in Germany, in the theater of Max Reinhardt. At the beginning of the 1930s she went to the United States. Her best roles were played in the films of J. von Sternberg, *The Blue Angel* (1930), *Morocco* (1930), *The Blond Venus* (1932), and in recent years − in the films *Witness for the Prosecution* of B. Wilder and *The Nuremberg Trial* by S. Kramer.

11 Joseph von *Sternberg* (1894−1969), American director who began his activity in Holland in 1925. The film *Morocco* (based on the play of Benno Vigny, *Ema Jolie*) was shot in 1930.

12 He has in mind the performances of *The Inspector General* (1927) and *Woe from Wit* (1928) produced by V. E. Meyerhold.

13 Abel *Gance* (1889−1981), French film director, poet, author, philosopher, and actor. He is famous for his films *La Roue* [*The Wheel*] (1923), *J'accuse* [*I Accuse*] (1919), *Napoleon* (1927), and others.

14 *Jourdain*, hero of Moliere's comedy *Le Bourgeois Gentilhomme* (1670). It is mentioned in the article of K. Marx and F. Engels, *The Holy Family* (chapter entitled "Critical Criticism as the Merchant of Secrets").

15 The conception of Eisenstein, characterizing the first fifteen years of Soviet film (1919−34), had been discussed by him in an address at the Creative Conference of Filmmakers in 1935 (Vol. II of Russian edition) and in the article "The Middle of Three" (published in Vol. VI of Russian edition).

16 Eisenstein probably has in mind the following statement of Karl Marx in his work *Eighteen Brumiere of Louis Bonaparte* (International Publishers, New Year, 1935): "Bourgeois revolutions as, for example, the revolution of the eighteenth century, dash impetuously from success to success; the dramatic effects of one are more blinding than the other, people and things seem to be illuminated by a Bengal fire, every day breathes with ecstasy, but they are transitory, quickly achieve their apogee, and a long hand-over seizes society before it is able to soberly assimilate the results of its period of storm and stress."

17 Louis-Antoine *Saint-Just* (1767−94), participant in the French Revolution of the eighteenth century, one of the leaders of the Jacobin party, a brilliant orator.

18 Jean *Jaures* (1859−1914), member of the international socialist movement, historian and leading orator, author of a four-volume *History of the French Revolution*.

19 Romain *Rolland* (1866–1944), French writer, musicologist, political figure, and author of the novels *Jean-Christophe* (1903–12) and *L'Ame enchantée* (1922–33).

IV. Nonindifferent nature

1 He has in mind his research "On the Structure of Things."

2 Arnold *Schönberg* (1874–1951), Austrian composer, theoretician, pedagogue, and Expressionist, later inventor of "atonal" music.

3 Camille *Saint-Saëns* (1835–1921), French composer. C. Saint-Saëns, *Portraits et Souvenirs*, Societe des Editions Artistique, Paris, 1900, p. 284.

4 The discussion is about Man Ray's film *The Sea Star* [*Etoile de Mer*] (1927), apparently about the film of Cavalcanti *Nothing but Time* [*Rien que les heures*] (1926) – characteristic of the French avant-garde experimental works, in which the emphasis on optical expressiveness was not combined with an interest in assimilating real life (as in Man Ray) or connected with it externally (as in Cavalcanti). Man *Ray* (1890–1976), French artist and photographer, who in the 1920s, joined dadaism and surrealism. He participated in making surrealist films. Alberto *Cavalcanti* (1897–1982), Brazilian film director who worked in Europe until 1949. In the 1930s he appeared as a leading master of documentary film (in England).

5 Anatoly Dmitrievich *Golovnya* (1900–   ), Soviet cameraman, professor. He shot Pudovkin's films (*Mothers, The End of St. Petersburg, The Descendant of Genghis Khan*), which made him one of the founders of the Soviet School of Film–cameramen.

6 *Mother*, a film based on M. Gorky's novel. The author of the scenario was N. Zarkhi, director-editor, V. I. Pudovkin, cameraman, A. D. Golovnya. Made in 1926.

7 *The Overcoat*, film based on the short story by N. V. Gogol, directed by G. M. Kozintsev and L. Z. Trauberg, cameraman A. N. Moskvin. Made in 1926.

8 Pietro Gottardo *Gonzago* (1751–1831), famous Italian set designer and architect who worked for a long time in Russia.

9 Fillippo Tommaso *Marinetti* (1876–1944), writer, head of reactionary Italian futurism.

10 Tristan *Tzara* (1896–1964), French writer, one of the creators of the dadaist movement.

11 *Confucius* (551–479 B.C.), ancient Chinese philosopher.

12 Geoffrey *Chaucer* (1340–1400), English writer, author of the *Canterbury Tales*.

13 This is about the most ancient form of writing, designating objects and actions by conventional drawings. Eisenstein's interest in pictographs and hieroglyphics was connected with research on the laws of montage.

14 Katsushika *Hokusai* (1760–1849), great Japanese painter.

15 *Prosody* (Greek), in verse composition, the system of interrelationships between syllables.

16 *Tristam Shandy*, novel by the English writer Laurence Sterne.

17 "*The Future of Sound Film: A Recommendation*" [op. cit.].

18 William *Thackeray* (1811–63), English novelist.

19 George *Cruikshank* (1792–1878), English graphic artist and book illustrator.

20 An analysis of the dawn scene from *Aleksander Nevsky* appears in the article "Vertical Montage," in *Film Sense*, J. Leyda, ed. and trans., Faber & Faber, London, 1953, pp. 87–156.

21 *Vorschlag*, a musical term [English: grace note], meaning a small note put at the interval of a tone or half-tone below the harmonic.

22 Nikolay Yakovlevich *Marr* (1864–1934), Soviet linguist, creator of a theory of the origin of language.

23 *Wu Ch'ao-ch'u* (A.D. 700–60), one of the most famous artists of ancient China.

24 *Sesshū* (1420–1506), important artist of the so-called Japanese Renaissance, follower of the Chinese "Northern" School of Painting.

25 *Kuo Hsi* (1020–90), Chinese artist.

26 *Siu-jan*, Chinese artist of the tenth century.

27 *Chu-jan*, apparently he has in mind Tszuyi Zhan, Chinese landscape artist of the tenth century.

28 *Lu Ssu-hsün* (650–716), head of the "Northern" School of Chinese Painting.

29 *Wang Wei* (699–759), a very important Chinese artist and poet.

30 *Sung Epoch* (907–1270), in the cited text there is a mistake: the years of the Sung Dynasty are 960–1279.

31 *Ming epoch* (1280–1643), the years of the Ming Dynasty are 1268–1644.

32 Nikolay Konstantinovich *Churlyanis* (Churlionis) (1875–1911), Lithuanian composer and artist-symbolist, striving for "musicality" in painting and who considered it possible to convey in colors sounds and melodies.

33 *Taoism*, the teaching of the ancient Chinese philosopher Lao Tze (604–531 B.C.), whose basic category is Tao: "Law," "The Way," nonbeing, containing in oneself all the possibilities of being and achieved by contemplation. Taoism includes elements of a naive dialectic.

34 See *K. S. Stanislavsky, My Life in Art*, 8th ed., Izd. Iskusstvo, Moscow–Leningrad, 1948, pp. 363–4 [*My Life in Art*, J. J. Robbins, trans., Little Brown, Boston, 1968, p. 417]: "'Listen, not Víshnevy but Vishnévy Sad,' he stated triumphantly...This time I understood the great and yet delicate difference. Víshnevy Sad is a commercial orchard that brings in profit. Such an orchard is necessary to life even at the present. But Vishnévy Sad brings no profit. It hides in itself and in all of its flowering whiteness the great poetry of the dying life of aristocracy. The Vishnévy Sad grows for the sake of beauty, for the eyes of spoiled aesthetes. It is a pity to destroy it, but it is necessary to do so, for the economics of life demanded it."

35 James *Whistler* (1834–1903), American artist, often called his landscapes and portraits by musical names.

36 See the article "E!" – "On the Purity of Film Language."

37 *Sepulchre of Wu-Kung-tse*, burial of the family Wu in the province of Shandun (147 B.C.).

38 *Fujiwara Takayoshi*, Japanese artist of the Yamato-e school, who worked in the middle of the thirteenth century.

39 William *Hogarth* (1697–1764), English artist, author of the essay *The Analysis of Beauty* (1753).

40 Robert *Delaunay* (1885–1941), French artist who asserted the concept of "simultaneity" in painting (the principle of the simultaneous perception of an object from several points of view). *The Eiffel Tower* is one of the early canvases of Delaunay – and is mentioned by Eisenstein later (see the section "Color").

41 *José Guadalupe Posada* (1853–1911), Mexican graphic artist, progenitor of contemporary representative art of Mexico.

42 Hans *Holbein* the Younger (1497–1543), German artist of the Renaissance, who worked in Switzerland and England.

43 David Davidovich *Burliuk* (1882–1967), artist, poet, critic, one of the founders of Russian futurism.

44 Here the author is turning to his ideas on Joyce's methodology, which were connected with Eisenstein's attempt to create the technique of "inner monologue" by the properties of realistic art.

45 *Mei Lan-Fang* (1894–1961), leading Chinese actor, director.

46 George *Cuiveau* (1769–1832), French naturalist who first restored the construction of missing aspects of animals by parts of the skeleton that had been preserved.

47 *Miracle plays*, religious dramas, very widespread in Europe in the thirteenth and fourteenth centuries.

48 See the article "Beyond the Frame," in J. Leyda, *Film Form*, pp. 28–44.

49 He has in mind Puccini's opera *Cho-Cho-San* (Madame Butterfly).

50 *Pythagorean*, of the philosophical school in ancient Greece founded by Pythagoras; the teachings of Pythagoreans asserted universal repetition and gave a mystical meaning to numbers.

51 Anthony *Asquith* (1902–68), English film director.

52 The novel of the French writer Choderlos de Laclos (1741–1803).

53 *Pointillism*, current in late impressionist painting, conveying the appearance of objects by strictly developed relationships of colored dots and tiny dabs.

54 Edgar *Lee Masters* (see note 45 to *Pathos*).

55 William *Faulkner* (1897–1962), American writer, Nobel Prize winner.

56 Herman *Melville* (1819–91), American writer and his novel *Moby-Dick* had a great influence on a series of contemporary writers, for example, Hemingway.

57 Wilkie *Collins* (1824–89), English writer, author of the famous mystery novel *The Woman in White*.

58 Orson *Welles* (1915–86), American director and actor. His film *Citizen Kane* (1941) played a great role in renewing the compositional and representational possibilities of cinema.

59 E. T. A. *Hoffman* (1776–1822), German writer, one of the most important representatives of romanticism. The novel *Katere Murr* was published in 1820–2.

60 Mary Roberts *Rinehart* (1876–1958), American novelist.

61 James Fenimore *Cooper* (1789–1851), American writer, author of adventure novels about the colonization of America.

62 Paul *Feval* (1817–87), French man of letters.

63 *Dumas*, referring to Alexandre Dumas-père (1802–70).

64 Vsevolod Vladimirovich *Krestovsky* (1839–95), Russian writer.

65 Sherwood *Anderson* (1876–1941), American writer.

66 William *Saroyan* (1908–81), American writer.

67 Eugène *Scribe* (1791–1861), French playwright.

68 Claude *Mellan* (1598–1688), French engraver. He probably has in mind *Eccehomo*!

69 Albrecht *Dürer* (1471–1528), very important German painter and engraver.

70 According to legend, the ruler of the Phrygians, Gordius, attached a yoke to the pole of a wagon with an intricate knot. The wagon was put in the temple of Zeus. The oracle predicted that the one who untied this knot would become ruler of Asia. Alexander the Macedonian untied the knot with his sword.

71 He has in mind Dicken's *Christmas Carol* where, in the course of Christmas Eve, a sharp change in the character of the miser and egotist occurs.

72 *The Deluge*, play by the Swedish playwright G. Berger (1872–1924), presented by E. B. Vakhtangov in the First Studio of the Moscow Art Theatre.

73 Joseph *Conrad* (1857–1924), originally Polish, but wrote novels in English. Several books were written by Conrad and Ford Madox Ford (1873–1939). Ford Madox's monograph on Conrad came out in 1924.

74 John Boynton *Priestley* (1894–1984), English fiction writer and playwright.

75 *Lillian Hellman* (1905–84), American writer, playwright. Author of *The Little Foxes*.

76 *Convivio* [*The Feast*], this treatise (1307–9) by Dante was mentioned quite often by Sergei Eisenstein in his lectures on directing.

77 Donato *Bramante* (1444–1514), great Italian architect, author of *The Belvedere in the Vatican* and the design for St. Peter's in Rome.

78 Michelangelo *Buonarroti* (1475–1564), the great artist who was also an architect of St. Peter's.

79 *Minotaur*, according to Greek myth, half-bull half-man who ravaged Athenian maidens and young men. He was killed by Theseus.

80 Jean Marie *Guyau* (1854–88), French philosopher-positivist, one of the most significant sociologists of art.

81 Vasily Vasilevich *Goryunov* (1908–   ), Soviet makeup artist.

82 Andrey Nikolaevich *Moskvin* (1901–60), Soviet cameraman. His films include *The Overcoat*, *The Trilogy about Maxim*, *Don Quixote*, *The Lady with a Dog*, etc. In the film *Ivan the Terrible*, Moskvin directed most of the shooting in the studio. [See the true story of what happened to Eisenstein's "permanent" cameraman E. Tisse in Part XVI of *Immoral Memories*.]

83 Eisenstein has in mind the words "Noli tangere circulos meos" [Don't touch my circles], which, according to tradition, Archimedes addressed to the Koman legion threatening him with death.

84 Eisenstein once intended *Nonindifferent Nature* for a collection devoted to the twenty-year-old *Potemkin*. The collection was published after his lifetime. See *Battleship Potemkin*, Herbert Marshall, ed., Avon, New York, 1978.

85 *Comedy of masks*, a form of Italian folk improvisational theater that arose in the middle of the sixteenth century. At the beginning of the twentieth century the comedy of masks attracted many Russian directors, particularly V. E. Meyerhold.

86 Pierre *Marivaux* (1688–1763), French playwright.

87 Pierre Augustin *Beaumarchais* (1732–99), French satirist.

88 *Lazzi*, a word meaning the form of comic jokes characteristic of comedy that is built on stage conflict, play of words, gestures, etc.; gags.

89 Thomas *Carlyle* (1795–1881), English writer and philosopher, affirming the romantic "cult of the hero."

90 Eugène *Sue* (1804–57), French writer. *The Cockroach* is a "colonial" novel on the exotic material of the tropics.

91 Joris Karl *Huysman* (1848–1907), French writer. *Des Esseintes*, hero of the novel *Au Rebours* [*Against the Grain*], 1884.

92 On the fruitful side of the conception of the "montage of attractions," see the commentary to the article "The Montage of Attractions," J. Leyda, *The Film Sense*, pp. 168–8.

93 Andre *Le Notre* (1613–1700), author of *The Plan of the Park at Versailles*.

94 Eugène *Delacroix* (1798–1863), French painter. His *Journal* was an important literary-artistic document of the nineteenth century.

95 *Andrey Bely* (1880–1934), pseudonym of Boris Nikolayevich Bugayev, Russian writer. Prominent representative and theoretician of the symbolists.

96 Gilbert K. *Chesterton* (1874–1936), English writer, master of the so-called psychological detective story.

97 Victor Borisovich *Shklovsky* (1893–   ), Soviet writer, critic, writer of scenarios, and film theoretician.

98 Aldous *Huxley* (1894–1963), English writer-satirist. Eisenstein looks at his novel *Brave New World* in his work "On Stereo Film."

99 William Randolph *Hearst* (1863–1951). American newspaper publisher whose name became a byword in designating the principles of an arch-reactionary press.

100 *Jingoism*, a word arising in the 1870s, signifying Anglo-Saxon chauvinism.

101 Peter Leonidovich *Kapitsa* (1894–1984), Soviet physicist, member of the Academy of Sciences, USSR.

102 *J. J. Thomson*, see note 157 to section "*Pathos*."

103 *Prokimen* [modern Greek], line of a psalm sung at matins before the Evangelia.

104 Ilya Ilvovich *Selvinsky* (1899–   ), Soviet poet. These lines are taken from *Notes of a Writer*.

105 Jules *Renard* (1846–1910), French writer and playwright.

106 He has in mind the words, "How to take a man –· this is the main thing."

107 Aleksander Nikolaevich *Veselovsky* (1838–1906), Russian literary historian.

108 Leon *Feuchtwanger* (1884–1958), German writer.

109 Michael Aleksandrovich *Chekhov* (1891–1955), Russian actor who created the figures of Khlestakov, Hamlet, Eric XIV, etc., on the stage of the Moscow Art Theatre and the First Studio of the M. A. T. Emigrated to the West.

110 Gordon *Craig* (1872–1966), English director and theater designer.

111 Isadora *Duncan* (1876–1927), American dancer, creator of new forms of the modern dance.

112 Joseph Frantsevich *Gertovich* (1886–1953), double bass performer, professor.

113 Abram Lvovich *Stasevich* (1907–   ), Soviet conductor. Author of the concert edition of the music of S. S. Prokofiev for *Ivan the Terrible*.

114 Boris Alekseyevich *Volsky* (1903–   ), sound engineer, colleague of Eisenstein and Prokofiev in the films *Alexander Nevsky* and *Ivan the Terrible*.

115 Velimir *Khlebnikov* (1885–1922), Russian futurist poet.

116 Ludwig *Klages* (1872–1956), German philosopher of idealism. In 1905 he organized a seminar in Munich on the study of means of expression [*Ausdrucksbewegung and Gestaltungskraft*, 3/4 Ausgabe, Leipzig, 1923].

117 Gustave *Stresemann* (1878–1929), German political figure, once leader of the government.

118 Heracles Luarsabovich *Andronikov* (1908–   ), Soviet writer and literary critic, master of oral speech.

119 Charles Augustine *Sainte-Beuve* (1804–69), French literary critic and poet.

120 *Dupin*, hero of Edgar Allan Poe's (1809–49) "The Murders on the Rue Morgue," "The Mystery of Marie Roget," and "The Purloined Letter."

121 *Rémy de Gourmont* (1858–1915), French writer and literary critic.

122 D. H. *Lawrence* (1885–1930), English novelist and poet.

123 Gustave *Courbet* (1819–77), French painter, active figure in the Paris Commune.

124 Albrecht *Altdorfer* (1480–1538), German architect, painter, and engraver, known especially for his landscapes.

125 Wolf *Huber* (1485/90–1553), German painter.

126 *Goven and Simerden*, heroes of V. Hugo's novel *The Ninety-third Year* who bear the two principles – the "ideal" and the "practical" truth of the revolution.

127 François *Coppée* (1842–1908), French poet and dramatist.

128 Charles *Leconte de Lisle* (1818–94), French poet, one of the main representatives of the literary group "The Parnassians."

129 Catulle *Mendes* (1841–1909), French poet, dramatist and critic.

130 William *James* (1842–1910), American philosopher and psychologist, founder of pragmatism.

131 *The Vulgate*, the Latin version of the Bible.

132 *Poor Lazaruses*, from the Gospel.

133 From the Biblical story of Ruth.

134 *Louis Philippe* (1773–1850), King of France (1830–48).

135 Francois *Guizot* (1787–1874), French historian and political figure, prime minister in 1847–48.

136 Henri Claude *Saint-Simon* (1760–1825), French thinker, one of the most important socialist utopianists.

137 Etienne *Cabet* (1788–1856), French utopianist, author of the novel *The Journey to Icaria* [*Voyage en Icarie*] 1840.

138 Charles *Fourier* (1772–1837), French utopian socialist.

139 Louis *Blanc* (1811–82), one of the last representatives of French utopian socialism.

140 *Novalis*, Baron Friedrich von Hardenberg (1772–1801), German romantic poet.

141 *Grimm brothers*, Jacob (1785–1863) and Wilhelm (1786–1859), German philologists and folklorists, authors of the famous children's fairy stories.

142 Henry *Laube* (1806–84), German writer and dramatist.

143 Percy Bysshe *Shelley* (1792–1822), English poet. Eisenstein cites his famous treatise *The Defence of Poetry* written in 1821.

144 *Pan*, in Greek mythology the God of Nature.

145 ...*are essentially Calvinist*, Calvinism, a Protestant creed (Huguenots in France and Puritans in England) preaching "worldly asceticism."

146 ...*decisions of the Dordrecht Synod*, at a Synod held in Dordrecht (Holland) in 1618–19 the Calvinistic symbols of faith were ratified.

147 ...*top hat on the head of an Eton boy*, at the famous Eton College, England.

148 *The medieval guard of "Beefeaters,"* dressed in medieval costumes and guarding the royal palaces of England.

149 *Bobbies,* a slang name for London's policemen. Also known as "peelers," from Sir Robert Peel, their founder.

150 *Demiurge* (Greek), a Platonic Subordinate deity.

151 *Lautréamont* (Isadore Ducasse) (1846–70), French writer, whom the surrealists declared to be their precursor.

152 *...that very deceased Marquis,* Eisenstein means the Marquis de Sade (1740–1814), notorious for his pornographic works that gave birth to the term "sadism."

153 Luigi *Pirandello* (1867–1936), Italian writer and dramatist. Particularly famous for his play *Six Characters in Search of an Author.*

154 *Captain* (John Augustus) Sutter, a Swiss emigrant to the United States who discovered gold in California. When in America, Eisenstein proposed to make a film on the history of this discovery, *Sutter's Gold,* but was unable to. Script is in Ivor Montagu's *"With Eisenstein in Hollywood."*

155 Upton *Sinclair* (1878–1968), American writer famous for his "muckraking" novels and campaigns. At one time a socialist candidate for Congress.

156 *Bayreuth,* a town in South Germany where a special theater was built for the production of Wagner's operas.

157 *"Well, are we obligated to you, Alexander Nikolayevich, for this good weather?"* A joke on A. N. Scriabin attributed to P. M. Plekhanov. (See the anthology: *A. N. Scriabin,* Muzgiz, Moscow–Leningrad, 1940, p. 69).

158 Johanne Joachim *Winkelmann* (1717–68), German historian and art critic, researcher into ancient cultures.

159 Gaston *Maspero* (1846–1916), French Egyptologist.

160 Jean François *Champollion* (1790–1832), French archeologist and Egyptologist pioneering the decoding of Egyptian hieroglyphs.

161 *The Thief of Baghdad,* an English feature film, directed by Zoltan Korda, a London Films Production, 1940.

162 *Mowgli,* English feature film based on Rudyard Kipling's *Jungle Book,* directed by Alexander Korda, London Films Production, 1942.

163 *Bathing Beauty,* American musical comedy, produced by Metro-Goldwyn-Mayer in 1945.

164 *Bambi,* animated color cartoon film produced by Walt Disney, 1942.

165 Walt *Disney* (1901–66), American artist, director, and producer, outstanding master of animated cartoons.

166 *Chopin,* the American biographical film about Chopin called *A Song to Remember,* Director King Vidor, produced by Columbia Pictures, 1944.

167 *Silly Symphonies,* a series of animated color cartoon films created by Walt Disney in the 1930s.

168 *In the Mickey Mouse series,* Disney's famous animated cartoon films whose central characters were Mickey Mouse and his girlfriend Minnie.

169 *Chopiniana,* a classic ballet based on the music of Chopin, first choreographed by the Russian ballet-master M. M. Fokin (1880–1942) on the stage of the Marynsky Theatre in Petersburgh in 1907.

170 *...Romeo and Juliet,* SME has in mind the ballet starring Ulanova with music by S. S. Prokofiev.

171 *Thérèse Raquin*, a feature film directed by the French director Jacques Feyder in Germany, a DEFA Film Production, 1928.

172 *Money*, a French feature film directed by Marcel L'Herbier, 1927.

173 *Nana*, a French feature film directed by Jean Renoir, 1926.

174 *The Human-Beast*, a French feature film directed by Jean Renoir, a Paris-Film Production, 1938.

Index